André Alexis • Margaret Atwood • Russell Banks • David Bergen
John Berger • George Bowering • Marilyn Bowering • Joseph
Boyden • Di Brandt • Barry Callaghan • Lynn Coady • Susan Coyne
Michael Crummey • Margaret Drabble • Bernice Eisenstein • Howard

Writing*Life*

Engel • Damon Galgut • Jonathan Garfinkel • Greg Gatenby •
Camilla Gibb • Charlotte Gray • Elizabeth Hay • Michael Helm
Sheila Heti • Annabel Lyon • David Macfarlane • Alistair MacLeod •
Margaret MacMillan • Alberto Manguel • Yann Martel • Anne
Michaels • Rohinton Mistry • Lisa Moore • Shani Mootoo • Alice
Munro • Susan Musgrave • Michael Ondaatje • Anna Porter • Eden
Robinson • Marilynne Robinson • Peter Robinson • John Ralston Saul
Shyam Selvadurai • Russell Smith • Rosemary Sullivan • Susan Swan
Madeleine Thien • Jane Urquhart • Michael Winter • Patricia Young

André Alexis • Margaret Atwood • Russell Banks • David Bergen
John Berger • George Bowering • Marilyn Bowering • Joseph
Boyden • Di Brandt • Barry Callaghan • Lynn Coady • Susan Coyne
Michael Crummey • Margaret Drabble • Bernice Eisenstein • Howard
Engel • Damon Galgut • Jonathan Garfinkel • Greg Gatenby •
Camilla Gibb • Charlotte Gray • Elizabeth Hay • Michael Helm
Sheila Heti • Annabel Lyon • David Macfarlane • Alistair MacLeod •
Margaret MacMillan • Alberto Manguel • Yann Martel • Anne
Michaels • Rohinton Mistry • Lisa Moore • Shani Mootoo • Alice
Munro • Susan Musgrave • Michael Ondaatje • Anna Porter • Eden
Robinson • Marilynne Robinson • Peter Robinson • John Ralston Saul
Shyam Selvadurai • Russell Smith • Rosemary Sullivan • Susan Swan
Madeleine Thien • Jane Urquhart • Michael Winter • Patricia Young

Writing *Life*

Celebrated Canadian and International

Authors on Writing and Life

EDITED BY CONSTANCE ROOKE

Proceeds to PEN Canada

McCLELLAND & STEWART

Library and Archives Canada Cataloguing in Publication

Writing life : celebrated Canadian and international authors on writing and life / edited by Constance Rooke.

ISBN 13: 978-0-7710-7625-1
ISBN 10: 0-7710-7625-8

1. Canadian essays (English) – 21st century. 2. Authorship.
3. Autobiography – Literary collections. 4. Authors, Canadian (English) – 20th century. I. Rooke, Constance, 1942- II. International P.E.N. Canadian Centre.

PS8367.A8W75 2006   c814'.608   C2005-907275-X

We acknowledge the financial support of the Government of Canada through the Book Publishing Industry Development Program and that of the Government of Ontario through the Ontario Media Development Corporation's Ontario Book Initiative. We further acknowledge the support of the Canada Council for the Arts and the Ontario Arts Council for our publishing program.

Typeset in Minion by M&S, Toronto
Printed and bound in Canada

This book is printed on acid-free paper that is 100% recycled, ancient-forest friendly (100% post-consumer recycled).

McClelland & Stewart Ltd.
75 Sherbourne Street
Toronto, Ontario
M5A 2P9
www.mcclelland.com

1 2 3 4 5   10 09 08 07 06

CONTENTS

INTRODUCTION

Constance Rooke

This anthology, conceived as a fundraiser for PEN Canada, gives us many points of entry into the writing life, into what it means to *do* this sort of work or to *be* a writer. What kind of life does a writer have, and what are the connections between time spent in the act of writing – that intensely private part of the writing life – and all the rest of one's time? To what extent is the writing life different from or similar to other lives? How do writers feel about promoting their work, public readings, and literary prizes? How does one *write* life? What are the writer's responsibilities? What are the greatest challenges, miseries, and joys? And what lies at the heart of the author's need to write?

Each of the essays collected here opens a door into a large space in which the partial answers given by individual writers gather and circulate. It's quite a crowd, and the opportunity this book affords for access to their conversation seems to me extraordinary. For each reader, even before the door is opened, there will be some points of entry that are more compelling than others – simply because of the name on the door, the chance to hear what a writer in whom we are particularly interested has chosen to say.

And, of course, readers will like some pieces better than others; and their preferences will vary, which is just as it should be. But for me it is the book as a whole – the combination of all these separate voices, the often startling individual decisions made as to subject or tone – that speaks most powerfully to the writing life. It is as if each voice helps the others to tell a larger story that is both fiercely individualistic and communal.

The curiosity many of us have about writers, both *en masse* and as individuals, seems to me an entirely natural thing. It follows from our having touched their minds, from having had our minds touched by them, in our capacity as readers. The two previous PEN Canada anthologies, *Writing Away* (1994) and *Writing Home* (1997), had wide readerships and raised a good deal of money for PEN Canada in part because of that curiosity – the desire for a new sort of encounter with the contributing writers, a fresh angle of vision on the writers themselves. The stature of the contributors, general interest in writing about travel and the idea of home, and the quality of the essays themselves all contributed to the success of these anthologies. But there was something else at work as well, something that helped them to deliver on the promise of a significant encounter between writer and reader. In the Introduction to *Writing Home*, I put it this way: "The attraction of *Writing Away* as a title had partly to do with the idea of 'away' as a direction in which writing points. But if that is one pole for the energy of writing, surely home is its other. We yearn both ways. 'Away' and 'home' are the destinations of writing, the places we get to inside ourselves through writing and also through reading." By indirection, as it turned out, these essays spoke eloquently both to the writing life and to the immense personal ground that is shared by writers and readers. This time, I thought it would be interesting to ask writers to address the subject of writing directly.

Writing Life (like the titles of the previous anthologies) is a title that works grammatically in two ways, with "writing" as an adjective modifying the noun "life," and with "life" as the noun object of the verbal "writing." So our title refers to *the* writing life – what it's like – or to writing *about* life, and the intersection of writing and life in either case. I was endlessly surprised by the individual essays as they came in. I would be astonished that *this* particular writer should say *that*, stunned by a writer's frankness, surprised by the choice of subject or the way it was approached – or simply knocked out by the quality of the writing.

I was *not* surprised that the book as a whole would reveal great intensity of feeling about life and about writing as a vocation, or that it would speak so forcefully to the relationship between reading and writing. But I was impressed by how differently these passions were articulated and by how they are felt to combine and cohere as the heart of the writing life. Again and again, we encounter the writers' foundational and continuing experience as readers, their wonder at the imagination and skill of other writers – other people – that somehow, miraculously, succeed in taking us into the presence of life. We see how that feeds the desire to write, which becomes a need as the writer's own creative powers are discovered and developed; and we see how the act of writing holds out the promise of an ever-deepening connection to the heart of life.

I believe very strongly in the force that unites writers and readers. When people in university English departments were first discussing with great enthusiasm the Death of the Author – a death, reported by Roland Barthes, that accorded new power and freedom to critics and readers working on the author's textual remains – I rebelled. I didn't want the power to be taken away from writers and given to me. I didn't *want* the author to be dead, or exiled from the relationship between reader and text; for me the idea of the writer as a human being – the *individual,* living or dead, who wrote these words and was mysteriously present in them – was indispensable. There was the book, there was me, and there was the person who wrote the book; I read alone, and the writer writes alone, but the words connect us. Take the writer out of my own reading experience, erase the splendid fact of a person needing to write just these words, and my lights would go out. The world, depersonalized and bereft of urgent voices, would shrink horribly. In truth, though, the theory of the Death of the Author had no power over me. My faith was too strong. Still, I was worried about other readers, especially new, young readers, about what they would lose if this death sentence on the writer as secret sharer were to persist. And I wrote an essay called "Fear of the Open Heart" in which I sketched out something I called a theory of intimacy and tried to describe the very peculiar and precious kind of relationship with a writer that may exist in a reader's heart.

So this book is for readers who are curious about writers – about particular writers, but also about writers generally. Taken as a whole, it offers a map of the writer's journey, revealing the complex interplay between the writing and the reality it seeks to express, at various stages both of the writer's life and of the creation of particular works. The individual essays provide pieces of a larger story, casting light for us on the diverse phases and aspects, tribulations and satisfactions, and anxieties and ambitions of the writing life. Together, they reveal a profound, inescapable commitment to what writing can do – to the intersection of writing and life, to the heightened sense of life that writing can deliver. And this is the groundwork that connects writers to readers who are not writers, to all other writers, and to anyone who wants to write.

If all of this sounds too desperately earnest, or idolatrous or mystical or whatever else, I can only ask for your indulgence. The anthology itself is brilliantly varied. It is, for example, often wildly funny. There are raucous complaints about interruption or the need to bend oneself out of shape to promote the writing. There is also deep appreciation of the ordinary, personal life lived outside of writing, its wonderful mess and vitality, the blessed relief it offers, its insistent, competing claims and essential complementarity. There is tremendous self-doubt and palpable misery, but also calm assurance and glee at success. There is ample praise of other writers, but there are also comic blasts of the competitive spirit. The work of writing is seen to bring everything from agony to bliss. The solitary and collaborative and public and political dimensions of the writer's life are explored, together with the life that is abundantly shared with family and friends. We are given detailed accounts of how a particular work came into being, or the special challenges it entailed. Several of the essays speak to the risks and responsibilities that must be negotiated when writers borrow from the lives of people close to them or address a foreign culture or deal with historical fact. Some speak about the research, about other kinds of excavation, about imaginative as opposed to factual truth, about profound experiences that precede the actual writing, and about scruples and doubts and the arduous process of revision. Several address the gap between one's first immaculate conception and the achievement of the work itself.

The precariousness of the writer's life is made very clear by the essays in this book, a precariousness that is not, as one might expect, related primarily to the notorious difficulty of making a living from writing. Hard as those issues are, they are seen to pale next to the precariousness of the writing itself, the passionate, often frustrated will of the writer to get it *right*, to achieve the vision, to write life truly. Often, in reading the essays that make up *Writing Life*, I found myself thinking about what a splendid but impossible profession this is, how very different it is from most others.

What makes it so terribly hard, I think, is the lure of greatness – and the special difficulty for the writer of distinguishing between success in life and success in work, because "life" is what one writes, because one writes against death, because writing may or may not endure, because life is always on the line. Writers are led to the desire for greatness by their knowledge of what writing *can* do; and the passion for excellence – including the hope of greatness – is a necessity of the writing life. Many people are ambitious about their work, believe in its value, want it to be first-rate; and reputation and the respect of our peers matters to us all. But something else is afoot in the case of writers, something that is externally imposed and that must be fought against. An expectation of *fame* exists in the public imagination for writers (and artists generally), an expectation that does not exist for teachers or doctors or engineers or business people. The work of doctors, for example, is understood by everyone to be important, and it is well-paid; everyone knows that we need a great many highly skilled doctors. But what of writers? What of the vast majority of writers who make very little money from work that is read by very few? Are *they* important, or only the few who achieve fame? Do we need the many only for the sake of discovering the few, perhaps the *very* few? Is writing a lottery with long odds, a good bet if you win, but largely useless (quixotic or self-indulgent) if you do not? And to what extent is "winning" in the public eye a true measure of excellence?

Writers know that they must be on guard against the poison that follows from an interiorized need to win the Giller Prize or the Governor General's Award or the Griffin Poetry Prize or the Booker or the Nobel, or to sell vast numbers of their books. At the same time, they have a perfectly natural, honorable desire for the work to be read and its merit recognized. They also need to make a living. They want to do so, if possible, from writing what they need to write, giving to that as much of their time as they can. And all of this means that prizes matter and that writers must care about and participate in the effective promotion of their work. Seeing how writers negotiate this perilous terrain is one of the many fascinations of this book.

Looking back now at *Writing Life*, I am struck by the honesty and courage and rigour of the writers assembled here. Their absolute dedication to the writing itself, to writing truly about life, moves me deeply. And I love the humour and self-deprecation and ordinary humanity that shines through as well, the leavening – the lightness of touch – that complements and takes nothing away from the seriousness of the writer's mission. My hope is that readers will be similarly moved and delighted.

❋　　❋　　❋

The writers who have contributed their work to *Writing Life* were invited to approach this broad topic in any way they liked. They could be funny or deadly serious or both. They could write at length or very briefly. Any take on the subject, any aspect of it from the most mundane to the sublime, would be appropriate to the task at hand. This time, in contrast to the two previous PEN Canada anthologies, and in recognition of the international context within which both writers and PEN Canada work, I asked a few distinguished writers from beyond Canada to participate. Still, the great majority of the writers assembled here are Canadian. Most of these writers are well-known; several are just embarking on the writing life. The contributors include a publisher, an historian, the past director of Canada's most celebrated literary festival, writers of memoirs, biographers, playwrights, poets, and fiction writers.

The contributing authors have interrupted their own busy writing lives to answer the call of PEN Canada, and we are intensely grateful to them. None of the essays assembled here has appeared previously in book form, and all but a few were written especially for this anthology. As with the two previous anthologies, the generosity of the contributors – and of others involved in making this book possible – demonstrates a remarkable breadth and depth of commitment to the work of PEN Canada. Again, McClelland & Stewart – which is celebrating its centenary year as this book is launched – is contributing all of its resources in the publication of the book. Again, a number of suppliers and printers are donating their services, or providing these at a significant discount, to ensure that as much as possible of the anthology's cover price will go directly to PEN Canada. Booksellers, too, are doing their part to help us promote the book and to sell as many copies as possible.

There are so many people to thank – the writers, of course, above all. I want to express my gratitude here to Amber Wilson, who gave me invaluable logistical help and astute editorial advice. At McClelland & Stewart, profound thanks go to Doug Pepper, President and Publisher, for his strong support of this project, and to Ellen Seligman, Publisher (Fiction), for her unfailing support and expert guidance in the development of all three PEN Canada anthologies. I am grateful to copy editor Jenny Bradshaw and to all those involved in production, design, sales, and publicity for their energy and expertise. Finally, it would be impossible for me to give sufficient thanks and recognition to Anita Chong, who worked with me on the anthology from its beginnings through to the end. I can only thank her, fervently, for *everything*: in particular, for her great ideas at the start, and for the editorial skill, immense hard work, patience, enthusiasm, and perfect grace that she exhibited throughout our collaboration in the making of this book.

✳   ✳   ✳

The goal of *Writing Life*, the reason that so many people have worked so hard to make it possible, is to raise badly needed money for the work of PEN Canada. Ultimately, of course, it is the readers who may choose to buy this book who will determine the success of our common venture. And so I want here, finally, to tell you something about PEN Canada and its work.

PEN Canada is one of the most active of the 141 centres of International PEN operating around the world. We are a human rights organization of writers and other supporters of free speech, and our mission is to defend "freedom of opinion and the peaceable expression of such opinion." Enshrined both in the Universal Declaration of Human Rights and in Canada's Charter of Rights and Freedoms, freedom of expression is a fundamental human right that is vital to the protection of all other human rights. We see this every day in the work for which PEN is best-known: our struggle on behalf of writers in prison around the world. Overwhelmingly, these are people living under oppressive regimes who have chosen to speak out about abuses in their own countries. Jail is intended to silence them and hide them away.

Our primary goal is to secure the writers' release from prison, and to do this we mount various public campaigns and seek the support of our own government to exert pressure on foreign governments. The close monitoring we provide and the very public light shed on the case of each imprisoned writer adopted as an honorary member of PEN Canada also sometimes helps to protect the writer from torture, or to ensure that medical help is provided or that the writer's family is not also victimized. Some of our members become "minders," writing letters to these writers that let them know someone far away is watching closely and trying to help. A huge amount of our energy is directed to this, and we often fail. I think, for example, of the case of Ken Saro-Wiwa, executed in Nigeria about a decade ago on trumped-up charges, but in fact for his fiercely articulate support of his people's most basic human rights. An intense political campaign was mounted to prevent that outrage, a campaign in which PEN Canada played a leading role. I remember his words of encouragement to us, not long before his death by hanging, his concern to assure PEN that its efforts had not been wasted, whatever the outcome. But there are clear successes too: in the last three years, PEN Canada has helped to secure the release of twenty-seven unjustly imprisoned writers. And all of it matters.

The two other principal areas of PEN Canada's work are home-based. For many years, an essential part of our mission has been to stand up for freedom of expression whenever threats to it have arisen within our own country. We take action, for example, in cases where written material is seized at the border, books are banned, journalists are compelled to reveal their sources, or proposed or enacted legislation poses a threat to free speech. And in recent years we have taken on a third major area of activity in support of writers in exile. In this work, PEN Canada has been the world leader, chairing this effort for International PEN and making great strides within Canada. There has been a good deal of talk in Canada about the desperate situation of immigrants whose credentials are not recognized here. Our Writers in Exile program addresses the particularly difficult case of writers who have fled oppressive regimes (often with the assistance of PEN) to take up a new life in Canada. Writing, as we know, is a precarious profession at the best of times. Imagine, then, what it is to try to begin again, often in a new language, and without the support of one's fellow writers or any recognition of one's past achievements. Imagine, too, how much the rest of us can learn from hearing the stories of these writers in exile. PEN Canada seeks, in a variety of ways, to support and welcome them into our community. (For example, with assistance from PEN Canada, twenty-three Canadian universities, colleges, libraries, and towns have so far provided placements for these writers.)

This is our work – which all the writers in this book and about seven hundred more writers across Canada have chosen to support with astonishing generosity and in many different ways. It is work funded entirely through members' dues and fundraising efforts such as this one. You can help by buying and urging others to buy this book – and also, very importantly, by choosing to become a member of PEN Canada. Please think hard about this, and consult the membership information you will find at the back of this book. A high priority for us now, for political as well as financial reasons, is to increase dramatically the number of *readers* who are members of PEN Canada. The more members we have, the better our chances of being heard.

And it just feels *right*, the bringing together of writers and readers – secret sharers in the pain and affirmation of life – in the work of PEN Canada. I think of something Saul Bellow said once about fiction, that it lacks everything if it lacks a sympathetic devotion to the life of *somebody else*. We do not write or read only to understand our pre-existing selves; we do it, we engage in this private, mysterious form of communication, in order to become larger somehow, to feel and embrace more fully the reality of others. We are all in varying ways and degrees in exile or in prison;

we are all in varying measure stifled in the expression of what is in our hearts. But sometimes there are words that pass through prison walls, words that by connecting us can help to free us. And PEN Canada's work merely takes this truth about the ordinary writing/reading life into the high danger zone, into a space where we know that human lives are literally at stake, and where we know that we *must* act. We act in solidarity with one another, and ask you to join us.

Toronto
April 2006

André Alexis • Margaret Atwood • Russell Banks • David Bergen
John Berger • George Bowering • Marilyn Bowering • Joseph
Boyden • Di Brandt • Barry Callaghan • Lynn Coady • Susan Coyne
Michael Crummey • Margaret Drabble • Bernice Eisenstein • Howard

Writing*Life*

Engel • Damon Galgut • Jonathan Garfinkel • Greg Gatenby •
Camilla Gibb • Charlotte Gray • Elizabeth Hay • Michael Helm
Sheila Heti • Annabel Lyon • David Macfarlane • Alistair MacLeod •
Margaret MacMillan • Alberto Manguel • Yann Martel • Anne
Michaels • Rohinton Mistry • Lisa Moore • Shani Mootoo • Alice
Munro • Susan Musgrave • Michael Ondaatje • Anna Porter • Eden
Robinson • Marilynne Robinson • Peter Robinson • John Ralston Saul
Shyam Selvadurai • Russell Smith • Rosemary Sullivan • Susan Swan
Madeleine Thien • Jane Urquhart • Michael Winter • Patricia Young

André Alexis • Margaret Atwood • Russell Banks • David Bergen
John Berger • George Bowering • Marilyn Bowering • Joseph
Boyden • Di Brandt • Barry Callaghan • Lynn Coady • Susan Coyne
Michael Crummey • Margaret Drabble • Bernice Eisenstein • Howard
Engel • Damon Galgut • Jonathan Garfinkel • Greg Gatenby •
Camilla Gibb • Charlotte Gray • Elizabeth Hay • Michael Helm
Sheila Heti • Annabel Lyon • David Macfarlane • Alistair MacLeod •
Margaret MacMillan • Alberto Manguel • Yann Martel • Anne
Michaels • Rohinton Mistry • Lisa Moore • Shani Mootoo • Alice
Munro • Susan Musgrave • Michael Ondaatje • Anna Porter • Eden
Robinson • Marilynne Robinson • Peter Robinson • John Ralston Saul
Shyam Selvadurai • Russell Smith • Rosemary Sullivan • Susan Swan
Madeleine Thien • Jane Urquhart • Michael Winter • Patricia Young

ANDRÉ**ALEXIS**

Are You a Writer and
Other Unanswerable Questions

When I was younger, I read an interview with Clark Blaise. I very much admire Clark Blaise's work, but what stayed with me was his confession that, when *he* was young, he decided he'd think of himself as a writer only after he'd published six short stories. I thought that a realistic standard and I took it seriously. At the time, I'd already published a short story, but I was unsure I had the right to call myself a writer. Here was an objective way to assess my standing: 6 stories published in literary magazines equals 1 writer.

As I said, I took this seriously. It wasn't that I was looking to make a career as a writer or that I dreamed the piles of cash my stories made would liberate me. I'm a Canadian writer, after all, and for Canadian writers of my generation, the thought of making a living from writing is something like the thought of walking on the moon . . . it doesn't happen often. Rather, I wanted proof that my writing was more than scribbles, that if I were to suffer it would be for the chance to produce a work of art. I thought publishing six stories would bring me the confidence to go on, to call myself a writer.

The milestone passed in an unexpected way, however. I published five stories in literary journals (*Descant, Ambit, Event*) and, then, I was invited to prepare a collection for Coach House Press. So, in effect, I published my first book before I managed to publish six stories.

I'm not sure I would have felt like a writer, even if things had gone to plan. I've since published a novel and a play, and my work has appeared in anthologies and magazines, but I have not, until very recently, felt I was a writer. It wasn't just that "writer" referred to artists I'd admired and whose works had inspired mine (Tolstoy, Beckett, Queneau). It was also that I couldn't help feeling the word was not the kind of thing one said of oneself but, rather, described an aspiration.

And then, halfway through the writing of my second novel, *Asylum*, I became a writer by finally accepting that "writer" is a less solid thing than I imagined. It happened like this:

In 1998, I began a novel that was an experiment with form and constraint. I wanted to write a novel that was formally strict, a novel like *Cigarettes* by Harry Mathews or *Le Chiendent* by Raymond Queneau, a work written with what are called constraints or, better, obligations. There were to be 100 chapters. The novel was to take place over a period of 10 years (from 1983 to 1993). It was to be divided into 24 books, because it was a mock-epic and 24 is the number of books in *The Iliad* and *The Odyssey*. What else? There were to be 24 covert descriptions of early Italian Renaissance paintings, 24 quotations from writers whose last names began with *A*, 24 covert references to pineapples (the symbol of hospitality), and *Asylum* was to be, on top of all that, an homage to Saltykov-Shchedrin's *History of a Town*, itself a mock-epic retelling of Russian history.

There was more. In *Asylum*, time was to be told by descriptions of constellations (as Dante did) and each of its 24 books would cover 152 days (10 years divided by 24). The novel was, in other words, a somewhat overdetermined mock-epic and the biggest surprise to me now is that, for three years, I worked at it diligently, happily, fulfilling all its obligations, dealing with characters and story and re-inventing the city of my dreams: Ottawa. I was writing and things were going well. (And by "going well," I mean that when I wasn't writing, I was engaged in a long, imagined conversation with Peter Gzowski (God keep his soul) on the subject of my work. Peter's death has, strangely, failed to interrupt our conversations about literature. The other presence to whom I justify my decisions is Leonard Cohen whom I have never met but who is, when we speak, always interested, though not always approving.)

And then, in 2001, the first inkling something was "off" came in the form of a dream. For weeks I had a recurring dream in which I was at my desk happily writing. From time to time, I would look at the last sheet on the pile of typed pages and read its number, just to see how I was doing. The first time I looked, the last page was number 400. That made me intensely happy. The next time I looked, after having typed for what seemed like a short while, the last page was number 800. That made me nervous, because I was working hard and the novel should have been finished. And, finally, the last time I looked, after what seemed like even less time, there was a pile of 10,000 sheets beside my typewriter. This number filled me with such anxiety, I'd wake up terrified, convinced I would spend my life trying to finish the work.

A second moment of doubt overcame me at my mother's house. It was night and I was alone. I had been writing well, but I was bothered by something I couldn't quite name, a vague question. I remember the night well. I had stopped writing and gone out for a cigarette. It was autumn and cold. There were clouds, but you could see parts of constellations and the moon. I walked to the end of the driveway and looked down the hill at Peterborough, Ontario, which is in a valley. The city looked beautiful and a little mysterious, like a crèche of white and yellow light. And I was admiring it when it occurred to me that I did not know if I were on the side of life or not. I mean, I couldn't decide if life was a "good" thing or a thing to be borne until death released you from it. Yes, this occurs to me all the time, and I've never been able to answer the question straight, but on this night it was slightly more complicated: If I was on the side of death or darkness, what was the point of writing? Why bother to "capture" life, either mine or the life around me, in words?

It was a strange moment, a moment when the world was neatly broken in two.

No, that makes the *moment* sound unusual when, really, the unusual thing was that, for the first time in my life, a literary question was indistinguishable from a moral one. What I felt about "life" was, in this moment above Peterborough, Ontario, inseparable from what I felt about "literature."

Mercifully, the moment did not last long. The idea that literary and moral decisions are inseparable is frightening. But its effects were immediate. First, looking down on the city, I felt an intense love for "life": for the lights beneath me, for my family, for my countrymen, for the world. And, in light of this intense love, I felt strongly that what I now needed from *Asylum* was different from what I'd needed when I began the novel (on January 5, 1998). I'd begun a work that was an homage to Harry Mathews, a work dedicated to formal play. I now wanted something more helter-skelter, something "wrong," the way life is "wrong." And so, from that night, I abandoned *Asylum*'s underlying structure, the constraints and obligations that had produced around one hundred thousand words, and I finished the book, years later, in a more traditional way, fumbling around with theme and ideas, characters and story.

This may all sound a little convenient, as if I were, in retrospect, justifying a change in approach, or as if I had, following a moment of inspiration, arrived at a "better" novel. Not true. I've felt strongly, over the last few years, that I've betrayed my own vision, that the novel called *Asylum*, by André Alexis, to be published sometime in 2007 or 2008, is not *Asylum* by André Alexis. I mean that, as I looked down on Peterborough, Ontario, I did not gain anything that made my work "better." And if *Asylum* is the work for which I've felt the deepest ambivalence, it is because I'm not certain (will never be certain) that I was right to abandon the obligations, structure, and play that generated the first half of the novel. *Asylum 2* contains the ruins of *Asylum 1*.

So, why should all this have made me feel like a writer?

Well, first, having abandoned a work halfway through its writing, I "saw" rather clearly a version of my own imagination. I briefly (and intensely) saw myself in the work I abandoned. I understood how the abandoned work related to me and to my imagination, and it was as if (however briefly) I got a kind of objective look at myself and the things that had gone into *Asylum 1*: Harry Mathews, Dante, Ottawa, a number of women (three actually) I've loved, and so on. In giving up *Asylum 1*, I came to see (and feel kindly toward) Alexis 1. I mean, I felt respect for the writer I had been, because I did not doubt that Alexis 1 was a writer, though I would have argued about his merits. To put it simply: in betraying my original aspirations for the novel, I saw my *literary* self as clearly as I have ever done, saw myself as a writer. And I understood that the way I'd chosen to write *Asylum* was not adventurous, as I had imagined, but another effort to escape doubt, to try to find confirmation of my being a writer. In creating an OULIPO-inspired work[*], I could point to my predecessors and place my work in a tradition I admired. (The irony, of course, is that for Harry Mathews or Italo Calvino, the use of constraints or obligations was a way to *question* tradition, to find something new, to choose the chaos that is "life.")

And then, second, though I don't believe aesthetic and moral questions should be confused (a confusion that would be bad for morality and worse for Art), I finally understood how important the *question* was for me. I had begun, while writing *Asylum*, to ask myself the kinds of questions that make the *number* of my publications meaningless. The questions I now ask myself are such as would take a lifetime to answer, a lifetime during which the work I produce is not the all-important object but, rather, the by-product of my commitment to a prolonged meditation on a handful of moments, places, ideas, emotions, voices. In this situation, doubt (not truth, which is the death of a question) is an aesthetic necessity. It allows the work to go on.

If I were committed to melodrama, I suppose I'd say "I became a writer by killing off the 'writer' inside me or by reducing him to pieces." But it's all so much more banal than that. During the writing of *Asylum 1* and *Asylum 2*, most of the concerns I had when I began to write simply receded. It isn't that the number of my publications, or the number of books I sell, is unimportant or insignificant. The numbers are crucial to the social mechanism

---

* OULIPO is an acronym for the Ouvoir de Littérature Potentielle. It was founded in 1960 by the French novelist Raymond Queneau and the mathematician François Le Lionnais. Its goal was to explore how mathematical constructs could be used to create literary works. Its members include the writers Harry Mathews, Italo Calvino, and Georges Perec, whose novel *La Disparition*, written without using the letter *e*, is one of the group's most notorious accomplishments.

that allows the writer to go on writing, to prolong the meditation. But the numbers are, obviously, unhelpful in bringing me to an understanding of the things that matter most and most deeply to me as a writer. For instance, what force is it that keeps me so in love with that accidental plot of land that is Ottawa, Ontario, Canada?

There's a third thing that happened while I was on that hill above Peterborough, but it's the most difficult one to express and the most easily misunderstood. That is, the moment I fell in love with life, etc., the idea of "perfection" died within me. This had nothing to do with OULIPO or constraints or any kind of formal experiment. My love for the work of Harry Mathews or Italo Calvino for example, is not even a little diminished. (If anything, my feelings for *Cigarettes* or *If on a Winter's Night a Traveler* are deeper now than when I first read them. They seem like pure marvels to me, these days.) "Perfection," here, has nothing to do with the OULIPO. Rather, what I mean by "perfection" is something like "the achievement of an exact correspondence between the work as conceived and the work as executed." The striving for that is what died within me.

Well, yes, of course. Having abandoned my original conception of *Asylum*, it's obvious that I would have had to abandon this version of "perfection" as well. Really, if I weren't such a slow learner, I'd have abandoned that idea of perfection long ago. Very few writers consciously hang on to it beyond their first story, poem, or novel. But, in my case, it was unshakeable because, of course, the achievement of "perfection" would be proof I was a writer. It was tied to my need to know, to publish six stories, to claim my place in a literary lineage, to know that I am an artist.

W.S. Merwin, in a poem called "Berryman," wrote of an encounter with the poet John Berryman, who had been Merwin's teacher at Princeton:

I asked how can you ever be sure
that what you write is really
any good at all and he said you can't

you can't you can never be sure
you die without knowing
whether anything you wrote was any good
if you have to be sure don't write

Yes, there, in a few words, is part of what I learned while writing *Asylum 1* and what I came to embrace during the writing of *Asylum 2*. (I supposed I would have learned it all sooner, if I'd had John Berryman to kick me around, but there you go . . .) Still, it isn't easy to accept doubt, unknowing, imperfection. What does one aim for, if not the ideal? And what is the ideal, if not the bright image that one has of the work when it first comes to you? What to pursue, if not some version of the ideal, some version of certainty?

I'm not sure, but I'd begin an answer by wondering about the "ideal."

One's first conception of a work is rarely unchanging or persistent or even clear. It's chimerical, in my experience, the kind of beast beginners stalk. And until *Asylum 2*, that's more or less what I did: chase after a chimera. With the writing of *Asylum 2*, that chase ended (or has ended for now). I'm ready, thirty years after I wrote my first short story, to be ignorant of my work's objective worth, if it has any at all, to remain in darkness. None of this, of course, makes me any happier, and none of it makes it easier to write. One still has to hold to standards, but I see them differently, these days. They're a convenience, a fiction, something to go toward for the sake of the work, to get the work out, but dangerous as soon as they think for you, as soon as one allows them to answer questions instead of provoking them.

There's at least one interesting example of what I mean about standards thinking for us. In Martin Amis's *Experience*, Amis gives approval to his father Kingsley's dictum about Shakespeare (I'm quoting from memory): "To write or to suggest that the writer known as Shakespeare is not the greatest writer of English is the mark of a mediocre mind." The first thing I thought on reading that was that its opposite ("To write or to suggest that the writer known as Shakespeare is the *greatest* writer of English is the mark of a mediocre mind") is equally true and that, in any case, either assertion allows us a certainty that is murderous to Shakespeare's work. If the work is what matters, the question of its merit can't be decided before an unbiased experience of it. You can't know his worth as a writer; you have to live it.

As it is with Shakespeare, so it has to be with us, I think. *Writer* and *artist* are words that designate a state of suspension, something eternally in abeyance. And so, after thirty years, I can call myself a "writer" because I finally understand the word as an open question, a question that suggests both the place from which it is asked (the individual) and the only place where it might be answered: the work itself.

MARGARET**ATWOOD**

Five Visits to the Word Hoard

My title is a tribute to *Nine Visits to the Mythworld*, Robert Bringhurst's amazing translations of the Haida poet Skaay. It's also a tribute to our Anglo-Saxon poets. "The word hoard" is what they called their well of inspiration, which overlapped with the language itself; and "hoard" signified "treasure." A treasure is kept in a secret, guarded place, and words were seen as a mysterious treasure: they were to be valued. And so I hold them to be.

When people ask "How do you write?" I say, "With a pencil," or something equally terse. When they ask "*Why* do you write?" I say, "Why does the sun shine?" or, if I'm feeling crabby, I say, "People never ask dentists why they fool around inside other people's mouths."

Let me explain why I'm so evasive.

No, let me not explain why. Instead I'll tell you a true story. As the creative writing teachers are always saying, "Show, don't state."

Here's the story: I have a friend who is a magician. He began in magic as a teenager, and did magic shows onstage, and from there went into radio, and then into television, and made a lot of money. But at heart he remains a magician, and he has invented many tricks and has contributed greatly to the literature of magic. Every year there's a magicians' congress in Toronto that revolves around him. Magicians come from far and near, and after the public part of the congress, there's a party for the magicians. Sometimes non-magicians are there too. At this party you can hear the magicians talking to one another.

Among the magicians, things are the same as they are among the birdwatchers, or among the poets, or among the jazz musicians, or among the members of any group of people who value an art, a craft, or a skill: that is to say, the usual social hierarchy – based on wealth or ancestry or company position or such – all of that dissolves, and individuals are valued by their peers according to their levels of accomplishment.

What are the magicians saying to one another? They're talking shop. Sometimes they'll split into pairs and trade secrets, one on one. The secrets they trade are trade secrets: they exchange tricks.

You've seen those TV programs on which magicians tell you How It Is Done. Those are immoral, as far as I'm concerned, because people go to magic shows to be dazzled and fooled and amazed – just as they read novels to enter into another world, and to be convinced that everything in that world is real, at least within the covers of the book. People don't want to know How It Is Done about magic, because that spoils the illusion. There's sometimes a smart kid in the audience who says, "I know how you did that!" And maybe, when we think about it, we do know. (Though not often, in my case.) But here's the point: even if we know, or think we know, *we can't do it ourselves.*

There's knowing what and there's knowing how, and the how comes from years of practice, and failure, and dropping the egg that was supposed to come out of the hat, and crumpling up

Chapter One for the twentieth time and throwing it into the wastepaper basket. Robert Louis Stevenson burnt three finished novels before he magically produced *Treasure Island*. Those incinerated novels were the three eggs he dropped. But the three broken eggs did not go to waste, for by dropping them he learned how to make the next egg appear out of what seemed like thin air.

Sometimes that never happens, of course. There's nothing inevitable about it. You can work away for years, but – alas, and to return to the metaphor of the magician – you've either got the hands or you don't, and if you don't have the hands, you'll never rise above the level of the merely competent. Sometimes it's just one uncooked omelette after another.

But also: you may have the hands – the talent – but not the motivation. In that case, you'll abandon your art quite soon, because you won't be prepared to put in the work – the work of the craft. I was once given a wonderful breakfast at a small Irish inn. When complimented, the man who ran the place said he'd worked as a chef at a restaurant that had now gone downhill. By coincidence, we'd eaten supper there the night before. I said that the meal had been very good.

"Ah yes," he said. "Anyone can cook a good meal . . . once."

We've all encountered those first novels that shine with the freshness of dew, and the second novels that wilt, and even the third novels that cause the briefly dead author to rise from the grave. Then there's the fourth novel, and the fifth, and the sixth – these are the ones that separate the sprinters from the marathoners. But art is cruel, and there's nothing necessarily more virtuous about a wondrous sixth novel – virtuous, that is, than a wondrous first novel. It may demonstrate character and perseverance in the practitioner – his or her ability to look in the mirror and ask "Why am I doing this?" and to keep on writing anyway – but that's all it demonstrates. As with magic, an unforgettable performance is an unforgettable performance, whether or not it's ever followed by another.

The poet Dylan Thomas has a poem that begins, "In my craft and sullen art." He names both art and craft: art, which requires some talent to begin with, which is why I will never be, and could never have been, an opera singer; and craft, which requires that the talent be honed and polished by focused discipline, which is why some people with marvellous voices will never become opera singers, either.

Robertson Davies had something to say about all this in *Fifth Business*. The character speaking in this passage is a young boy who's enamoured of magic – the conjuring kind – and longs to be able to do it. But he is clumsy, whereas Paul, the much smaller boy watching him practise his tricks, is not:

> I cannot guess now how many weeks I worked on the sleight-of-hand pass called The Spider. . . . But just try to do it! Try it with red, knuckly Scots hands, stiffened by grass-cutting and snow-shovelling, and see what skill you develop! Of course Paul wanted to know what I was doing, and, being a teacher at heart, I told him.
>
> "Like this?" he asked, taking the coin from me and performing the pass perfectly.
>
> I was stunned and humiliated, but, looking back on it now, I think I behaved pretty well.
>
> "Yes, like that," I said. . . . He could do anything with his hands. . . . There was no sense in envying him; he had the hands and I had not, and although there were times when I considered killing him, just to rid the world of a precocious nuisance, I could not overlook that fact.

It's much the same for any art – you need the hands. But you need more than the hands, too. Here is Alice Munro, in a short story called "Cortes Island":

> – it seemed that I had to be a writer as well as a reader. I bought a school notebook and tried to write – did write, pages that started off authoritatively and then went dry, so that I had to tear them out and twist them up in hard punishment and put them in the garbage can. I did this over and over again until I had only the notebook cover left. Then I bought another notebook and started the whole process once more. The same cycle – excitement and despair, excitement and despair. It was like having a secret pregnancy and miscarriage every week.
>
> Not entirely secret, either. Chess knew that I read a lot and that I was trying to write. He didn't discourage it at all. He thought that it was something reasonable that I might quite possibly learn to do. It would take hard practice but could be mastered, like bridge or tennis. This generous faith I did not thank him for. It just added to the farce of my disasters.

The narrator and her husband Chess are both right: you can work at a thing, and you can learn it – that is Chess's point of view. But only up to a point. Beyond that point comes the talent, which is a given. It's there or it isn't there, in varying quantities; it's not reasonable or predictable or demandable, and it can be with you at one point in your life and then vanish. Practising a craft can awaken a dormant talent. Conversely, too much practising can kill it. Such matters are incalculable, and much depends on coincidence. Much also depends on teachers, for all artists have teachers.

Sometimes they are living people – writers or not – and sometimes, more often, they are dead writers, or writers known to the aspiring young person only through their books. Often, when they think back over their lives, writers can remember the exact book they were reading – the exact moment – when their talent was first called into life. Frequently this happens in youth. But not always, because every life is different, every book is different, and every future is unpredictable.

So what can I tell you that will be of any use to you, if you want to write or are already doing so? Read a lot. Write a lot. Watch and listen and work and wait.

Apart from that, I can't tell you what to do. I can only tell you a little about what I myself have done. I'll describe some of my own visits to the word hoard: five of them. I won't tell you too much about the dropped eggs. You'll have to trust me on this: sometimes there was egg from wall to wall.

My first novel to be published was not the first to be written. That one has never seen the light of day, which is just as well. It was a dark book, not to say a lugubrious one, and it ended with the heroine wondering whether or not to push the male protagonist off a roof. I was twenty-three when I wrote it, and living in a rooming house – the room cost about seventy dollars a month – and cooking my dinners on a one-ring hot plate. They had plastic packages that you could boil, then, and that is what I did. The rest of the food I kept in a bureau drawer. The bathroom was shared with others, and it was there also that you had to wash the dishes, which gave rise to the odd frozen pea or noodle in the bathtub. I had a day job – that was how I paid for the room in the rooming house. I had a typewriter at the day job, and I could do the job itself in half the time I was at work, so after I'd finished what was required of me I would just roll my novel into the typewriter and type away at it. This gave me a pleasingly industrious look.

When I had finished this novel I sent it out to publishers, such as they were in Canada in those times. Several of them expressed interest. One publisher indeed took me out for a drink. He suggested that maybe I might change the ending to something a bit more cheerful. I said no, I didn't think I could do that. He leaned across the table and patted my hand. "Is there anything we can *do*?" he said, as if I had some kind of lingering disease.

That was Visit One. Here comes Visit Two. My day job while I was writing the first, unsuccessful novel was with a market-research company of considerable eccentricity, and it was this material – material, just as in sewing, is anything you use to make the thing you are making – it was this market-research office material that got into the next novel. By this time I had a different job: I was in British Columbia, filling a university teaching job on the lowest rung of the ladder. I taught a survey course – from Chaucer to T.S. Eliot in tiny bite-sized chunks – and I also taught grammar to engineering students at eight-thirty in the morning in a Quonset hut left over from the Second World War. The baby boom was hitting the universities then – it was 1964–5 – and there was a shortage of space. I made the engineers do writing exercises based on Kafka's short parables, which was good for them, I felt, since I was sure it would be of use to them in their future careers.

Meanwhile I continued with my secret life, which was the life of a writer. Like vampires, I had to pursue this life at night. I had a real sink of my own now in which to put the dishes. Like many young people, I would use every dish until they were all dirty and the first ones to be put into the sink were sprouting mould. (Vancouver is a damp place.) Then I would wash them all at once, in a burst of energy and desperation. There's not much about Kraft

Dinner with hot dogs cut up into it that I don't know. The rest of the time I ate at Smitty's Pancake Houses, especially on mornings when I did not have to be in the Quonset hut with the engineers. Sometimes, in a spurt of reckless hedonism, I went skiing.

I began my second novel in the spring of 1965. I wrote each chapter with a pencil in empty exam booklets left over from my teaching duties. These booklets were a convenient size – a sort of chapter size. I sat at a card table to do this writing, beside a window that looked out over the harbour and the mountains – it isn't always a good thing for a writer to have a lovely view, it can be distracting. If the writing came to a halt or I couldn't get started, I might go to the movies. Luckily I had no television set; indeed, I had hardly any furniture at all. I didn't see the point of it in those days – furniture was a thing parents had – and anyway I couldn't afford it.

I wrote on the right-hand pages, and on the left-hand pages I drew little pictures when I wanted to visualize more completely what one of the characters was wearing. Or I would make notes there. Then I would type the handwritten pages, an act complicated by the fact that I couldn't really type. (I used a typist for the final versions of novels until the personal computer became available. The last book I wrote in the old way was *The Handmaid's Tale*, in 1985.)

Using these imperfect methods, I cranked out my novel in roughly six months. A helpful hint: it's easier to go without sleep when you're younger. Then I sent off the retyped version to a publisher who had shown interest in the earlier one. (We didn't have agents in Canada then; now you'd have to go through an agent, no doubt, as there are a great many more people writing, and the publishers use the agents as a kind of sieve.) The publisher accepted the book, somewhat to my surprise. But then I didn't hear anything more about it for quite a few months.

By then I was back at Harvard studying for my Ph.D. Orals. I knew I would have to support my writing somehow, financially, and university teachers were in short supply then. I thought university teaching would be better than waitressing, which I'd already tried (I got very thin: looking at food already messed around by others has that effect), and also better than the few other things I might have been able to do. I'd been turned down by the Bell Telephone Company, and also by both of the publishers who subsequently became mine. All were quite right to reject me: I wasn't equipped for the jobs they were offering.

Once I'd passed my Orals, I went in search of my vanished novel. It turned out that the publishers had misplaced it. But they found it again, and after a revision, which I did in yet another location – Montreal, in 1967–8, while teaching both day and evening classes in Victorian and American Romantic literature – it was published, in the fall of 1969, just in time for some, though not others, to hail it as a product of the newly forged Women's Movement. It wasn't, of course. Its composition predated the en-masse advent of this movement by four years. But it did sort of fit in, since it ends with . . . but then, you should never tell the ending.

By this time I'd moved again, to a place where the Women's Movement had not even been heard of – Edmonton, Alberta. It was there that I did my first-ever book signing, in the men's sock and underwear department of the Hudson's Bay Company. I sat at a table near the escalator with my little pile of books, with a sign proclaiming the title: *The Edible Woman*. This title frightened a lot of men – ranchers and oil tycoons, I like to think they were – who had wandered in at noon hour to buy their Jockey shorts. They fled in droves. I sold two copies.

This was not my vision of the writing life. Proust never had to flog his books in a women's lingerie department, I reflected. I did wonder whether I might have taken a wrong turn on my career path. Perhaps it was not too late to go into insurance, or real estate, or almost anything other than writing. But then, as Samuel Beckett said when he was asked why he'd become a writer, "Not good for anything else." So I took my chances, and kept on going.

The third novel-writing experience I'll describe is somewhat more complex. We are now in the year 1994, and I have become a grown-up, at least to outward appearances. In spring, while on a book tour in Europe, in Zurich, city of Karl Jung, and while staying in a hotel with a view out over the water – always so conducive to controlled hallucinations, I have found – I began writing the first chapter of a book. I hadn't intended to start a book right then, but the choice of starting time never seems to be up to the writer. Another helpful hint to aspiring writers might be this: if you keep waiting for the perfect circumstances before you begin, you'll probably *never* begin.

As often before, I'd been trying to write another, quite different book just before this. But I found myself in the book that would eventually become my 1996 novel, *Alias Grace*. By this time I had evolved the following working method: I would write by hand for ten or fifteen pages. Then I would alternate between typing up those pages and continuing to advance, in handwriting, at what you could think of as the front lines of the book. It was a sort of rolling-barrage technique. That way I could keep in mind where I had just been while covering more new ground at the same time.

When I was about a hundred pages into the book, I realized that I had started it wrong. This happened on the train to Paris, where I was going to do some promotion for an earlier book. I was keeping a journal at the time, and here is what I wrote: "I had a sort of electrical storm in my brain – it came to me on the train that the novel was not working – but after two days of [here there is a drawing of clouds and lightning] I think I have the solution – it means throwing out some characters and stuff and rearranging, but it's the only way, I think – the problem is and always has been – what is the connection between A and B?"

Looking at these notes now, I can't remember exactly what A and B were. I think I'd been trying one of those in-the-present/in-the-past structures, but I threw out the present timeline and got right into the past, which was a lot more interesting and peculiar, since *Alias Grace* is based on a real-life double murder that took place in 1843. (How I came to know about this murder is another story.) I also changed the person in which the book was written from the third person to the first, and here is another helpful hint: if you're blocked, try changing the tense or the point of view. Frequently this will work. Also: if you have a really bad headache, go to sleep. Often you will have an answer in the morning.

As a rule I start out writing slowly, feeling my way into the cave, if you like. Then I gather speed and increase the hours until by the end I'm writing for eight hours a day and can barely walk without bending over, and can no longer see straight. By April 4, 1995, I had 177 pages of *Alias Grace*. By September 1995, I had 395 pages. You can see I was chugging along, rewriting as I went. I submitted the book to the publishers in January 1996, at which point I went to Ireland and became ill. This often happens when you finish an intense stretch of work of any kind: the body has wanted a rest for some time, and you haven't given it one, so it waits patiently until there's some breathing space and then it takes revenge.

The fourth visit to the word hoard involves *The Blind Assassin*. I set out with a sort of vision, induced probably by the family photograph albums. I was intending to write about my grandmother and my mother – both of their generations, which together would span the twentieth century – but my actual grandmother and mother were far too nice to be put into a book by me. So I started writing about a more problematic old lady who was dead, and who'd had a secret second life that was being discovered by a still-living character through some letters found in a hatbox. That didn't work, so I threw out the hatbox and the letters, but kept the secret life.

Next I was writing about the same old lady, but now she was still alive. She was being discovered by two other characters – nosy people, they were – and there was a container in this book too: it was a suitcase, and inside it there was a photograph album. But this didn't work either – the two other characters started having an affair, and the man was married and had just had twins, so I could see that the affair was going to take over the book and eclipse the old lady, who was the one I really wanted to write about. So into a drawer went the adulterous pair, and away went the suitcase – though I kept one of the photos.

At last the old lady began to speak for herself, and then the book could go forward. This third version had a container in it as well – it was a steamer trunk, and inside it were all of the things you will find inside it to this very day, in the chapter called "The Steamer Trunk."

I'm aware that the way I've told this story makes it sound a lot like "Goldilocks and the Three Bears," but there's something to that. You have to keep trying one chair after another until you find the just-right chair – the one that fits – and hope that not too many bears will come out of the woods while you're doing it.

The fifth visit to the word hoard took place in the summer of 2004, and resulted in a book that has been published very recently. It's part of a series called The Myths Series, which now has almost twenty writers and thirty-four publishers around the world involved in it. I got talked into doing this in Edinburgh some years ago, because I was ambushed at breakfast by a young, designer-stubbled publisher named Jamie Byng, and I hadn't had any coffee yet. These are my times of weakest willpower. The idea was to take a myth – any myth – and retell it in a book of a hundred pages or so. This is a darn sight harder to do than you'd think, as I soon found out.

I did give it a try. I tried it this way and that, with no results. I couldn't seem to get the kite to fly. As every writer knows, a plot is only a plot, and a plot as such is two-dimensional unless it can be made to come alive, and it can only come alive through the characters in it; and in order to make the characters live, there must be some blood in the mix. I won't sadden myself by detailing my failed attempts. Let's just say there were so many of them that I was on the point of giving the thing up altogether.

"Do you think Jamie Byng would mind very much if I just gave back the advance and cancelled the contract?" I asked my British agent. By this time I was embarrassingly behind deadline, and the first page was just as blank as it had always been. True, I had quite a few thirtieth pages, but they were crumpled up in the waste bin.

My agent's upper lip is nothing if not stiff, but I detected a quavering over the telephone as she said actually she expected that he might in fact mind quite a lot. But I shouldn't let that influence me one way or the other. And if I couldn't I couldn't, she added staunchly. But Jamie would probably be gutted.

I am susceptible to British slang. I did not want to be responsible for gutting anyone. "Give me a couple of weeks, then," I said. Desperation being the mother of invention, I then started writing *The Penelopiad*. Don't ask me why, because I don't know. Let's just say that the hanging of the twelve "maids" – slaves, really – at the end of *The Odyssey* seemed to me unfair at first reading, and seems so still. They were all hanged from the same rope – how frugal. As

The Odyssey says, their feet twitched a little, but not for long. So although Penelope herself, wife of Odysseus, is the main narrator of *The Penelopiad*, the second narrator is the Maids. They keep interrupting; like the chorus in a Greek tragedy, they comment on the main action, and act as a counterpoint to it. Sometimes they do this in popular song. I'm afraid I have called them The Chorus Line.

So that's five visits done, and I'm sure I've said enough about the way I write. Or about the way I've written so far. It can all change. It can all stop. The blank page is always pure potential, for everyone, me included. Every time you begin, it's just as frightening, and just as much of a risk. The magic can always fail, and the eggs that come out of the hat may end up on the floor.

I'll close by telling you another true story. I was in a café the other day, getting some takeout coffee, caffeine being my evil drug of choice. Quite a few people now recognize me, especially since I let myself be talked into impersonating a goalie on Rick Mercer's television show, and a man working in the café did too. He was from the Philippines, he told me. "You're the author," he said. "Is it a talent?" "Yes," I said. "But then you have to work very hard." "And you must have the passion, as well," he said. "Yes," I said. "You must have the passion as well. You must have all three things: the talent, the hard work, and the passion. If you have only two, you won't do so well." "I think it's like that with everything," he said. "Yes," I said. "I think it is." "Good luck," he said. "Good luck to you, as well," I said.

And now that I think of it, that's the other thing we all need. We need luck.

This essay is an amalgam and reworking of several speeches and one small piece.

RUSSELL**BANKS**

On Research

It's happened numerous times, but even so, I'm still surprised when, after I've read in public from my novels, a member of the audience – or sometimes someone from the press – comes up and asks me how I managed to do my research, how much had I actually done anyhow, and how much of the fiction was based on my own personal experience.

Surprised, I suppose, because the folks who pose these questions are usually serious readers of serious fiction and poetry. They are sophisticated and intellectual people, and thus one would expect them to understand that these questions are more reasonably directed to scholars, historians, social scientists, and journalists than to fiction writers and/or poets.

Actually, I wonder, are poets, too, thought to do research?

I'm reminded of a story told of the poet – Robert Creeley, I believe it was – who, having read to a university audience a particularly long poem, long for him, a poem describing the rise and fall of the narrator's marriage, was asked afterward by a member of the audience, "Was that a real poem, Mr. Creeley, or did you just make it up?"

So I guess, yes, in a sense, poets, too, are thought to do research – whatever *that* is, my purpose here being to try to look at what that is, at least for a writer of fiction. But the point is, I do feel sometimes that I'm being asked, "Was *Continental Drift, Cloudsplitter, Affliction, The Darling*, etc., a *real* story, Mr. Banks, or did you just make it up?"

I'm doubly surprised, although probably shouldn't be, when I realize, on attempting to answer the questions and watching emerge on my questioner's face a look of utter puzzlement, that the questions regarding research arise in large part from what I *look* like. That I, a late-middle-aged, bespectacled, befuddled ex-professor, should have written *The Relation of My Imprisonment* – a novel narrated by an abstracted, moralistic, obsessive-compulsive coffin-maker from the land of Plod on the Planet of the Puritans – is clearly less perplexing to my questioners than my having written *Rule of the Bone*, a novel narrated by a homeless, drug-abusing fourteen-year-old wanderer from upstate New York who journeys into the ganja-growing backwaters of Jamaica. But the fact is that I have done just as much and as little research to write the one as to write the other.

Well, surprise sometimes prompts reflection, and I've actually been reflecting on research in general and going back over my own particular backlist, as it were, those books whose process of composition I know best, trying to recall how I myself engaged in research while creating that backlist of novels and stories, so that for once, if only for myself, I might answer that apparently simple but deceptively deep and telling set of questions that come at one so frequently, usually after readings and in press interviews, but even from friends and students: how did you manage to do your research, and how much did you do anyhow, and how much of the fiction was based on your own personal experience? (Before you began that story or novel, what did you know, when did you know it, and how did you come by it?) These are questions that especially trouble young or beginning fiction writers, I think. They are serious questions, often put forward shyly and with other people listening impatiently for their turn, questions that, out of politeness, the constraints of time, and perhaps simply because we either don't know the answers or don't want to know them, we older, more experienced writers tend to deflect rather than answer. Or simply, we lie.

Then there is this – and fiction writers are as subject to it as any mere reader, and it may invite in us a bit of shame or lead us to exaggerate somewhat the nature and degree of our research: there is something in all of us that loves a *fact*, admires a "real" poem instead of one made up, prefers the *roman à clef* to the conjuration, ranks the thinly disguised autobiography above the literary vision-quest. It's an especially American hierarchy of value, I think – the predilection for "Just the facts, ma'am." Europeans and Canadians don't seem to worry much about it. But here in the U.S., agents, editors, publicists, film producers, all of them, when a new fiction manuscript starts to make its way slowly along the long, switch-backed, pocked and pitted road toward the solitary reader, all of them are secretly (and sometimes not so secretly) hoping against hope that the manuscript will turn out to be "Based on a True Story!" How much more eager we are, it sometimes seems, to see a fictional film, read a novel, story, or even a poem when it's advertised or even rumoured to be based on a true story. And if it can't be based on a true story, then we want it to be based on years of arduous research. We don't care where the research is done, and a university library is as good as the Himalayas. We probably don't *really* care if a novelist learned how to travel upriver into the heart of darkness from a book or by boat, so long as he did the research.

Actually, that's not true: we prefer him to do his own fieldwork; we Americans do, and for us, after all, there's no substitute in our minds for eyewitness testimony. He's the real man, or woman, he was there, the Old Man taught himself Spanish and caught that fish himself, learned to sail on Long Island Sound and went around the Horn from there, so call him Ishmael, give him the ears of the bull and the red badge of courage. Read his fiction, folks, and weep. It's okay. Even if it's not based on a true story, it's at least based on fact and personal observation. He did his research in the field. Or in a library.

The time has come to tell the real story, to spill the beans, at least my beans, and answer that simple set of questions honestly. In the last forty-some years, I have published fifteen books of fiction, set in places as far and different from Saratoga Springs and Keene, New York, where I live, as Haiti, Jamaica, South Florida, the decaying milltowns of upstate New York and northern New England, Liberia, and even a place not unlike a seventeenth-century English midlands parish village; and I've written a thousand-page historical novel which is set among anti-slavery agitators and abolitionists in mid-nineteenth-century America; and I have told short stories about, and even from the point of view of, Edgar Allan Poe and Simón Bolívar, Haitian peasants, oil-burner repairmen, parttime cops who dig wells and drive snowploughs for a living, Vietnam vets who run filling stations, middle-aged female bus drivers, paraplegic teenaged girls, a female ex-weatherman on the lam in West Africa, Rastafarian drug dealers, and yes, coffinmakers and mallrats.

And I have not done any research. Or not what I'd *call* research.

I'm not trying to sound positively Whitmanesque here, as if I contain in myself multitudes, or to suggest either that the curious circumstances of my childhood and a peripatetic early youth provided me with everything a fellow needs to know so that, later on, as a sedentary adult fiction-writer, I can write convincingly of Poe, Bolívar, small-town well-drillers, teenaged girls, Rastafarian drug dealers, and mallrats, etc.; or that my father's work as a plumber took the family from New Hampshire, where I was raised, to South Florida, Haiti, Harpers Ferry, Liberia, and mid-seventeenth-century England. Sadly, I was not so fortunate as to have had that unhappily disrupted a childhood or that interesting a life as a young man. Didn't happen.

No, what I'm trying to say is that when questions about research are put forward, they are actually questions based on what is generally known about how a journalist or scholar does research. And given that, my answer *should* be, "I'm sorry, but I don't do research."

It's not like, "I don't do windows." I wish I *could* do research. I wish I could *allow* myself to do it. Which is to say, I wish it were somehow *necessary* to my fiction, or could improve it, even a little. How I envy the scholar in his carrel in the bowels of Princeton's Firestone Library, poring over musty, tattered texts, filling his or her 3 × 5 cards with lost lines, forgotten connections, obscure allusions, and unsuspected collisions, totally clear about her subject and what information she will need in order to master it, which will ultimately come, she knows, when she has read and annotated everything that has ever been written or said about the subject. When she has become an expert on John Brown, the Kansas Border War, Harpers Ferry . . .

And how I envy the anthropologist in the field, tramping through trackless jungles to encamp for months and even years with half-a-dozen naked extended families, living the neolithic life alongside them, learning their clicking, humming names for the beasts and plants that surround them, deciphering their choreographies and rites, transcribing their creation myths, mapping their cosmologies, and observing the peculiarities of their mating rituals, wearing a loincloth, even, and body-paint and all-over tattoos and facial scars.

Not just the scholar and the social scientist: when it comes to the role research plays in their work, I envy the non-fiction writer and the journalist, too. Who wouldn't want to ride a train from London to Vladivostok for thirty days, or interview a serial killer, or hang with the camo'd gun-toting Freemen and militia pals of Timothy McVeigh, making interesting, shrewdly observant notations in a notebook, asking questions and tape-recording the answers, learning the *factual* truth, and cutting, shaping, planning, and honing it on a word processor back home into a five-thousand-word article for the *New Yorker* or fifteen hundred words for the *New York Times* travel section? I've done it a little myself, some modest attempts at scholarship and at journalism, and loved doing it, and will no doubt do it again. But I have to confess, it's not at all what I do when I'm behaving like a fiction writer.

Let me try to recapitulate how in three specific cases I obtained certain information *not* given to me by the accidents of my birth, childhood, and young adulthood, information which has usually been thought to have come into my possession by means of "research" (in quotes from here on). Let me describe how, but also, more to the point, *why* it came to me – that's very important – and what the information actually provided when it arrived – that's important too.

In the novel *Continental Drift*, there is all that Haitian lore concerning *voudon* (or voodoo), all those details and descriptions of the Haitian characters' flight from Haiti's north coast up along the Caribbean archipelago to South Florida, and the scenes set in Miami's Little Haiti section; there is the Haitian Creole that the characters sometimes speak to one another, paraphrased in English but left untranslated; there are the Haitian characters themselves, who obviously could not be less like me, especially the main character, Vanise Dorsinville, a young, black Third World peasant woman.

In a later novel, *The Sweet Hereafter*, we hear the story of a number of parents in a small town in upstate New York who have lost their children in a terrible schoolbus accident – which, thank God, has *not* happened to me – a story told from four points-of-view: that of the middle-aged schoolbus driver herself; a Vietnam vet who runs the local service station and has lost his twin children in the accident; a teenaged girl who was injured in the accident and is now a paraplegic; and a fast-track New York class-action litigator (some might call him an ambulance-chaser) who only coincidentally is in the process of losing his daughter to drugs.

And in *Rule of the Bone*, we hear – in language as close to my protagonist's spoken speech as I could get it – the story of a year in the life of a homeless, abused teenaged boy trying to survive in the malled-over world of mid-1990s America and who in order to do it has literally to leave the country.

When I began *Continental Drift* in 1982, I was living in Concord, New Hampshire, not far from towns just like the fictional Crawford, New Hampshire, the decrepit, closed-in milltown where the novel begins, from which a man named Bob Dubois, a white, thirtysomething oil-burner repairman packs up and flees for a better life in Florida. It's a town not unlike the one I was raised in, and Bob Dubois' situation and solution are not unlike those of my father, various male cousins, and more than a few uncles. So I knew almost first-hand what it was like to be inside Bob Dubois' skin and look out on the world; I knew what he would see out there in New Hampshire, what it would mean to him, and what it would not mean. And when he got to Florida, where I had wandered in my late teens and not much later felt trapped by early marriage and fatherhood there, I knew, once he arrived, what Bob would see of the world in Florida, too, and what that would mean to him.

The initial inspiration for the novel, however, was not my or my family's personal past. It was a photograph in the *New York Times* of the bodies of several Haitians washing up on the sands of Palm Beach, Florida. Within days of seeing that photograph and reading the accompanying account of how an American smuggler had tossed his human cargo into the sea when his boat was accosted by the U.S. Coast Guard, I was excitedly inventing a story that required a life and a world that converged with Bob Dubois' – the life of a Haitian peasant woman risking everything to get to America. It never occurred to me to make her a Haitian *man*, even though I am a man: the form of my story and its themes wouldn't have permitted it; or a *Jamaican* woman, even though I had lived in Jamaica in the mid-1970s for two years, had made many Jamaican women friends, and at that time had never been to Haiti at all and knew no Haitians personally; it was the Haitian migration I needed – for reasons of language, religion, and history, for reasons of drama.

Write about what you know, we're constantly told. But we must not *stop* there. *Start* with what you know, maybe, but use it to let you write about what you *don't* know.

The best fiction writers seem to be great extrapolators; they start with a cue, a clue, an iceberg tip, and are able to extrapolate from that the hero's entire soliloquy, the motive for the crime, the entire iceberg. How does Joyce Carol Oates, for instance, know so much about the sexual secrets of lusty, irresponsible, working-class white men? Or of African-American, inner-city male adolescents, for that matter? I mean, come *on!* Joyce is my good friend and longtime colleague at Princeton; she's a shy, reticent, decorous person who, to the best of my knowledge, does not hang with the homeboys. She's *got* to be extrapolating all that information from some small bit of only marginally related information close to home, conjuring an entire world of quotidian data, speech, night-moves, anxieties, sweaty desires, and hormonal after-effects, drawing it out of what . . . ? A pair of men's undershorts flopping in the wind on a backyard laundry line, glimpsed by her from the passenger's seat of a car speeding down the New Jersey Turnpike? I suspect so.

I needed more than that for the Haitian half of my story. You will note, however, that my story, its bifurcated form and its twinned but opposite central characters, and the controlling themes of immigration and the American Dream of perpetual self-renewal have preceded my need to know. They have in fact *created* it, not vice-versa. It was strictly on a *need-to-know* basis, then, that I took notebook and tape recorder in hand and went into the Haitian bush, returned to the U.S., and buried myself for weeks in the Columbia and then Princeton libraries, then flew to Miami and for several more wandered the streets and alleys of Little Haiti and rode fishing boats in Florida Bay. I even made a second trip into the Caribbean and island-hopped my way north from Haiti to the Turks and Caicos and Grand Bahama Isle, looking for locations, as it were. I worked like a film director with a script already written and actors already cast, looking to see what my Haitian characters would have seen and heard and smelled, and in that partial, limited way getting inside their skin.

We Americans usually associate the phrase "need-to-know" with a politician's desire to protect himself from future investigations into "what did you know and when did you know it?" Nixon and Watergate, Reagan and the Arms-for-Hostages scandal,

Clinton and Whitewater, George W. Bush and Weapons of Mass Destruction. As fiction writers, our motives are different, naturally, but we probably should instruct our staff the same way Ronald Reagan instructed his (as Nixon and Clinton should've instructed theirs): "Don't tell me anything I don't need to know." George W.'s staff probably needs no such instruction.

E.L. Doctorow, asked by an interviewer how much research he did for his novels, answered, "Just enough." As a fiction writer, one has no need to master a subject, to become an expert on it, or to report or otherwise testify on it later. In fact, quite the opposite. Because if I had done as much research to master a subject as would be required of a scholar of *voudon* or of Haitian migration to the U.S. in the mid-1980s or of vestigial cultural practices among second-generation Haitian-Americans in and around Miami, Florida, then it's very likely that my novel would have died a-borning. Its form and structure would have served no purpose but to organize data more or less coherently; its characters would have been case studies instead of complex, contradictory human beings; and its themes would have led me, not to the acquisition of a comprehensive vision of the larger world, but to a narrow, parochial didacticism and/or ideology.

Here's a second example. When *The Sweet Hereafter* was first published, I went out on the dreaded Book Tour, and in every city I visited, in Minneapolis, Portland, Oregon, Denver, and Miami, people would ask, "Is your novel about *our* school-bus accident?" Well, yes and no. Actually, it, too, took its inspiration from a newspaper article. I'd read a *New York Times* follow-up piece about how, a year after an awful school-bus accident in a South Texas Mexican-American town, the community had come undone, mainly due to the Bhopal-like arrival of out-of-town lawyers and the resulting lawsuits. Due to the belief in and search for that spurious post-traumatic condition called "closure" by means of establishing blame and exacting compensation for the victims, families had split up, finger-pointing neighbours had fought with one another, a whole town had broken down. A community had been atomized. I wanted to know how and why this had happened, and I wondered if it was the same thing that has happened to our culture and country generally in the last half-century – I wanted to know if that small South Texas town was somehow a metaphor or emblem that could stand for the whole.

I know little or nothing about South Texas Mexican-American communities, but a lot about upstate New York small towns, so, rather than do the research, I simply moved the bus accident there. I tapped into what I know. But I didn't write about it; I extrapolated from it. I happen to have lost a teenaged brother in an accident thirty-five years ago, and when I was a kid in New Hampshire, I had a vivid, tough-talking, soft-hearted woman school-bus driver, and my other brother is a Vietnam vet, and one of my four daughters spent a year in a wheelchair. The character of the lawyer, however, was a bit more problematic. As a man his age with grown daughters, I could get to his fears and desires – his psyche – fairly quickly. But, since I had a novel that would require a deposition scene and had never myself been deposed, I needed to know legal language, specifically the language of a deposition. So I turned to an acquaintance, a New York litigator who had represented a number of parents over the years who had lost children in accidents and were suing those agencies and individuals who were presumably responsible for their loss. I read forty or fifty of these depositions – not happy reading, believe me – and discovered in the process, not merely the legal language I needed to know, but also the voices of parents who had lost children. And in that way I discovered the four voices that control my novel. The unexpected gift.

For *Rule of the Bone*, you would think, since I am now eligible for Medicare and senior citizen discounts, that I would have nowhere to start, if starting with what you know is what I was supposed to do. Not true, however. The child is father to the man, after all, so all I had to do was renew my connections to the child I once was. My narrator, like me many years before, was a turbulent, angry, confused fourteen-year-old boy, alienated by divorce, violence, alcoholism, and disabling neurosis from his family and any larger community, a boy unprotected, uninstructed, and unloved. My novel would take him to the same place where, too frightened to go on, I myself had turned back and made the best of things at home for a little while longer.

I think generally novelists suffer from arrested development anyhow, so it wasn't difficult for me to return to the nest of snakes that passed for my emotional state when I was sixteen and stole a car and ran off from my Massachusetts hometown for three months with my pal Dario Morelli, only to be turned over to the cops in Pasadena by the priest that Dario, a Catholic, had confessed to.

Once back there in memory, which is to say, once I was properly situated emotionally, certain aspects of my old 1950s teenaged language returned to my listening ear, aspects that are perennial in teenspeak – generally characterized by a defensive, flattened tone that can shift meaning from irony to praise by adjusting in micro-tonic degrees, can move inflection from one syllable to another and turn putdown into wonder, all of it conveyed by means of a syntax that reflects suspicion and mistrust of the listener, sentences that withhold the important, self-revealing clause to the end, sliding qualifier escape-hatches into nearly every adjective and adverb. The essential aspects of my narrator's voice weren't far from my own long-muted adolescent voice, once I started listening to it.

Also, since I wanted my story to take my narrator, Chappie, a.k.a. Bone, gradually out of his family, then out of his town, and finally on to Jamaica, and perhaps complete the journey that I myself had only begun when I was sixteen and had thus been obliged to complete in other ways many years later – because of that, I knew that in the course of his journey he would be obliged to deal with themes of race and class. He could not travel to Jamaica and escape them. And, too, I knew the traditions I was tapping into, their forms and norms, their powers and limitations.

What I needed to give me full, easy access to Chappie's voice, then, to fill out the blanks in my knowledge of teenspeak, was mainly lexical. I needed to know the names of the things that filled his world, his names for them. For, even though he was a white, lower-middle-class fourteen-year-old dropout from another one of those upstate New York milltowns, as I had been myself, it was now forty years later, and American society had been profoundly altered in the intervening years, so for a few weeks I made it my business to imitate an anthropologist of the mall, encamping there as much as possible and learning gradually my subjects' names for the many things that surrounded them – the words they use for the herbs they use for medicinal, recreational, and religious purposes, their native foods, their articles of clothing and adornment, even their weapons. I studied their native dances, read their master-texts, diagrammed their kinship patterns, and observed their sexual rituals.

What was surprising and in the end far more valuable to me, however, was that by having placed myself where I could see the world of family, community, school, even the larger culture that surrounds all Americans, and having seen it from a kid's perspective, I was able to understand and clarify for myself the larger implications of my themes, especially the theme of America's lost children, who, as far as *they* are concerned, are not so much lost as abandoned.

Let me try to wrap this up more or less neatly by returning to my claim that I don't do research. I can't. I mustn't. Not in the way that people who don't write novels do research. For a novelist, research must always and exclusively serve the purposes of one's characters, one's narrative forms, story, theme, plot, and style. Not vice-versa. From my point of view, scholars and journalists have got it all backward.

Of course, later, when the novel has been published, one is often thought an expert – on Haiti, or on *voudon*, say, or negligence suits, or mallrats and drug use, or pre–Civil War U.S. history, on West Africa – which has its occasional pleasures and perks, until you meet someone who really is an expert on these matters.

But then there is always the mystery of the thing you got right, the thing that no scholar, no anthropologist, no journalist ever could have known about. There is the mystery, for instance, of how I knew solely from a photo in the *New York Times* and the accompanying news clip that the captain of the boat that brought the Haitians across from Grand Bahama Isle, the man who had tossed the Haitians into the water to drown a few hundred yards off the coast of North Miami, had a Jamaican mate who'd encouraged him to do this terrible thing. The news clipping that inspired the novel had made no mention of a mate; yet years later, there comes a letter from a Bahamian lawyer congratulating me on that particular detail and wondering how I did my research. "How'd you know that?" he wants to know. Because he was the very lawyer who had defended that Jamaican and got him off and deported – and he'd had the man's record erased.

And there's the pleasure of learning that the novel about the school-bus accident is being taught in several law schools, strictly because of the accuracy of its portrayal of a negligence lawyer and the complex moral issues that these people must deal with as professionals. They want to know if I'm one of those novelists who went to law school.

And there's the pure delight of hearing a sixteen-year-old girl with a shaved head and nose rings telling me, "Dude, you got it right. You got how it *feels* to be a kid. How'd you do your research, anyhow?" she asks.

The only honest answer is, I don't *do* research. I write fiction. I tell stories. They are real stories, and I make them up.

DAVID**BERGEN**

And You Arrive on the Other Side With Nothing

Ten years ago when my wife and I and our four children moved to
Vietnam, we found ourselves, temporarily, in a hotel in the heart of
the country. We thought ourselves lucky to have two TVs and two
refrigerators, until we discovered that none of them worked. We
appeared to be the only guests in the hotel, save a rock band from
Hanoi whose ten members slept all day and in the evening waltzed
across the cement floor of the great empty dining room. We took
our meals in a tiny café across the street and we woke each morning
believing that today we would have the house we had been promised and that soon we would fall into the life we had imagined.

We had arrived in the country, vainly enthusiastic and hopeful,
and discovered early on that, perhaps, we had chosen badly. For
the first time in my life I felt strangely lost and out of control. I
wept one night; deep unbeckoned gulps. My oldest son cried too,
out of the blue, while talking about the women and men grabbing
his penis in the market. The town, Quang Ngai, was rural: the
dress, the food, the style. The market swam with cone hats and
smelled of fish sauce and wet chicken feathers. And yet, what did
I expect?

We had spent the first week in Hanoi and on Sunday had attended the ecumenical service at the United Nations' building, where a priest in jeans and a T-shirt gave the sermon. He had a habit of leaning back against the wall and making a tent with his fingers in front of his face. Thinking. He talked about free will and quoted Augustine: *Myself I willed it, and myself I nilled it: it was I myself. I neither willed entirely, nor nilled entirely.*

Though I fought the tendency, I felt that we had failed in some way. And though I disliked Augustine, I kept thinking, *It was I myself.* I knew about the difficulty of arrival, we had done this before in another country and succeeded, but we had not counted on the uncertainty here, the intransigence of the local government, the lack of a house, a kitchen, a pot, a bottle of oil, or a simple hot plate.

One morning in Quang Ngai we celebrated our son Luke's fifth birthday. At 5:30 a.m. I went out to the market and purchased, with much haggling and gesturing, a Russian hot plate, frying pan, bowl, sifter, spatula the size of a shovel, oil, flour, eggs, milk, and salt. As I walked back to the hotel, a man squatting beside the road spit in my direction. I ascended to the third floor and mixed up pancake batter, plugged in the Russian cooker, poured oil in the pan, placed the pan on the cooker, and promptly received a shock.

Our translator, Mr. Kiet, had joined us. He laughed. "No problem. No shock," he said. He explained that the plug was, indeed, inserted upside down. He turned it right side up and smiled, "There." I gave him an oblique look, but for his sake had another go. I was again jolted. Undaunted, I put on rubber flip-flops and produced a marvellous mass of pancakes which the kids devoured, dressing them with a syrup purchased in Hanoi. Mr. Kiet tried one. He didn't like it much. Too sweet.

Later, Luke searched for his presents, we sang "Happy Birthday," and by 8 a.m. the party was over. We sat around until Kiet suggested the beach. We went and burned our shoulders and feet. The beach went on endlessly, a stretch of sand laid out millions of years earlier as if in preparation for our arrival. We ate Choco pies, an imitation of a chocolate Wagon Wheel, and drank warm water. Our youngest slept in a hammock. The surf fell. Time seemed prodigious. The moon grieved in the sky. We were all alone.

From that first hotel we moved to a guest house and then to another hotel and, eight weeks after arriving in Vietnam, we moved into a house. It was a small bungalow enclosed by a brick wall rimmed with barbed wire, and on three sides neighbouring houses rose within one foot of our windows. On the open south side, beyond the wall, was a small lane in which young children played marbles and the husband and wife next door did battle, voices raised, dishes rattling. To the north, just past the landlord's hut, was the pig farm where at night five or six men made rice noodles, talking loudly.

Our landlords, out of goodwill and wanting perhaps to celebrate the amount of money they were making on rent, had us in for supper. A couple arrived, people we'd never met before. They were introduced as Lan and Binh. Lan wore a red dress with a long scarf and Binh had on a light blue suit. Silent, smiling. An artist, who spoke English, was present as well. He wore a white shirt and his face was dark and scarred and long. He was an eloquent drunk. He quoted Kalil Gibran a lot and Ernest Hemingway. He said, "I read *The Prophet* years ago when I was in school. How do you say his name, Kawleel Zibrun? Like that. And Hemingway, you know that one about the fish where the old man comes back with nothing? That's it. You fly over things, you must, and you arrive on the other side with nothing. Take God for example. Not Buddhism or Catholicism, but just God. You ask me. Do I believe? I love the tiniest flower, that rock, that tree, the blue moon. I am not a Communist. I can believe. But that's a big question. Everyone's question."

Later, after he'd finished talking, the artist left, and the rest of us settled down to eat tripe, headcheese, a frightening-looking greasy soup, wonderful spring rolls, and salad. And we drank beer and Coke and poured whisky from a bottle shaped like a golf ball. Conversation was dominated by monosyllables and lots of grins. Huynh, the landlord's daughter and an architectural student, seemed embarrassed by her father's mix of garbled French and Vietnamese.

"Have some tripe," he said. "Beef, beer, whisky."

I accepted all four, and later asked for water.

Ba Bich, the landlord's wife, was dressed in her finest, a kimono-like outfit of raw silk. She touched the boys' heads and whispered to them. Huynh left and came back with chocolate. And watermelon. Before supper she'd been cooking in the chicken coop, fanning the coals with a piece of cardboard. She'd been wearing an old T-shirt and jeans. Now she was wearing new overalls and a sweater. She minced, pouted, and preened.

We praised the food and were given more. The boys devoured the chocolates. More beer was drunk. We gave gifts: cookies and a Sheryl Crow tape. Nam, the teenage boy, seemed pleased. He rose, dipped slightly, and said, *Thank you, David, thank you, Mary.* He proceeded to clean up then and he managed to do it all by himself as his sister slipped away to visit with two boys who had shown up at the gate. The rest of the evening we could see her through the slats in the brick wall, holding court, waving her thin fingers through the air and giggling.

We went to bed that evening thinking that good things were

beginning to happen to us. We had a house, we had eaten well, we were liked by our landlords. Still, beneath all the goodwill, there was the understanding that deliverance does not come that easily.

In the morning I went to get bread. By the bakery there was a soup stand. Bit of a hovel. Huge black tureen. Plastic stools stuck in the mud. Tiny tables all hurly-burly. On one of the red stools sat a woman. Her blue hair was thrown up in a chignon poked through with two carved sticks. A few wisps fell to her neck. Bright red lipstick. White teeth. Long neck. High heels. Skirt. She was eating soup, a dead chicken at her feet.

Our landlord beat his wife. We didn't hear anything, no argument, no fight, no blows. But in the morning he left on his bicycle and we caught a glimpse of Ba Bich. She had toilet paper bunched up in her ears and one side of her face was swollen. She explained she fell against the wall. The son agreed, "She fell against the wall." The landlord came home and he looked sheepish, almost contrite. He was a hard, balding, wiry man, a former war-hero. He came into our house later and stood by the map of the world and pointed at various countries as if he were blind and trying to guess by touch where he was or what actually existed beyond his reach. He talked to me then in his strange language, and I ended up agreeing and nodding, "Va, va. Oui, oui."

That same day we caught a butterfly in the garden. We looked in our butterfly book and decided it was a variation of the *Common Rose Swallowtail*. Turned out it could have been poisonous. It was reddish blue with rounded wings and robust, club-shaped tails.

And then one afternoon we rode our bicycles up past the Pissing Wall to Ong Ich Khiem Street and then turned left toward the river. The traffic was thick and children played along the side, their brown legs kicking into the sky. An old woman with sticks for ankles wiped herself beside a tree. Two dogs were backed into each other and three boys tried to beat them apart with a metal rod. Hawkers called out their own special sorrow and chickens rolled on the dusty sidewalks. Pigs hollered from a living-room-turned-sty as a young woman washed clothes at the edge of the road. A cyclo passed carrying two teenage boys holding hands. In the doorway of a welder's shop an arc of blue light offered a mother cradling a baby. We boarded the ferry. A blind man sang, in a terrible voice, songs we did not understand. His plastic bowl held a small amount of cash. Once across the river we disembarked and rode up a small busy lane toward the beach.

The ocean was heavy and the waves irregular and large. Fishing boats in the distance. I took the two older children out into deeper water. We held hands and fought the surf.

"Come, my sweet little chickens," I said.

And then we went under. And came up. Choking, I called the children to me. I held each by an arm. We were swamped again and again by the waves. The shore floated away. I looked back to the open water and wondered if we could reach the outer calm and tread water until a boat arrived. We were hit by three waves in succession and then I was standing on a sandbar, holding my children. A fisherman waded out to help us. We had travelled a great distance down the beach.

Mary appeared. "You were gone," she said. I let go of my son's arm. My grip had bruised him. His eyes in the bright light were black.

"You just disappeared," Mary said.

The fisherman scowled and scolded us. I was tired and embarrassed and salt water ran from my nose. I wiped at it with my forearm. A small crowd had gathered; it turned out a boat had been called. Our subdued assembly walked up to the nearby restaurant. My daughter wanted to go home. I ordered two Cokes; they remained unopened. We showered and climbed on our bikes and rode down to the ferry. It was dark when we reached the other side of the river. We rode up Bach Dang, past the whores on Quang Trung Street, and one, her face powdered white, became the moon which pulls at the tides in men's hearts.

I was baptized on a Sunday morning at the age of seventeen in front of three hundred people in a small town in Southern Manitoba. Pastor Abe Konrad held me as I went under the water and then he drew me back up again and gave me a slight push to aid my exit from the tank. The rug in the church was blue. There were large open rafters of varnished oak holding up the church roof. Narrow windows ran high along the side walls. It was impossible to see anything through these windows save the occasional clump of leaves or a pigeon strutting beside the eaves. I believed, at that age, that salvation was extremely personal, that conversion was marked by a specific time and place, and that baptism by water, the going under and returning, was a testimony to the world, to my world, of my newness.

Though I am a different man today, and no longer believe in a selfish salvation, I am still taken with the idea of pushing a new Christian under the water and drawing him forth again. I cannot imagine, if this is your desire, any better way to proclaim redemption.

My brother, who lived in Nigeria, wrote that every day he had to stand in line for petrol, bread, and water. But with the arrival of the hot season, when the wind blew dry, and sand coated the insides of the houses and got into the sugar bowl, water had become more important than bread or petrol. One day, after an hour of waiting, he received his two buckets of water and proceeded home. On the street, a jeep approached, swerved out of control, and in avoiding the jeep, my brother spilled his two buckets. He said the water fell onto the sand, and though he attempted to scoop it up with his hands, it disappeared. He was left with nothing but damp sand. What surprised and frightened him was not the quick evaporation of the water, but his own desperate act of attempting to salvage what was already lost.

What we have on our hands is always enough. Though I counselled myself, I was still illogical and fearful, especially for the children. A prescient parent's fear. One night my son dreamed that he was drowning, except that he was all alone this time. He woke, calling out, and my wife went to him. I dreamed that I was in a large house, running from room to room, and that a child of mine, nameless and faceless, was needing to be rescued. Of course I could hear the calls but I could not find the room. I woke to the screech of a pig and the bread lady calling in the lane, "*Bang mi, oy!*"

One afternoon, I sprayed the house with Baygon because of the recent onslaught of mosquitoes. At night, in bed, I could still taste the poison in my mouth and I thought how stupid I was, killing my children slowly. I saw dangers everywhere. On the roads riding our bicycles, the crazy teenage boys speeding by, the trucks, the hard pavement coming up to meet a soft skull. I saw danger in the rats, the dogs, and, of course, the ocean. I imagined electrocution, snakebite, dengue, choking, rabies. I would lie awake at night and think of how we still had to fly back up to Hanoi on an ancient

Tupalo, the Russian-built airliner, one of which had crashed in Danang the previous week.

In the past I had imagined the possibility of one of my children dying, yet in Vietnam the chances seemed augmented, inevitable, as if God's grace were less present, as if the country's official absence of belief had left my own family open to disaster and the whims of misfortune. I wanted to believe that mercy or God had little to do with our fate. I was raised in a home where my father, the pastor, invoked the Lord's will for whatever happened in life, especially miraculous escapes from death. In fact, we had called my parents and told them about the incident at the beach, and my father, signing off, suggested Isaiah 55:6-10. *"For my thoughts are not your thoughts, neither are your ways, my ways," saith the Lord.*

I allowed him that belief, that escape, and in some ways I too believed in miracles, even if it was the simple miracle of waking up anew each morning. However, that week, I could not let go of the fear that came with the uncertainty of life in that country. And so I hungered for routine, however small, because it was the quotidian that made an existence more bearable: riding out to buy bread every morning; drinking three-in-one coffee at the breakfast table; boiling up water for instant soup; building Lego; riding bike down to the harbour to sit and crack peanuts in the early afternoon while most of Danang rested; reading to the children under the mosquito net and falling into a world that was mercifully elsewhere; playing badminton in the front garden while butterflies and bees hummed and dipped; all those things took away the fear for the moment.

Unlike my father, who believed in an angry but forgiving God, I wanted to hold to the mysterious and if that was my only form of faith, so be it. Yet faith seemed distant those days and I wondered if my children saw me as an angry, frustrated man. My daughter said that I yelled too much at the younger boys. For that, I was sorry. Still, I suffered the weight of the days and nights, the domesticity, the uncertainty, the immediacy of the children I had sired, of my own choice. More and more it felt as if we were completely alone.

The thing was, we were not travellers and so it wasn't about to end the next week or even the next month. A brief madness descended. One day I hit my youngest son, Levi, across the head with a book and he cried miserably and gasped, "You hit me, Da Da. You hit me." After he calmed down I read him *Jelly Belly*, which he loved and held dear. And then, for no good reason, one evening I left the supper table in a rage. Held my head in the corner bedroom and rocked back and forth. Levi came to curl up beside me. He did not cry or talk. Just touched my leg.

Jacob Boehme, a Protestant mystic and philosopher, made the classical statement that all things are rooted in a Yes and a No. You cannot have one without the possibility of the other. On fear and anxiety, Paul Tillich wrote that courage can overcome fear because there is always an *object* of fear, but courage cannot necessarily overcome anxiety because anxiety is naked and so has no clear outline at which we can point a finger and say, "There, there, there it is."

I was suffering from some absurd fear, brought on by the faltering of our own lives and perhaps the near drowning of myself and Hilary and Nicky. But, there was also anxiety, and anxiety fell into the realm of the unknown, of what happened *after*, and in this sense I was not worried about myself but thought only of my children. At that point I would gladly have given up my own life to save theirs. Only, I did not know how to do that, and I was keenly aware that I had failed, or that failure was imminent.

The rain fell for eighteen straight days. Our sheets were wet, the wind was cool. Then, by chance, I happened upon a man who, riding his bicycle beside mine, pointed at a procession ahead of us and said, "A Vietnamese funeral." We talked for a while, he was an older man who seemed to understand what life had given him, and then he said goodbye and disappeared. It was those surprising and uncalled-for acts of kindness that buoyed me, and it would be that man who would change our lives in Vietnam, for he had not disappeared, he would return: to feed us and give us gifts of chokecherry wine, light bulbs, and dates. And we would talk together. Sometimes his wife would join us and sit quietly in the corner, her oily forehead shining, and her husband would raise the ubiquitous glass of water and say, "Let us toast." And we would.

The days passed. And the madness passed as well. It disappeared with the rains and so at night, through the window, instead of the beating of water against the walls and the trellis, I could hear the passersby just beyond the wall that enclosed our garden. Motorcycles, pedestrians, cyclists, young children crying, people talking. The language I heard was more beautiful because I did not understand it.

These are some days from my life. There was no writing in those days, but they made the writing that came after possible.

JOHN**BERGER** • MICHAEL**ONDAATJE**

A Conversation

MICHAEL ONDAATJE: I wonder if, as a writer, you are influenced more by writing than by art.

JOHN BERGER: I think maybe I'm most influenced, only when I'm writing fiction, by the cinema and neither painting nor writing.

MO: Why cinema? What does that give you that inspires you or leads you into something?

JB: Three things. First of all, and you know everything about this, cinematographic editing, which seems to me something very, very close to a form of written narrative. Also, that one can have long vistas and close-ups one after the other. And lastly, because of the relationship of the cinema to its public; there are two things very special about that. First of all, it's in the dark. Secondly, there are frequently quite a lot of people together and yet each is listening and looking alone. People can't look at paintings like that; they can't read books like that and somehow, that image, not really of a public, it's [more] an image of collaboration, the collaboration of the spectator who is no longer a spectator but who is part of the telling of the story; that image which comes from the cinema is, to me, more encouraging than the other two.

MO: Yet there's something about reading that is a wonderful, private, secret thing, which is exactly opposite to that more democratic group audience response.

JB: But don't you think being in the cinema is private and secret?

MO: Oh it is. But I'm not sure that will influence *me* as a writer, because I think, in order to write, I need to go somewhere that's excessively private in myself and so, even to think about an audience or a group response would make it very difficult for me to write even one paragraph.

JB: Yes, I understand that, but you sometimes make films for yourself, yes? Is that a very different you that makes those films from the you that writes?

MO: I think it is. I think there's a limit to what films can do in getting below the surface of things. Obviously they're wonderful, and I think that great films like *La Jetée* or *The Tree of Wooden Clogs* are equal to the major fiction of our time. I'm not saying one is better than the other, but I think that to write, sometimes you need to escape that kind of place where you are conscious of the audience or of a response. Although when I'm editing a book, like you, I am very conscious of what I've learnt perhaps from film editing, which *does* take the art of editing *very* seriously, almost microscopically. It takes it much more seriously sometimes than a novelist does.

JB: Yes. And when you have that need, which I fully recognize, to be intensely private, to withdraw, are you withdrawing into yourself or to somewhere else? Where is that place that you find yourself when you withdraw?

MO: I don't think it's withdrawing. It's more like descending, in the sense that I'm trying to descend to a level that I haven't gone to before. If I began to write something that I already knew, it would be a problem for me, so I'm trying to accept the given of what I know and *begin* by writing something I don't know. That's why that privacy and secrecy, which in a way I'm obsessed with, is necessary, and it becomes a time of discovery as opposed to clarification.

JB: And when you make that descent, and if we take for a minute the image of the diver, and you need oxygen for that descent, is the oxygen language or something else?

MO: It's curiosity. But I think I need, at least in the longer works, at the same time as I descend or withdraw, a real place and situation – Venice perhaps, in 1926 – some small fraction of a situation that I can begin with, and then within that place I can become as intricate or as private as I want to be in what I'm writing. But I do need that situation, otherwise I think it would be like surrealism for me. I'd never be touching the earth. But there is also the essential curiosity at, say, what went on between two people, or why did this person go mad in the parade in 1911, something like that, it begins with that question of curiosity, I think. But something like your novel *G.* Did that begin with an image or a scheme, a plan? Was there a *structure* somewhere in your head? Was there a landscape? A time period?

JB: Do you find that a book *has* a beginning point?

MO: I tend to find that beginning at the end. When I finish the book, then I realize where the book should begin.

JB: Ah yes, in the book, but before, before writing, in your head or in your imagination, isn't it very difficult to date or really be precise about how . . .

MO: It's a very unfair question.

JB: No, it's not an unfair question, because it's the kind of question that everybody asks. It's quite a reasonable question. I have a feeling that of course there is that beginning point, but I'm not sure that we ever know it in a way, and it seems to me it surfaces usually in a completely false form. For example, about G., if I just try to remember my conscious thought . . . not so long before, I'd written a book about Picasso [*The Success and Failure of Picasso*] and sometime in the writing of that book, I thought of Picasso as a kind of Don Juan in relation to the rest of painting. It's just an image, there's no need to analyze it, it's a rather stupid image, but nevertheless it was there and so then I started thinking about Don Juan in the twentieth century, about Don Juan and history. Okay, but I don't think that's where G. began really at all. I think that was a kind of signal coming up into the discourse that was going on in my head and which used that to say, "Hey, listen to something else." With *Anil's Ghost*, your last novel, I don't think it began because you made a trip to Sri Lanka . . . ?

MO: No. When I asked about structure before . . . Well, what I love about your books is that their structure is as thin as skin. We're not conscious of it, we're not conscious of an edge to the story. So when I'm reading one of your books, there's a feeling that you can just take us all over there for two or three chapters and bring us back. And I think *G.* was the first book in contemporary fiction where I saw it happening, where you describe a crowd and suddenly you come in and say that they're not ready to talk, that we don't know how to describe this crowd yet . . . I can't remember the exact lines but I held on to that moment in *G.* and you held that note of "explanation" back for another 150 pages, and then during a later scene, you said, "*Now* we can describe the crowd . . . ," so there's that sense of having a guide who's not constantly handcuffed to us but who can come in every now and then. We have a form that is so open you can go into discourse, you can go into essay, you can go into drawings on the page, you can go into past history . . . that's the kind of structure that your book surrounded me with. So I'm just wondering where that structure comes from, if it's something that's naturally invented as you write the novel, or do you see parallels in art or music for instance?

JB: Well, I can only describe what happens, which doesn't make much sense, but before I really start writing a story, like you there is something there. There is Venice or a date or a character, but that's only a starting point. The story in my mind is absolutely not verbal. There are no words for it at all. Nor is it visual, it's not a series of shots or a painting. It has something in common with music in the sense that it is complex and can be held in the head like a whole musical composition, although it can never all be there at any one given moment. I haven't any words for it. It is perhaps in a way geometric, but it's not, because I think that implies an incredible precision. Perhaps it is algebraic in a way, but it's much more chaotic than that; and the strange thing is that, for a long, long time when writing, I check it against this inarticulate, totally amorphous thing, and *it* can say with certainty, "no, what you've just written is false" or, occasionally, occasionally, "yes, perhaps that's not too far away."

MO: I think that's a wonderful description. When I begin a book, I have in my head as well that it's an unfinished ideal, and it's not all verbal, it's sort of like a tone of music.

JB: That's right, that's right.

MO: You go toward that tone.

JB: Yes. Is it the same when you write poems?

MO: When I write poetry, I think it's more to do with language. The source is language. Not that language isn't there with fiction . . .

JB: You asked me a few hours ago to read something I've written about Caravaggio and, in *The English Patient*, for me perhaps the most important character is called Caravaggio. Tell me, why is he called this?

MO: Well, whenever I think of you, of your work, the first thing I always think about is that piece on Caravaggio.

JB: Yes?

MO: I love that section about power and about the avoidance of people with power. To me, it's such an intimate portrait of someone and, again, it's this ideal made out of someone who was in no way ideal in real life, one suspects. When I was writing *In the Skin of a Lion*, there were two things. I must have read that essay in a magazine and then I saw the Caravaggio show in New York. I just never forget walking out of those rooms that had his paintings and through the rest of the gallery where everything else, centuries of work, seemed so pathetic compared to those images that were leaping off the canvas at us. I was about halfway through the book and the character of Caravaggio was born. It was almost like a flamboyant gesture to call this character Caravaggio, and I had to somehow rationalize his existence and his name. He was this out-sider, this character who stormed into the story halfway through. Most of my most essential characters come to me halfway through a book, like Kip [in *The English Patient*] and Gamini [in *Anil's Ghost*], so I sort of wait for these people. And the artist Caravaggio was for me this kind of person, where you know there are no boundaries between him and everybody else that he paints. There's a kind of furious democracy in him, which is perfect for the thief in a way.

JB: When one of these characters breaks into the story halfway through, does she or he do it suddenly? Or does he infiltrate himself in?

MO: They just seem to enter. There's a line, "Hey, Caravaggio," which someone yells out in the book, when they're working on the bridge. That line came up much later on, but I moved it up close to the front. And with Kip, there is a scene where Hana is very depressed and she goes downstairs and plays the piano. And while she's playing, there's a thunderstorm and these two men walk in. At that point I didn't know who they were. Are they dangerous? Are they allies? Are they the enemy, or what? And one of them was Kip. So then I had a situation where I had to decide, do I invite this person in or do I keep him out of the story. And I think Hana goes off to make him a sandwich while I was still forming the decision to keep him or not. Gradually I was delighted to keep him in the story and in a way I'd been preparing his entrance, because the whole place was mined with bombs and he was a bomb disposal expert. So again it seemed essential for me to bring him in, but at the time, these characters seem to be gate-crashing.

Do you let characters do that in your works?

JB: Yes, I think they do, sometimes, but maybe a little differently, and it's something I want to ask you about. Because it seems to me that at a certain moment, when one's writing a long story perhaps; if it's a very short story of a few pages it doesn't work, but it must be a work that is taking months or years – of course even a very short story can take months or years, we know that – but at a certain moment, actually when perhaps you're very tired, but at a certain moment life begins . . . well, normally life is absolutely opposed to the activity of painting or to the activity of writing or to all, all creative activity. I mean life has a total continual conspiracy against creativity. We know that and we have to fight for it all the time, but there are certain moments when life, just everyday life, comes and helps. And you never know when it's going to happen and then it's amazing, because you just do the same things that you do every day, you go out to do some shopping or you look at somebody on a train or whatever, and it *speaks* and it contributes an actual idea, an actual image, a colour or something, or a whole sequence of things, to the story. Does this happen to you?

MO: Yeah, I think that happens a lot, and it is almost like moving from documents to fiction in a way for me. I think that conspiracy against writing or painting *does* exist, but for me it's about finding that kind of accidental occurrence in the real world that can enter the story in a way and kind of double its value.

JB: Yes. An accident is very important, isn't it?

MO: All my writing is hopefully based on accident. When I'm writing a scene, I will not know the eventual arc of that scene at all. I am waiting for something to happen, waiting for someone to say the wrong thing, change his or her mind, do something odd, pour some milk over somebody's hand. Odd things like that that are outside the normal behaviour of a scene.

JB: Yes.

MO: But the art of drawing, the pleasure of drawing, which I know you do all the time, the pleasure of painting and all the different structures you find in painting that you don't find in fiction, I would think all that would be important to you. I tend not to learn from fiction, from my own art. Perhaps I do, but not consciously.

JB: What do you learn from?

MO: If I am reading I will find myself totally immersed in the world of that novel, whereas I can look at a painting and recognize a device. When I was writing *In the Skin of a Lion*, I was very conscious of Diego Rivera's murals and how someone's holding a wrench on this wall, and someone's holding a pencil over there – that they were composed with exactly the same hand gesture. I learned a lot from that kind of echo. So the structure of a novel becomes a repetition or a recognition of echoes perhaps.

JB: Yes. That's very important, Michael. I see that, because echoes and repetitions, I don't know what they are in the body of a story, but no story exists without them. They're an incredibly important part of its body.

MO: Even the repeat of that crowd in *G.*, it's like a huge musical note that is brought up to the surface again to remind us.

JB: But now, because you asked me what drawing was to me . . . when you are drawing, anyway when you are drawing something which is alive . . . no, I'm saying that, thinking of a plant or an animal or a face and dismissing a bridge or a pile of stones, that is a completely false distinction, because they are also alive in another sense. They're inanimate but they're not dead. Okay. When you are drawing something which is alive, finally you are drawing the traces of what has happened to it until that moment at which you are looking at it. I mean, the traces of how it has physically become itself. For example, if it's a face, how it has, by its experience or the soul behind it, become the face it is. So the drawing is, it seems to me, an observation of how the thing that you're looking at has become itself. And that of course does have a lot to do with what we're talking about, and storytelling.

MO: I would never have thought about that in terms of drawing. That's fascinating what you're saying . . . Is that a normal response in an artist?

JB: Well, I'm saying that's what drawing is for me. It seems to me it's perfectly possible that Hockney, whose drawings I love, might say something very different for instance.

MO: Well, that picture you showed me of Katrin [Cartlidge] this morning is a wonderful example. You're seeing the whole life in that one still life . . .

JB: But it's not that I see it, that's the point. It really isn't. It is that the life, those traces, really come and almost take your hand or your shoulder as you are drawing. And it's not that you see something and put it down, it is that something is coming and now I will try to let it come through until it rides on the scraping noise and gesture of that charcoal on the paper or whatever.

Michael, I would like to ask you something because it's a pre-occupation of mine at this moment, so maybe your answer will help me. And it's a bit difficult to ask, not because it's embarrassing but because it's difficult to define. Okay. A writer like you, you write in deepest secrecy and privacy and that's absolutely under-standable. And then, when the work is there more or less, it's not really that it's quite addressed to people exactly, although of course one wants it to be read, but it has in it a kind of appeal; not an appeal to people but an appeal, not for a cause or anything; indeed, most of the stories that we write, perhaps most of the stories that have been written are in fact laments, but they are laments that have a curious, small cargo of hope in them. Okay, that's how it is but why I ask you this question is that, in your books and your whole life story, you move between several cultures, cultures geographically and ethnically apart but also within a given, very diversified society like North America.

Okay. My key question is this. In the predominant world around us, that's to say, the world of information, the world of the media in general, I ask myself whether it is possible to launch that appeal and I tend now to think that the appeal is to another period or another culture, one that is not immediately present but which is perhaps potentially present, not nostalgically for the past necessarily, perhaps just laterally in the present or perhaps even, dare I say it, it has now become an absolutely taboo word, perhaps even for the future. If you agree with me so far, what do you feel about the address of that appeal, not that *we* make but what has finally made itself through us?

MO: Probably, the privacy that I write with I leave behind at a certain stage in the writing of the book; and then I turn back and look at what I've written for the last three years and I spend a year or two essentially reshaping it, re-cutting it, reconstructing the novel, so that it has a voice outside of myself. I'm not saying it's simplified or it's publicized in any way but, in the reshaping of the book at that point, I think you are in a way trying to see what you have invented in a larger context, trying to see whether it now can be read with some clarity of sharpness or dramatic power in North America as well as South America, or in Asia as well as England. So it's not altering the moral, if there's a moral in it, or the argument, but it's making it clearer. It's like a theatre, then making sure that every corner of the stage is lit, so that an audience from all over the world can witness the minor characters as well as the major characters.

JB: That's marvellous what you are saying. Yes, yes, that at one moment its voice changes . . .

MO: It's interesting to me what I keep discovering about these large political questions and how that balances with the intimacy of the story or, say, the love affair. How those two things can merge. And can double a meaning. I read, far too late in my life, Turgenev's *First Love*, this amazing, amazing story and then in the last half page he opens it out to describe the death of another woman who has nothing to do with the story. And suddenly the compassion and the intimacy of that personal love story is expanded and enlarged to include this woman who is a complete stranger. That's one of the remarkable things a book can do that I think film cannot. If you switch in the last five minutes of the film to something else, it feels like someone's put the wrong reel in. [The film editor] Walter Murch says you can have just two and a half ideas or conversations going on at any given moment in a film. The audience can listen to you talking and they can listen to somebody else at the next table of the restaurant talking and maybe they can half hear a conversation behind them, but nothing more. But a novel can have five or fifteen . . .

JB: Yes, yes, and I like very much what you say about every square corner of the stage being lit and how, after it's changed, its voice will change. You move things around a lot . . .

MO: I move things around *a lot*. In that sense, like you, I think that I have learnt from film, because you can literally move a scene, a shot that was part of the fifth act can now appear in the first act or in the prologue. The art that influenced me most when I began to write longer works was collage. *The Collected Works of Billy the Kid* wasn't chronological in plot and certainly didn't appear in the order that it was written. So the juxtaposition became very important. So scene F put beside scene A was more powerful than scene B being put beside scene A; and that allowed me in later works, even when the plot was more evident than in *The Collected Works of Billy the Kid*, to move things and re-dramatize them, and so in a way reconsider them.

JB: Have you ever made physical visual collages?

MO: I have done a few collages, sometimes I will try and begin with a collage, very minimal things, where I use two objects . . .

JB: That's the first thing you do?

MO: Well, sometimes. I remember doing one when Louis Malle died. I had a picture of him and a piece of music. I don't remember what the music was but I just put those two things together, a little shrine for him. I did one recently of a picture of Peggy Lee singing so she is now looking toward the handwritten manuscript of E.M. Forster's *A Passage to India*. I love collage. I went through the new Museum of Modern Art in New York and what I really wished to steal were two small ravishing collages by Kurt Schwitters. Also, I think I always wanted to illustrate things like *Westward Ho!* or *The Count of Monte Cristo*. I've always loved those illustrations in nineteenth-century novels.

JB: If you could with a magic wand, and I don't know whether devil or fairy, if you could swap the talents you have for another of any kind, do you know what you'd choose?

MO: Oh yeah, I would want to be a piano player. What would you do?

JB: I would want to be a singer.

MO: What kind of singer?

JB: It doesn't matter. The devil or the fairy can decide that.

MO: Well, we'll meet in the next life and join up . . .

GEORGE**BOWERING**

The Twilight of the Gods

"Since baseball time is measured only in outs, all you have to do is succeed utterly; keep hitting, keep the rally alive, and you have defeated time. You remain forever young."
– Roger Angell

I grew old in the Twilight League.

It is a commonplace that when it comes to writing about sports in North America, the poets and fiction writers write about baseball. Some write about boxing, but most of them write about baseball. I have seen various theories about this – what is there about baseball that resembles poetry and fiction, and so on.

Some say that it is because most of the game of baseball goes on inside the heads of the players and fans. Hockey and car-racing enthusiasts complain that baseball is slow. Maybe they are the same people who watch television because they think that books are too slow. A lot of people in the baseball grandstand are not fans – they are spectators. They make noise when the electronic scoreboard tells them to, or when someone is throwing free T-shirts into the crowd.

The baseball fans among them are busy thinking about the next opposition batter, and how he normally does against left-handed pitching in day games on the road. These fans resemble novelists just the way they do not resemble the people making the "wave" that goes by them.

Some writers like to point out that unlike football and hockey, baseball is a game in which time and space do not insist on your mortality. You can play outside the lines, whether on offence or defence, and if the game is going to come to an end, human beings will decide that, not some clock. Can you imagine applying football rules to writing? There you are, hunched over a beautiful page in a late chapter, and you hear the two-minute warning? You step outside the iambic pentameter line and a guy in a striped shirt whistles a stop to your poem?

How many muses are there? Nine. How many innings are there? Nine. How many players are there in a lineup? Nine. Do not talk to me about the designated hitter. That rule was brought in by some fan of football, where they like "specialty" teams. Baseball is a field of green surrounded by dark Satanic banks.

I personally think that an awful lot of poets and fiction writers wish that they were baseball players. And I think that most of them play softball. In softball things happen faster than they do in most sports, including baseball. Maybe that's why poets and fiction writers like to play softball with their friends.

They played softball at Black Mountain College, where Joel Oppenheimer would be barrelling toward third, and the third-base coach Charles Olson would be discussing pre-Socratic philosophy with someone on the bench, and Oppenheimer would get thrown out at the plate. Mordecai Richler played softball with his friends on Hampstead Heath. The writers play softball in Central Park and High Park. In the seventies the writers played ball with the painters

in Vancouver's silly but talented Kosmic League. Then a couple of
decades slipped by.

At first, the Twilight League was made up almost entirely of people involved with published words. There were reporters for the Vancouver *Sun*. There were magazine editors. There were magazine distributors and booksellers, columnists and movie reviewers. Then there was my team, made up of poets. Boy, we had fun! Boy, we lost a lot! Not that poets are not good ballplayers. Poets are the unacknowledged batting champions of the world.

Boy, the years went by!

Maybe it's a good thing that my diaries are packed away where it would be too much trouble to dig them out. The stuff that happened in the Twilight League would fill a book and then some.

Back in the days of the Kosmic League I admired Glen Toppings, sculptor and first baseman for my team, the Granville Grange Zephyrs, for playing at the age of forty! But then I played in the Twilight League when I was fifty. I played in the Twilight League when I was sixty.

I'd switched my admiration from Glen Toppings to David Alfaro Siqueiros, the great Mexican muralist. People know that Siqueiros was an artist and a labour organizer and an assassin and a Communist, but most people do not know that, like Glen Toppings, Siqueiros was a first baseman.

Siqueiros spent a lot of his life in jail or in exile. When he was out of jail, he was machine-gunning Trotsky's house, or organizing miners, or painting great Marxist murals. When he was in prison, they would not let him paint the walls, so he did thousands of easel paintings that will cost you a lot of money these days.

In the late 1950s, Siqueiros was given the project of creating a grand mural on the walls of Maximilian's magnificent castle in

Chapultepec Park, from which that Hapsburg ruler was hauled for his execution by the Mexican insurgents after whom the grand boulevard Insurgentes is named. The castle was headquarters for one of the U.S. invasions of Mexico, in which the invaders were decimated by the armed Mexican children now remembered in the name of the grand boulevard Niños Heroes. Maximilian's castle was also the residence of the hated dictator Porfirio Díaz. Siqueiros's mural would take as its subject the overthrow of Porfirio Díaz.

Well, Siqueiros had to do a lot of his sketches for the mural while he was a prisoner in the nearby Lecumberri Penitentiary. The sixties were a time of dissent in Mexico as they were elsewhere. In Mexico they would culminate in the army's 1968 murder of university students whose protests the president thought might endanger the success of the Olympic Games and suggest to the world that it had been a mistake to grant the games to such a volatile nation. A lot of people were going to be coming to these games, and tourism is very important to Mexico City. It would not look good, then, to have a half-finished mural at Maximilian's castle and the artist in jail. So it was decreed that David Alfaro Siqueiros should be let out of jail again in 1964.

Thousands of people were waiting for him outside the jail. Four thousand people were waiting to throw him a party at the biggest movie theatre in town. I was living in Mexico City then and wanted to go downtown, but I have a problem with crowds, so I stayed home in Churubusco.

Siqueiros did not show up at the prison gate at the advertised time. The huge crowd that was waiting to carry him to the cinema theatre had to wait a couple of hours. Why?

Because Siqueiros's ball team had an important game that afternoon, and he was their starting first baseman.

He was seventy years old.

That's even older than I am now, if you can imagine.

And to think: I officially retired from the diamond when I was sixty-six.

Glen Toppings died in 1972.

David Alfaro Siqueiros died in 1974.

There were changes, amalgamations, and withdrawals over the years in the Twilight League. For years I didn't even know that it was called the Twilight League. If it was mentioned in the newspaper, if, say, a player was being written about in his other disguise as an editor or writer, the organization was just referred to as the "Media League."

A lot of former Kosmic Leaguers were around: Leaky Fawcett, the poet, Fast Eddie, Gill Collins, Popcorn Naylor, Laura Stannard. Sometimes there was a great temptation to do something goofy and theatrical, and I do remember that there was a pitcher who had never worn shoes in his life, and that there was a team that played a game under protest because the opponents' team dog had peed on someone's glove, and that once in every game I would pull the old snot-ball routine.

The snot-ball. This would entail my approaching the pitcher's position (we always called it "the mound," though a softball pitcher throws from the flats) from my infield spot, and taking the orb from Fast Eddie or Jim Allan or whoever was hurling that day. Then I would place it under my nose, and make a huge snotting noise and, holding the ball delicately between thumb and middle finger, hand it back to the chucker, who himself would then hold the ball with great respect. The disgust on the faces of the batter and his companions (and our catcher) made the manoeuvre one of the highlights of any game tape.

We do not have reliable stats, but it is believed that batters facing the snot-ball fared significantly worse than dry-ball batters.

In general, the Twilight League did not feature the theatre (or circus) of the Kosmic League. Because its main organizer, Vancouver *Sun* movie critic Marke Andrews, was a kind of anal-retentive pitcher-commissioner, the scores and standings were kept in a big book, and the season-ending championship tournament insisted on a clear adherence to League rules, whatever they were.

So skill was approved. But Jockism was still frowned upon. There were obvious signs that companionship was more important than competition, especially in the clothing favoured by the pitchers. There was the barefoot boy, of course. And there was Marke Andrews's hat. It was a kind of fuzzy hunter's hat, a heavy wool item in a brown plaid, with a peak, earflaps, and a big bushy ball on top. Marke wore this atrocious headwear on the hottest July day, along with shapeless cotton shorts of no colour known to designers, and a torn and faded Red Sox T-shirt. Opponents would routinely protest the hat, but as Marke was the League's ultimate authority, such protests always met with failure.

Three pitchers, Jim Allan, Fast Eddie, and a southpaw from Richmond named Steve, wore tiny gloves from the earliest days of baseball, flat little leather items without padding or pocket or even laces. These gloves were said to be designated for the Hall of Fame.

Actually, clothing was always one of my favourite things about the Twilight League. A lot of players were known for their signature attire. My friend Darryl always wore pants that had distressful rips and holes in them. In addition to his tiny ancient glove, pitcher Jim Allan wore hospital operating-room greens and who knows what in his enormous afro.

Back in the day Jim had been a rock-and-roll promoter. Now he was the most prominent gink at the Granville Book Company, a co-operative that was sort of my team's sponsor. We were officially the Paperbacks, but because of our age and physical imperfections we were generally known as the Bad Backs.

The Bad Backs. Sometimes we won. More often we blew an early lead. (I'll never forget the fun some Kosmic League teams had with my *Georgia Straight* headline: "Zephyrs Blow Early Lead." They kept asking who this lucky lad was. I guess they were thinking of the great American League pitcher Early Wynn, 300–244, 3.54.) It didn't matter. Everyone made the playoffs, just like in the NHL.

We all grew old in the Twilight League. But there came a time when I figured that I had to be the oldest person in the seven-team loop. I was our David Alfaro Siqueiros, but I couldn't paint. I once remarked that if I were to retire, the average age of the league's players would drop by five years. I remember games in which I was four times as old as our left fielder. With Jim Allan and Brian Fawcett and Fast Eddie and me, we had the slowest baserunners on the North American continent. There was a lot of talk about issuing us walkers.

Often the vocalizing on the diamond would go like this:

"I got it!"

"Oh, Jesus!"

Our home venue, which we shared with our opponents The Friendly People, was the famous Needle Park. (A lot of the parks on the east side of Vancouver are called Needle Park, I suppose, but ours was one of the older Needle Parks in town.) Its real name is Woodland Park, and it's the two blocks of grass that sit between hip working-class Commercial Drive and East Hastings, the most heroinized street in Canada.

It wasn't the sixties any more. We didn't say Cricket Chatter

Park and Daisy Beanblossom Stadium. Needle Park is not Kosmic, and certainly not funny, but we say it as if it were sometimes. Most of our games were on Sundays, which occurred shortly after Saturday nights, which are big around Woodland Park. When we arrived at our home field, we would have to groom the playing area, meaning that we would search the outfield grass for hypodermic needles and carefully dispose of them, near but not inside the garbage barrel, in case anyone should rummage through it with bare hands.

Playing ball in Vancouver in the late twentieth century.

When it came to drugs, people might have lived dangerously around Woodland, but they must have practised safe sex. We found an awful lot of used condoms every Sunday. We also found high-heeled pumps and undies and the odd pair of slacks.

We also found a lot of dog caca. Outfielders at Woodland Park had to keep their eyes on the ball *and* on the grass.

Jim Allan kept the team equipment – bats, balls, bases, orange plastic cones, catcher's armour – in his horrible beat-up car. Throughout the history of the Twilight League, he had a series of horrible cars, including a yellowish van that had the door on the wrong side, a blue pickup truck that would not start on level ground, and a little nondescript hatchback that may have been made in Latvia. In these vehicles Jim Allan carried the Bad Backs' equipment – and a shovel and a hoe and a pickaxe.

It rains in Vancouver, and after it stops raining, it is still wet. The nice high-school diamonds on the west side have drainage, and a day after a week's worth of rain, these grassy diamonds are ready to go. On the east side, where none of Vancouver's alderpersons live, there are wide puddles at home plate and elsewhere on the soil diamonds such as the one at Woodland. Jim Allan and the other early-arrivers dug little trenches in the soil in an attempt to encourage the wide puddles to run along behind the backstop. Then they tried to find some relatively dry soil to fill up the muddy hollows where batters left-handed and right would be required to stand.

We all liked dry spells.

There were other characteristics of Woodland that made it a special place in which to conduct sporting contests. There were, for example, many immigrants from non-baseball-playing countries who did not know that it is perilous to conduct picnics or Tai Chi sessions in left field, caca or no caca. Then there were people of many national heritages who have consumed some product that alters the level of awareness in their brains and bodies and causes them to walk in imperfect gaits across areas also occupied by relatively stationary outfielders. It is even worse when these folks are pushing or pulling heavily laden grocery carts, because these are difficult to wheel over uneven grass, caca or no.

Luckily, we also played road games across town, even in leafy BMW country, Kerrisdale, site of my second eye injury, and above False Creek, site of my first eye injury. The Kerrisdale diamond, at the back of the Magee high school, was also the site of my broken left wrist, come to think of it. A lot of my injuries happened in the Twilight League. They say that between your early fifties and your mid-sixties, your reflexes might start to go.

One of my favourite moments in softball happened at the Magee diamond. The Magee diamond was just about the exact opposite of our home diamond. It had thick, well-mowed grass. It even had grass in the infield. It had no proper bench, but there was a lovely big tree near third base, a place to sprawl and look good. In the Twilight League, a pop-up that hit a tree limb in foul territory was a foul ball, while a pop-up that hit a tree limb in fair territory was declared no-pitch. At the Seventh Avenue diamond above False Creek, home diamond for the Write Sox, whom we all called the Soreheads, the nearest tree was in deep right field and up a little hill.

Magee was home park for The Secret Nine, an athletic and pretty young crew who had team shirts – each with the number 9 on the back. Their centre fielder was a tall, young guy who had lots of talent but not much in the way of smarts. He could really hit the long ball, despite the fact that he had but one working eyeball. Not much perspective on the game, we said over and over among ourselves. Once he stroked an impressive home run, and on crossing home plate, he missed the high five, delivering a palm to the face of his congratulator, and taking one in his own mug.

But this guy, like a lot of individuals who are bothered by the perception that other people know more than they do, had a surly attitude. There are genial men who have natural baseball talent but lesser knowledge of the game. But this guy seemed to resent any unspoken suggestion that he was short of savvy.

Well, one of my great joys as a player or fan is to know more than the other guy, and, if possible, to convert that greater knowledge into victory. That, in all likelihood, is a flaw in my character, but one that I quickly forgive.

Once during the TL championship tournament, I was playing first base and had to dive (all right, flop) to my right to snag a skipping grounder. Unable to rise to my feet in time to retire the hustling runner in a conventional fashion, I flopped back to my left and touched the base with my bare right hand. I beat him by a heartbeat. This gink loudly maintained that he was safe because I hadn't touched the bag with my glove wherein was nestled the ball. I guess he was confusing the situation with another in which a tagging of the baserunner might be involved. The umpire hesitated.

"What," I inquired with professorial calm, seeing as how I was a professor during the weekdays, "would be the case were I, the first baseman, to have touched said base with one of my feet?"

There were many such moments on the sandlots of Vancouver and Burnaby in the late twentieth century.

But back to my treatment of the ignorant young athlete who patrolled centre field for The Secret Nine.

There are a lot of admonitions to ballplayers, simple bits of lore that they should commit to memory. Many of these have to do with running the bases, perhaps the most likely activity to show the intelligence of a ballplayer. Do not make the first or third out at third base, we runners are told.

If a ground ball is hit in front of you, and you are not forced, do not try to advance, we are advised. Well, the guy I have been describing was on second base, having smacked a nice double to left centre. There was one out, and we were in the middle innings of a tied game. I was playing shortstop, just waiting for my chance, and praise be to Marty Marion, here it came. I grabbed a one-hopper and went into throwing mode. Ho ho, the galoot took off for third, and I had him cold. I tagged him politely, and turned my attention to the business at first.

Boy, he was pissed off!

I did not smile.

I'll bet that he has forgotten all about it.

I made one concession to geezerhood on the diamond. After the age of sixty I quit playing in shorts. This happened soon after my daughter, subbing at second base that day, asked the famous question: "Are those your legs, or are you riding a chicken?"

At about the same time, my team, the Bad Backs, started giving me retirement presents. I got a framed photograph of the team, all in our nifty team shirts. I got a giant-size bottle of Geritol. I got a lawn chair. For the first several years my teammates would present me with my gift right after we got eliminated from the season-ending tournament. After that they started giving me my retirement present at the *start* of the season.

In the pre-season of 2002, *Vancouver* magazine ran a story by Guy MacPherson about me and the Twilight League. First he quoted me on my second eye injury: "Smashed my glasses to smithereens and blinded me for a few days. But I don't care. Baseball's important. More important than eyesight."

Then MacPherson quoted league commissioner Marke Andrews to the effect that I was "the biggest bench jockey in the world," which is, I guess, true. I could never stop the flow of witticisms that passed through me. "It's like having a stand-up comic for the game. You get this cheap, live entertainment."

It's all true. That's why I was so proud of my kid and her chicken remark.

I gave MacPherson a shot at the end of the piece. He wondered what would happen if I were to retire.

"I think the league would just more or less disappear without me, to tell the truth," I am quoted as saying.

I was (mostly) just kidding.

In the summer of 2002, I kept waiting for my skill at getting the ball out of the infield to return. Then I felt that sad realization I had read so often about – they always say, the real ballplayers, that there comes a time when you know that it's time to hang them up.

In July I quit the Bad Backs.

In early August I was coaxed out of retirement by The Friendly People, our opponent pals, and played a few more games. Then I hung them up for good (I think).

During the off-season the Twilight League folded. There are rumours that Jim Allan is trying to get it going again, in some form. But they'll have to do it without me.

I'm headed for the Hall of Fame.

MARILYN**BOWERING**

Famous Writers

It's 1977 and I am living with Michael, the Scot who will become my husband, in Peter the Gardener's former cottage in Glen Lochay – the Glen of the Black Goddess – near the village of Killin in Perthshire, Scotland. The cottage is Tighnacriag. From the minute table at which I work in a tiny attic, I have a view, through a narrow skylight set into the roof, of the heather-shrouded shoulders of Sron a Chlachan, the mountain that rises immediately behind the house. Although I've lived here only a short time, I've climbed it and many of the other hills, and have an intense feeling of belonging to this place. I'm in the right place at the right time and so I'm not at all surprised that my poems are accepted by the magazines I send them to. One of these magazines is particularly long-established and highly respected. The editor writes and invites me to visit the next time I'm in Edinburgh. So I do.

The editor's house is one of those solid, stone, cold Edinburgh residences I'll become familiar with soon, but this is one of my first visits to the capital, and it strikes me as surprising. It has a stone fence hem, a small garden, and window gables; it's on a street that Michael tells me is respectable. I'm not vastly experienced in anything, but the experience I do have of writers and editors is that they live in cabins, or in houses of ill repair, or, in any case, they live surrounded by a clutter of valuable paintings, scavenged artifacts, letter presses, excellent or abominable pottery (but pottery nonetheless), and with books overflowing shelves, stacked on chairs, holding up windows, and propping open doors; for some reason, their children go without diapers. This is what I expect behind the sandstone facade. Instead, the hallway is narrow, stone-floored, and neat, the sitting room (to the left) is small and decorated in pastel pink and beige. I examine the room first, and then the editor, for signs of passion and do not find them. I crack open my mind.

He talks to me about my poems, and we drink some whisky; he shows me some of the extraordinary oral literature he and his wife have recorded and published; he piles back issues of the magazine into my arms. We drink a little more, but not that much, and then he begins to talk about himself. He's fifty-five years old. He's not only an editor, but a poet, anthologist, and translator. I mention the handful of Scottish writers I've read. They are all friends of his – poets I'll soon meet, like Norman MacCaig, Robert Garioch, Sorley Maclean, Hamish Henderson.

I'm enthralled to be in the presence of "literature," and it takes me longer than it should have to understand his tone. He has never received the recognition he deserves (I glance at the publications, the framed awards and citations); each and every one of his contemporaries has been given far more attention than he; *he* is better than most of them but *they* are friends with all the people who matter – the critics, the prize-givers, the purveyors of canon and commentary on Scottish literature. I'm simply unable to reconcile the evidence around me, and my reading experience of the wonderful magazine he edits, with this bitterness. Would that I might someday be as lucky, as productive, as treasured! I leaf once more through the brilliant anthology he's given me: yes, it is brilliant, pioneering, important, a contribution that is bound to be lasting – it *has* lasted, too.

Eventually we say our thanks, our pleasure at the meeting, etc., and the solid wooden door of the stone house shuts behind us. While Michael starts the car, I take a moment to look back: with what expectations I arrived and with what confusion I leave. I swear to myself that whatever happens to me, however the literary life I'm just embarking on turns out, I will never allow myself to be bitter. Not for an instant. It's a promise that, as time goes by, is sometimes difficult to keep.

The dark side of the literary life is that many aspects of it *outside the writing itself* can nurture bitterness and disappointment; a sense of failure shimmers at the edges of the auras of even the most extraordinary writers. You'd be astonished at the poets and novelists who express pain at the disregard of their work or a perceived diminishment of their reputation. It astonishes *me*, at any rate.

Obviously, what fuels any writer's sense of neglect and isolation is real isolation and real neglect. This happens. Many books are never read beyond the narrowest of circles. A work may have the potential to inform and enlighten thousands – but that audience, for that writer, remains beyond reach. Reasons for this may include distance from a literary centre of power, lack of a championing publisher, poor distribution, shyness, and an "un-promotable" personality, as well as the general market changes that have affected readers and reading taste. Any writer worrying over this one will come up with a very long fault list indeed; and it's true that an analysis of the forces at play in the industry – note the term

– can only underline how much is beyond the writer's (and pub-lishers') control. People whose job it is to connect books and readers sweat blood over this: any writer who doesn't fit neatly into a niche is going to suffer, and the publisher with her. We shouldn't forget, though – and this is hardly a comfort – that no matter how famous a writer is now, sooner or later he or she will be ignored, forgotten, passed over. An icy wind will blow through his or her heart too. If not today then soon, when the next generation of readers (or non-readers) comes along. Writers, like any other living creature, flourish and fade. So why is it hard to cope? Why do so many who could unroll an arm-and-leg-length scroll of "honours" still feel the ache of "not good enough"? Don't they know what they've achieved? Don't they know who they are?

It's sometime in the late 1980s and I'm at a party in Victoria with a group of cricketers, a friendly, merry lot, on the whole. I've run out of introductory conversation and am looking round the cricket pavilion when I realize that a short, stocky bald-headed man is staring at me. Perhaps he's seen my picture somewhere? Maybe I preen. I've had a little flurry of local fame and have been fielding compliments all evening along the lines of, "Saw a great piece about you, heard you on the radio, etc." Not that anybody's read or gone to see whatever it was – but it's a party, and what do I care whether anyone's *literary*!

The bald-headed stranger shifts his elbow from the bar and makes his way over. "Hi, remember me?" No, I don't, but it turns out we went to school together. (Christ, what time does to some people!) "So, what do you do?" he asks. I tell him. "Is that so? I've never heard of you." There's a beat not quite long enough for me to take this in before he goes on: "How does it feel," he says, "to spend your life doing something nobody cares about?"

He's a jerk – he's certainly not a cricketer – and I don't really take him seriously. But he has hit a nerve, the nerve that tells me that what he says is true in a way I don't really want to think about. Most people don't care about what I or most writers do; but most people do care about what some writers do. And so? If most people haven't heard of me, could it mean I haven't done my job?

A few years later, I struggle through an interview with a newspaper columnist who is not as far removed from the bar-leaning bozoid as she probably thinks she is. Over and over she returns the conversation to the same point: *You've been writing for many years, but this is the first time I've heard of you. Don't you feel all those years were a waste?*

No, I tell her. I try to explain why I write, who my readers are, and that what my readers think about what I do matters more to me than having reached or not reached her, um, particular circle, but she won't accept what I have to say. She can't see it.

The *I haven't heard of you* type of encounter is based on solipsism – people who think that since *they* haven't heard of you, *you* can't be any good, and nothing you've written could be important. A solipsistic outlook is the antithesis of the bridging, network-making, insightful, solace-bringing, stimulating, mind-widening exercise that constitutes literary culture. Solipsism, though, has juju – the power of the individually self-regarding mass. It is strong magic, because it works like a battery: single cells joined together engender power. The power is mainly social and (of course) economic, and publishers naturally want their writers to be inside this magic circle: but this self-regarding world is not writing's natural home. The Nobel Laureate Gao Xingjian, who wrote for many years in exile, says that "... literature is neither an embellishment for authority nor a socially fashionable item, it has its own criterion of merit: its aesthetic quality. An aesthetic intricately related to the human emotions is the only indispensable criterion for literary works."

Remainders, anyone?

I've never seriously been expected to adjust what I write to suit "the reading public." It could be because nobody thinks I could, or it might be that my readership is too small to bother with. It *was* suggested that I explain all my metaphors: I considered it, too, until I saw how it flat-lined the book. A linear death. I was asked to do this to make it easier for the reader. Easier? But what about the contract? The one I have with myself and with my reader? My part is to write with clarity and integrity and with as much craft as I can. I'm saying, in effect, *Come with me and you won't be sorry; trust me.* My reader's part is to begin with the assumption that I might have created a world worth entering, and to endeavour – on an experimental/experiential basis – to accept its premises.

A writer friend told me recently about the editing process he went through with his latest novel. His editor had directed him to change his depiction of the main character, an historical figure, to one that was more positive, more friendly. Knowing something about his fascinatingly devilish subject, I thought that a revision of this type was not only revisionist but dishonest. It would be a little like changing Genghis Khan into Elmer Fudd – much less threatening, no whiff of evil, a domestication of the pathological. Why did my friend acquiesce? Because he was afraid. Because writers who don't sell enough books can be dropped by their publishers; and because his editor had convinced him that the marketplace (of the solipsistic magic circle) would be more comfortable with a positive view of this character (no matter how historically inaccurate), and that it didn't matter anyway because most people wouldn't know the difference. Is there anything wrong with this? Not from this editor's perspective, but from the writer's, surely?

In my view, my friend has relinquished his right to the reader's trust. That trust is an endowment, I believe, from the past and for a future which is hopeful – not cynical – about the possibilities of human beings. It takes the position that literature, although it may be many things – scurrilous, scatological, satirical, sublime, serious, silly, whatever – is the result of a compulsion to draw from the resources of the human spirit and with some sincerity.

As I've been considering this box of snakes, as one pops up and I shove it back down only to have three more anxieties on the slither, I wonder if I will ever have done with it. What's this all about? What are my obligations as a writer, to what am I not measuring up? Why this worm of discomfort? I have my duty to myself and my art, to my reader and . . . what else?

You could break your heart trying to understand it – it's heart-break I hear when wonderful writers tell me how they've been ignored. Your writing instincts tell you one thing, your writing-life business associates and the man at the bar tell you something else. You feel like you're caught between generosity toward yourself and your writing, which includes a fierce desire to measure yourself against the immeasurable in this beautiful world, and some literary weigh-in in which you've never agreed to take part. But here you are. And the requirement you haven't fulfilled (and which you'll continue to fail to fulfill), the only thing you could do to be a *real* success and to reach those readers who could do with a pinch of your storytelling or poetry to release them from the solipsistic bubble in which they've been captured . . . is to be famous. (And how can you think, let alone say, *that* without being offensively self-serving?) But I do see that behind the Scottish editor's bitterness, behind the puzzled grief of the ignored writer, is an understanding that he or she is not famous enough, hasn't been famous enough, will never be famous enough. Celebrities understand this and hire people to take care of it. The writer keeps writing books in the hopes that that will do. Silly writer. If you want to succeed in this game, if you really want to, better take your clothes off, or kill somebody, kill yourself.

Once, after I wore a pair of red stockings to a poetry reading, a member of the audience began writing to me, and calling, and following me. That's obsession. It's not a literary accolade and it isn't pleasant. But it does have something to do with celebrity.

It's 1999: I'm on the shortlist for the Orange Prize. I do not know, because no one has thought to tell me, that the week of interviews, readings, parties, lunches, dinners with the other nominees and with the members of the prize jury, is part of the selection process. I've been on display in a way I haven't understood: I'm out there in my bathing suit and I'm not holding my stomach in. I'm enjoying myself, for heaven's sake – I'm reading everyone else's books! I have no idea I'm in a pageant.

I remember the moment I almost get it. It happens just before a reading at the British Library when the finalists are informed that we're obligated to attend a pre-reading reception. I don't want to: I'd rather think about what I'm about to read, but we're shooed out of our corners and into a room of canapés, wine, board members, and the prize winners of a magazine contest. Guess what? We're the prize. Meeting us is the prize.

The following afternoon I've got some spare time and I spend it at a museum. I'm examining a heap of bones when I have a strange sensation: something inside me is turned inside out like a purse and shaken empty. I look at my watch – the sensation is so peculiar that I note the time. I sit down on a bench and I know that a decision has just been made. When I check, later on, I find out that it was at exactly this time that the prize was decided. If this were an interview, I'd be asked, "How did you feel?" I didn't feel anything, I just knew what I knew.

Knowing what I know, not being overly concerned with what I don't know, and refusing to guess at the unknowable is how I stay sane and resilient enough to write.

It's a fact that there is almost never fair recompense for the effort put into creative work. It's a fact that it's a struggle to maintain balance in a milieu that insists it's the writer's job, *even more than to write*, to acquire and maintain fame. If I'm to keep my promise to my long-ago self, I have to remind myself of certain things: of the importance of sincerity and of the fact that arrogance gets in the way of just about everything. I have to remind myself because I'm not always good at it. What I am good at is writing toward something I'm certain is there. Something that someone else can feel too. The life of the book. Life.

It's today. I open up my email and there's a letter from a stranger, Mox, in Finland.

> *i read your book slowly only, because i want the injoy it*
>   *piece to piece,*
> *feeling to feeling.*
> *good day, good ewerything!*

Yes, Mox. Good Everything.

JOSEPH**BOYDEN**

Killing a Rock

Excuse the blood on this page. It certainly isn't moose blood, despite a moose being what my brother, my best friend, and I are currently tracking. It's human blood. My own, to be precise. I was filleting a really big pickerel I caught earlier today out on the Abitibi River. My hand slipped. That easy to make a mistake.

An admission. I'm drunk on rye whisky. Hunting moose in the Hudson Bay Lowlands is partially an excuse to drink whisky and smoke cigarettes. Maybe this is why we still haven't killed a moose this trip. But we have only been out on the river for a day, in all fairness, with five or six or even seven days still to go. As long as the whisky and cigarettes last.

In the last six months I've travelled across Canada, the United States, England, the Netherlands, France, and Spain, primarily to promote my first novel. It's a wonderful life. That's not the name of my novel, but this life I've been introduced to is pretty great.

I've written very little in these last six months. Don't tell that to my publisher or agent or mum. I'm told I'm a writer and I'm supposed to write. But travelling is too much fun, too full of adventure to be some boring guy sitting in a little room in Paris with a type-writer when Paris is outside waiting.

Another admission. Even the excitement of being in a new place each day and meeting people who like you (or at least act like it) can begin to wear you down. Don't get me wrong. I've lived the life these last months, a dreamy life. Not a regret, except maybe for beginning to feel out of shape – oh – and not writing much. But by the time autumn had started to wane, I began to dream of James Bay, of the black snake of the Abitibi River, of snow hissing on water, of shore lunches of goose and pike roasted *sagabun* over a fire, of falling asleep exhausted at 9 p.m. and waking two full hours before sunrise to drink cowboy coffee with my great friend and Cree legend William. No cities, no readings, no interviews, no air-planes. Just a freighter canoe, William, and my brother Francis scouting the shores for signs of life.

On our third day, the signs of moose are abundant. Even tipsy on rye I can spot them. How to track a moose, you ask? Everyone has his or her favourite way. Some will build tree stands and sit perched and shivering like foolishly dressed birds of prey, syn-thetic moose urine sprayed all about, plastic moose call clutched in hand. Others choose to stalk the bush, hoping desperately to be in the right place at the right time.

But William has taught me the best way. Scouting the river and creeks by freighter canoe, looking for the most obvious signs – tracks on the muddy shore and stretches of red willow.

Around James Bay, and indeed throughout most of Northern Ontario, moose rut in October. The males go mad with desire during this month, desperately searching for elusive females. Females only go into heat for a very short while, and so the bulls will travel miles every day on their own hunt, sending out powerful grunts from deep in their huge chests. If a bull is really lucky and a horny cow is within earshot, she will respond with a bawl that is both frightening and a little sexy, a long moan of want ending in something akin to a howl.

The river hunter's job is to find those spots on the shore where the tips of red willows have been nibbled off so that the white ends stand out against the blood colour of the willow. A horny moose is a hungry moose, and this is the time of year when the succulent tips of red willow are at their most tasty. And so if you find these sprays of red willow with the tops all gone, you will – you hope – also find fresh tracks, and then you will break camp at a place across the river.

As soon as dawn breaks, the spotting begins. You with a cup of hot coffee – maybe with a shot of rye in it, but don't mention this to the Ministry of Natural Resources cops – and your rifle and scope. Then a hopeful wait as you scan the riverbank across from you for the moose to come out and feed. Follow said procedure again at dusk. Over the years, William has shot dozens of moose in this way, but I want to make it absolutely clear for the record that William would never, ever hunt while drinking. That's illegal, you know, and William is a law-abiding man. He's also the best hunter I've ever met.

And what does one do during the day? My favourite thing is patrolling up and down the river in the hope of surprising a moose drinking or wandering the shoreline. I love stopping at the mouths of the creeks that feed into the Abitibi and fishing for pickerel and pike and sturgeon. This also offers the perfect opportunity for a couple of drinks with your brother and your best friend, a chance to smoke cigarettes and talk, albeit quietly. Moose have big ears for a reason. And when you're not fishing or drinking and talking, you perfect your moose call. None of those plastic moose-calling jobs for us. We do it the Cree way, with birchbark peeled and shaped into a cone, held together by duct tape. I'd do a female and a male moose call for you now, but you'd probably think I'm drunk, and a little weird.

Living in a prospector's tent on the shores of the Abitibi River as November approaches is something all Canadians should try at least once. By the fourth evening, I've fallen into its rhythm. An hour or two before dusk we find a good location across the river from the right signs, somewhere flat and with poplar, one of the smaller poplars becoming the roof beam for the tent. We tie off the tent against other poplar, unroll our sleeping bags, and get the propane heater going inside (no fires – moose have a good sense of smell, too), hang our damp clothes on a line across the ceiling, and then begin scoping. When it becomes too dark to see, we head into the tent, which is just tall enough for us to stoop inside, and prepare dinner, say some pan-fried pickerel if you've been lucky, pan-fried Klik (our northern Spam) if you haven't. Eight p.m. feels like midnight, and by 9 p.m., Francis is snoring loud enough to make the tent walls puff out.

On this fourth night out, I stay up really late, until almost ten-thirty, then fall asleep with my head in my sleeping bag. Sometime in the middle of the night, I awake startled, feeling as alert as I've felt in years. It must be near time to rise. I check my watch in the blackness with a lighter and see that it's only 1 a.m. William and Francis duel snores and so, quiet as I can, I climb out of my bag and crawl out the flap.

With the half moon behind a cloud, the night is black enough that I must walk carefully toward the water, watching for the steep bank. Only when I'm a few feet away does it appear, tumbling down to the rocky shore. I steady myself against a poplar while I pee. Boy, must have drunk a lot last night. It goes on and on, echoing out into the darkness, loud enough in the stillness of this evening that I begin to worry I might wake William and Francis.

And that is when the sound booms over my head, so close it might have been only yards from me, and I almost fall over. At first I think of the burp of a tugboat's horn. No tugboats around here. I hear the snap of sticks across the river, the breaking of tree limbs, a grunt, and, finally, a splash. Not until I hear the snorts of a big animal breathing heavy and swimming in awkward lunges does it sink in that it's a moose. I stand in momentary awe, my eyes peering across the 150 yards of river and into the black trying to make sense of this.

Am I the one being hunted? The bull moose continues to splash across the river, straight toward me. He's mad. You can tell by his breathing, angry rushes of air as he struggles against the current. As I turn to make my way back to the tent and rouse the boys, I realize he must have heard me relieving myself and assumed I was another bull moose on his turf. Now, he's coming to defend it.

William hears me trip into the tent. I can see his outline sitting straight up. "William," I say. "You're not going to believe this but . . . just grab your gun and come."

Francis wakes to the noise of us struggling for our gear. "What?" he asks.

"Just come on," I say. "Moose." That's all it takes for the three of us to be up and out and making our way to the shore as quick as we can. The moon's out from behind the cloud now. I'm worried it was all just a crazy hallucination until we reach the spot and hear the bull, much closer now, still angrily working his way right to us.

"I was peeing," I explain, out of breath, but trying to speak in a hush, "and the moose must have heard me and assumed I was another bull in his territory."

"That or he thought you were a cow," William says. We can see its form three-quarters of the way across now, his antlers swaying as he kicks toward us.

"Never assume," Francis adds, still a little sleepy-eyed. I don't think he believes me. "It makes an ass out of you and me."

Quiet as we can, we slip our magazines into our rifles. My heart beats madly. The moose struggles onto shore. We can see him clearly now, twenty yards below us, steam rising from his wet fur as if he's on fire. He tenses to bound up the hill, black and hulking in the moon's light. And it is only at this moment that he realizes he's made a grave error in his testosterone rush. He can smell us. He turns, presents his profile to us, not sure what to do. We raise our rifles and fire.

Gutting and field-dressing a moose in the darkness is not an easy chore. The slip of the sharp, hooked gutting knife along the length of the large animal's belly, the stink of innards and the sound of them spilling out onto the rocky shore, the skinning and quartering and wrapping of the meat in gauze is not an easy thing to accomplish, even in daylight. But it must be done.

Afterward, after we load the canoe with the bloody meat and wash our hands and arms in the cold river and toast our success with a drink of rye, William and Francis return to their sleeping bags for an hour or two of rest before dawn.

But I can't sleep. I sit on the shore by the canoe and smoke a cigarette, watch for signs of first light. I sprinkle tobacco from my cigarette onto the ground and thank the moose for his life, for his meat that will feed William's family and my own.

Alone here by the water, my thoughts turn to what I've been avoiding. The time has come for me to write my second novel. It's a strange thought way out here in the middle of nowhere, so far away from the world of writers and of readers. But I am a writer. It is what I do. And to begin the journey of writing a novel is a lonely and frightening one. I can smell the tinny scent of fresh blood and the richer smell of fresh meat. I'm fresh meat in the publishing world. A writer with a first, successful novel. I've heard the horror stories of following up with a second. I don't worry about critics, though. I have a moose rifle.

The party's over, and my travels, novel in hand, are dying down. I face the inevitable. Time to write every day again. Time to create another world.

A final admission. And this one will affect you more than the others, if only just a little. I didn't shoot the moose. In fact, we didn't shoot a moose at all on this particular trip. But it is a true story. Just not one that I own.

This true story happened to my oldest brother, Bruce, a few years ago, in the morning, not in the night, but in the same area. Humans, like moose, are creatures of habit. We hunt the same areas. They feed and rut in the same areas. I'm a habitual fiction writer. If not much had happened, you probably would have been bored. And, for me, one of the cardinal rules of writing is not to be boring.

Don't get me wrong. Everything else that I've described really happened. I really have been travelling on my first book tour for months. My friend and my brother and I hunted. We slept in tents. We fished and drank and smoked cigarettes. We just didn't get a moose on this particular trip. Maybe I fictionalized – my aggrandizement, my borrowing, wasn't a lie, was it? – because I feel that, as a writer, I need to fulfill certain expectations. If I go hunting, you want me to get something. Maybe not an animal if you're a conservationist, but at least I should learn a lesson or gain some better understanding. An epiphany.

My epiphany? I'm not sure, beyond what I've told you. But I can tell you that my brother Francis had to head back to work and so I stayed on with William for a few more days.

William and I continued hunting the elusive moose whose tracks we'd found by the nibbled red willow. On the final morning, only hours before we were to head out of the bush, and knowing we were not going to be successful this time, we decided to have a shooting contest. We chose the appropriate target – a rock about the size of a Margaret Atwood or a Michael Ondaatje, smaller than a calf moose, two hundred yards upriver.

I shot first, the bang and kick of the rifle echoing through the stillness of morning, over and over. I imagined animals with heads bent to feed startled by the noise and darting away. I watched through my scope as the bullet ricocheted on the water a yard or two in front of the rock. William took his turn and nailed the rock in the centre, leaving a white divot in the brown stone. I tried again with my rifle, and again, I fell short, this time at the rock's base. With his second turn, William once again killed the rock, more chips of stone flying.

On my third shot, I placed the crosshairs of the scope higher on the rock, at its tip, and this time, after the boom and echo, saw through my scope that I'd hit it neatly in the centre. "Scope's off," I said to William, meekly. On his third shot, William hit the rock once again. He's a fine shot, William.

Holding a heavy rifle while standing and aiming at a rock two hundred yards away is more difficult than most would imagine. Once you've placed your crosshairs on the target, even the slightest breath or movement in your body sends the crosshairs jiggling all over the place. You have to take into account wind direction and speed. You have to be calm, and not rush. You have to be confident. A tiny jerk of the trigger will send the bullet askew. It's hard, that's my excuse. Like writing.

DI**BRANDT**

So this is the world, & here I am in it

I grew up in a house without books, other than The Book, which was more of a talisman, a sacred object, than a book in the way we think of books nowadays, surrounded by paper, texts, as we are in this culture, centuries, eons away from the village of my childhood. My dad read to us from The Book every morning at breakfast, in German. He was a traditionalist Mennonite prairie peasant, with thick fingers and sunbrowned leathery skin. He loved farming, he leaped out of bed every morning, eager and energetic, to tend to his beloved farm, the cows in the barn waiting to be milked, the pigs snuffling to be fed, the crops in the fields waiting to be tended, the machinery in the sheds needing oiling and polishing, the granaries bursting with grain, or standing empty, waiting for the new summer crops. He was a brilliant farmer. He grew up in a large poor family and didn't inherit land, as most Mennonite children did. My mother was given twenty acres and a cow as a wedding gift, and he pieced the rest together, bit by bit, a dozen acres at a time, stroking, cajoling, seducing the neighbouring farmers into selling him a field here, a field there, when someone died, over the course of his lifetime. It was high-risk, back-breaking labour. He was in his element. He scoffed at "city people" who sat tamely at desks in little offices all day, with predictable little paycheques waiting for them at the end of the week. He felt sorry for people who got their exercise in gyms, futilely punching rubber bags or running tread-mills, instead of wrestling fiercely, robustly, with the sensuous earth, animals, weeds, weather, daily, seasonally, as he did. He would come in from the fields rimed with dirt, his white teeth gleaming against the red-brown blackened leather of his face. Joyful is how I remember him then, sizzling with energy. He never read operating manuals, he figured out how everything worked with his hands. He built all his own barns and sheds and granaries and even our new house himself, with help from relatives and neighbours. By the time I left home at age seventeen, my parents owned a flourishing thousand-acre debt-free farm, fully modern-ized, with gigantic brand new tractors and combines and harrows resting in the sheds, the barns filled with silver gleaming milking machines. His literacy level was approximately grade two. He fol-lowed the words across the page with his thick sunbrowned finger as he read, slowly, in a language he understood but didn't speak. We would sit, sullenly eyeing the porridge steaming in our bowls, waiting for the reading to be over. My mother was restless during the readings, fussing with the coffee pot, the toaster, the grapefruit, the sugar bowl. He was displeased. He wanted reverent attention. Reading was a sacred act to him.

Once every six months or so, my dad would reach The Book ceremonially across the table and say, Mary, why don't you read today. We were reading our way through The Book, from Creation to the Apocalypse, and then all over again, a chapter a day. None of the extravagant stories in The Book seemed very relevant to our rambunctious sweaty village lives, told in a language we heard in church but never spoke. Many of them didn't seem at all credible, though our salvation from eternal damnation apparently hinged on believing in their facticity. My mother would reach for The Book with a small flourish, and begin to read. My mom had completed grade nine before she was called home to work on the farm. She was the eldest daughter in a family of ten children, and my grandmother badly needed her to help with the cooking and cleaning and looking after the children. She was a formidably talented farmwoman, a whiz at elaborate Mennonite cooking, gardening, canning, baking, sewing, embroidering, crocheting, quilting, entertaining, looking after children. In this way my parents were an excellent match. She also had the gift of an extraordinary memory, and for this reason served as the keeper of stories in our large extended family; whenever someone wanted to remember something, they'd ask Mary. Her oral archive included a large repertoire of folk tales, nursery rhymes, sayings of all kinds, in Plautdietsch, our mother tongue, and also in German and English, which she liberally sprinkled into ordinary conversation, with wit and panache. I didn't realize then how special that was, to receive so much delightful literary education so casually, while kneading the dough or weeding the carrots or mending men's trousers. She loved reading poetry and novels, though it was hard to come by books, or the time to read them. Tante Jay, my mother's youngest sister, who was a schoolteacher and lived in "the city," in another world, an hour and a half away by car, had read all kinds of interesting books and seen Hollywood movies, which she recited to us in fascinating detail in the kitchen over my mom's fresh-baked apple pie. Sometimes she brought novels for my mom to read. My mom and I were fascinated by her stories and shared a secret yearning to travel and see the exotic world beyond our peasant villages, thus tantalizingly glimpsed. My sister wasn't there, she was usually outside playing with the boys or tagging along with the men. My dad definitely wasn't there, Tante Jay certainly wouldn't have told her lively stories of city life if he was. I was a clumsy kid, prone to breaking dishes and cutting myself accidentally with kitchen knives. This made my mom impatient. On the other hand, I was good at school, bringing home high grades and prizes, which made my parents proud. For these reasons I was the only kid in the village allowed, and even encouraged, to read books even during the busy spring or summer or fall seasons. I consumed Tante Jay's novels with ravenous hunger and curiosity and lustful pleasure. I knew I wasn't staying in the village when I grew up, and this was a great way to begin to find out about the world outside our village community. My mother's readings from The Book at the breakfast table were dramatic and elegant, and quick. Suddenly we were in Egypt, or Palestine, or Babylon, among shepherds and sheep and treacherous kings and magic mountains and devious beautiful women. My mother would hand The Book back to my dad across the table with a small smile. This exchange, we knew, wouldn't happen again for awhile.

When I was fifteen, my Uncle Henry, who was also a schoolteacher and had attended university, gave me a book of stories by Anton Chekhov, with an introduction that cited the Russian writer as saying, "I had to wrestle with the serf in every cell of my body in order to become a writer." This statement was like a bucket of clear ice water poured over my head. It startled me into awareness, identification, dreaming. I wasn't the only person with an illiterate lowly heritage foolish enough to want to become, of all arrogant, unachievable things, a writer. Who did I think I was? But still. It hadn't stopped him, why should it stop me? There were many years between that event and the volatile moment of my stepping off the cliff of my life into print. But that was the moment perhaps when it began, my underground writerly aspiration, though, if I think about it, it was there from the beginning, from the earliest moments of my memory, the fascination with language, words, images, cadence, rhythm, intonation, as was the determination to get away, to leave the narrow enclave of my ancestral culture, with its strict separatist rules against the mainstream. I'm thinking now that both of these things were hatched to a great extent by the style, intelligence, and simmering restlessness of my mother, for whom village life was not large enough, not stimulating enough, though it's taken me most of my life to recognize her as an ally, so divided was she in her loyalties, encouraging her daughters to break away, on one side, and chastising, even actively betraying us for it, on the other.

I loved school. I loved the spectacular imaginative explosion that happened in my head entering grade one. I loved having my own desk, my own space, in our little village school. I adored my beautiful teacher, Rita Klassen, who wore pretty dresses and read poetry to us and drew fascinating pictures for us on the chalkboard with coloured chalk, to illustrate her stories. I wasn't physically robust, I didn't mind sitting still for hours on end, as many of the village children did. Indeed, I was happy for it, to get away from the rough and tumble of farm life. I bruised easily, I was always getting hurt in one way or another, at home. Mennonite child-rearing practices at that time included violent beatings in early childhood to instill passive obedience in us, and I had received large doses of extreme violence in my early years that have haunted me ever since. I was mentally and imaginatively robust, though, endlessly curious and fascinated by everything bookish. School opened me to the world. There were books to read, not many, but some, a tiny library in the corner of the room. Six months after entering the classroom, I could read and write and speak both English and German, and soon read my way through the entire library. Some of our relatives moved to Mexico and Paraguay in the 1920s, to establish pioneer farms all over again in inhospitable landscapes in the Mexican desert and the Chaco, "the Green Hell," in protest against the enforcement of English curricula in Manitoba schools. They were worried about the effects of an English school education on their children, the loss of tradition and culture that would result. They were quite right. I'm sad now to see the enormous losses that did occur in my generation, which I enthusiastically helped to enact, but then, I just couldn't wait to get away, to throw it all away. I embraced the otherness of English culture eagerly and joyously. Though it didn't always make sense. I remember in grade four we were taught how to introduce people to each other in an English school text: Mr. Smith, this is Mrs. Jones. Mrs. Jones, this is Mr. Smith. Mrs. Smith, this is Mr. Jones, Mr. Jones, this is Mrs. Smith. Such conversations seemed astonishingly nonsensical to us, who knew everyone in our village and the neighbouring villages intimately, where introductions were made in advance, elaborately, contextually, obliquely, so that by the time you met someone face to face, you already knew their name, their immediate and extended family and their specific place in it, where they lived, their purpose in being here, their relation to you, their current business. Our lives were nested, protected, ritualized, in a way the lives of *de Englische* apparently were not. I have sometimes reflected on the way our humble peasant lives offered many of the privileges only the very rich or famous can afford in modern urban life, a wide community, a rich storehouse of ritual and musical performance, a thousand people at your funeral. On the other hand, *de Englische* wrote books, gorgeous amazing books, and I was hooked on literature, stories, essays, poetry. Books offered the possibility of a whole other world, a richly inspiring, poetically inflected one, a grand getaway. Only children poised between cultures, with access to art and literature, can imagine the future filled with so much freedom and promise and hope.

I'm remembering the precise moment I became conscious of myself as an individual conscious being. I was sitting at my desk in grade five, writing answers to history questions in my notebook, enjoying the sun coming in through the window, and suddenly I thought, I am sitting here, at this desk, writing in this notebook, and all these other people are sitting at their desks, and they are not me, they have their own inner lives and plans, they are thinking about completely different things than I am. The philosopher Rudolf Steiner believed that the moment of coming into individual consciousness was a more significant growing up moment than puberty; perhaps he was right. I remember it as a breathtaking moment, filled with awe and loneliness, and a deeply felt, if dimly understood, sense of responsibility. People don't talk about "vocation" much anymore, but if there is a "calling" involved in one's life choices, that is when it came to me, writing in my notebook, knowing that what I was thinking was somehow relevant, important beyond myself. Grade five was special in many ways. Our second-room teacher, Valentine Thiessen, loved literature and taught it eloquently to the grade sevens and eights on the other side of the classroom, while I eavesdropped, guiltily but mesmerized. *Julius Caesar*, *Jean Val Jean* (Solomon Cleaver's English retelling of Victor Hugo's *Les Misérables*), and *A Midsummer Night's Dream* filled my mind with grand recognitions of treachery, and heroism, and desire. In order to preserve Mennonite customs, we received supplementary courses in the village schools, German, catechism, Mennonite history, and of course choral singing. The German course in grade five consisted entirely of memorizing German poetry, reciting it out loud, and writing it out for the final exam. Many children and parents complained about the course, finding the poems hard to memorize and perhaps hard to stomach, and the course was changed to something more colloquial and superficial a few years later. But for me it was a feast of imaginative pleasure. And terror. No one thought to explain any of the poems to us, it was straight mainlining into the blood. Goethe, Schiller, Hölderlin, Heine. I still shiver at the spectre of the implacable Erlenkönig, haunting the forest and stealing children from their father's arms, and the heartbreaking Lorelei, luring sailors onto the rocks along the Rhine with their unearthly singing. The rich vein of German Sturm und Drang, of full-bodied expressionism, palpable in the poems, fed my Germanic spirit in a way that English writing, with its streak of puritanism – with the brilliant exception of Chaucer and Shakespeare – could not.

And then everything broke open. One of our teachers decided I should skip a grade, so I finished the curriculum in our little village school, grade eight, a year earlier than my twin sister. Few village kids went on to high school after grade eight. Those that did were either sent off to boarding school somewhere, or enrolled in correspondence courses, with occasional tutoring from the school principal in a little room in the back of the school. The year I hit grade nine, high-school instruction in the village schools became consolidated, and widely encouraged. I found myself on an hour-and-a-half-long bus ride every morning and evening to attend Garden Valley Collegiate in Winkler, only twelve miles away, but with many villages to stop in, without my friends, and most importantly, without my twin, from whom I had never ever been apart, for even an hour. I was fascinated by the new world of town life, which was radically different from life in our villages, considerably more cosmopolitan. My sister felt left behind and did not want to hear about my exciting experiences in grade nine. The town kids and teachers discriminated against the village kids with our unsophisticated *Darp* ways, in both subtle and blatant ways. My parents were alarmed by my blossoming sense of independence and disapproved of everything I said and did. I felt deeply bereft, in shock, as if my arms and legs had been cut off. Perhaps it was my sense of exile, coinciding so exactly with the moment of adolescence, that propelled me into an intellectual life and took me, unwaveringly, as far away as possible from the world of my childhood, my people, my homeland, though I have spent much of it mourning for the great deep loss of them. I spent two years at Garden Valley Collegiate, then transferred to Mennonite Collegiate Institute in Gretna, Manitoba. This was a boarding school with a rich music and sports curriculum, and strict rules. We were locked in our little rooms for four hours every evening for study period. We were not allowed to cross the campus to talk with boys. We wore uniforms with strict hemline requirements. Miniskirts were just coming into fashion then, and blue jeans, and sandals, for girls. Our mothers had carefully measured our hemlines, while we kneeled on the floor, to reach just below our knees. When we got to the school, we raised these carefully sewn hems up several inches with safety pins, or Scotch tape or staples. They would often come undone while we walked from math class to music, a minor embarrassment that was mostly a joke. We experimented with makeup, which we wore all week and washed off before visiting our families at home on the weekend. It was a strictly controlled environment, but I loved every minute of it. My sister was there then too, and we shared a room in the student residence, but we were no longer twins. Our deep childhood connection had been severed; we knew we were headed in different directions.

My parents somehow didn't see it coming, they didn't see that having encouraged me to excel at school, and discouraged me from being very involved with the farm, would mean I'd want to leave the village community and village life after high school and not come back. Everyone "leaves home" nowadays, so my parents' irrevocable grief over my departure is perhaps incomprehensible now. I arrived in urban Canada in the heyday of the sixties counter-culture, and leaped enthusiastically from the Middle Ages into the psychedelic world of peace marches and sit-ins and folk festivals and experimental European films and hippie communes and free love, all of which suited my lurking anarchist rebel genes just fine. I am, after all, a descendant of Anabaptists, who were reviled and hunted all over Europe in the sixteenth century for their sectarian utopian views. People in Canada don't readily understand this radically political side of the Mennonites, and we don't always understand it about ourselves, given how meek and merely old-fashioned we've become, though it comes out loudly and clearly in certain situations, such as war, when our radical anti-nationalist pacifism kicks in energetically and cheerfully, despite its obvious costs. But it is also there, latent, lurking, in everyday activities, we are stubborn and independent minded, we "bow down to no one," we refuse to assimilate to modernity and its puritan, hierarchical, universalizing assumptions. We insist on our traditional peasant customs and sensibility and ways of being in the world.

I don't think my dad ever really got over it. He was heart-broken, he was inconsolable. He had failed, he thought, though he had done his utmost very best to instill the old ways in us, to preserve the traditionalism he so cherished. My mother was of two minds about it, as was typical of her. Her internal dividedness contained a certain treachery to us, most of all to me, who alarmed her so with my independence of spirit, growing up. I see it now as one of her greatest gifts to us, her children, she was a dreamer, a revolutionary, without allies or strategies to enact what she wished to become, and fed our spirits, our creativity, our imaginations with the underground river of her unhappiness. Of course everyone else left after that too, my twin sister, and eventually my other siblings, and most of the village children of that generation. I had been the first one to reject Plautdietsch in favour of English, the first to attend university, other than to get an education or nursing degree in order to come back to serve the community, the first to leave Manitoba to pursue a graduate degree in Toronto, the first to stop attending church, the first to go secular, assimilationist, mainstream. The whole edifice of our Mennonite separatism, preserved so carefully at so high a cost through four centuries of exile and migration and hard labour in harsh, inhospitable landscapes, was coming, as he rightly perceived it, crashing down. My father held these things darkly against me, though he tolerated them in the others later on. There are certain privileges attached to the difficult role of scapegoat, as I have long experience to know: you get blamed for everything, but in exchange you're granted a certain precarious outlaw freedom that is much admired and envied, as well as heavily punished.

He died when I was twenty-seven. I wasn't finished fighting with him yet. We had argued loudly and bitterly about everything since I was about twelve or so. He was an excellent peasant intellectual, a farmer philosopher, but I was quicker, more articulate than he was, I could talk circles around him. This delighted and astonished and infuriated him. And then he was gone. Virginia Woolf said she was thankful her father died young, otherwise she couldn't have become a writer, he simply took up too much space in her life, her psyche. I believe that was true for me too, though I say this out of great love for him, and great grief, who was such an inspiration to me, and such a foe. Perhaps he needn't have worried as he did. Even though I ran away from my Mennonite upbringing, as far and fast as I could, I never really left it, it never really left me.

Eventually I was shunned by the rest of the family, as I had long feared I would be, for my iconoclastic writing, for breaking the centuries long taboo against print culture, for breaking open their separatism, their stowed secrets, betraying them, as they saw it, to the world. That is another great grief, ongoing. Like James Joyce, who lived his entire adult life in exile from his loved and hated mother country, and wrote about nothing else, like Leonard Cohen, who threw away his noble rabbinic lineage for bohemian excess only to recapture its grandeur in his poetry and contemplative practice, I put myself in their grand company to claim that I've been faithful, are you listening, daddy, grandma, somewhere among the stars, I've been true, trying as hard as I can to understand what that idealistic, crazy, stubborn, ecstatic, beautiful, terrible heritage was about, and what it means to me, and to everything, now. *So this is the world, & here I am in it, one of the many lost & found, if you can believe it across all this space, & I think I can say this from so far away, that I love you, I love you.*

BARRY**CALLAGHAN**

Paul Valéry's Shoe: A Story About Storytelling

I have tried as hard as I can to tell stories, not necessarily what I'd call true stories, but stories that have a true feel to their endings, true to how I feel in my heart. What happens is I start a story with a particular face, a particular phrase, and soon I have a page or two – or ten or twelve – but coming to where the story has to end the only thing that ends is my knowing what more there is to say. I sit staring at the dance of dust in the light. Sometimes I'll keep typing, searching for that shoe that Paul Valéry said is out there waiting for the story that's true to itself, the perfect fit. But no matter how bold my start has been, there's finally nothing more to say and I end up shelved in my own head. So the hours pass and I try to peck out a line, a paragraph, I keep trying to look for the ending back in the beginning. I refuse to take the easy way out of the story by just killing off the main man or the woman because that is not an ending. That's just death. That's just having absolutely nothing to say. So what do I do, caught between nothing to say and no ending because I don't understand my beginning? I sit here in this room with these ridiculous old curtains on the window, curtains that remind me of my childhood because they are worked with an

appliqué of the letters of the alphabet, the promise that the alphabet is. I am sitting in this dark room lit only by a lamp beside the
stand-up mirror on the bedside table, trying to tell this particular
story about a writer who is actually starving to death while he is
writing the story of how he is eating himself alive – refusing under
any circumstances to quit on himself or his story because he is too
much of an optimist, as all storytellers have to be, because they
believe that there is that shoe out there that fits – they can't help
themselves from starting a new story because they know that
somewhere in the beginning there is an end – just as I believe that
there has to be an end even for this tawdry, shameful story that I'm
trying to write – a story as cramped as these two tiny rooms where
I sit and catch inadvertently an appalling glimpse of my sneaky
little face in the bedside mirror, the face of a dolt sneering back at
me – sneering because that dolt knows that I still believe the phrase
"a petal falls" is a touching, moving phrase – sneering at me, his
eyes shining bright in the gloom, as I'm sure my own eyes are
shining, the eyes of a starving man, chewing like an anxious girl on
my knuckle, too stupid to feel pain, and then chewing on another
knuckle, as if coming to an agreement with that dolt about a phrase
could save me, could spring open the light that is in all the little
phrases I have hidden away in notebooks – the lines of conversation overheard and written down, lines so quick and easy to
whoever said them, quick as the curl of a lip, quick as an eye
dropped in sleep, all, all of them, the words, seeming at first as fresh
and alive as fireflies at night but turning to ash in the morning,
ashes in the mouth whenever I've sat here like I'm sitting here now,
day-after-day, TAP TAP on the keys, hearing "a petal falls," "a petal
falls" – not eating for nine days now – stroking my wrists, stroking
the mildew-like tracing of my own veins in the skin, so delicate,
not believing that any of what is now happening is true. I mean,

could I actually die of hunger, die out of want for a story, die at the only point in my storytelling life where I actually have an ending, die because in fact I have absolutely nothing left of myself, I mean, could I actually end by eating my own heart out? Could I end up, after more pages pile up and pass, being so light-headed from hunger and typing and licking between my tendons in this hour that is so cold that it takes my breath away, eating what is necessary, possible, getting down to the heart of who I am as I ease one word, and then another, into a shoe – a shoe that fits as I end my story, yes, end it by saying, yes, with utter storytelling simplicity, yes, how much I hate the words, "Once upon a time . . ."

LYNN**COADY**

On Behaving Badly

When I am nervous about performing some kind of writerly action in public – reading from my work, participating in a panel, or even just sitting around looking sage – I have this ritual I go through. It is not a deliberate ritual, like saying the rosary or rubbing a lucky rabbit's foot. It is more of an instinctive ritual. I've only become aware of it in the same, gradual way that women (often with the tentative assistance of their male companions) will become aware of the peaks and lows of their monthly mood swings. Just before P-day, for example, it is my sad time. A few days later, it is my exhilarated, creative time. Middle of the cycle, during ovulation – this is my angry time. But in the last few years, I've realized I have another angry time, every bit as irrational, destructive, and inopportune as the hormonally induced one – if not more so. This is the rage I experience just before making a public appearance.

And so I have this thing I always find myself doing. I will stomp around the house for a few days, kicking the cat out of my way and feeling generally owlish, until one night, I'll blurt to the person I live with: "I don't wanna do that goddamn (library reading, dinner, writer's festival, etc.) next week."

The person I live with will know enough to jump right in, pounding his fist on the table and rejoining: "To hell with those losers! Who do they think they are, anyway, paying for your flight and accommodations just so you can read from the novel you desperately want people to read."

"The hotel will probably suck."

"Of course it will."

"I've asked for the dairy-free meal. You think they're gonna remember?"

"Big bowl of fettuccine alfredo – that'll be the first thing they put in front of you. With a glass of milk."

"And cheesecake for dessert. Then they'll expect me to be all: Oh la la. Hello, so nice to meet you."

". . . When what you really want to do is punch them in the face."

"That's what I should do when I get there."

"Don't read. Just punch everybody in the face."

"But first I'll have to get up there and explain why I'm punching them in the face."

"That's only fair. They're your hosts after all."

And then the person I live with and I will kill a bottle of wine as we put our heads together and come up with an appropriate speech to replace the reading I have been asked to do.

Greetings, morons. Thank you for inviting me to your shitty little (town, library, festival, etc.) I can't express to you the loathing I feel gazing down at all your pasty, slack-jawed faces. My hotel room looks out over the parking lot and I haven't gone to the bathroom in two days because the organizer thinks "lactose intolerant" means "put cheese on everything." Please, please, everybody. I implore you: go to hell. Because you suck VERY MUCH.

Now gimmie money.

Those are all terrible things to say, and I hope I don't need to add I would never say them in any circumstance other than killing a bottle of wine with the person I live with. It is, simply, my private ritual. It makes me feel better, because I think it's funny. Not everybody would find it funny, but those people would be wrong. Those people wouldn't be getting the joke: encapsulated in the above speech is everything that a writer – these days – is not supposed to be. To break those things down: insulting, profane, ungrateful, complaining, illiterate, inelegant, and – worst of all – flagrantly money-grubbing.

It's a lot of pressure, knowing you are not allowed to be any of those things. Especially when you're the kind of person who suspects she was born with a natural predisposition for at least four of them. It wasn't always thus for writers – although it was usually thus for women writers, which strikes me as doubly unfair. People like Charles Bukowski and Canada's "people's poet" Milton Acorn made a career of bad behaviour – indeed, it got to be expected of them. I'm not one to romanticize alcoholic hijinks, but at the same time, I couldn't help but feel wistful when, after a reading I gave in Saint John, my host Anne Compton told me about hosting Acorn years earlier, and how he had fallen off his stool in the middle of his reading. There I was, thirty years old, on the last leg of an exhausting tour of Atlantic-Canadian universities, in my nice neat clothes, with a new haircut and shiny shoes and a fever of about 101 (I had gotten steadily sicker during the tour). I was sitting having dinner with various kind, lovely people, just trying to hold up my end of the conversation while seeming gracious, pithy, and deeply engaged, when what I really wanted to do was go up to my room and immerse myself in a tub of rum toddies. Except for the rum toddies, nothing had ever sounded so luxurious to me: "Milton fell off his stool." Imagine being such a writer at such a time! You're bored, you're sick, you're tired, you're drunk – you can just fall off your stool, simultaneously living up to your audience's expectations while providing them with dinner-table conversation fodder for years to come.

Back in the old days (and you'll forgive this lazy generalization), before the days of the Harry Potter empire and movie deals being enshrined in book contracts before said books are even written, it was mostly okay for writers to come across as the grimy, petty, foul-mouthed little shits they were. That's because the stakes were so low. Now the stakes are marginally higher, but with the lure of Big Money looming for whoever hits the jackpot with the next international bestseller or Miramax deal. Only then is the writer permitted – indeed expected – to revert to his or her natural jerkdom. It's this heady promise that keeps the rest of us on the straight and narrow. There are publicists to be appeased, for example, publicists who, it turns out, will refuse to work with you if you become known for screaming: "WHAT PART OF 'HOLD THE CHEESE' DON'T YOU UNDERSTAND??" at them three times a day. There are television and radio personalities to be sucked up to, people who will ban you from their programs if you sanctimoniously insist upon reading a prison rape scene during their morning show on the basis that the scene in question is "the most representative of the book as a whole." There are festival organizers who will drag you off the stage with a cane (this is actually true) if you continue reading that same prison rape scene well past your designated twenty minutes (because to shorten it would be to "betray your vision").

Despite these strictures, however, I still have my passive-aggressive moments. I expect most writers do. I'll be preparing for a reading, I'll get nervous, the nerves will immediately translate themselves into hostility, and next thing I know, I'm combing my book for the most foul-mouthed, scatological passage I can find. Aha! The intestinal-parasite-hits-in-the-middle-of-foreplay scene! That'll show those complacent bastards! This is why it is advisable to select the passage you will be reading well in advance and stick to it, which I almost never do.

You'll notice I began this essay with reference to my womanly cycles. That's another passive-aggressive technique, because what writer, in her right mind, would begin an essay with reference to something so gross and personal and off-putting? Normally, once my initial skittishness about writing the essay had abated, I would edit the reference out. But I will leave it in, this time, to be instructive.

The question I've often asked myself, though, is from where does all this pent-up hostility and aggression spring forth? Why am I so deeply angry at people who are interested in my writing? To be honest, some of it is explicable. Sometimes you really do get the feeling that people are not so much interested in you as they are in your potential to fill a slot in their itinerary. Some people even go out of their way to make this clear. Oh yes, writers do not have the lock on passive-aggression, believe me. I have a friend who was told by her host that he believed there really hadn't been any good writing since Shakespeare. He then went on to lecture her, a novelist, on the dearth of readable contemporary fiction.

But even when the hosts are lovely, the venue is lovely, the audience is lovely – which of course is more often the case – I still grapple with an irrational impulse to turn around, bend over, and moon the bunch of them. Sometimes I put it down to my upbringing as a hick. When you're a hick, you are taught to react to anything strange or new – anything that makes you feel remotely uncomfortable or threatened – with vociferous loathing and contempt. You scorn the thing loudly whenever it comes up in conversation and make it clear to one and all that this is a thing you absolutely "don't care for."

But I could never kid myself on this front. I enjoy reading my work out loud. What I don't care for, clearly, is being afraid, afraid of the same thing everyone who lives in terror of public speaking is afraid of – looking and sounding like an idiot. This affliction certainly isn't limited to hicks, but it might be worth noting that some of the worst-behaved writers in history have been from rural or working-class backgrounds. Acorn and Bukowski are two such types, both raging alcoholics, and I tend to believe they honestly didn't know how else to behave in the alien world of "literary" activities. Imagine being raised to fear and loathe such a world, knowing you have pretty much no alternative, as this is clearly a world to which someone like you would never be permitted entry. And yet one day, there you are. Invited to read your private, fevered, semi-pornographic scribblings in front of the kind of people you always assiduously feared and loathed for being so conspicuously better than you.

But are they? Clearly a re-evaluation is in order. Looking around, it becomes manifest that these people are stupider and lower-class than you once assumed. After all, look at them gazing back at you with their respectful, attentive smiles. A queasy-making wave of cognitive dissonance sends you swooning. What the hell is wrong with these people? You thought they deserved your contempt for their assumed superiority over you, but now it's obvious they deserve your contempt for having allowed you to put this huge joke over on them – this joke you've been perpetuating for the last decade or so. That you are a real writer, worthy of being taken seriously, the kind of person who is invited to speak in public and trusted to entertain and enlighten – as opposed to horrify and disgust – with your words and actions. Yet here they sit – happy, expectant – perhaps even having paid money for the privilege of listening to someone like you.

God.

What a bunch of losers.

SUSAN**COYNE**

Writing Together

Now that I make my living as a writer (more or less), people ask me whether this was something I'd always planned. "Not exactly," I say. The truth is, I haven't planned much in my life.

I left university with a history degree, and while my classmates went off to law school, I came home to my parents' house, got a job in a restaurant, and took some courses in theatre. Acting seemed to be something for which I had a knack, and so I auditioned for the National Theatre School of Canada, where, in my final year, I was firmly assured that I would never play leading roles. But shortly after graduating, I was cast as Juliet at the Stratford Festival, and soon added Regan, Olivia, Helena, Ophelia, Rosalind, Portia, and Hermione to my resume. For the next fifteen years I was steadily employed, performing in new plays and old, in theatres across the country.

The joy of this work, for me, is in the collaboration. I love theatre people: their stories and jokes, their complicated personalities. I love the rehearsal period: the research, the discussions, the way the words of a great writer seep into your imagination. I dreaded opening nights, at first, because they meant the end of this enjoyable process, but I have come to look forward to the audience's participation, the way it lifts one's game.

Acting, it seemed, was my life. Then, sometime in my late thirties, just as I was beginning to think that I knew something about my craft or art, offers of work became more and more infrequent. I had an identity crisis. What is an actor without a show? What was I, if not an actor?

Around that time, a close friend became seriously ill. John was a witty and gifted actor in our Young Company at Stratford, where he had played Paris in *Romeo and Juliet*, the Fool in *King Lear*, Puck in *A Midsummer Night's Dream*. A group of us formed a care team, cooking interesting meals for him, watching movies with him, laughing and gossiping with him, as if we could keep him alive with our gaiety. When he died, six months later, we were in shock. For many of us, it was our first serious encounter with death.

The wake was a piece of theatre, poignant and hilarious, with moments of sudden and surprising intimacy. And so it was that after a few glasses of wine, I confessed to a writer friend that I had been harbouring an idea for a story. A story that I had been thinking about as I sat by John's bed, and that I wished I could have shared with him. "Write it down," he said, withdrawing ever so slightly from my glassy-eyed intensity. "Don't you want to know what it is?" I asked. "No. Write it down." "But – I'm not a writer," I said. "I wouldn't know how to tell it." He looked at me pityingly. "Oh, for God's sake. Get over yourself. Write it down. You can't know until you try."

This was hard to refute. The story was about my childhood friendship with a man who had been a neighbour of ours, a retired schoolteacher named Mr. Moir. He had written me a series of letters in which he had created an entire world furnished with bits of folklore and song, and poetry from Shakespeare, Shelley, Keats,

Swinburne, and others. It was an extraordinary gift that I felt called upon to repay.

And so, in my tiny upstairs office, in the hours when my children were at school, I set to work, reading and rereading Mr. Moir's letters, and marvelling once again at his patience and his gift for encouragement. It was Mr. Moir who taught me how to play chess, repair a loose board on the dock, and tell whether the moon was waxing or waning. It was he who first told me of Queen Mab, of Ariel and Puck and the rest of their ilk, of the great Hummingbird God of Peru, and of the customs of the Babylonian kings. And it was Mr. Moir who once asked, in response to a childish fable I had written: "How does it feel, Susan, to put a few marks on a piece of paper and see a kingdom and all its people rise up in front of you?"

All of this I had forgotten, until I opened the box in which my father had preserved the letters for me.

After I had put them in order, I ventured to sketch in a little narrative: memories of our summers at the cottage, descriptions of my family. A few humorous anecdotes, the kind that were told around the dinner table. Nothing that could give offence.

When I had finished a draft, I sent it to my family who were pleased, but puzzled by my portraits of them, which seemed to them fantastically distorted. My mother summed up the general mood, saying, "Well, they say the first thing a writer has to do is try to kill off her mother." I began to understand how thin the membrane is separating autobiography and fiction.

Friends to whom I showed the piece were deeply affected by the story of the kind old man and urged me to send it to a publisher. But I felt unready, and probably would have worried away at my manuscript until I was sixty if my husband hadn't submitted it on his own to an agent. And soon after that, I found myself sitting at a table, staring at a lineup of people wanting me to sign their copy of my book, thinking, "What am I doing here? I'm not a writer." It was a mortifying experience.

It may seem odd, this shyness, considering my vocation. But I am comfortable onstage precisely because it's someone else's words I'm saying. An actor has a ready answer to the question: "Who do you think you are?"

For a writer, the question seems infinitely more complicated. Especially if one is coming to it late in life, trailing dogs, kids, and all the rest of it. How could I be a writer in the midst of such mundane chaos? A writer speaks in her own voice. What could I possibly have to say?

A writer, however, is what I seem to have become. Since that book signing, four years ago, I have adapted two of Chekhov's plays and written a radio drama, two original plays, and three seasons of a television miniseries. I even have a room at the Tarragon Theatre with a sign on the door: "Writer's Office." Writing seems to be a part of everything I do, now. It has permeated into every cranny of my life. I'm not quite sure how this happened. It's as if by revisiting my wise old mentor, I passed through a magic door and into a whole new life. Now I give *other* people words to say.

My latest project is a case in point: *Slings and Arrows* is a six-part TV series set in the fictional world of the New Burbage Shakespeare Festival. Each season we (co-writers Bob Martin and Mark McKinney and I) take a different play and watch our theatre company attempt to stage it while negotiating the politics of a major cultural institution.

We created our characters with an eye to the people in Shakespeare's plays. Geoffrey, our hero, has a touch of Hamlet's melancholy and is haunted by a vengeful ghost. Richard, our Macbeth, is an arts administrator itching for bigger things. Ellen, our leading lady, is a narcissist obsessed with aging – clearly our Cleopatra.

Over the years, however, the characters have grown in ways none of us could have imagined on our own. They are the children of our collective imaginations. All three of us are actors first. All three of us are married. All three of us are in middle age. And all of this is reflected in our story. This is what writing together looks like:

Interior. Kitchen. Day. It is twelve-thirty on a September afternoon. The door is open, the dog sits on the back deck sniffing the warm air. I am making sandwiches while arguing with my colleagues over a scene in which Ellen falls into bed with her brother-in-law. I accuse them of being heartless. They imply that I have lost my sense of humour. A break is declared. Tea is made. The dog is furiously petted. After a time, our discussion resumes.

Around three o'clock, my daughter appears at the door, throwing off her coat, "MOM! Where's my form for running club?" "In your knapsack." "No, it isn't." "Yes it is, and say hi to Bob and Mark." She does. Mark asks: "What do you think, Julia? Should Richard and Anna get together?" "No way. Anna should marry Geoffrey."

Moments later, my teenage son arrives home and heads straight for the fridge. "Jamie! Say hello to your surrogate uncles." Jamie glances over his shoulder. "Hi, Bob. Hi, Mark." He returns his attention to the fridge. "Technically, Mom? They're my co-writers once removed." The doorbell rings, the dog barks, the meter man appears. Someone opens a laptop, and an outline begins to take shape.

Interior. Third-floor office. Night. Unable to sleep, I am sitting at my computer, staring at the script I am meant to be writing. I compose an email: "Holly and Richard confess a dark secret: they hate Shakespeare." I make a few more notes, then send another one: "The auditor should be in the audience for *Macbeth*." Minutes later, I receive an email back: "Go to bed."

I have been working this way with Bob and Mark for five years. Having to share our first drafts with each other, an experience of such excruciating vulnerability, has created a blood bond between us. We are each other's best advocates and worst critics.

Interior. Day. On location at The Sanderson Theatre in Brantford, Ontario. While a winter storm rages outside, Bob and I huddle in an unused dressing room, rewriting a scene in which our two middle-aged lovers remember their youth. We are arguing about the dialogue, but we are also talking about our own experience of love and longing and disappointment. Between takes, Mark appears in his Richard costume to add his two cents. Somehow, over a long day, as the streets of Brantford fill up with snow, the scene transforms itself, and the pages are printed off for the actors to learn by the next day.

In the course of this unusual partnership, the three of us have endured all the predictable and not so predictable vicissitudes of midlife, and shared them together in my kitchen, in bars and coffee shops, over Korean and Greek food, while drinking tea and wine and vodka martinis. Our scripts are full of these anecdotes, changed, but still recognizable: the speech a minister gave at a wedding, a destructive director, the nightmare of stage fright, falling in love with your leading man, the perils of success, the bitterness of failure.

Since I began this kind of work, I have learned that, if you have to, you can do it anywhere: at the orthodontist, on the road, in hotel rooms, at the hockey game, on trains and planes and buses, on a moonlit beach, in the streets of Old Montreal. The time at the laptop is only part of the story. So much depends on a willingness to switch back and forth between the currents of life and one's own interior world. Sometimes in the very same moment.

I wonder, sometimes, what it would be like to fly solo, like a novelist. I wonder if I would enjoy it, the loneliness and the responsibility. Could I wall myself off from the ongoing distractions that make up my life? Is that the necessary price for being a writer?

Then, I think of Anton Chekhov, who lived for many years in a crowded apartment with his wreck of a family. There was always a crisis of some kind, usually involving money or alcohol. Every day, there were hordes of visitors to be fed, impoverished relatives to be entertained, young writers seeking advice. In his letters, Chekhov complained bitterly of all this, but the minute he had built a house of his own in the country, he begged his family to join him, friends to spend weekends with him. He never resolved the ongoing internal conflict between his two vocations – medicine and literature – and was unable to decide which had the greatest claim on him. It was Chekhov who said, in one of his letters, "It is time for writers to admit that nothing in this world makes sense. Only fools and charlatans think they know and understand everything." I take a strange comfort in that. Perhaps this crowded, messy way of being a writer is just as it should be.

Interior. The Regent Theatre. Day. It is June. The cast and crew, writers and producers, family and friends, a small army of people, gather to watch the final assembly of our series, the six episodes which will go to air in the fall. The lights go down, the show begins, and I am suddenly in tears: remembering how all this began sitting around my kitchen table, arguing and laughing, in the midst of dogs and children, meter men and laundry. In the midst of a noisy life.

I think of John, and his passion for all that makes life a *life*: friends, conversation, and laughter.

I think of Mr. Moir and the question he once posed: "How does it feel, Susan, to put a few marks on a piece of paper and see a kingdom and all its people rise up in front of you?"

How does it feel? Lucky. Astonishing. Miraculous.

MICHAEL**CRUMMEY**

The Fish, the Fish

The wind was up that morning, sweeping in over the bay, lifting a heavy lop on the water. I wore jeans, sneakers, two sweaters under a life jacket. Dad had on steel-toed rubber boots, an old pair of coveralls. Mom shook her head as we headed down to the stage, unlikely looking fishermen, the both of us. "Don't catch a whale," she said.

"If I don't throw up," I told her, "I'll be happy."

Eric, a family friend, was taking us out in his open eighteen-footer. He'd made his living off the cod before the government-imposed moratorium ended the commercial fishery in Newfoundland due to the cod stock's near-total collapse. He drives the local school bus now, but still has his boat and the stage just below his house in North Bay.

He kept the skiff to the calmer water close to shore as we headed out, the bow slapping above the waves, the spray blown back at us bitter, salt and cold. Halfway to open ocean he turned parallel to the troughs, gunning then easing off the motor as we rolled over each successive crest, before cutting the engine altogether in the middle of the bay and throwing out a grapple to hold us steady in the pitch.

We were there to hand-line for cod, during the one weekend a year set aside for the "food fishery." Fathoms of nylon threading through our fingers over the gunnel. I sat facing Dad, Eric standing behind him in the stern, each of us jigging our lines. Dad looked up occasionally to watch me, something like a grin on his face.

I had never caught a fish in my life. Grew up in a mining town in the interior of Newfoundland, hundreds of miles from salt water. I was also afflicted with a susceptibility to seasickness, which has always felt like a personal failure, a laughable weakness. And which might have accounted, I thought, for my father's grin.

Dad started in the fishery as a boy of nine, spending the summer months of his youth on the Labrador coast with his father. Working in all but the worst weather, out to the cod traps in open boats before first light, all day then at the splitting table to clean and salt the fish. Often just making ends meet after settling the crew's wages and what was owed the merchant at season's end. When his father died, Dad quit school to take over the crew, sixteen years old then and he fell quickly into debt. Took a job at the mine intending to pay it off and go back to fishing, but wound up working in Buchans thirty years and more.

After half an hour we had only the one small cod brought up by Eric and he decided to move us farther out, a small crowd of gulls chasing the boat to the mouth of the bay. The wind and waves heavier out there, the rise and fall like flying through turbulence but steady, a false kind of soothe to it. I stood in the bow, legs braced against the wood, letting out my line. The first hint of nausea was an odd niggle in the gut, a heat that was almost pleasurable, and I ignored it, hoping it would pass. Tried to will myself not to succumb. Left it nearly too long, raced to get the line up, the blood draining from my face. Sat just in time to hold down the surge of vomit.

"You sick?" Eric asked, surprised.

Dad just shook his head, that grin on his face again. Not mean at all. Bemused.

Sitting down settled my stomach some, but I still felt miserable. The foul acid in my mouth and I spat repeatedly into the water, wanting only to get ashore. But I wouldn't ask. Let them go on fishing.

This was the summer of 2001, just before my first novel was published. Dad was already sick then with the cancer that would kill him a little over a year later. I know he worried about me. He was never sure what to make of the writing exactly, why I did it, or what it did for me. I was thirty years old before I published my first book, a slender volume of poetry after nearly a decade of slogging it out in the little magazines. I remember telling Dad the news when the manuscript was accepted.

"How much are they paying you?" he asked. And after we'd laughed off that question he wanted to know what the book was called.

"*Arguments with Gravity.*"

An abbreviated nod as he tried to take it in. "That's a queer fucking title," he said finally.

Even that summer when we took our one and only fishing trip together, after I'd sold the novel, making enough money to quit my day job and move home to Newfoundland for good, he worried. "Who's going to take care of him?" he asked my mother when they lay in bed at night. After they were gone, he meant. To his mind writing was something more uncertain and mercurial than the whereabouts of the cod, an occupation to rival fishing for its insecurity, its monumental unpredictability. He never said as much but he must have expected, as I often do, that it might leave me someday, migrate somewhere else or simply dry up.

They had no better luck after the fish in the mouth of the bay. When Eric gave up and took in his line, he gutted the single cod, heaving out bloody handfuls of offal that the waiting gulls screeched and fought over. Washed the split fish over the side of the boat. Finally, mercifully, started the outboard.

I was still pale and clammy-cold as we headed back in. Still without a cod to my name. Dad and I were facing each other where we sat on the tauts, him smiling at me. "Better to be a poet," he said then.

And at that moment I could not disagree with him.

MARGARET**DRABBLE**

The Wickedness of Fiction

As I grow older, I realize that writing is perhaps necessarily an invasive and intrusive activity. When I first started to write fiction, at the age of twenty-one, it seemed a harmless occupation. It cost next to nothing, it kept me company, and it hurt nobody. Or so I thought. Of course, I must have deceived myself. My intentions were surely malign. Now, nearly forty-five years later, I look back at that lost sense of innocence with tears of regret. For I have come to suspect that the writing of fiction is an act of aggression. And if so, my occupation is gone.

I am left to reconsider the catalogue of my past crimes. I know now that writing involves aggression and betrayal and appropriation. I am guilty of these charges. The "writing life" is a life of crime.

The awareness of my wickedness came to me gradually. I knew from an early age that novelists had always used characters and incidents out of "real life," and that such use and abuse could cause pain and even lasting damage. I thought little of novelists who, with "a nervous disinclination for responsibility" (I think the phrase is Doris Lessing's, from one of the Martha Quest books), pretended that they never used "real people" or real events, though I did not go as far as the late B.S. Johnson, an experimental novelist who claimed to believe that telling stories was telling lies, and that only autobiography held truth. (Why he became a novelist, starting from this premise, remains unexplained by novelist Jonathan Coe's recent and in some ways unsatisfactory biography.) My position was somewhere between these poles. Fiction, I believed, draws on real life and real experience, but it transforms and conceals. Certain stories are to be avoided altogether; others are to be softened or disguised. I believed that I had no wish to cause pain to the living, and there were some subjects that I thought I would never use.

I did not write about my mother until many years after her death, when I felt I had earned the right to try to explore the difficulties of her life. She had been dead for nearly twenty years when I published *The Peppered Moth* in 2001, and I had thought the distance great enough for me to be able to write about her. I was close to my mother, or she was close to me, and in her angry later years we spent a fair amount of time together, time which relieved my father of her exhausting and demanding company. She was a manipulative woman, with a gift for making others feel guilty for her unhappiness. As I discovered while researching the details of her childhood and trying to discover what took place before I was born, it was not so much her family who was to blame as the times that she lived in. There was a sociological explanation to her distress. Her story was representative of the lives of a generation of women born early in the twentieth century, who were tantalizingly offered higher education and raised expectations, and who planned to pursue independent careers. But war intervened, and their hopes were disappointed. They lived lives of frustration, frustration which often turned to bitterness and bad temper.

I knew this story was important and worth the telling, and because I am by trade a novelist I used the device of a memoir-novel, mingling fact and fiction, rather than attempting to write a factual memoir. I thought this would enable me to avoid issues which I did not feel free to confront, and to edit out family members who might not wish to be implicated in my personal interpretations of family history. Not surprisingly, this device was not wholly successful, and the book aroused much hostility within the family and beyond. It is small comfort to me to know that writing any kind of honest factual account of my mother's life would have aroused even more hostility. It would have been more diplomatic to avoid the subject forever.

Yet what are writers to do? Their lives are their raw material. *Heart of Darkness* and its dark message would not exist had Conrad not visited the Congo. Melville would not have written *Moby-Dick* had he never gone to sea. Some novelists make no secret of being inspired by marital shipwreck or amorous vengeance. Saul Bellow and Philip Roth do not make it all up, and sometimes their disguises have been very thin. Most of Kenzaburo Ōe's fiction is directly and overtly inspired by his brain-damaged son, whose condition he describes again and again, with a repetition verging on obsession. (He has pointed out, however, that this son does not read his books.) Biographers have written thousands of pages on how long Dickens spent in the blacking factory, and whether or to what extent he traduced his friend, the poet and editor Leigh Hunt, in his portrait of Harold Skimpole in *Bleak House*. (Dickens immodestly claimed that his delineation of Leigh Hunt was "the most exact portrait that was ever painted in words . . . I don't think it could be more like the man himself . . . it is an absolute reproduction of a real man.")

Volumes on the subject of "Who's Who in Fiction" are regularly updated. If you know a writer personally, it is impossible to read the work without asking personal questions about sources and identifications. Clever, evasive, ambiguous authors like Henry James bury the clues deep, a practice which has inevitably inspired a good deal of detective work: the life and work of James have recently inspired and suggested, within the space of two or three years, no less than five works of fiction: Emma Tennant's *Felony* (2002), Alan Hollinghurst's *The Line of Beauty* (2004), Colm Toíbín's *The Master* (2004), David Lodge's *Author, Author* (2004), and Wendy Lesser's *The Pagoda in the Garden* (2005).

More flamboyant literary figures have attracted a different kind of attention. Lady Ottoline Morrell was rewarded for her generous artistic patronage at Garsington Manor by satiric depictions in the novels of various friends. She appeared as Hermione Roddice in D.H. Lawrence's *Women in Love*, a character whom she found "loathsome": she complained of a "ghastly portrait . . . written by someone I had trusted and liked" which horrified and haunted her for many months. Priscilla Wimbush in Aldous Huxley's *Crome Yellow* combines elements of Ottoline Morrell and Edith Sitwell, another figure who was a gift to the caricaturist. Larger-than-life Canadian-born newspaper proprietor Max Beaverbrook is to be found in the pages of Arnold Bennett, H.G. Wells, and Evelyn Waugh: in the work of his protegé William Gerhardie he becomes Lord Ottercove, an alias which was clearly meant to be decoded. The descriptions of fellow-Fabians Sidney and Beatrice Webb as Oscar and Altiora Bailey in Wells's *The New Machiavelli* are unforgivable and unforgettable. The long life and now neglected work of Wells's mistress, Amber Reeves, was overcast by Wells's vivid (and admiring) evocation of her as a passionate young feminist in *Ann Veronica*.

Writers are a treacherous crew, be they novelists or biographers, and it is wise not to tell them too many secrets. They may claim the privileges of art and truth-telling, but they do not always deserve them. Sometimes revenge is all that they seek, and the wounds they inflict are out of all proportion to the offence. In at least one literary life, however, we can see the process of the transmutation of raw material with exceptional clarity. Virginia Woolf's letters and diaries are rightly famed for their merciless and often spitefully petty observations of relatives, friends, and neighbours, but in her fiction she assumes a different tone altogether. Some use fiction as a disguise for comments that might otherwise be offensive or libellous, but Woolf appears to dispose of her harsh judgments in her more ephemeral (albeit carefully preserved, widely published, and heavily edited) prose: in her fiction and her critical works she writes with a far larger and more forgiving spirit. In major works like *A Room of One's Own*, *The Waves*, and *To the Lighthouse*, she writes with compassionate understanding of characters who, in "real life," might have been (and often were) the subjects of her mockery and wit.

Perhaps she offers us an example of how to approach the ethics of life writing. We could attempt to dispose of our resentments in our indiscreet journals, or in gossip to our friends, where they cannot infect our more serious or lasting work, and thus we might feel free to write our novels or our biographies with a liberated and elevated generosity. This procedure, in principle, would bear some similarity to the (minority) psychoanalytic view that dreams are the rubbish bin of thought: we dream of nonsense and trivia, thus liberating our working brains for better and more rational stuff. (This is not a view that I hold, but some do.)

Unfortunately, this approach doesn't seem to work for everyone. A habit of private malice may be carried over into public print. And some of us are incapable of telling some truths, even in a private diary or private correspondence. Each writer has to find her own way of finding an ethical balance between disclosure and discretion, between betrayal and sentimentality. Some of us are too nervous about causing offence: others indulge themselves too freely, and sometimes live to regret it.

A certain amount of pillaging from real life and real people is acceptable, and meets with no objections. Novelists are thieves and magpies, and always have been. I have a friend whose opinions, eccentricities, décor, and aphorisms have appeared in many of my works, recombined in different characters for different purposes, and I don't think she bears me any malice. I once gave a lecture in Sweden on her recurrent fictional manifestations, as a way of owning up and giving credit where it is due, and I don't think she minded that either. She wasn't in the audience, and the conference was in another country, but I don't think she would have minded anyway.

I realized that in attempting to write about my mother, I was taking different risks, although she was long dead, but I hoped I could resolve the problems both artistically and morally. Maybe I had attempted the impossible: I never achieved the resurrection that Virginia Woolf performed for her mother when she created Mrs. Ramsay in *To the Lighthouse*. When I read feminist critic Lorna Sage's remarkable memoir, *Bad Blood*, which appeared after my own memoir-novel, I saw that she had achieved what I had only hoped for: a sense of forgiveness and understanding, combined with a sharp-eyed and unsentimental frankness about family history. I wrote to tell her how much I had admired it, just before her death. I am glad I wrote that letter.

After the self-inflicted wounds caused by the publication of *The Peppered Moth*, I resolved to stay away from personal matters and allegations of appropriation. My next novel (*The Seven Sisters*) borrowed much of its plot from Virgil's *Aeneid*, but Virgil did not pursue me from the underworld, accusing me of theft and betrayal. However, I had not learned my lesson. After my mild little Virgilian novel about growing old in London, I embarked on another novel inspired by my reading of the memoirs of a crown princess of Korea, who had died in 1815. I had thought she was at sufficient distance, historically and geographically, for me to be able to respond in my own way to her astonishing story.

I could not have been more mistaken. Although, in my view, I proceeded openly and correctly and courteously in my negotiations with the most recent translator of these memoirs, I found myself embroiled in an alarming battle about Orientalism, multiculturalism, Edward Said, and cultural appropriation, and I began to wish I had never come across the works of the ill-fated princess.

One of the sentences which the lawyers wished me to remove from my text was a phrase that I have redeployed above: "*Novelists are thieves and magpies.*" I removed it, and other incriminating passages, and my novel, *The Red Queen*, was eventually published. But this was a cautionary experience. It made me feel very unhappy about the whole enterprise of writing fiction. Perhaps the great hostility I had aroused was justified. Perhaps writing is theft, and the using of the lives of others is morally, if not legally, criminal.

PEN, of which I have long been a member and for which I am now thinking about and writing about these issues, exists to protect freedom of expression, and of course I support the rights of writers to say what they want without fear of censorship and imprisonment. We should beware of and question closely any legislation which seeks to infringe our right to speak out about politics, religion, gender, race, and all the large and dangerous topics that preoccupy us. But, having said that, we know that writers agonize about other rights, and in particular about their right to use the lives and tell the secrets of others. Dan Chaon, in a

"Conversation" printed in the Reader's Guide at the end of his remarkable and poignant first novel, *You Remind Me of Me* (2004), describes the dilemma he faced. The novel is about adoption and identity, and Chaon lets us know that he himself was adopted. But he goes on to say "I really wanted to avoid direct autobiography.... So while I was drawing on fairly intense personal experience as I was writing, I was also creating entirely fictional characters and situations. I was worried about hurting the feelings of both my adoptive family and my biological family, and so I was especially careful that no one would mistakenly identify themselves as one of the characters."

This is an honest and elegant statement of the complex interaction between fact and fiction, source and current, and as a result of this process of transmutation Chaon has produced characters who are fictional but wholly credible.

Yet, in the spectrum of literary conscience, there are great writers distinguished by their ability to say the unsayable – writers as diverse as Jean-Jacques Rousseau, Theodore Dostoevsky, Jean Genet, Doris Lessing, Salman Rushdie, writers to whom the inhibitions of self-censorship seem alien. Great truth-tellers do not always write to their own advantage, and are sometimes forced into exile or imprisoned. The writing life is a dangerous life, on many counts: a dangerous life, a dangerous balance.

BERNICE**EISENSTEIN**

From Another Vein

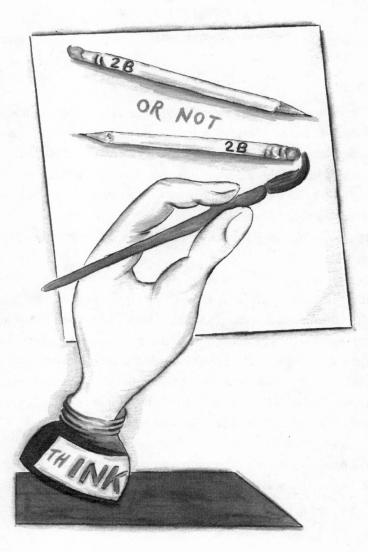

HOWARD**ENGEL**

Stroking the Writer

I've written a lot about my stroke. Too much, maybe. I've used it in fiction, talked about it in public, on radio, and on TV. And enough of my ego has survived the stroke to make me fear that too many readers of this piece will have heard too much of this already. I feel a bit like a public performer with a flawed fiddle and only one party piece, or an old-timer telling yet again how I whipped the rebels single-handed with my Gatling gun. Nevertheless, here's my story.

When I take an inventory of my physical resources, I discover that I am still mostly in this world. My arms and legs still work. I can cross the street without a walker. I know the name of the prime minister. My only problem now, as it was four years ago, is the fact that I can't read. Oh, I can work my way through a text, word by word, but when I say *read* I mean read with the old ease and pleasure that had stood by me since I first learned about John, Mary, and Peter in my primer, or Tom Sawyer or Huckleberry Finn.

It was Tuesday, the last day of July 2001. I was asleep at the time, so I have nothing to report on the nature of the advent or arrival of the stroke. I was asleep at the switch. There was no pre-dromal sensation, such as migraine sufferers recognize. No sudden blackout or blindness. No pain. It came like a burglar in the night and robbed me of Chaucer, Shakespeare, and Donne, Wordsworth, Byron, and Arnold, Hawthorne, Whitman, and Poe, but left me with Leonardo, Raphael, and Klee. I could still talk and follow an argument, but I couldn't read about it in the papers. The stroke was a poison dart that hit me where I live, in the centre of the brain that controls the recognition and interpretation of symbols like letters. Even short words like *the* and *for* escaped me in the beginning. At first I couldn't pick out my own name from a list of a dozen others. What I had was a rare sort of what professionals call an "insult to the brain." To me it smacked of more than bad manners. My personal insult is called *alexia sine agraphia*, which means not being able to read while still being able to write.

Of course, at the beginning, flat on my back in the hospital, I didn't test the second half of the proposition. Writing seemed a bagatelle. It was like being told by my surgeon that the left leg must be amputated but that I could keep the sock and shoe. Writing was what I did. It was part of me, it was my creative outlet, it put the jam in the fridge and made a summer vacation possible. It gave my life meaning; it had become bound up with my identity.

I know that no one forced me to become a writer. It was my choice, and it follows that it was my fault as well. A writer crying poverty before the world is like a man who has murdered his parents throwing himself on the mercy of the court because he is an orphan. I could have remained a teacher; I was one once. I could have chosen to stay in broadcasting; that had been my profession before I began publishing detective stories. No one held a gun to my head and said "You must become a writer or I'll shoot!" Like all writers, I have only myself to blame. Like Maggie Tulliver, I always hated blame. But while I was an active writer, I never used my choice of profession to excuse my relative poverty. I had made the bed myself: I couldn't now complain about the fact that it hadn't made me wealthy.

Writing was a corner of my life, an important corner, but not large enough to compare to the vast treasure of literature that I was now cut off from. When I looked at a printed page, it was like trying to make sense of alphabet soup. I resented the casual way in which my fellow patients in the Stroke Unit glanced through the *Globe and Mail*. I felt like a dreamy tortoise jealous of a soaring swallow. Or like a eunuch in a harem.

In fact, it began with the *Globe and Mail*. It was when I stooped to bring in my daily copy of the paper that I first became aware that something was odd about my vision. At first I thought I had been victimized by a practical joker. Who else would exchange my old reliable *Globe and Mail* for something written in Russian or Serbo-Croatian? I moved on to the inside pages and found that these were similarly distorted. I couldn't make heads or tails of it. Was I looking at it right-side up? Who was the joker responsible? It didn't take long to find that not only the *Globe*, but every scrap of paper with writing on it had become jumbled overnight. So I knew this was no joke. The only logical explanation was all too clear: I'd suffered a stroke. With my son, Jacob, at my side, I took a taxi to the nearest Emergency department.

That was the beginning of a new and unexpected chapter in my life. I was in two hospitals over the next month or so: first Toronto's Mount Sinai and then the Toronto Rehabilitation Hospital, one just below the other on University Avenue. In the Stroke Units of both places I learned the new language of illness. My stroke, as I've said, was an "insult" to my brain. In the hospital, and under the guidance of people who were learning to deal with this peculiar, rare, and frustrating condition, I was also learning new words to describe it.

There were "adjustments" to be made, "coping skills" to acquire. I was learning "strategies" for coping with my "deficits."

My stroke had not visibly wounded me. I could walk and talk, draw pictures, and look after myself. But in the hospital I was surrounded by people whose strokes had had visible impact on them: men and women with stricken limbs. I learned to respect these fellow patients who were coping bravely for the most part with far more debilitating problems than I had. Every day I saw signs of quiet bravery and decency. I watched men on crutches manoeuvring a friend in a wheelchair down the corridor to meals. People showed patience with the newly acquired stutter of a fellow diner.

The unit also brought to my attention cases of family neglect. One woman had been so isolated and forgotten that she talked back to the television set mounted on the wall. Others were carted off home by family members who seemed indifferent to the kind of care being given to their parent or grandparent. There was little anyone could do in such cases.

As time in hospital wore thin, I was marked down for therapy. First they decided to put my bruised brain in a healthy body, so I was taken to the gym every day, where I was encouraged to climb stairs, ride a stationary bicycle, and roll around on mats together with a throng of people who seemed far worse-off than me. The second line of attack addressed my reading disorder. With Lea Ayuyao and Marla Roth principally, I worked on my main problems. I learned again to read a map. I discovered the depth of my memory loss, which hadn't been evident until I found myself unable to introduce my hospital visitors to one another. There was a vacuum where my memory used to be. It was an exaggeration of the quirkiness of memory in people my age. I could not produce the names of my son and daughter when asked for them without warning. I forgot the name of the street I live on. I could no longer remember the names of my agent and publishers. I could, however, still give an interested visitor three causes for the Punic Wars and recite all of Hamlet's soliloquies and most of "The Cremation of Sam McGee."

My problems with memory did not begin with the stroke. As a middle-aged roustabout, I noticed, as many of us do, that memory is unreliable. Post-stroke, it just got a little worse. And the problem plagues me still. But now I have an excuse for mangling a three-way introduction at a book launch.

Perhaps more interesting than the memory loss itself is the fact that one is only aware of it at a moment of memory failure. It's like not knowing you're broke until you check at the bank. One is protected from the vacuum that memory has become. The empty shelves are not always staring one in the face. The functions of the brain seem to be elastic: they expand with new information, and contract when it is forgotten. One is never aware of the hole – the "deficit," as the hospital people would say. In the same way, it is not necessary to face the loss of all of literature from Rabelais to Thomas King all at once. A fine, calm passivity descends and takes charge. Panic is sent off on furlough, given walking papers, booted out.

My next bout of therapy came from the capable hands of Michelle Cohen, a transplanted South African who was working outside the health insurance system. She brought more than twenty years of experience in treating patients with reading and writing difficulties. She found or made a computer program that challenged my ability to recognize words. At first I found it nearly impossible to differentiate among similar words of three or four letters. Michelle says that I improved as time went on, but to me it seemed very slow going. In a straightforward reading test where we counted the number of lines in a text that I could read in a given time, I showed some progress that even I could see. The text she chose was the story of Mata Hari, the famed Red Dancer and First World War spy. What with reading only a dozen or so lines a session, it took months to bring her to trial for treason. Each reading session brought poor Mata Hari closer to her inevitable rendezvous with the French firing squad. My plodding reading drew out the suspense and prolonged the agony. In the end, we never got as far as the last shot of bracing rum and the refusal of the blindfold. I was glad to have been able to save her going through it all over again.

Before I left the Rehab, I was coaxed by Marla Roth to send a note to Dr. Oliver Sacks in New York. She and I had been talking about his books – such as *A Leg to Stand On* and *The Man Who Mistook His Wife for a Hat* – and about the film *Awakenings*, in which Dr. Sacks was portrayed by Robin Williams. My own case, we thought, when looked at dispassionately, might have come out of one of Dr. Sacks's books. She suggested I write to him. It was almost a dare. So I did, describing as well as I could how my acquired disorder affected me. Dr. Sacks, in his second letter to me, asked if he could quote from my letter in an article he was writing for the *New Yorker*. Flattered, of course, I agreed, and the article in question appeared in the October 7, 2002 edition of the magazine. After that, we corresponded frequently. In one of the notes came an invitation to visit him in Manhattan, should my travels bring me in that direction.

As it happened, my son, Dr. Anita Johnston, and I had planned such a trip, and we called on him in his Greenwich Village consulting rooms. I was surprised to see how much he looked like Robin Williams, and I liked the way he listened. There would be a long pause after I answered a question before he made an observation on my response or asked another question. I appreciated his simple, relaxed manner. And I was delighted by the chalkboard placed on the wall behind where I was sitting: there was my name, where he could see it easily. I thought what a straightforward, courteous way for a man who had many visitors to dispose of a small anxiety! He led me through the history of my illness and my treatment step by step. I tried not to repeat what I had already told him in my letters. I remember trying to describe the way a page of type appeared to me when I glanced at a page in a book. "It appears as though through a fog," I said. "Then I try to concentrate and give the page a Double-Whammy and look again." Then I interrupted myself: how could this Londoner know about the L'il Abner comic strip? Al Capp had invented such things as Lower Slobovia and the Double-Whammy, which was a look that disabled if it didn't kill. Even here in Canada fewer and fewer people remember these things. Now it was his turn to interrupt me.

"Al Capp was my cousin," he said.

During this visit, I asked the good doctor if he would write a preface or afterword for a book that was then only in the early stages. To my delight and surprise, he agreed that if, and it was a big fat *if* at that point, I completed the manuscript, he would read it, and if he thought the book merited it, he would write something. He also was generous enough to suggest that in the event there was an afterword, he might submit it to his editors at the *New York Review of Books*. I didn't believe such generosity was possible, and I returned home to Toronto with increased determination to complete the novel.

The promise of getting a piece by Dr. Sacks spurred me to work on the book. It was a detective story featuring my detective, Benny Cooperman, who had already appeared in a dozen stories, novels, radio plays, and a couple of films. This time I wanted to make use

of my recent hospital experience. I wasn't tempted to let Benny
suffer a stroke. One was enough in the family. But detectives are
always getting banged in the head – it is one of the clichés of the
genre – and in most cases, the detective wakes up after a few
moments of unconsciousness and continues his investigation. One
of the games I had been playing with the Cooperman series was to
bring a little reality to the myth of the gumshoe, as seen in characters like Lew Archer and Sam Spade. Spade and Archer never had
family connections, and they came from major American cities.
Benny, on the other hand, is Canadian, and a family man. Benny,
like me, is Jewish – and most fictional detectives aren't. So it
seemed to me that I would be continuing in this modest, anti-
traditional vein if I had Benny spend some time in hospital and
rehab after a bang on the head. It matched what I had been doing
with the character all along.

To Benny's head injury, which duplicated what I had experienced as well as I could record it, I added a dash of amnesia, the old
fictional standby. If Benny didn't remember getting hit on the
head, all the better for the book. So I began with not much more
than that fixed in my head. It didn't bother me at the outset that I
didn't have a plot. At that stage, I rarely do.

Although I couldn't read, I could still write. I could do it in one
or all of the ways I used to write – in longhand, on a typewriter, on
a computer. I could dash off short notes to my son or write letters.
There was no problem with my writing, I thought. What I hadn't
understood as yet – what I had briefly, incredibly ignored or
repressed or forgotten – is that a writer reads as he writes, going
back repeatedly as he goes forward, poring over the text to make
it consistent and to make it better. I began on the computer, where
I quickly got lost after a few dozen pages, searching for an early

reference. Trying to compare one text with another, I was at sea. Quickly I learned to manoeuvre my way by noting the different places where the pages were indented by new paragraphs. I learned to let the "search" function find earlier references to a particular word. In a large text I could use the same function to show me that a character who has appeared regularly in the early pages of a book is missing for most of the middle. Sometimes there's a good reason for this, but it's always something the writer should be on top of. By checking the words on the left-hand margin and comparing them with the margins of an earlier version of the same text, I could quickly find where the texts diverged from one another.

I've had less luck with mechanical aids. People – friends – have been my best helpers. When I tried one electronic system for reading my text back to me, I ran into trouble right away. For instance, in the Cooperman books, Benny often refers to his mother and father as "Ma and Pa." The electronic helper read this back to me as "Massachusetts and Pennsylvania."

Sometimes I got confused and had to call for help. That brought my son, Jacob, to the rescue. He could correct most of my computer blunders, and though the nightmare of losing large chunks of text because of an error continued to hover over my head, it never, happily, descended on my computer.

I've been asked if the efforts I made to recapture what had been lost landed me in despondence or depression. I think that the trauma itself brings with it a calming anodyne, a cushion against despair. It provides the scab that allows healing to go on underneath. It is as though the situation closes in on you, closing off the path to hopelessness. This sort of vision might cut one off from seeing total reality, but it allows one to see what is tolerable. I wasn't floating on an unreal cloud, nor was I seeing my life as a litany of broken shoelaces.

The main thing I needed was for someone to read back to me what I had written. That way I could check on the tone and flow of what I intended to put down. To read the text back to myself would take me far longer than to write twice that much again. No, I needed to hear the words in a normal way and at the speed at which normal people would read them. Jacob read to me from time to time, but he was busy with school. That was when I recruited Griffith Cunningham, a friend from the neighbourhood watering hole, Dooney's Cafe on Bloor Street. Grif is a retired professor of geography, a founder of the Karma Co-op, and the president of the Native North American Plant Society. For years we had been having coffee together once or twice a week. It was at Dooney's that I discovered we both came from St. Catharines, Ontario, and had attended the same high school at the same time. Since then, after travelling miles and miles in my various texts, we have revisited together the scenes of childhood. In my office at home, he was able to read the text of my book back to me while I made notes. When the work got too much for us, we adjourned to Dooney's for refreshment.

My old friend Don Summerhayes – poet, photographer, scholar, one of my best remaining friends from undergraduate years, and a fellow Hemingway aficionado – aided and abetted me in the same vein as Grif. Sometimes our conversations about writers, poets, and the very craft of writing got in the way of writing: a situation that only Gertrude Stein might appreciate. Don and I have mutual friends too, and we pay our respects to them while the keyboard growls at us.

Gradually, a text was assembled, edited, and sent off to the publisher. Penguin Books, which might have forgotten all about me in the years since my stroke, bless them, did not. They welcomed me, the reformed prodigal, back into the fold and lent me the skills of the editors I had worked with in the past: Cynthia Good, the former chief editor at Penguin, and Mary Adachi, who has saved my grammatical bacon down the years.

In the meantime, Dr. Sacks's afterword arrived and was incorporated. I admit that it took a long while for me to get up the courage to read it. After all, he was talking about my naked brain. When I did, finally, I was delighted, of course. Here was the same thoughtful voice I'd first heard in his consulting room, in prose that breathed sanity and calm intellect.

When the book finally appeared, it did so to good reviews and brisk sales. My friends were kind to me personally and cheered the book. Gradually I began to get the feeling that I had gotten away with it. Once again I had publicly committed literature.

While the novel was working its way through the press, I began work on another novel featuring my sleuth Benny Cooperman. This time I sent him to somewhere on the Malay Peninsula, where it doesn't matter that the still ailing Benny can't read: he doesn't know the language anyway.

DAMON**GALGUT**

The Man with the Spade

Some years ago, when I was homeless and very poor, I was offered the use of a house in the country. Friends of mine had recently bought a small place for themselves in a rural village. They didn't want to charge me rent. They lived in London, and it would suit them, they said, to have somebody staying in their house, to keep an eye on things. The arrangement would be to our mutual advantage.

Of course I accepted. There wasn't much choice: I had no money, no job, no other options. Although I had never considered a move to the country, I would be able to live cheaply and without distractions, and I would do nothing but write. I pictured myself at a desk, under a window that looked out on rolling hills and fields. Words would proceed from my pen in a long, unbroken flow.

Until then I had never lived outside a city. Barrydale, the little village where the house was situated, was about four hours out of Cape Town. I had no car, so I had to rent a van and conscript someone to help me drive. With my few belongings packed into boxes, I was taken and dumped at the beginning of my new life.

It was a shock at first. My friends had bought the house from a distance, unseen, and it was rough and old. It had concrete floors and a thatch roof and felt crowded with ghosts. There was the window I had imagined, with the rolling hills and even a field or two, but in the foreground was a broken windmill that creaked and thumped alarmingly. The most disturbing thing, however, was the back garden. It was a large area, about the size of a soccer field, and it was covered, from top to bottom, by an army of brown, dead weeds. Generations of them had sprouted and seeded and died, and then been baked solidly into the dry, iron-hard earth.

I told myself: This is not your problem. You have come here to write books, not to dig out weeds. Let them rustle and wave in the breeze. They have nothing to do with you.

So I set out my few possessions and bought a couple of items of furniture from a junk shop on the main street. Amongst these was a table which I set near the window with the view I had coveted. After a few days of procrastinating, I laid out my note-book and pen on the table and took up my appointed place. I had a few scattered ideas that might cohere, I thought, into a story of some kind, as long as I stayed in that chair and didn't give up.

I was there for two or three days. My ideas showed no sign of developing, let alone of fusing together into any sort of theme. But I didn't lose heart. I kept returning to my place at the table, laying siege to the paper.

Then, one morning, I saw a man through the window. He was working the ground of the property next door, digging furrows to lead water from a reservoir to an orchard. I could hear the sound of his spade, hitting against slate, and I could see the repetitive movement of his arms. He was as aware of me as I was of him, and yet we pretended that we couldn't see each other. He was absorbed in his task, but every few minutes he would send a quick, covert glance in my direction.

Then something happened to me. I felt suddenly, acutely con-scious of myself at the table, and of what I was doing there. I saw my work in relation to that physical labour outside, and the comparison made me feel absurd. The pen in my fingers was nothing like a spade, and the ground I was digging into was ethereal, invisible. I was inventing people who didn't exist, making up dialogue that had never been spoken, tossing around abstract moral problems in my head. For the first time, the act of writing seemed ridiculous, and worse: it seemed dishonourable. I felt ashamed.

It was a shocking moment. I had seen a flash of myself through the eyes of the man outside – though he had passed no judgment and was already losing interest in me. The judgment was all mine, a traitorous self-doubt I had stored up in my psyche. But once the seam had started to fray, I couldn't stop it unravelling.

I jumped up and closed the curtains and, after a while, I moved the table away from the window. But it didn't help. Though I returned to my place, staring now at the consoling blankness of the wall, my mind remained outside, on the man with his spade. I could hear him digging, the sound moving slowly away.

The writing was over. I stayed in that little house in the country for another two years, and I made several attempts to start a book, but it would be a long time before the block lifted. It only did lift, in fact, when I eventually moved back to the city and surrounded myself with people who were all, one way or another, making a living through work that felt as dishonourable as mine.

All of this happened, as I say, some years ago, and I look back on it now with a certain irony. But not entirely. There is still a quality of genuine revelation that attaches to the memory, and I am reluctant to consider it too directly. It is preferable to think about what followed on: later that day, or perhaps the next, I went down to the farming co-operative in the village. I bought myself a pick and a spade. I returned to the house and went into the back garden and started, like any honest worker, to dig out the weeds.

JONATHAN**GARFINKEL**

By Accident: A Young Writer's Life

When I was twenty-two years old, I dreamt that Margaret Atwood appeared before me wearing a white satin dress and a red silk scarf.

"So how's the writing going?" she asked.

"Not so well," I said.

I was sitting under an oak tree, gnawing on the eraser of a well-sharpened pencil. She grabbed it from my hand.

"What'd you do that for?" I asked.

"You should go to Mexico," she said, somewhat impatiently.

"Mexico?" I asked.

"It will help you write." Ms. Atwood wagged the pencil at me menacingly and added, "To use it, you have to earn it." Then she disappeared.

When I awoke from the dream, I opened the yellow pages to "Travel Agents." I picked up the telephone and booked an airplane ticket to Los Angeles. A week later I was in a car to Tijuana. Then I disappeared into the Mexican landscape.

❋   ❋   ❋

From as far back as I can remember, I've had a need to write: to put pen to paper, fingers to keyboard. I feel more like myself when I'm writing. Conversation has always felt like a strain, and I never say the things I want to. When I dedicated myself to the "writing life" at age eighteen, I made a promise to commit to it wholly, completely. There would be no turning back.

But deciding to be a writer is one thing, and writing itself another. What would I write about? My grade eleven English teacher, Mr. Wall, had taught the old adage, "Write what you know." But what I knew was uninteresting to me. I didn't want to write about my suburban, middle-class upbringing. I decided to write what I wanted to know.

I listened to the Atwood dream because I thought Mexico would provide me with interesting material. I also had this vague notion that a writer must listen to voices and follow them. I followed, expecting adventure, romance, encounters with history — the fodder my writing heroes had gone in search of. There was plenty of all of that during my six months of travel from Tijuana to Tulum, but my writings amounted to nothing more than poor renditions of Kerouac's *Mexico City Blues* or the regurgitated prophecies of Irving Layton or Allen Ginsberg. What I was lacking more than interesting content was an original voice.

In the mountains of Chiapas I contracted dengue, bonebreaking fever. I didn't know I had dengue, had only the distinct impression that I was losing my mind in the most unromantic of ways. I'd gone to visit some friends in a cabin near San Cristobal de las Casas, only to find a note telling me they'd taken off for a beach in Oaxaca, too bad I missed them. For ten days and ten nights I sat alone in the cabin hoping they'd return. I read Octavio Paz's "Sunstone" several times and decided I'd take advantage of the solitude to write something monumental, something *important*.

But instead of writing an epic poem I found myself shouting at a cat named Borscht and chain-smoking unfiltered Atlas cigarettes. My body was consumed by the chills of fever, my bones ached as if a hammer were pummelling them. *This is not a result of physical illness*, I thought. *This is corporeal punishment meted out by the muses for your complete lack of talent.*

I was depressed, unable to sleep. The insomnia lasted five nights. I cursed Margaret Atwood and her voice in my head, and I cursed myself and the facts of my life: I had no craft, no skill, and nothing to say.

One day I went outside to turn on the propane gas at the back of the cabin. I was finally catching up on sleep – Valium is an over-the-counter drug in Mexico. Half dead to the world, I didn't realize the gas valve was already open, and when I opened it some more and lit my match, the entire tank exploded in my face, catapulting me back a good twenty feet. The explosion blinded me. I held my eyes in pain, scorched from the flame. Inside the cabin I took two ice cubes and pressed them against my burnt eyelids while making a mental list of friends I could ask to read me the books I would never be able to read myself. I mourned the things I would no longer see – snow, the mating of dragonflies, heat rising off the pavement, my mother's face.

Blind, I walked to the field of the Mayan farmer Carlos who lived next door, holding my eyes closed with my hands. When Carlos found me, he tapped me on the forehead three times and removed my hands from my face. I could see.

"*Tu popotes, Juan, tu popotes!*" he exclaimed.

The explosion had singed off my eyelashes, burning them to their roots.

That night my fever climbed up to 104 degrees. I was like an alcoholic with delirium tremens, my hands shaking when I tried to pick up so much as a glass of water. I managed to slink on a scratched-up record on an old phonograph – Ray Charles. I lay down in my hammock. The accident had opened a door inside me. I felt vulnerable, terrified. The difference between sight and blindness, life and death, was as banal as the striking of a match.

There were voices loud in my head, messages clamouring – sometimes fighting with Ray and sometimes pushed along by the blind man's pain and glee and guts – but they seemed to come from me. *Cut the shit* was one of them. *Write!* But the hubris that surrounded being a "writer" was despicable. *You're alive, idiot. And you won't be soon.* I was completely alone, and the world was still there for me – unfathomable and precious.

A few nights later, I wrote my first good poem. I knew it the moment it was on the page and confirmed it upon rereading the next day. This wasn't Kerouac or Paz. I thought maybe it was me. Months later, I received some confirmation from outside: the poem had been accepted for publication, my first.

Back in Canada, great poems did not come spewing forth onto the page. I struggled. I forced. Did I have to get TB this time, blow my arm off to write something half-decent? I had somehow stopped being afraid of the voices of other writers, and knew I needed to read more, to learn what other writers were doing. So I read – a lot. And I loved what I read and I learned things, but the writing – my writing – was flat.

Then theatre director Paul Thompson gave me the chance to travel again. I thought it might be the jolt I needed. We would go to the Republic of Georgia to find the Shangri-la of theatre, a place where theatre was still an essential part of a country's culture, where the minds of its citizens had not been taken over by television, globalization, and the monoculture of capitalism. Four months later I was on a bus with Paul travelling from Istanbul through Trabzon to Tbilisi, Georgia. We knew very little about where we were going, and even less of the Georgian language.

The theatre in Tbilisi was unlike anything I'd ever seen before – when there was theatre to be seen. Yet another play had been cancelled for some reason I could not understand, so I headed alone into a café to kill time.

It was evening and I kept myself warm with sweet brandy and a wool scarf. The Russians, who control Georgia's gas supply, had turned off the heat for four days because of an outstanding bill. Outside the café six men carried an open casket, followed by a chorus of mourning women. I was alone on the other side of the world and felt constantly threatened. I eyed the bartender, who shined his pistol instead of serving the patrons. So-and-so was in the middle of a three-week drinking binge, and the neighbourhood prostitutes huddled together, laughing around cups of lukewarm Nescafé.

Suddenly the power went out.

I was trying to write a postcard to a friend to explain my situation – where I was, what I was doing – the usual tourist *drek*. And instead of waiting for the power to return (candles were in short supply), I continued to write.

A friend once told me that accidents provoke the most interesting events onstage. When a glass tumbles unexpectedly, the great actor will make a moment of the fallen object. Accident demands improvisation. It keeps the actor from becoming too comfortable onstage. The fallen glass provides a sort of wake-up call, one that demands a fresh response. In the plays I'd been seeing, I felt an "authenticity detector" existed in the Georgian audiences; they simply knew when reality had entered the fray. And the actors worked for surprise regardless of whether the glass fell or not.

For years I had wanted to write perfect poems, the perfect play. Anything less was not worthwhile. Perhaps this is symptomatic of youth. But the power failure in Tbilisi, the exhilaration of accident, made nonsense of this way of thinking. The tourist postcard became a poem. Darkness made me pay fierce attention to the details of the page and my environment. I tried to write the real poem: the threat of the bartender and his gun, the smell of the drunk pissing himself in the corner. And the power failure that proposed that art without accident is art without life.

When the power came on, a dark-eyed waitress asked me what I wanted.

I want to make this chaos into something beautiful, I said.

She didn't understand.

*   *   *

A year later I went to Israel with a clear purpose: to write a play about a house in Jerusalem. This was an actual house I'd been told about by a woman in Toronto, a house shared by a Palestinian family and an Israeli family since 1948. My idea was the obvious one: this house would offer a kind of blueprint for peace.

The street number I had been given did not exist. The street itself was in a maze-like part of Jerusalem where it seemed that no Palestinians lived. The one family name I had been given was unknown, unrecorded. I searched for three long days, asking people I met on the street for leads. "It could not possibly exist," I was told. "Not in one house, not ever." I consulted old maps, and found an archivist. Asked him if he knew of such a house, whether perhaps it *had* existed once. He knew only of an area nearby where there were a few houses that had been Arab. They were on a cul de sac without a name, across the railroad tracks. I got badly lost, but found in the end *two* houses. They faced each other, one house occupied by Israelis, the other by a Palestinian family whose name was the one I carried in my notebook. Although I spoke to him in Hebrew, the Israeli man who answered the first door was no help. He shouted at me that this house was his alone – he'd built it, his Palestinian neighbour was a liar and a thief – and he slammed the door. The Palestinian was more hospitable, leading me through the rooms of his large house, giving me sesame cookies and sweet coffee in a cracked cup. He said the man across the street was worse than Hitler. He said that the house across the street had been his father's, the Israelis would not acknowledge this, but the court had settled it. The Israelis would not go, and the Palestinian was waiting for the evil man to die.

Not wanting to call my play *The Cul de Sac*, I saw that the only exit from this situation would be invention. Theirs and mine. But I had not the slightest idea of how to build my house or what I would put in it.

I continued to walk the streets of Jerusalem. One day I was in the Qalandya refugee camp in the West Bank. I received a "tour" from three young boys from the UN school, walking through the dilapidated houses and streets, the cemetery and football field. They escorted me to the checkpoint so I could make my way back to my hotel.

Beaten-up cars lined the way for maybe five hundred metres, and people were milling about, waiting to get through the checkpoint. A spray of rubber bullets was suddenly, inexplicably fired into the crowd by Israeli soldiers. I was an instant, total wreck, the boys only a little nervous. They brought me a cold Orange Crush to settle me down and introduced me to their friend Sam, an older

Palestinian who was burning trash nearby. They said I was a Canadian and wanted to understand.

In spurts of broken English, Sam gave me a jumbled version of the last fifty years of Palestinian/Israeli history. The gunfire continued sporadically, and Sam increased the volume of his rant with each new volley. The bits of history came in no rational order, and I decided he must be mad. Suddenly Sam asked me what I did. I told him I was a writer.

"A writer has power," he said, "You listen and make people listen."

Sam presented me with a Western Union ad written in Arabic. "This ad," he said, "Bring this to the people of Canada. Tell them what is going on here."

I stared at the familiar yellow of the Western Union logo, the words that meant nothing to me. Then I saw: on the glossy page there was a studious-looking woman counting out American money. Was this what Sam meant? Send money? Or America's part in this mess? Did he want me to listen to *that*, speak to *that*? He might have given me the Western Union ad only to say that the story of what is going on here is urgent. Telegrams are sent in emergencies. It could be just that. Or it could be the Yankee Dollar.

I wanted to write Sam off as crazy. But the way he said, "Tell them what is going on here," glued me to where I stood. This was a command. It reminded me of what I wasn't doing, what I wanted to do and had no idea *how* to do. This place is a labyrinth with no centre to be found. A divided, haunted house. I would have to build a story with the hope of some answer at its heart. Justice in the world. Beauty in the work. I would have to move toward my centre by accident, in mortal peril.

I wanted to write something as important as Sam's conviction. But I couldn't even read the ad. What would I say, what was my message, and why in God's name did I think I could write anything about anything?

*   *   *

The violence I experienced at the Qalandya checkpoint did not go away. The day I returned to Toronto, I was hit by a car as I was riding my bicycle, and broke my left hip. I spent many weeks in bed, and began – very slowly – to write the story of the house. The old fears were still there: the terror of the empty page, the fear of rejection, the dreaded solitude. I did not expect perfection of the work, and thank God for that. I certainly did not expect to discover the key to peace in the Middle East. But I wanted not to lie. I wanted to do justice of some kind, and to make – or find – something of value, of which I would not be unspeakably ashamed when I held it up to the mirror of the world.

One night I remembered my old Atwood dream, and I fell asleep thinking that no one would believe me if I were to tell it. And this also is true: just before morning, I dreamt that Leonard Cohen was in the room with me. He was completely naked when he sat down at the foot of my bed with a pencil.

"What are you doing?" I asked.

"Writing," he said. He twirled the pencil in his left hand. There was no sign of a notepad.

"Do you really have to be naked?" I asked.

"My friend," he said, putting down his pencil, "I'm afraid there is no other way."

GREG**GATENBY**

The Golden Dolphin. Or, A Very Short History of Public Literary Readings

For as long as there have been writers, there have been readings. Longer, in fact, if by readings we include recitations from memory and, being even more generous, choose to include all events at which a storyteller recounts a tale to a gathered public. Scholars are generally agreed that the authors of our earliest tales practised for centuries, probably millennia, in pre-literate societies, and one suspects that those fortunate enough to have heard the author of Gilgamesh were enraptured even if there were no autographed books to be had at the end of that reading. Homer may never have written his poem onto parchment, but most people, if invited by the magic of a time machine, would be happy, I believe, to attend a reading by the Greek bard. Certainly another blind author of note, Jorge Luis Borges, told me by phone that he would be happy to come to read at Toronto's Harbourfront Reading Series if only the University of Toronto would deign to grant him an honorary doctorate at the same time. When I asked more pointedly what he meant by a reading, Borges said, "Oh, for me a reading is a recitation of my work, with some discussion of the writing – and of language." So for him, at least, the word *reading* was bigger than a literalist might insist. (Alas, the University, for reasons too embarrassing to its reputation to cite here, chose not to honour Borges with an LLD). A few years ago, in Reykjavik, I was fortunate to hold in my hands the thousand-year-old manuscript in which the *Greenlanders' Saga* was first transcribed – and in which, coincidentally, my country was first mentioned in literature. Thrilling as that was, I would have traded the experience in an instant for the chance to have heard its author give a reading of the saga, even though there was no book per se from which to read.

Of course, in our time, a reading has come to mean an author literally reading from his or her latest (usually just-published) tome. The frequency of such readings tends to vary by literary discipline. Most poets in the English-speaking world, for example, make far more money from reading fees and books sold at readings than they do from sales in bookshops. And the reading-life of poets tends to be much longer than that of novelists – the latter, especially as they become better known, tend to confine their readings to a few weeks or months after the publication date of their work whereas poets continue to be invited for years, and are usually poor enough, or hungry enough for a slightly larger audience, that they will accept paying gigs even into a very advanced age. Playwrights, though, are almost never invited to read, and yet, in my experience, are among the finest at the task. So, popular as they are in some places, in any discussion of the modern reading it is important to recall that today's various reading series and literary festivals are but the current endpoint of a tellingly long continuum.

As the founder of North America's first international literary festival, I met many people over the years who were unaware of this sustained and honourable history – a lacuna which never stopped them from making utterances about readings with all the authority of the ignorant. These pronouncements varied from exhortations to invite so-and-so ("I'm sorry," I would reply, "T.S. Eliot died many years ago") to queries as to why I never invited Mick Jagger since "he's a poet, man!" Then there was the board member who called me to say he was having drinks at that very moment with his brother-in-law, the author of a book about how to train your dog, and wouldn't it be wonderful if Bob were put on the same bill as Margaret Atwood and Saul Bellow. When I pointed out that the International Festival of Authors presented writers of fiction, poetry, drama, and literary biography, and had never placed dog-trainers onto its stage, there was an awkward pause at the other end of the line, and then a mumbled suggestion that featuring the author of a dog-training manual might attract new audiences. Somehow I resisted the offer.

There was always one exhortation from the apparently well-meaning on which I could count with painful regularity, and that was: *writers are the worst readers of their own work.* Not only was this falsehood uttered with great self-assurance, it was usually passed along while the speaker leaned in to me confidentially and, *sotto voce*, reported this truth with the same friendly tone a man might use at a dinner party when telling another diner that his fly was open. Early in my career I accepted these utterances with a nod and a short thank-you for the wisdom thus disseminated. However, with time, the suspicion grew that these people who thought authors were terrible readers had actually never heard an author read, or had listened to very few. I began to ask the pontificators upon what experience of readings they made their judgments, and, inevitably, the evidence was thin or worse: "Oh, I cannot possibly remember now, it was all so long ago, but I do remember the author was a terrible reader!"

Public readings, at their best, are much more, of course, than just an enunciation of vowels and consonants. Especially when eminent authors are involved, there is inevitably a sense of occasion and an air of excitement as hundreds, sometimes thousands of admirers gather in a single room to hear the great one speak. If the author is old, or from far away, the sense of occasion is augmented by the reality that this may be the only – or the last – time to see and hear the living author in person. One would hope on these occasions that the eminent author is also a good reader, but, ultimately, the thrill and the fond memory come from having been there on the night. Readings also have the merit of forcing us to listen to passages at a reading pace – we read much more quickly than we speak – and thus listen to passages which we might otherwise have skipped over. There are also many occasions when an audience will hear a story, as a group, differently than a reader would alone. Many authors I know were surprised when an audience laughed at certain passages during a reading – because they themselves had not realized the comic import of a phrase or delineation until the audience had responded. Raymond Carver certainly had this experience when he read his famous short story "Cathedral" in Toronto for the first time. Within a minute or so of his beginning, the audience guffawed, and I will never forget the perplexed look Ray hurled at me while I stood just inches away in the wings: a mixture first of anger that his words, to him so serious, were being laughed at, and second, of bewilderment at the realization that such a sophisticated audience might actually have seen something profound which he had not. As he came off the stage, Ray said to me, "That is either the smartest or the stupidest audience I've ever read to." A day later he told me the listeners had been right.

Over the nearly three decades I ran the world's largest program of readings, one of the pleasures of which I never tired was seeing people in a queue approaching the autograph-table after the reading itself. The smiles were broad on the eager faces as person after person finally drew near to the author, saying almost reverentially, "I've admired your work so much" or "I never thought I would ever have a chance to meet you" or even sometimes, "Your book changed my life." The approaches by the fans were respectful, but, I'm pleased to say, never fawning. These were usually happy occasions for the authors as well because, as writers, they work alone in rooms, far from the madding crowd, and rarely get to meet the people who actually read their published efforts. Strong is the writerly ego that is not puffed by compliment after compliment received in such queues.

This experience of meeting the author in the flesh, shaking his or her hand, chatting briefly, and then leaving with an inscribed copy of the latest book was a facet of every reading I produced, and was a crucial part of the pleasure for those in the audience. Again, one hoped that the author was a good reader, but for many in the audience the far more important aspect of the night was the opportunity to have come face to face with an artist whose work had meant so much to them, and to leave the event with the author's handwritten best wishes, an enduring souvenir of a memorable occasion.

Public readings by authors have been prevalent in the English-speaking world for so many decades now that most people think meetings with writers have always taken this form. And indeed, while the prevalence of autographed books is certainly new, the essential ingredient of words being spoken by an author and heard by an audience has an undeniably ancient history. Undoubtedly there were storytelling adepts who compelled listeners gathered around the campfire in the Cro-Magnon cave. And the recitations of the Greeks and their precursors were so common and well understood that there is next to no mention of them, per se, in the texts that have come down to us.

There is, though, one wonderful exception to this Classical-period vacuum of documentation regarding readings or recitations – Arion of Methymna. Born in Lesbos in seventh-century BC, he is the first *individual* in history whose public recitations have been accepted by scholars as fact. Arion's skill as a writer and reciter was acclaimed early, and he soon found work in the famous and wealthy court of Periander, the Tyrant of Corinth. It was probably in Corinth that he invented the dithyramb (an early form of tragic drama), and Aristotle among others regarded Arion as the father of Greek tragedy. His fame as a singer of his own songs and poems was so great that cities far and wide made outlandish offers to him for even the briefest of visits. One offer he could not refuse came from Syracuse in Sicily, and such was his triumph there that he decided to linger on the island and perform in other towns. Finally, homesick, he gathered the fantastic wealth he had garnered and set sail for Greece. Alas, the crew, seeing so much loot, conspired to throw Arion overboard. Before walking the plank, he convinced the sailors to let him recite his work one last time, and they, thinking they were going to get a free concert, as well as all the gold, agreed. Arion reached for his lyre and declaimed his favourite poems, enthralling his captors and, more importantly, attracting a pod of dolphins. When push came to shove, Arion splashed into the sea, miles from shore, while his looters sailed on, convinced he would drown. But he did not drown. The dolphins, discerning literary critics that they were, saved Arion by carrying him to land. He reached Corinth before the treacherous crew arrived, and had the pleasure of informing the Tyrant of what had miraculously happened. When the crew disembarked, they were arrested and put to death. Arion used much of the loot (which had been returned to him) to commission a life-sized sculpture of a dolphin – a dolphin made entirely of gold. The Roman travel writer

Pausanias saw it still *in situ* several centuries later. On his death, Arion and his marine saviours were placed by Dionysius among the stars, and the constellation of the Dolphin who saved the author is overhead every night.

It is odd that this first documented reading should also have been the best paid of all time. However, 2,500 years later, some British authors must have felt that they were giving Arion a run for his money, for it was in the 1800s that readings by authors once again paid huge fees. It is a paradox that these huge fees came as a result of an effort to help poor people.

John Anderson and George Birbeck were two Scottish professors based in Glasgow who held what were considered at the time to be radical views: the right to free speech, freedom of the press, and the right of every man to an education. Anderson taught at the university during the day, and, at night, taught working men wherever he could. When he died in 1796 Anderson left sufficient funds in his will to found a small college devoted to the mental betterment of what he called the "unacademic classes." Run by his colleague, George Birbeck, Anderson College was quickly successful in teaching practical science to the men known then as mechanics – a rough translation in our time would be blue-collar workers. Birbeck moved to London in 1804 but continued his interest in the education of the working class. With others he founded the London Mechanics Institute in 1824, a place that offered not only classes six nights a week, but a library of newspapers, magazines, and books – reading matter prohibitive for most people because of cost. Immigrants to North America brought the idea of the Mechanics Institute with them, and almost all cities on the continent had at least one in full operation by the 1840s.

Simultaneous with the rise of the Mechanics Institutes was the growth, especially in the USA, less so in Canada, of Lyceums. These had been founded by Josiah Holbrooke in the 1820s throughout New England, and while adult education was an essential part of their mandate, there was always the whiff of Temperance hanging over the programs. Despite this (or because of this), there were as many as five thousand Lyceums in America by 1839, and, although they were concentrated in the northeast, they ranged even as far west as Detroit.

With so many Lyceums and Institutes, there was a gargantuan demand for people qualified to lecture. Perhaps because the means of communication over continental distances were still so primitive, or perhaps because the competition between cities and individual organizations was so fierce, there was little coordination of tours by speakers before 1860 (even Charles Dickens in 1842 found the making of travel arrangements on this continent a real trial). Just as such coordination of speakers was beginning, though, it was killed by the eruption of the American Civil War. And with no promise of having one's travel expenses paid for, there was no incentive for serious speakers to move beyond their own neighbourhood. Also, it seems, few dared to ask for a large lecture fee. Ralph Waldo Emerson, for example, early in his lecturing career, asked only for some feed for his horse – and five dollars for himself!

In the years immediately after the Civil War, the public made it clear it wanted to be entertained as well as educated. So in addition to speakers who were high falutin', these institutions began to offer representatives of the lesser arts who would soon go on to be the backbone of vaudeville: comedians, minstrel singers, mesmerists, ventriloquists, jugglers, magicians, tap dancers, and child wonders. Popular as these were, there were always large and respectful audiences for authors reading from their books or talking about their work.

One such author was James Redpath, born in England in 1833, who immigrated with his parents to the States when he was seventeen. He quickly became an ardent abolitionist and through his writings against slavery was discovered by Horace Greeley, who brought him into a much wider world. Redpath then met John Brown shortly after the hero of Harpers Ferry had begun his guerilla campaign against slave-owners. The two men, Brown and Redpath, were of like mind, and Redpath agreed to write what became the first biography of Brown. As a journalist, Redpath had a good sense of publicity, and motivated by his passion to spread the gospel against slavery, he toured extensively, not for money, but to alert Americans to the evil in their midst.

As a result of his travels to promote the biography, Redpath realized there was a huge need for proper coordination of an author-tour. So in 1868, in Boston, then the publishing capital of the United States, he established the Boston Lyceum Bureau, the first for-profit organization in the world created to send authors on tour. Redpath's timing was fortuitous because the railway boom was just beginning, and it soon became possible for authors to move speedily between towns and cover distances that, hitherto, were too daunting to contemplate. Perhaps because he was from Britain originally, Redpath was not blind to the possibilities in Canada, and, from the beginning, his office regularly offered literary lights to the Institutes in Montreal and Toronto and, on occasion, to smaller venues in Ontario such as Hamilton, London, and Kingston.

Redpath soon changed the name of his agency to The Redpath Lyceum Bureau, by which time he was representing Emerson (no more five-dollar honoraria for him!), Mark Twain, James Whitcomb Riley, Booker T. Washington, George Washington

Cable, Oliver Wendell Holmes, and just about every other prominent or commercially successful writer in the USA. However, by
1875, he found his heart was not in the business (he wanted to
write full-time) and he sold his interest to a young partner he had
recently acquired: Major J.B. Pond. In a death appropriate somehow for a showman, Redpath was killed in Manhattan by a speeding vehicle while crossing Broadway.

Pond took control of the reins and led the firm off at a full
gallop. He began by recognizing that New York had become the
new publishing centre of America and moved his agency there
with dispatch. He expanded his client list beyond the literary to
include military brass bands and singers; and he made a small
fortune from having presciently bought the American licence for
Pirates of Penzance. But it was really his aggression in bringing
English authors to North America that made Pond the most
famous lecture-agent ever. Among the authors he presented were
some who were vastly popular in their day but whose star has
waned, and others whose glory remains, such as Arthur Conan
Doyle, Winston S. Churchill, Hall Caine, Ian MacLaren, Sir Edwin
Arnold, Anthony Hope, and Max O'Rell to name just a few of the
hundreds he promoted. Given the era, the fees he promised these
authors were astronomical. Ten thousand dollars, twenty-five
thousand dollars, and even one hundred thousand dollars would
be offered for a tour of three months, and many a British author
noted with some sadness that he made more in three months with
Pond than he did in a lifetime from royalties. Among his biggest
North American stars was the Canadian wildlife author Ernest
Thompson Seton. The audiences ranged in size from a few dozen
to, more frequently, two thousand.

Pond's success inspired competitors, of course, but his singular rapport with literary authors – he travelled as a companion

with the biggest names – meant that he was top of mind with British authors who had yet to venture across the Atlantic. He left us four volumes of delightful and candid memoirs which delight because they give both commercial and aesthetic insights into the author-touring of the day. Pond died of blood-poisoning in 1903.

Pond's presentation of authors on stage also inspired the spread of the Chautauqua movement in Canada and the USA. This movement had begun in 1874 in Lake Chautauqua in upper New York State as a means of augmenting the skills of Sunday-school teachers. The organizers soon noticed that the outdoor atmosphere encouraged informality and fun and an unusually fervent desire by the adult students to listen and learn. By 1880 the organizers had added to the faculty a number of speakers on various topics and the renown of the Chautauqua seminars became international. Many of the speakers were supplied by Redpath at first, and then by Pond, but in 1901 Keith Vawter bought a large share of the Redpath agency solely for the purpose of creating a Chautauqua circuit. Vawter and the Chautauqua movement were much less interested in making a profit than in the wholesome education of the masses, and so they sent their speakers into towns too far away and too small for the commercial lecture agents to consider. By the end of the First World War, Chautauquas organized by Vawter and his colleagues had taken place in nearly three hundred Canadian towns, almost all in the four western provinces. The eastern half of Canada, for reasons still unexplained, preferred independently run operations that were not part of a circuit. The late Canadian poet Earle Birney told me that as a young writer he had attended an independent Chautauqua in the Muskoka cottage country. He was struck, he said, by the very high ratio of women to men, by the fact that otherwise quite straitlaced women were dressed in diaphanous clothing that would have caused a scandal back in

Toronto, and by the fact that, after dark, many of the women demonstrated to him that they were not straitlaced at all. So perhaps not all Chautauquas were as wholesome as believed.

The arrival of movies and radio put an end to the popularity of Chautauquas, Lyceums, and Mechanics Institutes. While poets such as Robert Frost and Archibald Macleish would make individual forays, usually to universities, if the honorarium were big enough, it seemed that the author-tour as Charles Dickens, or Mark Twain, or Conan Doyle had known it was over. The 92nd Street YHMA in New York City had started in 1939 to present a few readings by authors, mostly poets, with some regularity, but most of the writers were local, or were visiting New York in any case, and in its first decade or so "the Y" did not organize tours. No other city anywhere in the world in the interbellum period had anything to match even the Y's limited program.

In the late 1940s, the Y began a search for a new director of what it called its Poetry Center. They chose a younger man, born and raised in Maritime Canada, who warned them that if he were hired he would radically change the whole nature of readings. To their credit, the executives of the Y hired John Malcolm Brinnin, and he quickly brought together a stellar roster, including a Welsh poet then practically unknown on these shores: Dylan Thomas. Thomas's reading created such a sensation that invitations poured in for him to read at colleges across America. Brinnin nobly and bravely assumed the task of organizing a North American tour, and despite its hardships and heartbreaks (caused by Dylan's alcoholism), the tour was a news sensation and a commercial hit. So much so that it made other poets see the financial rewards of such a tour, and, in the 1950s, as in the late 1800s, writers began once more to crisscross the continent, doing a series of one-night stands.

For most of the twentieth century, readings were something

poets did. A fiction writer might read a chapter of a just-published novel at his local bookstore or library, but novelists and short-story writers received nowhere near the number of invitations to colleges that poets did. Moreover, it was the custom of the first half of the twentieth century that fiction writers, rather than reading from their work, should pontificate aloud on the pressing political issues of the day. The ruminations on war by H.G. Wells and Anatole France, for instance, were front-page news in papers around the world. That started to change in the 1970s as publishers began to pay extraordinary advances, and, in order to recoup the huge sums they were paying, sent their newly wealthy novelists onto increasingly wide tours. In the 1990s and 21st century, the poets were shoved off college and bookshop stages by the novelists. But as the truth of how big (that is, how small) the market for literary fiction really is becomes apparent to the publishers, more and more of them are pushing the novelists aside and replacing them with diet gurus. In Canada the poets have held on longer than they were able to do in the United States because the Canada Council has played an important role in subsidizing the bulk of the costs of an author's tour. But with cutbacks to its budget, the Canada Council's role vis-à-vis readings by poets and fiction writers is now much diminished. Diet gurus and popular non-fiction authors seem set for a long run in North America. This will come as a relief to those authors who, while good readers, hated the travel and the inane press interviews. During my three decades at the helm of the Harbourfront readings, I could count on less than ten fingers the living literary giants who would never give readings, no matter how much money they were advanced, no matter how severely they were pressured by their publishers. As the financial pressure on them wanes, the reticent may be able to resist in larger numbers.

And yet, and yet . . . nothing can replace that singular thrill that comes from hearing an author recite a famous passage, or share the world premiere of a story just finished – to say nothing of the bonus of hearing, as one can only at a reading, how this poem came to him, or how that character or plot development or title came to her. Nothing can replace that bond that comes from having a personal inscription after the reading, a souvenir cherished by most for life. So while the payday from a literary reading may climb and fall with the book fashion of the day, I believe there will always be a place for a reading by a writer, for the magic and the excitement that come from hearing the work straight from the creator's mouth. Just as there was when shadows flickered across the walls of the Cro-Magnon cave. Or when Arion recited for the Syracusans.

CAMILLA**GIBB**

Truth Takes Up Room in the Imagination

Books one and two

I know a man who was cruel and strange and did cruel and strange things to his children. Perhaps you know this man too. Perhaps you were the child of such a man and loved him just as much as you feared him, leaving you tormented on bad days and angry and confused on good days, and on the best days, after a good few years on the couch, you found yourself capable of something more peaceful: call it sadness, compassion.

And if you grew up to be a writer, perhaps you'd feel it was something you had to write about, because writing is often about the had-tos, the have-tos. But the story you have to tell is one that implicates the man, a man who is still living, and that is where you are arrested, on the doorstep of decency, because for all that was not right, there is still a certain respect for the basic personhood of an albeit endlessly troubled entity, so you keep that material for your journals, journals you burn once it's all written down.

It's not over, but having it written down, you find it is over in a particular way. The clouds shift, and so too does the language.

You've become the author. Years later you find yourself writing fiction about a man who was cruel and strange and did cruel and strange things to his children. You give the feelings – the love, fear, torment, confusion, sadness, and compassion – to your characters, invented characters, in light of new "facts" – also invented.

Perhaps the story bears repeating. Perhaps not. But you tell it again anyway because you haven't yet seen it through to completion: the man who was cruel and strange has gone missing, and you need to write his end. On the page you create a character who is an eccentric inventor, clearly losing his grip. In real life you hire a private detective who confirms that the man is still alive, giving you the liberty to kill the inventor off in your fiction, or at least the liberty to try, even if he does manage to send your main characters a posthumous postcard.

Years later you happen to meet the man in a coffee shop in some city you've never before visited, and he surprises you by telling you he has read your books, but surprises you even more by telling you he thinks they operate at the level of metaphor, and that somehow makes it all okay, because metaphors are things we can all handle. They are literary. Devices. Not only can we choose how to interpret them, we can control the distance to whatever we choose to understand is represented there.

"But I'm still inventing," he tells you.

Book three

I know a woman who endured years of abuse in a country that despised her people, a country she was forced to escape only to land in another harsh country where she lived as a prisoner until she finally came to Canada. Perhaps you know this woman too. She might even have become your best friend, certainly your most important. Her story might have forced you into action, leading you to rail against the inhumanity of racism and the racism of humanity, giving you a direction that would change your life.

But what if after ten years of close friendship this woman confides she has no memory of her first year in Canada, including meeting you. She spent that year feeling like a ghost, she says. You'd feel the guilt of not having realized that while you were so moved and inspired by her that you even went to live in her country for a time, she didn't even have a sense of her physical presence, of having a body, let alone a passport or the freedom to return to the country she called home.

You would be forced to think about your friendship, question your motives, look at the inherent racism of your having exoti-cized/eroticized her difference and at the privilege that allows you but not others, not her, to cross borders. You'd find yourself impli-cated in some unbearable white middle-class truth.

You look to the writer in you for redemption. The writer speaks to your friend. *Tell me that story again. Let me hear your voice,* she says to her. And by this time your friend might no longer identify as a refugee, but as a proud American citizen living in some middle-class suburb, ready to tell a longer story, to have it put down on paper to pass on to her children, a personal history, one which you can transcribe.

It's not over, but having it written down, she finds it is over for her in a particular way. Why is it not over for you, then? You come to realize (perhaps because of the years on the couch and books one and two and your understanding of the cruel and strange things fathers can do to their children) that it is because, for all your differences, you understand that ghostlike feeling she once described, you are in fact still possessed by it. The story you have to tell actually has very little to do with your friend.

You project your story onto the canvas she first painted for you. You add characters to the scene and hear the voice of a white Muslim woman raised in Africa, now living in exile in England, who takes you through a new novel. A woman who doesn't belong anywhere, who has lost her lover to a revolution, a woman who feels like a ghost.

Your friend, who is not white, nor a Muslim, and has never been to England, might write to you after reading the novel that you have dedicated to her and tell you what she thinks.

"People who do not know [my country] may think this is fiction, but it is all real and factual. It depicts the reality of people's day-to-day life. This is the first book I have ever read and fully related to the stories."

Book four

I know a man who has been injured and it breaks my heart and it makes me angry because I love the man and he is my family in a complex chosen way. But I am just as angry at him because he is partly at fault, partly responsible for getting sick; we were going to have a baby, after all.

Perhaps you've been in such a place too, and can name it. Betrayal? To some extent yes, but ultimately something more like the collapse of a shared project, a dream, a certain narrative of the future. And perhaps feeling frustrated and helpless as the future is rewritten without your consent, you find yourself writing in retaliation, an essay, say, about trust and the families we make.

And perhaps you share that essay with the man who is your friend/family and he acknowledges it as an important portrait of who you all were in the moment before; who you can no longer be as a result. It is a private snapshot of a moment in history. Your friend has been injured, but if this were ever published, you'd cause a hell of a lot more damage – blowing up the entire village that surrounds him. And so it is written and you can keep it in a drawer for those times you wish to revisit your former life, if that is what you choose to do.

But the obsession with the details – the what-ifs and what-if-nots, not to mention the shoulds and the plaintive whys – drives you to more words: the beginning of a new novel. One about a community of people with a shared illness living in exile on an island: a story of good guys and bad guys and all the moral sludge in between. The injury of one man has taken you into a story of thousands who are afflicted by some mysterious condition, none of them your friend. You get stuck at some point and relate the plot to him. What if you bump off the priest? he suggests, changing the direction of a story that has nothing and everything to do with him. And so you bump off the priest.

And on

This is where the novel begins.

Once the journals are burned, the life histories have been passed on to the children, and the essays driven by guilt or retaliation or trouble have been written and put away in a drawer. Once the facts have been forgotten, or once you have sorted out why the facts that are not your own have resulted in feelings that very much are. I'm talking about the hard stories, the ones about the living, the ones that matter, the ones fuelled by feelings you cannot shake, feelings that beg for a more intelligible framework than real life affords: a fictional reality within which they can be exor/exercised.

Writing about life is a complex negotiation between external and internal realities. A story from "real life" moves or speaks to us and takes up residence in the imagination, where it develops a whole new set of attachments, imaginary or otherwise, and is, thereby, transformed. We might all be part of these stories, but it is actually fiction that owns the majority share, making them anyone's and everyone's.

We find ourselves in the stories of others, regardless of the particulars of our own life experiences. Certain stories possess us because they embody something recognizable, something desired or longed for, something that otherwise seems impossible to locate or see clearly. When something one has struggled to articulate or understand is given life in tangible form, even though that form may be entirely invented, it can result, potentially, in the most powerful rendering of the truth.

And this is where the novel ends.

CHARLOTTE**GRAY**

Talking to the Dead

When I am writing the biography of a dead person, I always hope for a few "Ah-ha!" moments – moments when the ribbon of time between past and present vibrates. Until I've had such a moment, I never really feel that I've come to grips with the person I'm writing about. Until that moment, all the careful reading and systematic research that I've done feel more like an academic exercise, a careful accumulation of facts that would make a really boring book. A good biography needs more than the tyranny of the card index or multi-linked folder. It needs that spark that will allow the writer, and the reader, to feel she or he has actually awoken the dead.

Of course, I don't want to minimize the reading and the research. They are crucial to a trustworthy biography, and also to priming me for the significant moment when it arrives. When I was writing *Sisters in the Wilderness*, a double biography of those two intrepid pioneers Susanna Moodie and Catharine Parr Traill, I conscientiously sat down, read and noted their books and reams of their letters. Their personalities were gradually revealed – Catharine, sunny and optimistic, always eager to be "up and doing" however dire the circumstances; Susanna, volatile and needy, pouring out in letters her loneliness. There were always more nuances to Susanna's prose. She complained more, yet she was also extraordinarily competent as she struggled to survive. She wrote with irony about her husband's lousy sense of business, while revealing in every poem and anecdote how much she adored him. After his death she never wrote another word.

The "Ah-ha!" moment? It came, one day, when an archivist at Library and Archives Canada asked me if I had seen Susanna Moodie's hair. "Susanna's hair?" I asked in surprise. Apparently, there was a lock of her hair preserved in the collection. The archivist gave me the little round box in which it was kept, and I reverently removed the tight-fitting lid. There lay a thick hank of coarse hair, about three inches in length. It was almost completely white, but it still had traces of its original colour – auburn. I shivered as (wearing white gloves, of course) I gingerly touched this relic of a woman who died 120 years ago. "Of course," I thought to myself. "Susanna was a classic redhead: capricious and passionate. She was bloody well determined to survive, just to show she could."

My "Ah-ha!" moments are usually triggered by an artifact that gives me a tactile connection with my subject. The most obvious, for all the books I have written, are handwritten letters. Handwriting of the nineteenth century (my preferred time zone) has a character all of its own. Most educated people had been taught to write in either copper-plate or italic script; they then customized the style to their own characters. Sometimes the script is bold and emphatic, with large loops. Other times, it is small and cramped, as though the writer is keeping her (always her, in this case) elbows close to her body. Sir John A. Macdonald dashed off many notes in a fluid, easy hand, and occasionally decorated the margins with witty sketches. Sometimes the missives themselves have a particular smell – the faint scent of lavender, for instance, in a late-Victorian valentine.

Then there are clothes. Pauline Johnson, the half-English, half-Mohawk poet who criss-crossed Canada in the late-nineteenth and early-twentieth centuries, was, in today's phrase, a performance artist. Reflecting her mixed heritage, she would give half her stage act in buckskin and feathers, and the second half in a ladylike silk evening gown. Many black-and-white photographs of her in both outfits have survived, so I had no shortage of visual prompts when I wanted to describe Pauline's performances. But then I discovered that the Vancouver City Museum had the buckskin outfit – fringed skirt, blouson top with silver trade brooches, plus the scalp and wampum belt that she wore at her waist. As the curator carefully unpacked it from its layers of tissue paper for me, I felt goosebumps on my neck. "Ah-ha!" The outfit told me so much about the flesh and blood Pauline that old photographs and newspaper reviews never could. She was *tiny*: five-foot-three inches, at the most. She worked *so* hard: the leather of the blouson top was brittle under the arms, where she had perspired in the stuffy heat of a hundred church halls and ramshackle opera houses. And, like too many of us, with advancing years she had thickened in the waist before her death, at age fifty-two. A hand-stitched insert had added a couple of extra inches to the waistband.

Now I am finishing a biography of Alexander Graham Bell. Best-known for inventing the telephone in 1876, this polymath also made contributions to medicine, genetics, eugenics, aviation, and marine navigation. He even recorded instructions on how to rig up a good ghost, and how to build a composting toilet. I am struggling with all the usual biographical challenges. I start with a huge advantage: there is a wealth of primary material – the basic building blocks of the kind of biography I like to write. Alec (we're on first name terms) was often separated from those he loved, and so he wrote copious letters to them and they replied. Moreover, his adored wife, Mabel, was deaf from the age of five. Since this clever, resourceful woman could never use her husband's greatest invention, the telephone, the Bells relied on the written word to bridge physical distance. When I entered the library at the Alexander Graham Bell National Historic Site in Baddeck, Nova Scotia, I was presented with 180 volumes of personal correspondence. Such plenitude is a biographer's dream, but requires rigorous selection. What themes should I tease out of all those letters, spanning more than seventy-five years? Which of all the people mentioned should I include, and which were extraneous to my story, and could be omitted so that a reader would not be overwhelmed by names?

Most crucial, how do I resist what the British writer Mark Bostridge, biographer of Vera Brittain and Florence Nightingale, calls "narrative greed"? Every biography has to tell a story as well as chronicle a life; otherwise, it is just one damn thing after another. "What's the story?" is the question that a journalist asks him or herself, before the fingers even hit the keyboard. Available facts are shoehorned into a compelling frame. But these days, a newspaper or magazine story is rarely more than three thousand words long, and the standard frame is a chronological narrative, topped and tailed with paragraphs of analysis. A chronological narrative is the spine of most life stories, too, but a biography is rarely less than one hundred thousand words. An imaginative biographer can weave into this large tapestry all kinds of themes – including themes that may not have been acknowledged by the subject in his or her own lifetime, themes that reflect concerns of today rather than the subject's own period. Victorians rarely wrote in their letters and journals about the kind of issues that fascinate contemporary readers: sex, for instance, or unhappy relationships.

One can pick up in a carefully muffled correspondence hints that the writer or her husband is, perhaps, an alcoholic, or that the marriage is on the rocks. An unscrupulous biographer, overcome by narrative greed, will make this "the story," because it is such a delicious revelation. A more responsible writer may acknowledge the possibility, but will put it into the perspective of the times.

Over the past three years, as I read my way through those 180 volumes of personal correspondence, I wallowed in Alec's and Mabel's lives. They met in Boston, where in the 1870s he spent his days teaching deaf people to articulate, and his nights fiddling with copper wires and batteries. Mabel became his student when she was only fifteen. At first, she was one among several students as far as Alec was concerned, although unusually self-assured and very bright. And then, in June 1875, he realized that, despite himself, he had fallen in love with her. It was a summer of extraordinary heat, passion, and excitement for him: the same sweltering month, he finally saw a way to transmit the human voice along telegraph wires. His emotions boiled over: he declared his feelings to Mabel's parents, who were shocked by his intensity, before pursuing Mabel herself to Nantucket, the island off Cape Cod where she was staying with a cousin. But he never saw her there. Instead, he poured out his love in a lengthy epistle that he entrusted to Mabel's cousin. Then he turned around and caught the ferry back to the mainland.

I am, of course, deeply grateful to Alec for committing his feelings to paper. I can write with absolute certainty about his private emotions as well as his public life. But there are other periods in Alexander Bell's life where I don't have such rich source material. These are the periods when he and Mabel are together, or after the death of Mabel's mother (Mabel's frequent letters to her mother contain marvellous descriptions of her married life in Washington and Cape Breton). There are gaps in the narrative – and gaps are another of the challenges that every biographer faces. Virginia Woolf distrusted biography: she said that what biography does is to "tack together torn bits of stuff, stuff with raw edges." However much evidence I can pull together about Alexander Graham Bell, or Catharine Parr Traill, there are always gaps between the reassembled pieces. I can produce only a patchwork. If I started making up the stuff that is missing from the written record, I would be pulling the material out of shape. In fact, I would be writing fiction.

Yet a good biography *is* closer to fiction than history, since it recreates a world and tends to be character-driven. I think this is why John Updike has called biographies "novels with indexes." I don't agree with this description: I am writing about real people. But biography does require an empathy between writer and subject – an empathy that, for me, is created by the "Ah-ha!" moment.

When I embarked on the biography of Alexander Graham Bell, I wondered not only when, but also if, I would have the required "Ah-ha!" moment. My previous books had all been about women, with whose lives I had felt deep empathy. Whether it was Isabel King's pride in her children's achievements, or Susanna Moodie's nostalgia for her English childhood, there were points of overlap in our lives. The artifacts that created the moments of empathy were all very feminine: a lock of hair, an outfit, a writing case. How would Alec and I connect? What overlap could there be between the life of a nineteenth-century Scots-born inventor whose head was full of diagrams and equations, and the life of a twenty-first-century writer with a sketchy grasp of physics?

The Alexander Graham Bell National Historic Site is in Baddeck, Nova Scotia, because Alec, Mabel, and their two daughters spent their summers there for nearly forty years. They built a palatial house across the bay from the village, on a headland that

Alec named Beinn Bhreagh ("beautiful mountain" in Gaelic). The site is in a purpose-built structure within the village, and it houses not only copies of the extensive Bell Archive (the originals are in the Library of Congress in Washington), but also a museum filled with Bell artifacts. On each visit there, I spent some time peering at early telephone prototypes in display cases, or at the elaborate paper kites that hang from the ceiling, or at the massive cigar-shaped hydrofoil that Alec developed a few years before his death. On my third visit, Aynsley MacFarlane, the manager, asked me if I would like to look at some of the items they didn't have room to display. "This is one of my favourites," she said, as she led me into a darkened room lined with shelves. She walked over to one of the shelves, crowded with model boats and complicated (and incomprehensible) wire structures. She pointed to an object that looked like a modernist sculpture: it consisted of beautifully finished mahogany slats glued together in such a way that they spiralled around a central axis.

When the Bells were furnishing their rambling mansion on Beinn Bhreagh, Aynsley explained to me, Mabel Bell sent off to Italy for a wooden Venetian blind for one of the bedroom windows. But she was away from Cape Breton when the blind arrived, so Alec opened the package. At the time he was immersed in flying-machine experiments, and doggedly trying to construct a propeller that would give a flying machine both lift and stability. By now, he was in his fifties – a wonderful avuncular figure, with bushy white hair and beard, who strode around his property in knickerbockers, flat cap, and a scruffy tweed jacket. He was held in great affection by the locals, who were proud to have this world-famous, and decidedly eccentric, inventor in their midst.

As I examined the strange sculpture in the museum's back-room, I could imagine Alexander Graham Bell slitting the string on the package, tearing off the brown paper wrapping, then pulling the wooden blind out of a box. I knew that when Alec was involved in a project, he was single-minded to the point of obsession. He would work night and day, forgetting to eat or sleep: Mabel would implore him to take rest, exercise, and regular meals, because she knew how often his unconventional, night-owl work habits drove him close to breakdown. The beautiful Italian workmanship of the blind must have enthralled him; the potential of its slats to fan out like a propeller must have entranced him. He would have stood in the library, oblivious to the magnificent view down Bras d'Or Lake from its window, as he twisted the blind first this way, then that way. Then, tucking the parcel under his arm, he must have stomped off to his workroom to incorporate it into his latest flying machine prototype. "Mabel was *not pleased*," Aynsley chuckled, "when she came home and found out what had happened to her expensive Italian blind."

It was the perfect "Ah-ha!" moment. I stroked those mahogany slats, and thought about a man for whom everything he saw and touched was a takeoff point for his next invention. Alexander Graham Bell loved science for science's sake. He was a hopeless businessman, and he had little interest in the commercialization of any of his ideas. He wanted to improve the world, to make communication easier for the deaf, to conquer time and space, to bring people together. He usually had several different projects on the go. His wife once remarked fondly that Alec's creativity reminded her of "the waves beating on the shore [that] fling seaweed on the sand and then retreat to fling more seaweed in some other wildly separated place." She deplored the fact that he tossed out "ideas, suggestions, accomplishments . . . recklessly and leaves them lying there to fertilize other minds, instead of gathering them all together to form creations to his own honor and glory."

The Italian blind was the trigger for one of his bursts of intuition and creative energy. I could imagine Mabel's exasperation when she discovered what he had done. But more important, I could imagine Alexander Graham Bell's dark eyes sparkling with excitement, as he realized he had everything he needed for the Next Big Thing. I was captivated both by the mangled Venetian blind and by the genius who had looked upon a piece of household furnishing and in his mind's eye seen it lift his newest flying machine toward the sky. I felt the ribbon of time tighten.

ELIZABETH**HAY**

My Debt to D.H. Lawrence

Until I was fifteen I didn't write, except, painfully, whatever essays and examinations and thank-you letters were required. A couple of weeks before exams, my father, who happened to be the high-school principal, would put my brothers and me into the car and drive us to school to spend Saturday morning, each in a separate classroom, studying until lunchtime. My father would be in his office down the hall. Gordon the Warden was his nickname.

Occasionally, one of my brothers broke out and came bounding up to my classroom window, pulling faces and carrying on. But I never broke out. Unless you consider the reading I did in my spare time a form of rebellion. It was my defining characteristic, this reading that no one supervised, for although my parents were very strict they left us alone in certain essential ways: I walked wherever I wanted to, I read whatever I liked. Only once was a book removed from my hands. I'd found a steamy paperback in the spare room closet. On the cover a very pretty woman with dark, wavy hair sat on the edge of an unmade bed, dressed in nothing but a yellow slip, while behind her slouched a man in a Brando T-shirt, cigarette between his fingers. My mother took it away: not the sort of thing that was suitable. Apart from that, I read whatever a small-town library had to offer. Lots of Taylor Caldwell and Frances Parkinson Keyes. I was willing to read hundreds of pages if, in one paragraph, a man's hand fondled a woman's breast.

Once, when I was about twelve, my father looked down at me curled up in a chair with my book and said, "You read so much. Have you ever thought of writing?" It was a kind and radical thought, but hopeless. Writing was inseparable from panic, from the strictures of having to write a certain way, from the essays that made me seize up when I did my homework at the dining-room table, or the exams that terrorized me, or those post-Christmas thank-you letters, the prospect of which left me whimpering.

Then something astonishing happened that opened up the world for me in two ways. When I was fifteen, my father moved us to England for a year, catapulting us from life in a small town, population 2,000, to the London of story and legend. I went to a girls' grammar school and one day my English teacher came in and without preamble asked us to do something we'd never done before. She was a young woman who wore shades of brown. My friend Artemis said she looked like a weak cup of tea. Not for the first time I was impressed – shaken would be a better word – by the audacious irreverence of English schoolgirls. They were not cowed. They were worldly and unruly and they had names that no small-town Ontario girl would ever have.

In through the door came our cup of weak tea (in fact, she was pretty, with a strawberry blonde's milky, freckled complexion). She asked us to open our books and read a poem by D.H. Lawrence. Then she told us to turn over our books and write down whatever came into our minds. I wrote easily, amazed that I had something in my head and that it had a way of coming out. Then she asked several of us to read aloud what we'd written. I read my piece and

I remember applause. But that can't be right; it must have been the feeling of applause. In any case, my classmates seemed to take note. I had become a little different, a little less the colonial hick.

That moment in the classroom was the great turning point in my life. From then on I wrote in private, thrilled to have discovered this new realm where things happened in ways I'd never foreseen. I would sit in the school library while it got dark (it got dark very early in England) and look over at the other girls who were studying. It seems to me I was in a window seat and therefore slightly apart, though again this could be simply a feeling, the physical aspect of a feeling. I see them in their green uniforms – skirts, sweaters, blue and green striped ties – heads bent over books in the darkening afternoon, a favourite time as the yellowy streetlights came on and the double-decker buses increased in number. Inside it became cozy, daylight gave way to a close and soothing quiet, and I wrote in my notebook whatever came to mind, one image leading to the next.

A year later we were back in Canada and although I continued to write, my writing gave me less pleasure. I didn't know what to do next. I didn't know how to turn my free-association poems into something else, something more, and I became convinced that I could write in only one very limited way. I lost my marvellous refuge – or it became less marvellous – although I remember a period of a few months when it came back. I was in my third year of university, living on the top floor of a rooming house on Brunswick Avenue in Toronto. I wrote poetry until ten every morning because my first lecture didn't begin until eleven. I remember being filled with the same sense of elation. Elated consolation, I want to say, but that's very awkward. Elation, certainly, coupled with a sense of three-dimensional light. Then I drifted back into the convinced self-doubt, the inhibitions, of my pre-fifteen years.

I was to all intents and purposes back at the dining-room table in my mind. The experience was very much like being behind the locked wheel of a car: the key is in the ignition but it won't turn and neither will the steering wheel. My father is an excellent driver; my mother is not and neither am I. To ride in the back seat when my mother was behind the wheel and my father in the passenger seat was to be at school again, watching my father give someone a failing grade. It was pitiable. The desperation of feeling stupid – a dim-bulb, nitwit, knuckle-head, dough-head, horse's ass – was something I felt all too often at my Chevy of a desk. At the opposite extreme was the moment when some slight movement, hard to say what, unfroze the key, the steering wheel, my mind, and they turned easily.

I say "hard to say what," but it isn't hard at all. It just took me a long time to figure it out. What exactly happened that day in the classroom when I found such an exquisite source of private pleasure, such a fine way of keeping myself company? I was reading a poem, and I didn't have time to think about myself. That's what made it possible to write. The poem not only gave me a starting point – and for a long time I thought that was the only point – but a way of forgetting myself. It distracted me into concentration.

I became a writer through an accident of reading, which never would have happened but for this other chain of lucky circumstances. Had we not been in England, had the teacher not had my class do that particular exercise, what would have become of me? I might have turned into my grandmother just as my mother feared I would. My grandmother was a capable but petty, self-involved, solitary woman with no outlet for her frustrated mind and considerable energies. She was the bane of my mother's existence.

I have a story about my mother and writing. This goes back to when I was six. By great good luck I was at a special Hallowe'en matinee, a double bill of horror movies. For that afternoon only, admission was six Pepsi-Cola bottle caps, and since my mother was never able to resist a bargain, we were allowed to go. My brothers and I scoured the back alleys of Wiarton and came up with the right number of bottle caps (we weren't allowed to drink soda pop ourselves, or to eat candy for that matter). By even greater good fortune, a miracle of sorts, my ticket stub turned out to be one of the prize winners at intermission. I strolled home with a magnificent walking doll in a blue satin dress. How well I remember the look of rapture on my mother's Scots face. The next morning I woke early and admired my doll in bed. Inspired, I took a pen and began to write my name on the doll's hard plastic neck. A long name. I started way back under her hair and worked forward, finishing at her Adam's apple if she'd had one. My mother was still lying abed on this fine Sunday morning when I took her my handiwork. She didn't have her glasses on and her face was soft from sleep and still favourably disposed to her winning daughter – until she saw what I'd done, and then she reared up in a paroxysm of outrage. She had a point, I could see that. My letters were unsightly and badly formed and huge. They snaked around the doll's neck in the greasy, smeared ballpoint ink of the day. I'd turned my beauty into an ink-stained wretch.

Such glory and such disgrace in less than twenty-four hours.

I put the sorry object away in the closet. I was never one for dolls anyway. Several years ago the doll came back to mind as something instructive, even a foreshadowing, not to put too fine a point on it. When you write you're putting your name to something. You're making it yours, often at its expense. More often than not, you alienate your family. You go too far, not that that's what you intended. Sometimes you disown what you've done, ashamed of yourself.

My mother, a painter, has minuscule handwriting. Her sense of aesthetics was deeply offended by what I'd done, and it would be again. She would find my transparently autobiographical writings hard to take. But how to leave oneself behind? How to enter a larger world?

Fiction beckoned, but I didn't know how to make the leap. After all, if I didn't know my own mind, how could I know the mind of an invented character? Years went by before I began to see that the moment of release in the classroom provided an answer. There's something life-giving about language if you can drop down into it. A kind of groundwater runs below the surface of everyday speech, and if you can just dip into it, you have something real. To slide beneath the surface of a character is a similar process. You get out of your own way. You concentrate on the outward appearance of this person taking shape. You work from the outside in. And then you have company. In a book people can be who they really are. Characters can relax and be themselves. A party empties out and leaves just a few behind, and you get to know them and they get to know themselves.

I know it seems contradictory, leaving yourself behind in order to write something you put your name to. It's part of an old riddle that I first encountered looking through some of my father's books. In his final year of high school he received a bundle of books as part of a history prize, and glued to the front page of each of them (*Seven Pillars of Wisdom* was one) was a book plate inscribed with the quotation "If I lose myself, I save myself." A paradox that intrigued me then and motivates me now.

It's impossible to write and not bang up against your limitations all the time. My mind is always going back to the sad, scared, discouraged blankness I associate with the dining-room table of my youth. Then – and this is the real point I'm trying to make – I pick up a book and that stimulated, competitive part of me wakes up again. By competitive I mean the feeling of *If they can do it, so can I.* A necessary feeling, since without it I'd be satisfied by reading alone.

I don't always start my morning by reading a page or two of fine poetry or prose, but if I'm stuck and mouldy in my mind, I pull down J.M. Coetzee's *Disgrace* or Michael Ondaatje's *Running in the Family* or Elizabeth Bishop's collected poems or her collected prose, or Margaret Avison's poetry – these are just a few examples – Anton Chekhov, W.G. Sebald, Alice Munro – I could give more examples. Penelope Fitzgerald. Marilynne Robinson. I live in a house full of books. I pull down one I love and read a page or two and invariably I'm absorbed and stirred and reaching for my pen. What I'm doing is catching a ride on the coattails of literature. The process is companionable and rooted in the past, my own and that of other writers. I'm returning to that moment in the classroom when I wasn't all alone, facing an exam, but with D.H. Lawrence in Mexico, astonished by the snakes and the red hibiscus.

MICHAEL**HELM**

Writing and the World Replaced

I intend to present myself here by disappearing, just leaving the room. The most personal thing I can say about my writing life is that the truest lines are often least apparent, and seldom the straightest (this is true of many lives, I know). Maybe I'm an unusually guarded person, and maybe if you knew me, you'd even conclude that my not speaking directly and at length about the things I hold closest, including writing and the life I live in order to do it, has less to do with reluctance than with incapability. Maybe you'd be right. Whatever the reasons for this guardedness, they likely contribute to my being a fiction writer.

At its best, fiction secures and communicates a kind of height-ened perception. Writers often put forward spiritual metaphors to describe this perception and the pursuit of it. The life of writing, for me, involves not so much the contemplation of transcendent things, as an attentiveness to the wonders in ordinary living and the superabundance of our experience. This attentiveness is a kind of grasping after the sacred, I suppose. There are even a few rituals attached, ceremonial robes (okay, favourite flannel shirts), mumbled invocations and prayers that mark an obsessiveness and at times irrationality. I find the act of writing itself exhilarating, but solemn. I can write other things in any common mood, but not fiction. Writing fiction is the way I go to church. It's a private place and I couldn't tell you how to get there or what goes on inside, other than to record in the novels what it's like when the music starts up.

It's important to have something in daily life about which we are dead serious. Many people who are outwardly happy and comfortable suffer in ways they don't understand because they lack this thing, or have lost faith in it.

I still have my faith, and it has its articles, my beliefs about the nature of the imagination and fiction itself. By turning the idea of "writing life" a little sideways, I'll now offer some of these articles to you, unnumbered, and flawed, though I'm still working them through, and will be for the full length of this life.

To begin, the things we find and sometimes love in novels – the characters, the food, the landscapes – they don't exist. What they do, rather, is *have being*. As readers we know what this means. We measure it mainly by a novel's emotional force, our physiological response to the rewards of belief. What we're believing in impresses us as not just true, but living. The idea is a metaphor, of course, but what it describes is very particular, and perhaps unnameable. We stare at the page and it stares back. How is this so? Why do the best novels seem organically alive?

Let's remove the writer from where he's hiding there behind the questions. A novel's seeming life has nothing to do with the writer's actual one. It's true that the well-travelled, well-read novelist, who moves easily between social classes and vernaculars, or between countries and languages, might have greater scope and better subjects. But living broadly, though it might make a writer more interesting at parties, won't help him dispose his experiences in fiction: it's one thing to know a lot of banjo tunes and another to play the instrument. It's also true that writing well is a political and moral act. Beyond this, if a writer chooses to use her public self for political ends, say, it may influence the way we read her work, but it doesn't enlarge the ontology of the writing.

So where does the *being* come from? The distinction to observe is between two kinds of language. Transparent language is common. It's in everything from advertising to instructional language to journalism, and it takes great skill to use it well. Poetic language (I don't mean flowery), the kind used in poetry, fiction, and (rarely) essays, draws on the same words but makes forms out of them that have elements of music and prayer. Transparent language belongs to specialized fields and popular media; poetic language to private minds. We should remember this when considering why so many literary writers are reluctant to talk publicly about their work or personal lives. Some are worried, no doubt, that they'll come off as self-fascinated and adoring of the art they pull from their beloved smithies, or they might prefer not to trade directly on their joys and sorrows, having perhaps traded indirectly on them in their work. But others don't want their work subsumed into what Don DeLillo calls "the middle range" of the culture, knowing their audience wants something that transcends crude commodification, the coy posing better suited to performers, brooding indie music stars, or actors on media junkets. On this simplest level, they seem to have attempted to replace their outward selves with written words, a substitution that even many gods have not survived, let alone the flawed creatures who write fiction, taking up the gods' creative work.

The idea of life created or renewed is connected to this sense of replacement. Acts of substitution are central to the imaginations of many cultures. In some psychoanalytic and anthropological theories, superstitions, rituals, and neuroses involve the substitution of one thing, a symbol or action, for another. Such models of understanding presume that there's a kind of rhyme to indirection. We need both math and metaphor to follow our own bending strata of the rational, irrational, and non-rational; we need science and poetry together to contemplate love, murder, totemic religions, or the newest consumer crazes. The poetry is in the replacements. In terms of the dominant mythic imagery which underlies much of Western literature, the so-called Penal Substitution strain of Christian theology, a second Adam replaces the first one, and his suffering is in place of ours. That the best novels enact this kind of replacement makes them necessarily affirmative, redemptive, even when their stories are bleak or apocalyptic.

But in other ways, too, writing is an act of substitution. Fiction writers describe one thing in terms of another, not just in metaphor (The old fireworks "exploded with stored energy or fizzled dangerously in clouds of smoke, the breath of a long horned animal on its knees"), but even in direct presentation ("The waitress stood tapping her pencil against the pad of tickets she held") because that's how language works, whether or not it's describing something actual. Writers put words *in the place of* things. Fiction is a kind of open deception in which the world outside the story is replaced by the world of language that is the story (though the world outside it has been altered by the addition of this story). If a writer hopes to write a novel to life, then, he has only the *figurative* means of language. So the central question is "What is life *like*?"

Admittedly, the question is unanswerable. Anything life might be like would have to be included as part of life itself; metaphor can't accommodate absolutes or abstractions. Yet novels and stories offer *seeming* answers, and these are always local. Life is like this in Yalta when the new woman appears on the esplanade. It's like this in the mind of Moses Herzog. And for the British Consul drunkenly preparing his death under a Mexican volcano, it's like this. But the answers aren't just local – they're comprehensively local. Like so many apparently self-evident truths about writing that are in fact false or misleading, the injunction to "get it right" can defeat any writer who accepts it too narrowly or ignores its ambiguity. Exactly what is "it"? The only answer is "everything." The uncompromising novel is one that gets everything right: the culture of 1950s Jewish Montreal, the way the felt wears along the rail, the image that holds an inflection of speech or a baffled expression, the line of dialogue that nails not just a character but her whole world, the sentence that renders a stumbling thought.

Over the last hundred years or so, fiction and poetry have revealed themselves to be the best means we have of inhabiting other people's subjective experience in something like the language and complexity of that experience. Novels remind us that our whole world is sensually perceived and held for durations determined by the imagining mind. Even as the novel's documentary opportunities increased with the growth of cities and the migrations of peoples, the thing that made novels fiction and not journalism was private consciousness. So if as fiction writers we're serious about pursuing the question of lifelikeness, we have to account for even more: memory, time, the need to see causality and resolution, emotions, the need to believe.

There's really no way of talking about even one of these briefly, but novelists have to (or should have to) take a position on them, and there are at least entry points to the positions. Of these elements, the first two are most clearly related. Personal memory provides fictional characters with dimension and gravity, and lets the storytelling dance in time rather than simply plod steadily forward like a movie zombie. The difference between the story and its telling is owed partly to the rift between reality and perception, which is often reality filtered through experience and memory. Those novels that have real substance carry their weight low, deep inside this rift, in the richest veins of subject and subtext. The readers who find those depths have been given a new way of seeing the world outside the book, the world of their own lived and witnessed lives. A novel is alive, then, when it proves an act of furthered perception, replacing, as it were, the world around us obscured by our prejudices and narrow habits of mind, with the world as it infinitely is.

Collective memory – both the unacknowledged kind and the public – allows history and mythology their places. The historical moment, the time and place coordinates, is in all things, of course – technology, politics, fashion, capital, all of it. To spare us both a thousand pages, maybe it's enough to say that if the writer is paying attention, the long history will be there on its own, even outside of historical settings or the current quotidian, even in seemingly unhistorical, fantastical things. As García Márquez once suggested to the Swedish Academy, his novels don't seem so magical when one accounts for the "outsize reality of Latin America," by which he meant the long, absurd, and bloody history of the region. Questions of plausibility fall away when a novel emerges from such a history, and these histories are not limited to Latin America, of course. Borges wrote of Faulkner that "the world he imagines is so real that it also encompasses the implausible."

You see the complications. I don't pretend to be managing them especially well. I'm ignoring debates about realism, representation, gender, influence, historicity, consciousness, loaded dice, faulty transmissions, reversible cloaks, the whole "tarnished brass" theory of "parade narratives." One consideration is barely met before another is upon us – there goes memory and here comes misremembrance. Lifelikeness requires us to account for this, too. Alice Munro's "The Progress of Love" gives us a character whose life has been determined largely by an early event misinterpreted and so misremembered. Here the reader's experience of the story parallels the character's experience of the memory. Notice the relation between the misreadings and the momentarily ambiguous pronouns (read the story, follow the *her*'s). Notice that we're *supposed* to be temporarily confused. Notice, in fact, that delays in understanding are part of human perception, and fiction that doesn't risk them is not just false and meretricious, but small.

And how does a writer convey not only the losses we can name but the absences we're unaware of, forgotten people and episodes that won't return unless triggered by chance? And what about things that don't ever return? How does a novel register an absence so complete? Imagine a character whose life has come down to her need to draw on an experience, a moment in the past, that is lost to her. Someone beyond the realm of unanswered prayers, or half-remembered prayers. Someone prayerless, beneath forgotten gods. But then isn't this our state, some of us? Isn't this part of the mystery we're writing toward?

We penetrate the mystery word by word until we see the thing taking shape there in the window with our own reflection light upon the glass, for though novels can deliver the world, they can also present a way of thinking about it, both rationally and associatively, as it plays in the mind. More than any other art form except poetry, fiction is interior. It's sounded out to us in the intimate voice of our thoughts, which brings us back to poetic language. How can we hope to write life if we don't observe the plain fact that, though novels may well employ the many forms of public language, where we actually live is in the language of consciousness, not the language of newspapers, advertising, business, popular culture, or well-struck argument? Everything we know is mediated through our minds, so how can we possibly ignore them? We sometimes hear it said that a good novel creates its own world, but of the best novels it's more accurate to say that they present a mind that beholds a world. The mind might be that of a character, or several characters, or it might belong to a master narrator, as in Tolstoy, or a storyteller who leaves the characters to their thoughts and presents them in a disinterested voice. The mind might be musical, mathematical; it might intone with the authority of divine utterance, or it might sleep drunkenly with its back to the lake and then wake like a floodgate at the milliontonne pressure of words.

That the words form stories lands us in causality (he did this because she did that), which, if you want something to believe in, could hardly be more inviting. There's so much evidence of it as a force in science, history, our day-to-day lives, that we don't always notice its complexity until one expert or another helps us out (it's always worth asking who's funding the expert, of course). But in fiction, causality seems to lead readers in two directions at once. We know the feeling of reading a near great novel that hasn't carried off its ending, a novel with the language, characters, emotions, ideas all working at once until the last pages, when the writer has either failed to resolve the story, or too neatly resolved it. At such moments we feel that cause and effect as it exists outside the novel has been misrepresented, looped into contrivance. We feel distanced, even duped, and often want to accuse the story – its building events, its dramas – of falseness. Yet when the novel works, we accept such dramas as true, and the story pulls us even closer. We all experience dramas, even if they don't daily involve daggers and bodies and bombs that tick like metronomes. There's nothing necessarily unlifelike about the novel's oldest devices and conventions, in that causality and a hunger for resolution exist in the world outside of fiction, as do daggers, bodies, and (unticking) bombs. No matter that we're forever looking back, we live moving forward with our eyes sometimes reluctantly on the finish. Even Sartre admitted that at some point novels had to provide "the consolations of received forms." But these forms – suspense, coherent character, story – are simply elements out of which, in the best novels, each new true thing is made. In fact, fiction is usually much more wary of contrivance than is life itself, in that life contrives to be full of unlikely event.

Many of the novels I like best aren't only alive, they're alive to the moment. What is life like here at the beginning of the new century? Well, some of it's familiar from history. Clashing theocracies, emerging sciences and technologies, unceasing violence, pandemics, barbers. But the cries of apocalypse, though they started to sound hollow a few centuries ago, lately sound more like the long opening notes of what will be a final, global chorus. Maybe "writing life" these days means replacing the whole planet *in extremis*. As for the human world, our baubles glitter more than they did in earlier centuries, and there are attached to the most powerful forces of information and bad government whole new kinds of noise. There are fewer solitudes, more encampments. From political platforms to news desks to seminar rooms, public utterance has grown suspect in its intentions. What's to be done with the human impulse toward faith when there's no place to direct it? Well, it can be directed toward stories, and stories can address the question in their way.

Novels themselves have been pushed farther to the margins of this new world. Literary fiction hasn't been the dominant narrative form for a long time now, and we're facing a loss not only of general high-literacy, but of the self-knowledge such literacy provides (anyone who finds this a quaint or conservative notion has never been hauled from the seas by language). We are less in need of stories about art or artists than we are of art itself. Is it any comfort that the best filmmakers are still the most literate given that like the best writers they may well lose access to their audience in the corporate dumbing down of arts industries? And though all arts have their strengths, movies can't do what novels do. Asking the real world to play itself falsely is different than replacing it whole with the resonant workings of belief, breath, and imagination. Here's a film scene of a man entering a bus station in 1950s Knoxville, Tennessee. We see the actor acting – he's good, just right for the part, and we liked him in the last thing he was in, the one about the Irish famine. We see him in the street approaching, opening the door. The shot changes so we see what he sees. We hear what he hears. What we don't hear is this:

> On Gay Street the traffic lights are stilled. The trolleyrails gleam in their beds and a late car passes with a long slish of tires. In the long arcade of the bus station footfalls come back like laughter. He marches darkly towards his darkly marching shape in the glass of the depot door. . . . The door swung back and he entered the waiting room. The shapes of figures sleeping on the wooden benches lay like laundry. In the men's room an elderly pederast leaning against a wall.

Now tell me you don't prefer this world, the one that replaces Knoxville, or even movie Knoxville, with the vertical wonder of poetic language. We don't need to note the subtle complexity of the rhythms created without punctuation, the tense shifts, the chiastic construction that mirrors the mirror imaging. We just hear and feel it. And as for the larger narratives, even the size, shape, and movement of the stories in great novels are truer than we find in most movies. The Russian filmmaker Andrei Tarkovsky wrote, "In my view poetic reasoning is closer to the laws by which thought develops, and thus to life itself, than is the logic of traditional drama." He was right about poetic reasoning, but because he made movies and not novels, he could only reveal his characters' interiors by defeating our expectations about pace and continuity. When they work, these effects are absorbing. When they don't, we're left wondering how something made of light can be both brilliant and dull. What the best filmmakers aspire to be, it turns out, are novelists.

In the end, a fiction writer hopes to find a story and a way of telling it that project all these elements – interiors and exteriors, pasts and presents – intelligently and poetically. But if the writer is replacing the world, there has to be something more, something true for being unresolvable, and very hard to reduce to language. The central paradox is this: great novels force us to believe in an absence. Because of their sheer abundance we feel the enormity of what has been replaced. Sensing the presence of an absence is a fundamentally religious feeling, not just in the post-theistic classes, but for any readers who live in doubt, as the best readers do. In short, the novels that are most alive suspend us in the best questions. One well-known but not always observed test of a writer's seriousness is his sentences (as Conrad wrote, "art should carry its justification in every line"), but another, slyly related one is a willingness to find these farthest territories of doubt.

What can be brought back alive from such places? As writers or readers, we know we've found it when it appears before us, as

Czeslaw Milosz writes, "as if a tiger had sprung out/and stood in the light, lashing its tail."

When the tiger sees us, there's nothing more to say. It stares back. Look up from the page, wherever you are, but the animal lines remain like a burning afterimage. Even the silence is made of words.

This piece warrants credits for what hasn't already been attributed. I've ripped off the following writers: William Gass for distilling the ideas of many poets and philosophers about the two kinds of language, and for seeing the novel as a mind that beholds a world; John Hawkes for the long horned animal on its knees; Cormac McCarthy for the waitress and the Knoxville bus station; and Seamus Heaney for the Milosz line.

SHEILA**HETI**

Mid-October Day

There are many machines in the world, so now we know something about machines.

They are what we like best until they fail us, and until we can figure out why they have failed us, there is nothing more frustrating than a machine. It is not that the power cord is unplugged. It is not that we have spilled Gatorade all over it.

Everything in a machine must be doing its little, private job if the whole machine is to be doing its single job, which is perhaps to turn out a bottle of Coke, or perhaps to let us send and receive emails, or perhaps to suck up dust and condoms from the carpet, or to turn out ten-dollar bills.

A person who works at an office is like one part of the vacuum cleaner, or one part of the machine that turns out six thousand bottles of Coke a minute, and so it is important that they work. But when what needs to be made is a story, then the machine is one person, and if the hands are able, and if the brain is not asleep, and there is no writing coming out, then one must detect what is wrong.

One thought is that we were wrong about this machine; we thought it was supposed to make books, but that was just vanity. It was to make children, or a fool of itself, or nothing at all, just to lie down on the sidewalk and die.

I have gone into myself tinkering and come out with nothing, no answers. I have not been able to find the element that is off, but to spend so long aware that every part must be working properly, and to not know what the parts are, or what is "properly," this is a strange maintenance job.

Motto: To work crookedly, then. To spit dust onto the carpet. To produce cars with three wheels. For the Coke to be on the outside, and the bottle on the inside.

ANNABEL**LYON**

Dropping Out

The joke was that my contracts professor talked like Marlon Brando in *The Godfather* – slow New York, oxymoron turned icon – and once this had been pointed out to you, it was difficult to sit through his classes with a straight face. And we liked him, my classmates and I, right from that first class at the University of British Columbia in September of 1997, when he drew a large, ovular *O* on the chalkboard over a small *a* with a trailing, spermy tail, and said these represented Offer and Acceptance, the essence of contracts. Then as the visual joke sank in, he erased the drawing in his bemused, measured, Don Corleone way. That was almost the funniest part, that erasing, because this was a law school, after all, and we knew some people couldn't tell sexual harassment from a hole in the wall, and because we all – budding lawyers – knew that he knew that we knew.

One year later, to the day, I stood in a lineup outside the registrar's office when he happened to walk by.

Annabel, he said. What are you doing?

Dropping out, I said.

He leaned forward intently, looking more interested than I had seen him during a whole year of contracts.

Good for you, he said. When you're done, come see me in my office.

The 1997–98 academic year: come on, remember it with me. Princess Diana had just died. I remember making banana muffins for the freezer, those first September days, listening to the news updates on the radio, guessing (correctly, it turned out) I would soon be too busy with school to bake. I like to bake. A couple of weeks before, I had gone day-tripping with my mom across the border to the outlet stores near Bellingham, Washington, and bought a navy blazer from Liz Claiborne; at a Body Shop in Vancouver I had bought a little bag of makeup – lipsticks and eyeshadow and mascara – that I didn't know how to apply. My uniform for years had been cut-off jeans and extra-large men's T-shirts. I liked to write and had published a handful of short stories in little magazines, but little magazines did not give you a pension and dental, and I was terribly afraid of slipping through the cracks. Law school would give me a solid footing in the world, that was what people told me and what I told myself too. Still, when I later tried to write a short story about going to law school, I made my protagonist a theatre student, a Beckett/Orton/Pinter fan who treated the experience both as a black farce and as an elaborate game of dress-up.

In February was the APEC summit – you remember, President Suharto, the pepper spray, all that – and the law school was on the front lines. Protesters filing toward Green College looked in through the big classroom picture windows and alternately jeered and invited us to join them. The Mounties came into the law building on their breaks to buy potato chips from the vending machines.

One wandered into one of my classes, a few minutes before it started, and asked hopefully if it was a criminal law class. When we told him no, constitutional, he looked disappointed. A senior professor offered an impromptu lecture, standing room only, on the various legal infringements of the government, the police, the University, and the summit delegates themselves. Many of my fellow students skipped class to go watch the violence at the front lines. My Real Property professor, who had spent time as a consultant in various troubled countries, paced nervously as he lectured, and ducked every time a helicopter flew overhead. Those were cold, grey February days, and I remember numbly attending class after class, too depressed to go and watch the reality that was being canned for the nightly TV news, or to enjoy the sixties *frisson* of being a serious student at a volatile place and time. All I wanted to do was go home – at that time, a basement suite off Alma Street, not far from Spanish Banks – and take off my nice law school clothes, scrub the store-bought colours from my face, and go down to the empty beach in the grey, drizzling twilight. During school hours I slipped away as often as I could to Nitobe Garden, a walled, classical Japanese garden in a secluded corner of campus. A couple of years later I wrote a story called "Every Little Thing" where the protagonist, a depressed medical student, hangs out in a similar garden, stark in its winter clothes, avoiding her fellow students and grimly questioning her career choice.

During reading week, as preparation for first-year moots, I went downtown to the courts to watch an appeal. My class (contracts, remember) was mooting a dispute over a fictional bagel franchise. One of the issues was that the franchisee had modified the franchisor's patented bagel boiling vats, potentially compromising the integrity of the brand. Anyway, I went to watch an appeal from a murder trial. It didn't have anything to do with bagels, or contracts for that matter, but it would almost certainly have a story. I was treating myself.

Because it was an appeal and not a trial, there were no accused, no witnesses, and not many observers. The only people present were the three judges, two defence lawyers, the Crown, a clerk, and a sheriff. I was one of the first observers to take a seat and almost right away the one defence lawyer – with the thick curly black hair, the florid face, the confidence – came over to chat. Ostensibly killing time before the process started, he quickly ascertained who I was and what I was doing there. He was slick, a pro, determined to control all possible factors in the room. He turned out to be representing the younger of the two defendants. The other lawyer was older, greyer, and considerably less sure of himself. His arguments were weak, his manner annoyingly diffident, and his client probably innocent. The judges tore him to shreds. The case concerned two teenage boys in a home invasion gone bad: when they came out, the old woman in the house was dead. Each boy accused the other. There was a third teen involved, a girl who waited outside in somebody's car with the engine running. She had not been charged with anything, or at least not that I could tell from that proceeding. The slick, curly lawyer at one point said that she had "had a sweetness for" the older boy, a phrase that stuck in my mind. I can't remember why he brought this up; to discredit her evidence, perhaps. At issue the morning I watched was the younger teen's psychiatric record, which the older teen's lawyer wanted admitted into evidence. Apparently the younger teen had a personality disorder and a history of violence. Because he was a juvenile, though, his medical records were privileged and could not be entered as evidence. The judges – particularly one woman known to law students as fiercely bright and hell on her clerks – were scathing, and once they got the gist of his argument practically refused to let him finish a sentence. I had a high old time watching all this, not giving a thought – for a few hours, anyway – to contracts or boiling vats or the fact that one day it would be me up there, stammering my case before the world.

Moots came; my partner and I got our bagels sent back for retrial. Our "judge," an alumna who had volunteered her time to the law school, kindly offered to take us out afterward for beers. That too stuck in my mind, the small, pining sadness of that plural.

A few weeks later, I got a summer job with a mid-sized law firm downtown. This was a classy outfit, with a dark green and silver logo, a lot of green leather furniture, and a couple of floors in an office tower overlooking the library. Too junior to article, I was hired as a research-and-writing student and spent an educational summer writing briefs and assisting one or two lawyers who wrote scholarly articles on the side. Students were encouraged to fear such positions as indenture to fickle sadists, but the lawyers I worked for were without exception kind, patient, and generous with their time. Their thoroughgoing niceness was all the more surprising since "my" firm specialized in a couple of particularly thankless branches of law (what most of us call "medical malpractice" they called "health law"). I had an office to myself, a secretary I shared with two other students, and a paycheque every two weeks. When I screwed up on the computer, I had tech support, in the form of a taciturn computer wizard who kept a plastic Marvin the Martian doll on top of his monitor. Someone else had a pair of goldfish named Dodi and Di. I myself kept a childhood tchotchke in the form of a small rubber monkey, a German TV cartoon character named Äffle, in my drawer with my highlighters. I also had all the free stationery supplies I could squirrel away, and meals in nice restaurants with the lawyers who wanted to make us students feel welcome and groom us for the future.

I was miserable there, but in a new way. Whereas at law school I had felt like an imposter, a kid playing dress-up, the firm fit me all too well. Long hours didn't bother me, and I was finicky about my work; I knew the challenges of the job would eventually sand away my shyness, such as my fear of the telephone. I could see the career I would have, the kind of lawyer I would be: a little too quiet and withdrawn but competent enough, with an acceptable sense of humour; the kind who was nice to students; the kind who gamely returned to the law school once a year to judge moots and drink beers with the kids.

Except, except. One day I took one of the firm's green notepads and wrote, "Two boys went into a house. A girl waited in the car." Now this was not good; this was quite bad. I should have been writing a brief. Worse, the short, declarative sentences were wilfully Hemingwayesque and amateurish and smacked of a kind of arch postmodernism that thought it cool to name characters "the boy" and "the girl." I found myself tinkering with this opening, racking up small variations all down the page. "It happened like this. The boys went into the house while the girl waited in the car." "It" was of course the appeal I had observed that spring, or at any rate how I imagined the events that led to the appeal. I decided to let the many openings stand, with the result that the story seemed to tell itself again and again, much as witnesses at a trial might tell the same basic facts again and again but with minute variations that gradually, over time, corrupted the whole. I hadn't had time for my own writing all that year, and to begin again with a style so jagged and odd gave me the feeling of clinging by my fingertips to something I could barely handle. Increasingly, up there in my posh office, I began to imagine an alternate future in which I abandoned law and wrote fiction for a living. I would be, what, thirty? forty? fifty? and still in my basement suite with the blinds drawn, still badly dressed, still weird, flossing like a demon to stave off the dentist I would have to pay out of my own pocket, still pensionless, still afraid of the telephone?

I would like to be able to say that my contracts professor's office had wood panelling and a blue-grey fog of cigar smoke and Venetian blinds leaking mellow old light through the slats, even as the sound of a wedding penetrated faintly from outside. But it was small, windowless, fluorescent, institutional, though well-booked: a typical UBC prof's office. My professor made green tea, hot and a little bitter, and we talked: about my unhappiness that past year, and about his own early ambivalence toward a legal career. He suggested that if I didn't love the law, I was right to get out before I bricked myself too far in. And when I told him I wrote fiction, he looked, in his bemused way, slightly incredulous. If I had something I loved to do, why didn't I just go and do it?

Two boys went into a house. The girl waited in the car. She felt sick. She tried to remember why money had seemed like such a good idea, what she wanted it for. CDs? Lipsticks? I don't want any more lipsticks, she thought. She sat in the car with the engine running, the exhaust going up like a white signal, thumbtacking them to the map of the cold curved street.

They walked out slowly. Marco closed the front door behind him and gave it a little tug to make sure it was locked. Neither of them was carrying anything.

DAVID**MACFARLANE**

On Not Going to a Party for Ian McEwan

There was a time, not so long ago, when the natural habitat of the writer was widely known. Libraries, the refrigerator – these were the kinds of places where you could be sure to check a few sightings off your lifetime list. But the traditional migratory routes can no longer be relied upon. These days, there are book launches, readings, parties, gala dinners – events at which writers can be found and that I seem to find difficult, for some reason. Let me give you an example of my confusion.

When Ian McEwan came to Toronto to mark the publication of his novel *Saturday*, his Canadian publisher decided to hold a reception for him. I was lucky enough to receive an invitation. Unaccountably, it paralyzed me for weeks.

On the one hand: why wouldn't I want to meet one of my favourite writers?

On the other hand: and that was the problem. I couldn't quite figure out what was on the other hand – even as I headed out the door.

But finally, whatever it was stopped me. I was on my way to the party, and I actually halted abruptly on the sidewalk two blocks from where the reception was being held. I stood there for a while thinking about Ian McEwan. I thought about the short stories I'd read, in a bed-sit in London, when his name first came to my attention. (I had decided that my syllabus that year, while working in a car wash near Russell Square and trying to become a writer, would simply be to read all Picador paperbacks – and McEwan and Flann O'Brien were two of the writers I read, without knowing anything about them before I opened their books.) Then I thought about *A Child in Time* and *Amsterdam* and about how clearly I could remember where and when I had read them. I thought about *Atonement*, and about what a partnership my avid attention and McEwan's skill as a storyteller had established. McEwan, like Julian Barnes and Philip Roth, is a writer for whom I will set aside ideal reading time (in the sunshine on a boathouse dock in Temagami; on a grey Sunday afternoon in downtown Toronto). I stood on the sidewalk, paralyzed, I realized, by how much I was looking forward to reading *Saturday*.

Irritated passersby hurried around me. Was it simply shyness that was stopping me? Or was it the silliness that so often attends the meeting of a celebrity? Or was it something else – some irrational but nonetheless stubbornly present notion that my relationship with Ian McEwan had already achieved a kind of perfection (on that boathouse dock; on those grey Sunday afternoons) and that meeting him might change that. Possibly, meeting him might betray that.

I turned around. I came home. I pinned the invitation to my bulletin board and have puzzled over it ever since.

My notion of where writers could traditionally be found may have had something to do with *New Yorker* cartoons. There was a recurrent theme – a kind of ongoing cautionary tale aimed, apparently, at anyone contemplating writing a book. There was some sexist presumption involved in these cartoons (although I was never clear on which sex was being belittled) for it was always a bleary, unshaven husband who was at his desk in a modestly furnished spare-room of an office. The floor was littered with crumpled pages, and his wife was at the door. She leaned there with aggressive nonchalance, as if that were the most natural place in the world to end up after a long, hard day of earning a living and raising a family. She had a newspaper open, and she was always saying something dry and devastating. Something like: "According to the *Times*, it took Richard Nixon seven weeks to write *his* book."

It was the doorway that was most interesting. The non-writing spouse leaned there – looking into the writer's domain, but never entering it. The geography that was implicit in these cartoons was that on one side of the door there resided the self-obsessed, the entirely impractical, the financially irresponsible, and the very foolishly undertaken. The writer at work, in other words.

On the other side, sanity prevailed. There, bills were getting paid, children were being looked after, phone calls got returned, birthdays were remembered. There was toilet paper.

It was regrettable, perhaps, that on that side of the door nobody was going to win the Nobel Prize for Literature. But that's the way it goes. Apparently, the people on that side are too busy matching socks and taking arthritic Labrador retrievers to the vet to ever get to Stockholm. However, it's probably worth pointing out that on that side of the door, there is food in the refrigerator. On that side of the door, there is somebody who knows what day of the week it is. On that side of the door, the car grows snow tires every winter and the bathroom sink hatches another tube of toothpaste just when one is required. It's kind of like a computer on that side of the door. I have no idea how it works. It just does.

It used to be said that writers could be spotted in bars – but I've always doubted it. I don't often go to the bar, and when I do I never meet another writer. Of course, I never meet anyone. I stare into my glass if it's full, and I rap it on the bar a couple of times if it's empty, and if anyone asks how my book's going, I tell them to fuck off. I just don't seem to be the type who easily strikes up friendships.

The truth is I have only the haziest idea of what other writers do when they are not attending book launches, or receiving prizes at gala dinners, or sitting on panels on television book shows, or standing around at receptions looking like they could do with a few fashion tips – which is as it should be. All my life, I have taken far greater pleasure in imagining the writers I am reading than in knowing anything specific about them. I prefer an author's biography to hover in the wings of a novel. Over the years, for instance, I've learned something of the life of Ian Fleming, but no actual biographical detail will ever be more vivid to me than the image of him that I constructed, at the age of eleven, as I stood beside the paperback rack of a drugstore in Hamilton, Ontario, and read a few surreptitiously turned pages of *Thunderball*. And, were he given the choice, I have no doubt that image is the one Sir Ian would wish me to have.

An author's presence in a book – the voice that is so precisely established, the sensibility on which the story turns – is the real presence of a writer, and not the one met a little awkwardly, a little artificially at a crowded reception. Certainly, that's the persona into which the author has poured heart and soul. It may not be quite as momentarily actual as, say, Ian McEwan standing in a room with a glass of wine in his hand, surrounded by admirers. But it is the author as he or she exists in the wings of a book – and not the one who shakes hands and says that yes, he's enjoying Toronto – that is important to me.

And so I prefer to keep writers a little mysterious. I prefer not to know too much. Do they write sitting at a card table in a spare room – à la the *New Yorker*? Or do they stand, like Dickens, at a grand wooden desk? I wouldn't care to hazard a guess.

Do they proclaim as they write – imagining their words ringing in the tones of a Brent Carver or William Hutt? Or, as those who have the great good fortune of being married to a writer sometimes point out, do they not speak at all? For decades? Do they write in furious bursts of energy? Are they crackling with cleverness in person? Or when you actually speak with them, and realize what a long, tortuous journey there must have been between the sentences that are naturally theirs and the ones that have ended up on their printed pages, do you realize (with a great heave of relief if you happen to be another writer) that they are far less bright than their books?

Do they solve the problems they encounter by doing what Philip Roth does – just staying at their desks? (I've read that Roth keeps a sign above his that says: "Stay put.") Or do they lie on the floor, or go to the refrigerator, or take a shower, or have a drink, or smoke a joint, or go for a long walk? Do they plough stubbornly through draft after draft until they find what they are looking for? Or does the answer to some question of voice, of narrative, of structure, of turn of phrase, come in the middle of the night, emerging from between the fitful dreams of those who spend their working days in the uncertain space between ambition and execution?

We won't ever know – not really. Even if we're fellow-writers we don't really have a clue. Writers keep their working time secret. And because, from the outside, writing looks so fantastically boring – look, there's Michael Ondaatje thrumming his fingers on his desk; look, there's Alice Munro staring into space – people tend to keep it that way.

During a book tour, or as fodder for interviews, or as dinner party chit-chat, the writer will trot out an anecdote about the writing process, maybe. But the chosen story will be after-the-fact. It will exist in relation to a finished book and not to one that is incomplete, troublesome, and that might get chucked into the fireplace at any moment. This is a crucial difference – one that virtually guarantees the eventual mummification of the anecdote in question. Over time and with repetition it will cease to have any real connection with writing. What a writer goes through to try to find the perfect story to tell and the perfect way to tell it, is a chaotic, messy, largely intuitive process – one about which writers are notoriously private. Many writers who are more than happy to walk under ladders, or are unshaken by whatever route a black cat chooses, are nonetheless "superstitious" about talking about a work in progress.

This could have something to do with the fact that a great deal of the progress is not in the least pleasant. It's not, as portrayed in movies, a cup of coffee, a cigarette, and (cut-to) a triumphant crescendo of typewriter keys. In real life in general, and with writing in particular, there are no jump-cuts. There are days upon days of one-too-many cups of largely useless coffee. There are weary afternoons of aimless walks and there are black nights when, by the time dawn breaks over the computer, it's obvious that staying in bed would have been far the more useful way to pass the time. There are occasions when a colonoscopy seems preferable to the difficulties of getting a story right. There are weeks of excessive, addictive, self-destructive behaviour. It could be cigarettes, or amphetamines, or dollops of opium, or bottles of beer. Embarrassingly, in my case it's entire packets of oatmeal raisin cookies – eaten with a kind of desperation, as if the secret of beautiful writing might be found, like a Chinese fortune, in one of them. Worst of all, there are occasions when a mind that seemed lively and interesting and imaginative a few days before, becomes dull and uncooperative and downright stupid, and there is often no easy way to know why this is so. Too little sleep? Too much? The wrong food for lunch? No food? Too many oatmeal raisin cookies?

Could the un-sparking of a writer's brain have anything to do with the half-bottle of whisky that was needed to quell the excitement of the few beautiful paragraphs written the day before? (And that, three days from now, will prove, in some new light, to be much less beautiful than imagined.) Could it be senility? Dementia? Depression? Or could it just be that I misinterpreted the signs that appeared to point toward a literary career? Possibly, what seemed, in the naive glow of youth, to be heading in the direction of Writing was actually leading to another destination entirely: possibly it wasn't Writing at all that was on my horizon as I worked my way through the Picador backlist. Possibly it actually was Working in a Car Wash.

James Boswell suffered on occasion from what he called "Dullness." He might have called it Melancholia – but "Dullness" seems as good a description as any, and Boswell recognized that it was about the last thing on earth a writer wants.

What dullness means to a writer is that words become just words: they are not lit from within, they do not reflect one another in new and captivating ways, they do not lead through the darkness, like a strand of lights, to a place known all along but that still comes as a surprise. James Boswell did his best to fend off his bouts of dullness – flapping around in his rooms with calisthenic-like exercises, or going for long walks, or hiring a prostitute or two or three – anything, it seemed, to get his heart pumping, his brain functioning, his spirit soaring with the excitement of his own work.

Of course (always worrisome) dullness might not be an arbitrary condition. It could be a response. It could be an entirely reasonable reaction to the work at hand. It could have to do with the very real possibility that whatever is being written is entirely without merit. I'm not sure that people who are not writers appreciate the sheer terror of this – that the difference between triumph and disaster can be only an adjustment in tone, a shift of voice, a structural re-ordering that, for some reason, the writer can't see. Writing is a kind of self-hypnosis, really – the ability of a writer to believe, completely, in the story that he or she is struggling to tell. That being the case, it's possible for a writer to believe almost anything about his own work: unfortunately, this includes believing that something that's really bad, isn't.

The world of the writer, writing – the only world in which the writer is entirely engaged – is largely unknown to most people, even to those who live with a writer, writing. "How did work go today, dear?" is not a question that writers welcome – not because they are too self-obsessed to communicate with the world beyond their own skin (an accusation often hurled, along with the occasional piece of crockery, in their direction), but because frequently it is not at all clear to them how work is going. Or if it's going anywhere at all. There are days when it appears to be going backward.

There's nothing wrong with book tours and shortlists and interviews on the CBC. The Canadian literary world is infinitely better off with the Giller Prize, the Governor General's Awards, the Charles Taylor Prize, and the Writers' Trust of Canada prizes than it would be without them. Those who finance, support, celebrate, and work toward the success of these events deserve a nation's thanks – because you don't actually have to be Methuselah to remember a time when a glamorous literary event and all the razzle-dazzle of its attendant publicity was the wildest of fantasies.

That said, it should also be quietly but insistently pointed out that this has nothing directly to do with writing. It has to do with marketing, which is important. It has to do with booksellers, who are crucial. It has to do with trying to make it possible for a writer to earn a living and for a publishing house to turn a profit – which is very important indeed. It also has to do with celebrating an aspect of culture that is important everywhere and which, in Canada at any rate, was unheralded for far too long. But in the end, no real writer – another way of saying: no good writer – has ever written a word for the purpose of winning a prize or publishing a bestseller. These may be the results of a writer's efforts, and there's no reason not to think of them as happy results. They may be hoped for, even longed for – but they are not part of the equation that is the work. They cannot be what a writer has in mind while engaged in that most secret and obscure of activities: writing.

The reviews, the jealousies, and the gossip that attend book releases, as well as the rankings that are always part of prizes and sales, are either distractions or advertisements, but they are oddly irrelevant to the connection between reader and writer. Writers always look slightly uncomfortable at literary functions, and I sometimes think it's because they realize that their real selves are elsewhere: moving like shamans through the pages they've written. And readers, I've noticed, often look awkward in the presence of writers: as if they, too, know that the most authentic version of themselves is the one that dances with the writer's story – and not the one standing in front of a stranger asking how he likes Toronto.

I've sat in the sunshine on a dock with the Ian McEwan I know. I've lost track of a grey Sunday afternoon with that Ian McEwan. He's always clear and precise. He's never dull, and when I'm in his company, I never am either. Sometimes it's best to keep it that way.

ALISTAIR**MacLEOD**

Some Thoughts on Writing

I have been writing for a long time. I was always interested in writing and reading, and I was someone who very much enjoyed going to school. I liked to discover new things and one of the ways to do so was through reading the thoughts and observations of others. I could always appreciate rhyme and rhythm and could always carry a tune. I suppose I was like someone who could sing but never thought of making music a career or, perhaps, like someone with athletic ability who never thought much about it – never fantasized about life in the NHL or the NBA or CFL (probably a good thing).

In college and university I wrote for the student papers. I had some poems published and some stories. I did not belong to the "creative writing clubs" for reasons I now find difficult to ascertain. Perhaps they were "by invitation only" or perhaps I was just not interested. I never was much of a "joiner" and this characteristic persists to this day. Whether it is a strength or a weakness I am not sure.

After some years of teaching in my native Nova Scotia I decided to apply for a Ph.D. This was in the early sixties and at the time there were not a lot of doctoral programs in English available within Canada. So I turned to the United States. I wanted to go to a university which was concerned with the "creation" of literature as well as the criticism of it and such a university proved difficult to find. I did, however, receive some very good offers and to this day I am appreciative. I was a good student and I was motivated but I did not have any money (or not nearly enough), and the offers I received presented a vista of possibilities that literally changed my life.

I decided to go to Notre Dame because people whom I respected said it would be a good place for me. There was a gifted creative writing teacher there named Frank O'Malley and one of his students, Edwin O'Connor, had recently published a novel called *The Last Hurrah*, which had received great critical acclaim. Unfortunately for me, Frank O'Malley had retired by the time I reached Notre Dame, although I did talk to him socially on a number of occasions.

In retrospect, it seemed two major things happened to me at graduate school. In the process of jumping through the hoops (passing the German exam, passing the French exam, passing the Latin exam, passing the courses, passing the comprehensives, finding an adviser, submitting a dissertation proposal, writing a dissertation, defending a dissertation, teaching undergraduates), one was constantly in "the presence of literature" and one did learn a lot about it. In my case my original interest in the creation of literature rather than the mere criticism of it was heightened by the whole experience. Instead of just writing another paper on James Joyce's "The Dead" or William Faulkner's "A Rose For Emily," I was drawn to the possibility of writing stories of my own.

Secondly, I was away from Canada and my home landscape for an extended period of time. I am not sure if it was a case of "absence makes the heart grow fonder," but I did become more thoughtful about where I came from and the issues that emerged from that particular geographical region. I decided to set any stories that I might write in the landscape that I knew best. There were a lot of precedents. Much of my graduate work involved British Literature of the nineteenth or early twentieth century, and there was a plethora of great literature written by people who did not come from urban backgrounds, including the Brontës, Thomas Hardy, and D.H. Lawrence, among others. By the time I made my decision, I was quite certain as to the path I would follow and so far I have not wavered in my commitment. That good literature can come from anyplace is something worth remembering.

It has been said that serious writers write about "what worries them." This may sound a bit extreme, but I believe that serious writers write about what they are most thoughtful about and obviously "worrying" is an aspect of thinking. No one worries who does not think. In a country as vast as Canada, concerns and worries vary across the landscape. Sometimes the worries are based on geography. Newfoundland people worry about the fishery, ranchers on the prairies worry about the "mad cow" issue and its fallout, B.C. loggers are concerned about soft-wood. As I write this in the autumn of 2005 there is great concern expressed in the Toronto papers regarding "what to do with our garbage." Many of these concerns are quite regional. Obviously no one in Medicine Hat or Iqaluit is very concerned about Toronto's garbage. In large countries it has always been so and the varied worries associated with different people from different geographical and cultural backgrounds present themselves in the literature emanating from such diverse sources. The protagonists of the early F. Scott Fitzgerald stories are often concerned with how they will fit in at Princeton. They worry a lot. No one, however, in the world of Flannery O'Connor ever worries much about Princeton and certainly no one does in the oeuvre of Richard Wright. Yet to write of the specific in the hope of striking the universal chord seems to me to be a fine idea.

I have long believed that writing is a communicative act; that the writer is sending out letters to the world, as someone once said, and that he or she is hopeful that the world will receive the letters and be affected in some way. Perhaps the world will write back!

I, myself, have been appreciative in that what I have to say has been so well received by the larger world. I have been impressed that stories set in Canada, or, even more specifically, in Cape Breton, have travelled so well and so far and, it seems, have been welcomed by the readership of so many cultures.

I would not say that when I was penning my sentences I was thinking that they would impress the Japanese, the Israelis, the Bengalis, the Turks, or any of the other cultures that have deemed them worthy of translation. But I am pleased. Pleased that such sentences have struck a responsive chord that sounds the note of our shared humanity. This may well be what the "writing life" signifies; that it is a life of communication which helps us to recognize the great within the small and makes us feel less lonely than we are.

MARGARET**MacMILLAN**

Writing History

Sometimes I hate it, the writing of history. I find myself in archives, sneezing because of the dust and feeling lonely. I tell myself that research is only for the young, who find it possible to concentrate for hours on end, and do not mind the boxes of papers that turn out not to contain anything useful at all. I wander around libraries looking for books. That's always salutary in a depressing sort of way – to see the rows of forgotten authors writing about obscure subjects. Why bother at all?

And then there is the period of trying to do something with all the bits and pieces I have carried back to my study. I shuffle through papers and I search my computer for the notes that I am sure I made, some time ago, somewhere. My brain hurts, or feels as though it ought to, as I wrestle with too much material, too many facts, too many interpretations by other historians. How can I sift them out and put what's left together to tell a good story?

Sometimes, of course, when it all goes well, I think there is nothing I would rather be doing than writing history. There is that feeling of relief and pleasure at being, at last, on top of the material and not under it. Of making a pattern. Of explaining, first to my own satisfaction, and then, I hope, to others, why the past turned out the way it did. Of grasping what it was like then. It is the times when it all works I remember best.

Who knows how we find our particular passions in life? I found history very early on. Perhaps it had something to do with my grandparents. There was the skin of the tiger that my maternal grandfather had shot in India, for example, which we played with until it became too moth-eaten. Then there was the hand grenade my Canadian grandfather brought back from the Great War. We rolled it around on the carpet and only years later found that no one had ever defused it.

I came to history early on mainly through books. My mother read to us from *Our Island's Story*, a wonderful Edwardian book about the British isles, which was all wrong by the lights of our own less bombastic age but had terrific stories. Boadicea (as we knew her; today she is Boudicca) led the local British against the Romans. The picture showed a pre-Raphaelite beauty with streaming golden hair at the reins of her chariot. King Alfred, the very model of an English public school boy, burned his cakes. The very wicked King Richard killed the two angelic boys in the Tower.

I read on my own, everything I could get my hands on. So I remember *Shadows on the Rock*, Willa Cather's extraordinary book about Quebec City. I also remember Black Hawk comic books, all about the Korean War and dreadful, now I think about it, when it came to who was good – always white Americans – and who was bad – always Orientals. I read the endless G.A. Henty books with titles like *With Kitchener in Khartoum* or *With Wolfe in Quebec*. The plots were always the same: a poor but good boy making his way in the world does something heroic and comes to the attention of Kitchener or Wolfe or a dozen other great heroes. I read novels about ancient Rome, the Crusades, and Elizabethan England. Then there was a series – I hope it still exists – on everyday life at particular times in history – in Egypt or Byzantium or China. It told you about what people ate and what games they played and what jobs they did, all those riveting details that make the past real.

I also started writing. At my public school, I wrote an historical play about St. Patrick. When the saint drove the snakes out of Ireland, my mother's stockings filled with paper wriggled across the stage on strings. I did three chapters of a novel, set, I think because I liked the name, in Revelstoke. It was heavily influenced by Enid Blyton, with intrepid and smug children getting the better of adult villains.

I learned to write by writing but I also learned much in school. In those days we learned grammar: I loved the drills where we had to choose "him" or "he" or the right tense of verbs. We wrote essays. When I was briefly at school in England as a teenager, we wrote easily an essay a week. I learned how to organize, how to move from one paragraph to another, and how to write clearly. Our essays came back to us, and not always with kind comments. I remember a dragon, a history teacher, who would not read an essay that did not start well. By the time I was ready for university, I had laid the groundwork for the techniques of writing.

I was also discovering my models: George Orwell, Evelyn Waugh, P.G. Wodehouse. None of them ever wasted a word or used one incorrectly. I loved more elaborate writers like Lord Macaulay but knew that I could not write those complex, orotund sentences. What I did learn from Macaulay, though, was how to balance one sentiment or one idea against another and how to sketch out a character. At the University of Toronto, I discovered Barbara Tuchman when a friend lent me *The Zimmermann Telegram*, one of her first books. All about the foolish attempt by the Germans to entice Mexico to attack the United States during the First World War, the book displayed her strengths as an historian: her ability to tell a story, her fascination with the follies of human beings, and her conviction that the past matters. Then she published *The Guns of August*, that wonderful account of those fatal weeks in 1914 when Europe slid past the point of no return. She has remained a model for me ever since.

Over the years, I have acquired others. William Eccles, a marvellous teacher, whose book on New France in the age of Louis XIV is still one of the best I have read on early Canadian history. Simon Schama, who is able to go from seventeenth-century Holland to nineteenth-century America and whose *Citizens*, on the French Revolution, made everyone look at that much studied event with fresh eyes.

I did not realize when I was younger that I was choosing history (or perhaps it was choosing me), but gradually I left other subjects behind. I liked science, but not enough. English was always fun but somehow it kept escaping me. I could never get a firm grip on it as a subject. I preferred history with its facts and its need for evidence to back up arguments. I was also fortunate that, when I started to take history at the University of Toronto, I found myself in a superb department with a solid and good curriculum. I was lucky too that my year included, although none of us realized it at the time, many future historians. We went to lectures and seminars together and sat in pubs drinking beer and eating cheap sandwiches (only five cents in those days) and talking about our professors and the history they were teaching us.

When I graduated, it seemed sensible to keep going. Anyway I couldn't think of what else I wanted to do. So I went to Oxford and, after a brief flirtation with political science, went back to history with relief. I studied the British in India during the heyday of the Raj, which, among other things, gave me the chance to live in India for a year and gather material for my first book. Then, although I had always said I would never be a teacher, it seemed practical to take a job for a year to pay the bills. I fell into teaching and never really fell out again.

I loved it. It was also the best way to learn history for myself. When you have to explain the Enlightenment or the First World War to students who may not have heard of either, you have to know the subject yourself. You have to be ready to answer simple and difficult questions. What is the difference between right wing and left wing? Well, it depends. On time, on place, on who is speaking.

Teaching made me a better writer because it made me explain things more clearly. It made me aware of how important the texture and feel of the past are if you want to make others interested in it. Barbara Tuchman talked about "the corroborative detail," the one that helps to fix a person or an instant in time. Once heard, how can you forget that story from August 1914, when, as Europe hurtled into a catastrophic war, the British Foreign Secretary, Sir Edward Grey, looked out his window and saw a lamplighter extinguishing the gas lamps in the park? "The lamps," he said, "are going out all over Europe; we shall not see them lit again in our lifetime." Or how can you not remember that Hitler was a vegetarian or that Mao Zedong never brushed his teeth?

I love history because of its richness and its variety and because it poses questions: big questions about war and peace, about how human societies work or could work, and smaller but equally interesting questions about why one culture prefers hot, spicy food and another bland. Why do Canadians eat so many doughnuts? What does tea mean in British culture? I love history for its gossip and for its limitless cast of characters.

I hate it when history is abused, as it so often is. It can trap us in prejudices and hatreds. Think of the Balkans or of Ireland, where memories of battles that happened centuries ago still reverberate, where neighbours do awful things to each other in the name of righting ancient wrongs. And how many times have we all heard someone say confidently that "History teaches us . . ." That Serbs are superior to Croats – or vice versa. That societies need to worship strong leaders. That humans will always make war. Such "lessons" from history are worse than useless. They are used to justify bad and wicked decisions.

Memories, and they need not always be based on fact, play a huge role in the present. History, sometimes very bad history, is used as a basis for claims, to land, for example. Greece claimed great swaths of Turkey after the First World War because in that Golden Age that began six centuries before the birth of Christ, there were Greek city states along the coast of Asia Minor and around the Black Sea. History is also used for validation, when people sharing a religion, perhaps, or a language, start to argue that they are a community deserving certain privileges. As Ernest Renan, the great nineteenth-century French historian and thinker, wrote, "A nation is a group of people united by a mistaken view about the past and a hatred of their neighbours."

We can learn from history, but what we ought to learn is understanding. What I remember of my life and what you remember of yours have helped to make us what we are today, and the same is true of societies. We act, individually or collectively, in certain ways; we make certain assumptions; and we fear certain things – all because of what has already happened to us. If we gain some knowledge of what the other remembers, we will have gone a long way toward understanding. How can we make any sense of the conflict between Jews and Arabs in the Middle East if we know nothing of the memories of both sides? Why is it so important for Jews to have a homeland and why do Arabs not want that homeland in their midst?

Dictators have always understood the power of history. That is why they have so often tried to expunge or rewrite it. The great and dreadful Qin emperor who first united China in 221 BC burned all the history books and buried scholars alive so that only his version of events would survive. Stalin wrote the early Bolsheviks out of the history of the Russian Revolution and made his own part more important than it had really been. As his colleagues disappeared into the Gulag, he edited and re-edited a famous photograph of them all with the revered Lenin just after the Bolshevik victory in 1917. By the end, Stalin, who had been far from Lenin in reality, stands alone beside him and slightly above, apparently pointing the way ahead.

When history refuses to go away or when it is recovered, it can help to bring down regimes. When the Soviet Union finally admitted in the 1980s that Stalin had done a secret deal with Hitler in 1939 to divide up Poland and other parts of Central Europe, that admission helped to destroy what legitimacy the Soviet Empire still had. Within the Soviet Union, Gorbachev's policy of glasnost, under which the horrors of the Great Purges and the famines of the 1930s were finally discussed openly, led many Soviet citizens to see their own regime as one based on lies and crimes. Today, in the People's Republic of China, the Communist Party tries to prevent any discussion of the Cultural Revolution. What, after all, does that dreadful period say about Mao Zedong, the great leader, and the Party itself?

Good history is the history that does not flinch from dealing with the difficult or shameful bits of the past. And good historians are those who keep on digging and asking the awkward questions.

Historians ought to challenge accepted versions of the past. Yet, at the same time they must always respect the evidence, even if it upsets some lovely theory they have painstakingly developed. History changes, as it ought, the more we learn generally. A hundred years ago British and Canadian historians mostly saw the British Empire as a force for progress in the world. We now have a much more complicated view, thanks in part to research by many historians over decades into what that empire actually meant for the African farmers or the Indian weavers who lost their livelihoods because of unrestrained competition from outside.

History can also help us to formulate good questions and to insist on proper answers backed up by good evidence. If we wonder why Iraq is in a chaotic and turbulent state today, we ought to ask about more than the present. Of course it helps to know who is who in that sad country, what its social composition is, and how its society works. But we also need to ask why the Kurds want their own state, and we will only learn the answer if we go back at least to the end of the First World War, when Kurdish nationalism was just beginning to take shape, and when, or so they thought, the Kurds were given a promise by the great powers that they would have a state of their own. If you go to Kurdish websites, you will see references to the Treaty of Lausanne of 1920 where a Kurdistan was mentioned. We also need to know what happened to the Kurds in the years after 1945, when the governments of the countries in which they lived – Turkey, Iran, Iraq – tried to obliterate Kurdish nationalism.

Mark Twain once said, "The past does not repeat itself but it rhymes." History can never be the same twice because it is not like a carefully controlled experiment in a laboratory. The ingredients – the individuals who are making decisions, or the cultures they are embedded in, their geography, economics, and technology – are always a bit different. What knowing history offers us is instructive parallels, the ability to answer the question "What if?" What is likely to happen if outside forces occupy Iraq? The British experience in the 1920s provides some possibilities worth looking out for. What if Russia feels itself ignored and despised by the West? Russian and Soviet history offers many examples of Russian nationalism and Russian leaders turning inwards. As John Gaddis, the distinguished American historian of the Cold War, put it, history is like using the rear-view mirror when you drive. If you only look back you will land in the ditch, but it helps to know where you have come from and who else is on the road. And history can sometimes keep us from making mistakes. Would President Bush have used the term "crusade" for the war on terror after 9/11 if he – or someone – had stopped for a moment to think how the Crusades are still remembered in the Arab world?

History can also teach us humility. Each generation likes to think that it is exceptional, perhaps this present one in the West most of all. An adviser to President Bush boasted about how they in the White House were creating a new world and one in which the United States dominated. "We're an empire now," he said, "and when we act, we create our own reality. And while you're studying that reality – judiciously, as you will – we'll act again, creating other new realities, which you can study too, and that's how things will sort out. We're history's actors . . . and you, all of you, will be left to just study what we do." Well, yes, but also no. We do indeed create the history of the future, but we are also caught up, whether or not we realize it, in past histories – and we ignore them at our peril.

We ought, too, to remember that the past is full of examples of intelligent, brave, and even good people who held views or pursued goals which we now think utterly wrong and absurd. I do not want to make history sound merely as though it is good for you. It should be fun, or so I have always thought. Read it for its entertainment value, though, and you might find yourself wiser as well.

Whether I have become wiser is another matter. Nevertheless I shall always be grateful that I discovered history. I have never regretted my own choice to teach it and to write it.

ALBERTO**MANGUEL**

Room for the Shadow

"No pen, no ink, no table, no room, no time, no quiet, no inclination."
    – James Joyce, letter to his brother, December 7, 1906

I wasn't going to write. For years the temptation kept itself at bay, invisible. Books had the solid presence of the real world and filled my every possible need, whether read out loud to me at first, or later read silently on my own, but always repeating their assurance that what they told me would not change, unlike the rooms in which I slept and the voices heard outside the door. We travelled much, my nurse and I, because my father was in the Argentine diplomatic service, and the various hotel rooms, and even the embassy house in Tel Aviv, lacked the familiarity of certain pages into which I slipped night after night.

After I learned to read, this storyland homecoming no longer depended on my nurse's availability or mood or weariness, but on my own whim alone, and I would return to the books I knew by heart whenever the fancy or the urge took me, following on the page the words recited in my head. In the morning, under one of four palm trees set in a square in the walled embassy garden; during the car drive to the large wild park where wild tortoises crept along the dunes planted with oleander bushes; especially at night, while my nurse, thinking I was asleep, sat at her electric knitting machine and, suffering from mysterious stomach pains that kept her agonizingly awake, worked until well past midnight. To the metronomic rasp of her machine, as she rolled the handle back and forth, in the dim yellow light that she kept on to work by, I would turn to the wall with my open book and read about an Aladdin-like hero called Kleine Muck, about the adventurous dog Crusoe, about the robber bridegroom who drugged his victims with three-coloured wine, about Kay and Gerda and the wicked Ice Queen.

It never occurred to me that I might add something of my own to the books on my shelf. Everything I wanted was already there, at arm's reach, and I knew that, if I wished for a new story, the book-shop only a short walk away from the house had countless more to add to my stock. To invent a story, impossible as the task then seemed to me, would have felt like trying to build another palm tree for the garden or model another tortoise to struggle across the sand. What hope of success? Above all, what need?

We returned to Buenos Aires when I was seven, to a large, amiable house on a cobblestoned street, where I was given my own room perched on the back terrace, separate from the rest of the family. Until then, I had spoken only English and German. I learned to speak Spanish, and, gradually, Spanish books were added to my shelves. And still nothing urged me to write.

Homework, of course, didn't count. "Compositions," as they were called, required one to fill a couple of pages on a given subject, keeping always closer to reportage than to fiction. Imagination wasn't called for. "Portrait of a Family Member," "What I Did on

Sunday," "My Best Friend," elicited a sugary, polite prose, illustrated in coloured pencil with an equally cordial depiction of the
person or event concerned, the whole to be scrutinized by the
teacher for accuracy and spelling mistakes. Only once did I diverge
from the imposed subject. The title given to us was "A Sea Battle,"
the teacher no doubt imagining that his students, all boys, had the
same enthusiasm for war games that he had. I never read the books
on airmen and soldiers that several of my schoolmates enjoyed, the
"Biggles" series for instance, or the short histories of the World
Wars, full of pictures of airplanes and tanks, printed on spongy,
coarse paper. I realized that I completely lacked the requisite
vocabulary for the task. I decided therefore to interpret the title
differently, and wrote a description of a battle between a shark and
a giant squid, no doubt inspired by an illustration from one of my
favourite books, *20,000 Leagues Under the Sea*. I was surprised to
discover that my inventiveness, instead of amusing, angered the
teacher who told me (quite rightly) that I knew very well that it was
not what he had meant. I think that this was my first attempt at
writing a story.

Ambition prompted my second stab at writing. Every year, just
before the summer holidays, the school put on a vaguely patriotic
play, exemplary and dull. I decided that I could write something at
least not worse than these pedagogical dramas and, one evening
after dinner, I sat down and composed a play about the childhood
of one of our ancient presidents, famous, like George Washington,
for never having told a lie. The first scene opened with the boy
facing the dilemma of denouncing a playmate or lying to his
parents; the second portrayed him inventing a story to protect his
friend; in the third, my hero suffered the pangs of a tormented conscience; in the fourth, his loyal friend confessed to the awful crime;
the fifth showed our hero repenting from his lie, thus adroitly

circumventing the real dilemma. The play bore a title that had the virtue of being, if not inspiring, at least clear: *Duty or Truth*. It was accepted and staged, and I experienced for the first time the thrill of having the words I had written read out loud by somebody else.

I was twelve at the time and the success of the experience led me to try and repeat it. I had written *Duty or Truth* in a few hours; in a few more hours I tried to write an imitation of *The Sorcerer's Apprentice* (inspired by Disney's *Fantasia*), a religious drama in which Buddha, Moses, and Christ were the main protagonists, and an adaptation of "Falada, the Talking Horse," taken from the Brothers Grimm. I finished none of them. I realized that if reading is a contented, sensuous occupation whose intensity and rhythm are agreed upon between the reader and the chosen book, writing instead is a strict, plodding, physically demanding task in which the pleasures of inspiration are all well and good, but are only what hunger and taste are to a cook: a starting-point and a measuring-rod, not the main occupation. Long hours, stiff joints, sore feet, cramped hands, the heat or cold of the working place, the anguish of missing ingredients and the humiliation due to the lack of know-how, onions that make you cry and sharp knives that slice your fingers, are what is in store for anyone who wants to prepare a good meal or write a good book. At twelve, I wasn't willing to give over even a couple of evenings to the writing of a piece. What for? I settled comfortably back into my role as reader.

Books continued to seduce me, and I loved anything that had to do with them. During my Buenos Aires adolescence, I was lucky enough to come across a number of well-known writers. First in an English-German bookstore where I worked between school hours, and later at a small publishing company where I apprenticed as an editor, I met Jorge Luis Borges, Adolfo Bioy Casares, Silvina Ocampo, Marta Lynch, Marco Denevi, Eduardo Mallea, José Bianco, and many others. I liked the company of writers and yet I felt very shy among them. I was, of course, almost invisible to them, but, from time to time, one would notice me and ask: "Do you write?" My answer was always "No." It was not that I didn't wish, occasionally, to be like them and have my name on a book that other people would admire. It was simply that I was aware, very clearly, that nothing that I could produce would ever merit sitting on the same shelf as the books I loved. To imagine that a book written by me might one day rub covers with a novel by Conrad or Kafka was not only an unthinkable notion but an incongruous one. Even an adolescent, in spite of all his overwhelming arrogance, has a sense of the ridiculous.

But I listened. I heard Bioy discuss the need to plot carefully the successive episodes in a story so as to know exactly where the characters are headed, and then cover the tracks, leaving only a few clues for the readers to think that they are discovering something invisible to the writer. I heard Silvina Ocampo explain why the tragedy of small things, of very ordinary people, was more moving than that of complex and powerful characters. I heard Marta Lynch speak passionately, enviously, of Chekhov, Denevi of Buzzati, Mallea of Sartre and Dostoevsky. I heard Borges break down a Kipling story into its many parts and reassemble it, like a clockmaker inspecting a precious ancient instrument. I listened to these writers tell me how the stuff that I read had been made. It was like standing in a workshop and hearing the masters argue about the strongest materials, the best combinations, the tricks and devices by which something can be made to balance at a difficult angle or keep on ticking indefinitely, or about how something can be built to look impossibly slim and simple and yet hold a myriad complex springs and cogwheels. I listened not in order to learn a new craft but to better know my own.

In 1968, having decided not to follow a university career, I left for Europe and did desultory freelance work for a number of publishers. The pay was abysmal, and I seldom had enough money for more than a few meals a week. One day, I heard that an Argentine paper was offering a five-hundred-dollar prize for the best short stories. I decided to apply. I quickly wrote, in Spanish, four stories that were readable, formally correct but utterly lifeless. I asked the Cuban novelist Severo Sarduy, whom I had met in Paris and who wrote in a rich, exuberant, baroque Spanish that resonated with literary allusions, to read them over for me. He told me they were awful. "You use words like an accountant," he said. "You don't ask words to perform for you. Here you have a character who falls and loses one of his contact lenses. You say that he lifts himself 'half blind' from the floor. Think harder. The word you want is 'Cyclops.'" I obediently wrote "Cyclops" in the story and sent the lot off. A few months later, I heard that I had won. I felt more embarrassed than proud, but was able to eat properly for a couple of months.

Still I wouldn't write. I scribbled a few essays, a few poems, all atrocious. My heart wasn't in it. Like someone who loves music and tries his hand at the piano, I undertook the experience less out of passion than out of curiosity, to see how it was done. Then I stopped. I worked for publishers, I selected manuscripts and saw them through the press, I imagined titles for other people's books and put together anthologies of different kinds. Everything I did was always in my capacity as reader. "David was talented and knew how to compose psalms. And I? What am I capable of?" asked Rabbi Ouri in the eighteenth century. His answer was: "I can recite them."

I published my first book in 1980. *The Dictionary of Imaginary Places* was the result of a collaboration with Gianni Guadalupi, whom I had met when we were both working for the same Italian publisher. The idea for the book was Gianni's: a serious guide to fictional countries, for which we read over two thousand books, with an energy that one possesses when one is young. Writing the *Dictionary* was not what I would today call writing: it was more like summing up the books we read, detailing the geography, customs, history, flora and fauna of places such as Oz, Ruritania, Christianopolis. Gianni would send me his notes in Italian, I would translate them into English and recast them into a dictionary entry, always sticking to a Baedecker style. Because we use words for a vast number of things, writing is easily confused with other activities: recounting (as in our *Dictionary*), scribbling impressions, instructing, reporting, informing, chatting, dogmatizing, reviewing, sweet-talking, making pronouncements, advertising, proselytizing, preaching, cataloguing, informing, describing, briefing, taking notes. We perform these tasks with the help of words, but none of these, I'm certain, constitutes writing.

Two years later I arrived in Canada. On the strength of the *Dictionary*, I was asked to review books for newspapers, talk about books on the radio, translate books into English, and adapt books into plays. I was perfectly content discussing books that had been familiar to my friends when I was young but were new to the Canadian reader, or reading for the first time Canadian classics that mysteriously mirrored others from far away and long ago. I found that the library I had begun when I was four or five kept growing nightly, ambitiously, relentlessly. Books had always grown around me. Now, in my house in Toronto, they covered every wall, they crowded every room. They kept growing. I had no intention of adding my own scribbles to their proliferation.

Instead, I practised different forms of reading. The possibilities offered by books are legion. The solitary relationship of a reader with his book breaks into dozens of further relationships: with friends upon whom we urge the books we like, with book-sellers (the few who have survived in the Age of Supermarkets) who suggest new titles, with strangers for whom we might compile an anthology. A book we loved in our youth is suddenly recalled by someone to whom it was long ago recommended, the reissue of a book we thought forgotten makes it again new to our eyes, a story read in one context becomes a different story under a different cover. We never enter the same book twice.

Then, by chance, because of an unanswered question, my attitude toward writing changed. I've told the story before, elsewhere. A friend who had gone into exile during the military dictatorship in Argentina revealed to me that one of my high-school teachers, someone who had been essential in fostering my love of literature, had willingly denounced his students to the military police, knowing that they would be taken and tortured and sometimes killed. This was the teacher who had spoken to us of Kafka, of Ray Bradbury, of the murder of Polyxena (I can still hear his voice when I read the lines) in the medieval Spanish romance that begins:

> A la qu'el sol se ponía
> en una playa desierta,
> yo que salía de Troya
> por una sangrienta puerta,
> delante los pies de Pirro
> vide a Polyxena muerta . . .*

---

* "At the hour of the setting sun/ On a deserted beach/ I, leaving Troy/ Through a bloodied door/ At Pyrrhus' feet/ Saw Polyxena lying dead." Polyxena, daughter of Hecuba and Priam, was sacrificed by Achilles' son Neoptolemus (also known as Pyrrhus) to appease his father's ghost.

After the revelation, I was left with the impossibility of deciding whether to deny the worth of his teaching or the evil of his actions, or to attempt to grasp the monstrous combination of both, alive in the same person. To give a shape to my question I wrote a novel, *News from a Foreign Country Came*.

From what I've heard, most writers know, from a very early age, that they will write. Something of themselves reflected in the outside world, in the way others see them, or the way they see themselves lending words to daily objects – to trees, skies, the eyes of a dog, the dim sunlight on a snowy morning – something tells them they are writers, like something tells their friends that they are doctors or dentists. Something convinces them that they are chosen for this particular task and that, when they grow up, their name will be stamped on the cover of a book, like a pilgrim's badge. I think something told me I was to be a reader. The encounter with my exiled friend happened in 1988; it was therefore not till I turned forty that the notion of becoming a writer appeared to me as possible. Forty is a time of change, of retrieving from ancient cupboards whatever it is we left behind, packed away in the dark, and of reconsidering its latent forces.

My intention was clear. That the result wasn't successful doesn't change the nature of my purpose. Now I wanted to write. I wanted to write a novel. I wanted to write a novel that would put into words – literary words, words like the ones that made up the books on my shelves, incandescent words – what seemed to me impossible to be spoken. I tried. In between my bread-and-butter jobs, early in the mornings or late at night, in hotel rooms and in cafés when an assignment forced me to travel, I cobbled together the story of a man of two natures, or of a single divided nature. *Dr. Jekyll and Mr. Hyde*, read during one terrified night when I was thirteen, was never far from my thoughts. I felt desperate for a long chunk of time to work continuously on my novel, so as not to lose the pace, the sequence, the logic, and the rhythm. I convinced myself that I could recapture the thread after days or weeks of interruption. I pretended that the lack of concentration didn't matter and that I'd be able to pick up where I'd left off, just as I'd pick up a story I was reading at the place where I'd left my book-mark. I was wrong, but lack of uninterrupted time was not the only reason for my failure. The lessons from the masters during my ado-lescence seemed now to be of no avail. A few scenes worked. The novel didn't.

Readers can tell when a sentence works or doesn't, when it breathes and rises and falls to the beat of its own sense, or when it stands stiff as if embalmed. Readers who turn to writing can rec-ognize this too, but they can never explain it. The most a writer can do is learn the rules of grammar and spelling, and the business of reading. Beyond this, whatever excellence he may achieve will be the result of simply doing what he's trying to learn, learning to write by writing, in a beautiful vicious circle that illuminates (or can illuminate) itself at each new turn. "There are three rules for writing a good book," said Somerset Maugham. "Unfortunately, no one knows what they are."

Experience of life everyone has; the knack for transforming it into *literary* experience is what we lack. And even if one were granted that alchemical talent, what experience is a writer allowed to use in trying to tell a story? The death of her mother, like the narrator in Alice Munro's "Material"? His guilty desire, as in Thomas Mann's "Death in Venice"? The blood of a loved one, like the master who sees his disciple beheaded and thinks how beau-tiful the scarlet colour is on the green floor, in Marguerite Yourcenar's "How Wang Fo Was Saved"? Is he entitled to use even the intimate life of his family, his friends, of those who trusted in him and might be horrified to find themselves speaking private words in front of a reading public? When Marian Engel, in the company of other authors, heard of something, however confidential, that appealed to her, she'd shout out "Called it!" claiming for her writing the juicy tidbit. Apparently, in the realm of writing, there are no moral restrictions on hunting and gathering.

I, too, tried to work from experience, seeking there moments and events to furnish the thing I was calling up from the shadows. I chose for my main character the face of a man I had once seen in the paper, a gentle, knowledgeable, kindly face which I later discovered belonged to Klaus Barbie. That misleading face suited my character perfectly as did the name, Berence, a name I borrowed from a strange gentleman I met on the ship from Buenos Aires to Europe, a writer who was in the habit of travelling back and forth across the Atlantic, never spending time in the port of destination, and who one night, when I was suffering from a bad cold and a high fever, told me the story of Lafcadio who commits the gratuitous act of pushing the unworldly Amédée off a moving train, in Gide's *Les Caves du Vatican*. I depicted Algiers according to my memories of Buenos Aires (another pseudo-French city on the sea), and Northern Quebec according to my memories of a visit to Percé. In order to bring the story to its close, I needed to describe the workings of a torturer, but not the torture itself. I imagined someone applying the brutal methods not to a person but to something inert, lifeless. My unattended fridge contained an old celery stalk. I imagined what it would be like to torture it. The scene, mysteriously, turned out to be exactly right. But I still had to give words to the torturer's self-justification. I didn't know how to do it. "You have to bring yourself to think like him," my friend Susan Swan advised. I didn't think I was capable. Humiliatingly, when I tried again, I found that I could think the torturer's thoughts.

But in spite of a few successful moments, the writing grated, stumbled, fell flat. To say that a man enters a room, or that the light in the garden has changed, or that the child felt that she was being threatened, or any simple, precise thing that we communicate (or believe we communicate) every moment of every day, is, I discovered, one of the most difficult of literary endeavours. We believe the task is easy because our listener, or our reader, carries the epistemological weight and is supposed to intuit our message, to know what we mean. But in fact, the signs that stand for the sounds that spark the thoughts that conjure up the memory that dredges up the experience that calls upon the emotion all crumble under the weight of what they must carry and barely, hardly ever, serve the purpose for which they were designed. When they do, the reader knows the writer has succeeded, and is grateful for the miracle.

Chesterton observes in one of his essays that "Somewhere embedded in every ordinary book are the five or six words for which really all the rest will be written." I think every reader can find them in the books he loves; I'm not certain that every writer can. As to my novel, I have a vague notion of what those words might be, and now (so many years after the fact) I feel that they would have sufficed, if they had come to me then, at the beginning.

The book was not what I had imagined, but now I too was a writer. Now I too was in the hands (in a very literal sense) of readers who had no proof of my existence except my book, and who judged me, cared for me, or, more likely, dismissed me without any consideration for anything else I could offer beyond the strict limits of the page. Who I was, who I had been, what my opinions were, what my intentions, how deep my knowledge of the subject, how heartfelt my concern for its central question, was immaterial to them. Like the Gnat in *Through the Looking-Glass*, always telling Alice that "you might make a joke on that," the writer wishes to tell the reader "you might laugh at the absurdity of this passage" or "you might weep over this scene" but, like Alice, the reader is bound to answer: "If you're so anxious to have a joke made, why don't you make one yourself?" Whatever I had not managed to convey in my novel wasn't there, and no self-respecting reader would supply the jokes and sorrows that I had left out. In this sense, I'm always puzzled by the generosity with which certain readers agree to mend the deficiencies of dismal writers; perhaps a book has to be not just mediocre but outright bad to elicit a reader's Samaritan response.

I don't know what – of the mass of advice given to me by the masters, of the books that set examples, of the exemplary events I witnessed and cautionary gossip I heard throughout my life – was responsible for my few successful pages. The process of learning to write is heartbreaking because it is unaccountable. No amount of hard work, splendid purpose, good counsel, impeccable research, harrowing experiences, knowledge of the classics, ear for music and taste for style, can guarantee good writing. Something, driven by what the ancients called the Muse and we bashfully call inspiration, chooses and combines, snips, stitches, and mends a coat of words to clothe whatever it is stirs in our depths, ineffable and immaterial, a shadow. Sometimes, for reasons that never become clear, everything fits: the shape is right, the point of view is right, the tone and colouring are right, and, for the space of a line or a paragraph, the shadow can be seen fully fledged in all its awful mystery, not translated into anything else, not in service of an idea or an emotion, not even as part of a story or an essay, but as sheer epiphany: writing that is, as the old metaphor has it, exactly equivalent to the world.

During the first half of the eighteenth century, it was customary in France for theatregoers, if they were rich, to pay for seats not in the orchestra or the boxes, but directly onstage, a practice so popular that often this intrusive public outnumbered the cast. During the premiere of Voltaire's play *Sémiramis*, there were so many spectators onstage that the actor playing King Ninus's ghost stumbled and nearly fell, thus spoiling a key dramatic scene. Among the ensuing peals of laughter, Voltaire is said to have stood up and cried out: "*Place à l'ombre!*" "Make room for the shadow!"

The anecdote is useful. Like the stage, the writing life is made up of carefully balanced artifice, exact inspirational lighting, right timing, precise music, and the secret combination of craft and experience. For reasons of chance, money, prestige, friendship, and family duties, the writer allows onto the stage, to sit in on the performance, a crowd of intruders who then become involuntary participants, taking up space, spoiling a good effect, tripping the actors, and who eventually turn into excuses, reasons for failure, honourable distractions, and justifiable temptations. Success in writing (I mean, writing something good) depends on tiny, brittle things, and while it is true that genius can override all obstacles – Kafka wrote masterpieces in a corridor of his father's hostile house and Cervantes dreamt up his *Quixote* in prison – mere talent requires less crowded, less constrained mental settings than those that most writers usually enjoy. The shadow needs room. And even then, nothing is promised.

For the time being, the reader I am judges the writer I chose to become with amused tolerance, as he invents strategies for his new craft. The shadow flitting in the gloom is infinitely powerful and fragile, and immensely alluring, and beckons (I think it beckons) to me as I cross from one side of the page to the other.

YANN**MARTEL**

Writing Death

Why am I writing about the Holocaust? I've asked myself that question many times since I've embarked on my current project. It's certainly not the easiest subject under the sun, if you're in the business of spinning stories.

For starters, stories operate on a number of well-known precepts. One of them is character development. In a story, at least one character must change in a significant way. This change may be only a hint of a change, a fleeting moment of illumination, but it must nonetheless lead the reader to see the character in a new light, as a new character, one transformed at least mentally. The reader sees this change in relation to his or her experience of life, and this parallel between character and reader, between reality and fancy, is the catalyst that makes a story work.

One of the many problems for the writer who seeks to deal with the Holocaust is the lack of character development among the Nazis. Take SS *Unterscharführer* Schillinger. His story quickly spread among inmates and was eventually set in print by a number of writers, including Tadeusz Borowski and Filip Müller. Another transport of Jews had arrived at Auschwitz-Birkenau and was about to be gassed. They were in the changing room next to the gas chamber and had been ordered to undress. At that moment, scanning the crowd of dazed Jews, Schillinger fixed his gaze on a particular woman, and something happened. There are variations in the details – understandable considering the intensity of the moment and the complete surprise of what took place next – but it seems to have been something quite simple: Schillinger felt desire. Was the woman a voluptuous beauty whose nudity he found exciting? It seems scarcely imaginable in the circumstances; the Jews in that room would have been of all ages – entire families, from young children to elderly grandparents – and they would have been oozing fear and humiliation from their every pore at having to strip to nakedness in front of each other and the guards. But Schillinger was an SS guard, after all, convinced that he was doing vital racial hygiene work, and he would have been as indifferent to the feelings of the Jews as a worker in a slaughterhouse would be to those of the animals he is about to kill. So why wouldn't he feel desire if the woman was beautiful? Or did the woman play a role? Did she lead him on? Some writers report that she began to dance in a seductive way. At any rate, Schillinger was aroused, and he approached the woman. Was he intent on raping her then and there? (Where? Had he thought of some nook, somewhere between the gas chamber and the crematorium, where he could help himself? Was this something he had done before? That other guards did?) Was he dragging her off to place her in the women's camp so that he could rape her later? The answer will never be known because the woman deftly grabbed the pistol from Schillinger's holster and shot him twice in the stomach. Such a fearless stand against an SS guard was astonishing. The woman died right away, some say shot by another guard, others say murdered with the whole transport, which, after much pandemonium, was pushed into the gas chamber and finished off in the usual way. But her feat survived, as a galvanizing tale to the prisoners and as a cautionary one to the guards. As for Schillinger, he was carried out of the changing room, clutching his stomach, mortally wounded. And do you know what he was whimpering? Do you know what his last words were, according to Borowski?

"O Gott, mein Gott, was hab' ich getan, dass ich so leiden muss?"

"Oh God, my God, what have I done to deserve such suffering?"

How can you tell a credible story with such a character? The man remained as obtusely evil in the last moments of his life as he was when he was first heard of. He was absolutely static, inhabiting a psychic morass that led not only to his own death but even to the death of any possible story about him. Or rather, to be more accurate, Schillinger's story is one that can be told *once*, accounted for, but beyond that, it strains the limits of fiction by being so flimsy, so one-dimensional. The ludicrously evil Nazi who barks away in German – while historically accurate – simply doesn't work in good fiction. It did for a few decades after the Second World War, while the historical accuracy – stench? – was still fresh in everyone's mind, but now? Now, it's stale. None of the Nazis, big or small, make for characters a fiction writer can develop in a compelling way. Even Hitler, surely the best-known political figure of the twentieth century, remains shrouded in impenetrable mystery. He is credible neither in myth nor in reality, but floats above them both, glowering in a nimbus of impossibly implausible evil. Perhaps it is in our curious nature as a species to be able to understand – but be dubious of – absolute good (Jesus Christ, to take only one of many possible examples) while believing without any doubt – but without understanding – absolute evil.

And the Jews remain as character-fixed too, although at the opposite end of the spectrum. No matter their individual moral character – no doubt some of the Jews who died in the Holocaust were liars, cheats, swindlers, thieves, murderers, whatnot – they nonetheless remain forever undeserving of their fate at the hands of the Nazis, who never bothered to ascertain the individual moral worth of the people they were killing. The Nazis famously did not kill just bad Jews; they killed *all* Jews. Including 1.5 million children. *1.5 million.* What do you do with that, as an artist, what *can* you do? If the SS guard is a coarse ball of the poorest quality wool impossible to unmat and spin into a narrative thread, then the child victim is the contrary: a ball of such light, ethereal wool that it simply vanishes between the fingers.

And that's only one problem, of flimsy, cardboard characters. Art also operates on a shared notion of meaningfulness. After reading a book or seeing a play, both artist and reader must feel that something meaningful has taken place. It needn't be something moral. Art simply records life, the experience of life, from one artist's point of view. That an artist's point of view might coincide with a moral point of view is just that, coincidence. But that art is morally neutral does not make it meaningless. On the contrary, art only works based upon some mutual understanding of meaningfulness. Thus the character who, Oedipus-like, fails because of his flaws, instructs us in how not to fail. We understand him, even if he didn't understand himself. We get meaning out of watching him.

But where is the meaningfulness with the Nazis? They did heinous evil zealously convinced that they were doing great good. What to us stands as unforgivable genocide was to them salutary nation-building. What to us is pathology was to them ideology. There's simply no common ground.

The matter is even more vexing when it comes to the Jews. How can you write a story – with a beginning, a middle, and an end, bounded by a nice framework – out of the killing of unknown person after unknown person after unknown person? Because that was an essential quality of the Jews in the Holocaust, their *unknownness* – not to themselves, of course, but to the Nazis and, alas, to us. How can you have a meaningful story with characters you don't know? This lack of a clear role affects not only the writer who wants to write about the Holocaust, but even affected the Jews themselves at the time, because the single characteristic – Jewishness – which the Nazis hated so much was one that was mostly irrelevant to the many Jewish victims who were assimilated. Hence the feeling of surreal meaninglessness about what was happening to them, which has been passed on down to us. Hence the fame of that anonymous memorial of a number: 6 million. Hence the weak role designation: *victims.* Compare that pale role to the roles people take on in war, another well-known epic tragedy. War is infinitely more amenable to artistic treatment because it is a tragedy literally full of character, of characters – officer, soldier, enemy soldier, resistance fighter, collaborator, nurse, villager, the women and children left at home, etc. – each instantly understood and metaphorically easy to grasp. Thus the multiple narrative possibilities of war. War is a broad stage upon which any number of plays can be set – adventures, historical dramas, romances, thrillers, comedies – with any number of characters and any number of resolutions. But the Holocaust? During the Holocaust, 6 million Jews were thrust into a role, and onto a stage, that meant nothing to them, before an audience who detested them with a passion. Of course, there were many instances of Jewish resistance during the Holocaust, instances that pulled them out of their status as victims, but to little significant effect. Any Holocaust story that isn't weighed down with the death of

6 million Jewish human beings risks the danger of trivializing their suffering. Indeed, a Holocaust story is defined by that weight. That is to say, the hallmark of a Holocaust story is its soul-destroying meaninglessness.

You try writing a story about that.

So what do you do with the Holocaust if you are a writer? What have others done?

The most common offering has been to take the stance of the witness, to turn the page into a sort of camera. In other words, to attempt to reconstitute what was rather than constitute something new. Which has meant much writing in the mode of social realism. Historical drama. Fiction that doesn't feel like fiction. Fiction that tries to make a space for itself chameleon-like amidst all the Holocaust diaries and memoirs.

But I – and I'm sorry to intrude with my little *I*, please forgive me, but it is in the nature of the artist to push forward his or her own artistic opinion – I'd like to try something different. To be a witness is not only good but essential. Where would we be in our knowledge of the Holocaust if it were not for the Primo Levis and the Anne Franks? But art is more than witness. Art is also artifice, invention, a creation of the mind independent of the world such that the world might be recreated in the light of that creation. Art then becomes memory. Art becomes human understanding at its fullest. I believe that we human beings are narrative animals and that if history does not become story to us – if it does not lose its first two letters – then it is not truly with us. So we must loose imagination from the strictures of Holocaust witness and see how it mixes with those dreadful events. Out of the blackness of Stalinism and its 20 million dead, George Orwell derived *Animal Farm*. Is there not some equivalent that might be squeezed out of the Holocaust, some narrative that works as art with characters that can stand on their own?

I'm trying. It's not easy. I've been wrestling for months on end now with the blackness of the Holocaust, and I have yet to see much light. But I think it's worth the effort.

ANNE**MICHAELS**

The Least of It

There are questions, two or three. They always seem most disparate, but something tells me they are not, though I cannot yet see how they connect. They haunt. I wait to see if they will fade or answer themselves. A year; longer. They become more insistent, not less. Every question is, of course, at its core, an idea. An image, very visceral, begins to grow in meaning. No longer an image: a metaphor – with ganglia attached to other metaphors. The image contains a character, then another character, then a third. I feel great compassion for these characters who need a language for their grief.

Every historical event of immense loss connects to other events in history. Sometimes it is very difficult to discern the connections. But if the questions are deep enough, they are always there. At the wrong depth, one finds nothing.

I begin to feel the shape, and who must do the telling. Many months are spent thinking before I begin to write. What is unimportant begins to burn away.

Research. Years of research. Books that lead to other books. Places that lead to other places. Wild goose chases, mad lateral jumps that only make sense later. Always the risk of time-consuming mistakes. But one must be sure. As the pile of books grows, my ignorance accumulates.

From the start, one renegotiates again, for the thousandth upon thousandth time, one's relationship with failure. Failure is inevitable; it cannot be otherwise. And one begins to glimpse what is at stake, the price that will be paid for going all the way, into material that eats one alive. Those are the only questions to follow, the ones that are unbearable, and whose "answer" has nothing to do with consolation.

As honestly as possible, I try to enter those questions without an agenda – political, psychological, philosophical, or emotional. One must grind one's preconceptions, biases, assumptions against every possible refutation. This is a very painful process. But in the end, one begins to understand something new.

The integrity of the ideas themselves forces one to give up the desire for solace. One longs for resolution, but only for the resolution that feels infinitesimally true – for those characters, for those events.

Nothing in the language of the book, not one comma, must ever betray those ideas, those events, or those characters. Nor stand in the way. A single whole, down to the last syllable.

If there is no hope – hope born in this way, to be given to the reader from this work – then I keep the book to myself. For me, it is essential that the reader reach land.

For the writer, true consolation is often shocking; it is cold water thrown on the fire of self-delusion. For the writer, false consolation is an unbearable idea. But, for a character, there are times when false consolation – conscious or unconscious self-delusion – is necessary, and the writer must allow her character the private mercy of wild hope.

It takes years for the worm of grief to eat its way through the brain and heart.

There are things one will never write about. To know this, the precise territory and destinations, is as important as what one writes about. That is part of the truth at the heart of every word written. No matter how "confessional" or "autobiographical." What is autobiography but everything written around what has been left out? The missing electron that gives the molecule away. Heisenberg's hide-and-seek. For the reader, this is everything; the way another's words illuminate our privacy. For the writer too. Whether we know or not. Much better to try to know.

One tunnels a passage. Where we arrive, if we arrive, words are the least of it.

ROHINTON**MISTRY**

Welcome to Acadan

There was a time and there wasn't a time when a young man from a faraway land decided to travel to the country of Acadan. He journeyed alone, but took with him a special attaché case besides the mix of hope and regret, optimism and doubt that all immigrants carry.

Upon arrival he presented himself to the immigration officer, who examined his documents and made vigorous use of a red inkpad and some rubber stamps.

"Okay, everything's in order," said the officer. "Next."

Clutching his documents, the young man remained at the counter.

"OKAY!" the officer repeated. "YOU – GO – NOW! EVERYTHING – OKAY!"

"Yes, but . . ."

"You need help? Speak Punjabi? Urdu, Hindi, what?"

"Why, yes," said the immigrant. "Indeed, I do speak some Hindi, but I'm afraid my accent is rather poor and my vocabulary quite limited. Do *you* speak it?"

"Of course not, I was offering to get an interpreter. You're holding up the line."

"Well, you see, I . . . people like me, in many parts of the world, have heard that Acadan is a land of opportunity, where hard work is rewarded, and human rights respected, where society has a vision of justice and fairness for all, whether they arrived four hundred years ago or four hours ago."

With his chin in his palm, the officer heard him out. "So why are you holding up the line?"

The immigrant looked bashful and fiddled with his passport. "Because you haven't said it yet."

"What?"

The immigrant leaned closer and whispered, smiling sheepishly, "Please, you know the words I mean."

"Haven't a clue," said the officer.

"Those three special words," pleaded the young man. "You know: welcome to Acadan."

"Oh. Those words. Sorry, can't do that."

"Why ever not? I was told on good authority you said it to every immigrant."

"Yes, in the old days. Not anymore, not since the cutbacks and departmental downsizing. They say it slows things down."

"But couldn't you, this once? Quickly and quietly? I won't tell anyone you broke the rule. This is such an auspicious occasion, the words would mean so much to me. And then all the rest will fall in place: I'll work hard during the day, go to school at night, I'll fight for human rights and universal healthcare —"

The immigration officer held up his hand and looked around: the supervisor was out of earshot. He gazed down at the counter and muttered, scarcely moving his lips, "Welcome to Acadan."

The young man thanked him and left the airport with a song in his heart, hope and optimism still intact.

※　　※　　※

It was indeed one of the credos of Acadan that education was not the preserve of the rich and privileged – even those who had to toil during the day could go to school at night.

This belief sustained the young immigrant during the first anxious months. And while he struggled to put together the pieces of his new life, the University of Acadan beckoned tantalizingly.

Now it was known throughout the land that the University of Acadan had a splendid Department of Gastronomy. The number and variety of courses listed in the prospectus made the young man's mouth water, for the art of food was his calling, his vocation, almost his religion. There were, of course, the traditional offerings in food sciences, in gourmet cooking and catering, and some more fashionable ones, such as "Introduction to Post-Modern Preparations" and "Kitchens Deconstructed: Mealtime Metaphysics and the Modern Menu"; also, "Comparative Studies in Post-Colonial Cuisines"; and a very advanced course called "The Phenomenology of Food."

Shortly after he had mailed in his registration form, the University of Acadan responded: because his academic qualifications had been acquired in a foreign land, it said, acceptance in the program was contingent upon his passing a test called the TOEFL, as described in the attachment.

But the attachment was missing. He felt it was safe to assume TOEFL was some sort of cooking test conducted by the Department of Gastronomy, and, though puzzled by the acronym, he went to the University of Acadan on the appointed day.

He took along the special attaché case that had accompanied him halfway around the world. The case, a rather large one, was not much to look at, but the contents – his cherished collection of cutlery and cooking implements – never failed to dazzle.

At the information desk, he asked for directions to the TOEFL examination hall.

"Which one? There are two types of TOEFL," said the woman.

"Oh?" said the immigrant. "The second page of my letter was missing, so I'm not sure."

"TOEFL type I," she explained, "is the Test Of English as a Foreign Language. It's meant for newcomers, foreign students who want to take things like history, anthropology, political science. What courses have you applied for?"

"Food-related – in the Department of Gastronomy."

"Then yours is the TOEFL type II."

"Which is?"

"The Test Of Eating in a Foreign Land."

"Pardon me?" said the young man, chuckling at what he thought was her little joke.

She repeated it; it was not a joke.

"What exactly is this test?"

"You sit before the examiner and eat different kinds of food. Marks are given for proper cutlery usage, for style, elegance – that sort of thing."

Indignation rendered him speechless for a moment. "But . . . but that's ridiculous! What does eating stylishly have to do with cooking and catering? Are you saying only immigrants eat sloppily, that there are no slobs born and bred in Acadan? Are you saying –"

"Oh, I agree with you," she said, cutting him off. "But I'm the Information Desk. You should visit the Admissions Office."

The immigrant made his way across the leafy campus and, minutes later, was in the presence of the Admissions Officer. "May I inquire about your Test Of Eating in a Foreign Land?"

"Ah, the TOEFL type II. A most entertaining test," smirked the Admissions Officer. The immigrant, meanwhile, let his eyes run up and down the man's pinstriped suit, which annoyed its wearer. "Look, is there something wrong?"

"No, it's just that . . . I thought only bankers wore pinstriped suits. Shouldn't you be in tweeds or corduroy?"

The Admissions Officer leaned back in his chair, laced his fingers over his stomach, and said severely, "Sweeping generalizations are the bane of civilized society." Then, leaning forward on his desk, "To be fair, we, in the University, are a bit like bankers, aren't we? Accepting in our care valuable assets like minds and personalities, nurturing and moulding them while investing in knowledge and wisdom."

"And I suppose," said the young man, "that like a mind, money is a terrible thing to waste."

"Exactly," said the Admissions Officer. "These days, we, in the groves of academe, have to watch our bottom lines just like the bankers. So we come by our pinstripes quite honestly. Now what was it about the TOEFL?"

"Well, I fail to see the point. Why should students of catering have to demonstrate their grasp of table manners?"

"We, in this institute, have very high standards. When our graduates go forth into the wide world, we want to be certain that they will shine not only while bending over the hot, greasy stove, but also seated at the starched, white tablecloth."

"How does the ability to do one influence the other? Would you disqualify a blind musician?"

"No. But have you heard the saying: physician, heal thyself? Well, master chef, feed thy face." He was terribly pleased with his reply, his florid countenance beaming with delight. "And why exactly do you oppose the test? Is it because your cultural background has left you ill-prepared for knives and forks?"

"Let me assure you," said the immigrant, with quiet haughtiness, "my skills at table would make your learned faculty seem a pack of dribbling fools. Be it nouvelle cuisine or roast beef and Yorkshire pudding, I make mincemeat of my competition."

Then, with a flourish, he threw open his attaché case. A glorious collection of knives, forks, and spoons ranging from Georgian silver to ultra-modern stainless steel were nestled in neat rows, along with a variety of chopsticks carved in bone and ivory. The cooking implements lay in a second tier under the tableware, hidden from view.

"My cutlery and I, sir, are always ready. Bring before me, if you dare, a slab of sirloin, done rare, oozing bloody juices, and my steak knife and I will tackle it like a Texan oil baron. Serve up trout à la meunière, and my fish knife and fork will treat the delicate, white flesh with the reverence it deserves. If it's Chinese food, my chopsticks shall demonstrate all the grace and charm of the East. In a bowl of spaghetti, I can rotate my fork with the dexterity of a Don Giovanni. And don't forget these," he waggled the fingers of his right hand before the man's face, "God-given cutlery, never in need of shining or sharpening. With these, I can roll a ball of rice and sambhar and pop it in my mouth, the nimble way they do in Kerala and Tamil Nadu."

Then, in a move that seemed quite out of character, the immigrant snatched a carving knife from the case and began brandishing it like a swashbuckler: "We have talked enough. Choose your implements, sir, name the time and kitchen."

Stereotypes of hot-blooded, irrational foreigners who came unhinged without warning were flashing through the Admissions Officer's mind. He grew a little nervous. Though he understood that the gleaming blade was being waved only as a metaphor, it did not help matters.

"Please calm yourself," he said. "It's un-Acadanian, debating with cutlery. Myself, I can barely boil an egg. Let us, instead, negotiate and compromise, the Acadanian way."

He relaxed visibly as the knife came to rest in its satin bed. "I must admit, the way you expressed yourself on the subject of table manners was quite impressive."

"That's nothing," said the immigrant. "You should see me perform with cooking implements."

"I'd love to. So why not just sit for the TOEFL type II and be done with it? Then we can move on."

"It's a matter of principle," said the immigrant.

"Ah, principles. They do make things awfully complicated, don't they?"

There was silence for a few moments. "By the way," said the Admissions Officer, "you have a fine command of the language. Ever considered taking up journalism or creative writing?"

The immigrant shook his head. "Words, words, words – they fill the mouth but not the stomach."

"Pity. You certainly have the talent. And there would be the added advantage of your ethnicity."

"Meaning what?"

"Well, the world is discovering ethnic writers, making them quite fashionable. Every publisher wants at least one."

"Should you be saying such things?" inquired the immigrant sternly.

"I mean no harm," said the Admissions Officer, afraid that a charge of racism might follow.

"No, I mean, are you qualified to recommend courses of study like journalism and creative writing? Isn't that the province of the Counselling Department?"

"Actually, I'm doubling as Guidance Counsellor due to the cut-backs," he explained, reaching for his telephone where a red button had lit up. "Excuse me, it's the hotline from the President's office."

Putting on a pleasant smile, he said: "Ee-yello." The smile disappeared the next instant, leaving his face ashen. "Oh my God, that's terrible! What a disaster!"

There was a click at the other end. He dropped the receiver and leaned back in his chair, clutching his forehead.

"Not good news, I take it," said the immigrant.

"The worst," he groaned. "A very important banquet is being hosted tonight by the President. For VIPs, captains of industry, CEOs of global corporations. All of them potential benefactors of the University. Now the catering is screwed up . . . some confusion about the date. And I'm ultimately responsible."

"You? Why you?"

"Well, besides being Admissions Officer and Guidance Counsellor, I'm also the Director of Special Events. Tonight's event is so special, the University's continued existence depends upon it. And VIPs don't take kindly to being sent home hungry. But how much can one person do?"

He was almost in tears now. "When will they stop these cuts? When will they see wisdom? And how am I to fill the gobs of those potential benefactors tonight?" He dropped his head on the desk and began sobbing into the TOEFL files.

The immigrant reopened his attaché case, held up the multicultural cutlery display, and coughed softly. "There is a solution," he murmured, shaking the case.

Hearing the comforting rattle of knives and forks, the Admissions Officer raised his head: "You mean . . . you are offering to –?"

"Yes."

"But do you have what it takes to prepare a banquet?"

"Do you have another option?"

No, there was none, the Admissions Officer knew. No choice but to roll the dice and gamble on this strange applicant sent by providence.

After they shook hands, all the culinary resources of the Gastronomy Department were placed at the immigrant's disposal. He spent the afternoon in the kitchen, in seventh heaven. The Admissions Officer lingered by the stove, agonizing over his decision. Had he gone mad, putting a student – and a foreign one at that – in charge of such an important function? Sick with anxiety, he tiptoed among the pots and pans, worried about being a nuisance, yet unable to tear himself away.

"Shoo!" ordered the immigrant, much too absorbed in his art to realize who it was he addressed thus. "You are hindering the creation of masterpieces! Begone!"

The Admissions Officer crept meekly from the kitchen to sit alone in his office till evening.

*　　*　　*

The fateful hour struck at last. The guests began to arrive. Each one was greeted unctuously by the President of the University, who had a curious manner of mingling stiff, formal phrases such as "pleasure of your delightful company" and "overwhelmed by your esteemed presence" with "attaboy" and "you betcha."

Drinks were served; the chitchat proceeded for the scheduled duration; and dinner was announced.

Despite its long tradition of grand dining and feasting, never had the University of Acadan served up such a sumptuous banquet. As the dishes materialized, the aromas and fragrances, the subtleties of spices from the four corners of the globe, conjured up a gastronomic symphony that no one wanted to end.

And then, out of nowhere, a strange ethereal music began to fill the air. There was no orchestra, no stereo system, no loud-speakers. But there it was, that heavenly sound, affecting the VIPs to the empty core of their beings.

Soon, a most delicious tingling took hold of their limbs. Hollowness that no hostile takeovers or mega-mergers had been able to cure was filling with something warm, with emotions never felt before. They dabbed their lips with damask napkins, pushed back their chairs, rose, and started dancing to that beautiful music which existed for their ears alone.

Captains of industry, CEOs of global corporations, cabinet ministers, powerful players from the backrooms of political parties – some of them burly men and others rather slight – were soon in one another's arms, blissfully dancing a food-induced foxtrot. It was followed by a brisk tango, a rather erotic samba, and a slow waltz during which the CEOs and powerbrokers closed their eyes and rested their heads tenderly on one another's dark-suited shoulders, all thoughts of world domination having fled their minds for the time being.

Still gliding on air, they regained their places after the Terpsichorean interlude. Now their chequebooks began popping out of their pockets, as rapidly as prairie dogs from their burrows on a fine spring day.

"Attaboy!" said the President of the University, and whistled under his breath as cheque after cheque was placed before him. The amounts made him utter things like "sonofagun" and "such munificence leaves us lost for words."

Once the donations were in, he waited impatiently for the banquet hall to clear, quite forgetting he was the host. The only man he wanted to meet now was the chef, the one who had worked the magic on this glorious night, when more money had been raised than from all their efforts in the last ten years.

The immigrant entered the room, and the President of the University of Acadan fell on his knees before him, to kiss his hand: "Maestro! We are in your debt forever! Singlehandedly you have rescued the University! Acadanians, regardless of race, religion, or sexual orientation, will sing your praises for generations to come! How can we ever repay you?"

"Well," said the immigrant, "I would appreciate being allowed to take some courses in your Department of Gastronomy. Without," he added, "the Test Of Eating in a Foreign Land."

"Maestro! Do not mock us," said the President. "You? Join as a student? You should be Head of the Department of Gastronomy. And I would appoint you this minute, except that the professors' union would descend on me like a ton of bricks."

"Please, a few courses, nothing more."

"If you insist. And we will waive all the silly requirements, tuition fees, miscellaneous charges. Except parking, of course. Even I am powerless when it comes to parking."

"That's all right," said the immigrant, "I don't have a car."

"Attaboy," said the President.

And ever after, or perhaps for a little while, the President, the Admissions Officer, and the immigrant lived happily.

Moral:

Never rush the simmering stew, nor over-stir the subtle sauce.

. And take dancing lessons: someday, somewhere, when you least expect it, you may get the urge to trip the light fantastic.

In a slightly different version, "Welcome to Acadan" was a convocation address at the University of Toronto in the spring of 1999.

LISA**MOORE**

(with Eva Crocker)

Yolk

The Second Person

On Christmas morning you sit catatonically rigid on the edge of
the couch thinking about Frank, a character in your novel. Frank
is trapped in a fire. Your five-year-old son, Theo, tears the wrapping paper off a Hot Wheels Race Track and begs you to help him
assemble it.

Ask Daddy, you say. Theo wraps his arms and legs around your
leg; he buries his face in your thigh. He begs for attention, but you
are absorbed in your novel. You head down the hall to the kitchen,
dragging your encumbered leg, because there's a pencil by the
fridge and you have to write something down. You wedge a palm
between your thigh and Theo's forehead. You shake him off.

Your fourteen-year-old daughter, Eva, stands before you and
says: Which dress?

She is holding up two dresses on hangers near her chin. You
realize she has asked three times. She has a hard glint in her eye.
You do not see the dresses. You have to get Frank out of the
burning house.

Your stepdaughter, Emily, is getting married and you have not returned her last three phone calls. You have to call her about the catering, and you will. You will call her really soon.

These are some of the crimes you have committed lately: You have offered to play hide-and-seek with Theo, and when he has gone to hide, you do not look for him. You have promised ice cream if he will just watch one more hour of television so you can write.

Just give me another half-hour in my study and I promise you'll never have to choke down another carrot as long as you live.

You have a deadline. Does nobody understand this?

And what happens when you finish the novel is that you find yourself in the shower, probably humming Leonard Cohen, "In My Secret Life," and you are overwhelmed with self-regard. You have worked so hard and sacrificed so much. My God, you feel good. You cry.

On the other hand – you have turned off the shower now, you are wrapped in a towel – you couldn't really call it work.

It feels like the novel just appeared out of nowhere. You don't remember writing any of it, because you were taken over by another you, a second person, while the writing happened.

The Real You

The real you is at the beach.

You are with Theo at Northern Bay Sands in Conception Bay, Newfoundland, and the water is so cold it makes you aware of all the bones in your feet and shins. Theo is fearless. He thinks he can swim. You hold his wrist and charge the waves, and there is a beautiful girl in a red bikini hanging upside down over a young man's bare shoulder. Her legs are kicking the sky and she's beating his back with her fists and he ploughs through the water and tosses her in the air. She goes under and comes up glossy and shocked and shrill. The wet red bikini is even redder, and she flings her hair. She smacks the water with the edge of her hand, and the young man arches his back as the splash hits his sunburn and the whole ocean contrives to drag him toward her so she can wrap her legs around his waist and grab a fistful of his hair and topple him over.

The sand beneath your feet is moving like a conveyor belt, and your son is lifted up on the back of a wave. He is laughing hard, his eyes wide open. While you are hanging on to that little wrist, hanging on for dear life, the second person is back home writing a chunk of the novel.

In the evening you and Theo are cuddling under a pile of sleeping bags, reading Harry Potter. You both smell like the sea and coconut sunblock and there is the whiff of burning lamp oil. Eva is outside on the lawn with your husband. She's doing a dance, and he is videotaping her shadow on the white clapboard. He raises a lamp with one hand, and her shadow stretches like a giant.

You dream that an elegant woman with broad cheekbones and silver hair offers you a gift; she opens her hand and there is a miniature panda, alive and curled up like a fetus – and while you are dreaming this, you feel your husband remove your glasses.

You have fallen asleep with the book in your hands and your glasses on, and you feel the arms of your glasses touch your temples as he lifts them away. In the morning you find a new part of the novel in your journal. Frank is out of the fire.

Truthfully

I have never really asked my five-year-old to play hide-and-seek, and then not gone looking for him. However, there have been big stretches of time when I am so thoroughly taken up with writing that I'm as good as gone.

Another Writer

I ask Eva to take care of Theo while I finish a piece I'm working on. She turns from the computer, distracted and half-deaf, and says, I can't, I'm writing.

What Eva Is Writing

When we arrived, someone ushered us upstairs and Jackie whipped a worn T-shirt over her head, slid into a black dress with overall-type straps that swoop over her bare back and snap just below her shoulders in the front. Angelina is pulling on red fishnet tights with big holes and runs in the thighs under a skin-tight, glittering dress. In the mirror we pass around a stick of sparkling silver lipstick and smear it over our eyelids.

Jackie had burned a series of CDs with smash hits from the nineties. Halfway through the first CD, a girl I had never met named Cassandra left for Wal-Mart to buy a strobe light on a whim. It was cheaper than I thought it would be, and while she was explaining how to work it, someone shot a cap gun off in her ear, and she had to go sit in the hall.

We fumbled with cords and switches and thin sheets of coloured plastic. When it started flashing, we turned off the lights and nobody walked any more, they glided. You took a step and before your sock touched the carpet, you had moved forward. We all clapped our hands because the noise came a second before our hands smacked. We danced hard, and jerky movements became slow and arced; people jumped and stayed in the air for longer than they could have.

Jackie got tripped up in the rug with her arms full of pillows. We turned the strobe light on at a slow pace and began battering each other with the pillows. Justin fell backward over a giant ribbed yoga ball. The pillows stuttered toward me. And you remembered the words as they came out of your mouth. Maybe writing is like this.

An hour later we stumbled upstairs, still dizzy from the lights, and poured half a bag of marshmallows into a ceramic bowl and put them in the microwave so they would grow. We all ate out of the same bowl with teaspoons.

A white trail hung off the bottom of my spoon like a synthetic, gooey comet's tail.

This Is Theo

I ask Theo if he wants to be a writer when he grows up.

He says, Nah, writers just sit down all day. I want to discover the cure for cancer, he says.

Oh no, I say. Don't do that. Be a writer!

The Eggs

Eva is out at a punk-rock concert. It's late and my husband and I are in bed reading when the windows in our bedroom start to rattle. There's a noise, like popcorn popping, and the glass shakes. It lasts a full minute and a half. My husband gets out of bed. The window is black and cold. He puts his face close to the glass.

It's eggs, he says. Somebody egged us.

Eva comes through the front door. The door slams, and she doesn't move. We listen. Then she's coming up the stairs two at a time. She's in the bathroom. She speaks through the closed door.

This is bad, she says. I open the bathroom door, and she's looking at herself in the mirror.

This is very bad, she says. I watch as a film of tears makes her eyes bluer than ever in the stark bathroom light.

They think I called the ambulance for a guy who passed out at the show and now he's got to go to court for underage drinking.

But he might have had alcohol poisoning, I say. Somebody had to call the ambulance.

That doesn't matter, she says. They're going to beat me up tomorrow at school. There's a whole bunch of them.

The Shoes

Emily hands Eva her bridesmaid shoes. The dress is champagne and arrived in the mail, but the shoes Emily delivers in person.

The shoes have a very long narrow heel and a few thin black straps.

Later in the evening I am writing, and Eva hobbles into the

living room. The room is dark except for the computer screen. She keeps the tips of her fingers on the wall for balance.

An earthquake in Asia, she says. What will happen to all those people?

The house is quiet except for when cars go past. Then the headlights move over the walls. The shadow of the lace curtain appears and moves over one wall, then it moves over Eva, over the other wall, and disappears. She is standing with her fingertips on the mantelpiece. Theo is asleep, and my husband is writing on the third floor.

She is much taller than me with the shoes on.

The whole world is in such a mess, she says. Then she turns and leaves the room. I listen to heels go unsteadily down the hall.

Virginia Woolf needed a room of her own. I need this house with its creaking staircase and the dryer tumbling and the lingering smell of cooking. The very faint sound of my husband practising guitar on the third floor. I need the chaos children bring to a life, the sensuality they bring and the imagination. I need the street outside too.

The Wedding

My stepdaughter, Emily, in front of the full-length mirror in the dressing room of the Masonic Temple on Cathedral Street. Her shiny black hair spilling over the embroidered, beaded dress.

Theo, in his tuxedo, tears down the hall to find me. His face is lit up, and he holds out his lapel and says, Look at me.

A white rose.

Each table in the hall has a white tablecloth and rose petals and a bowl with a goldfish. The goldfish a pulsing, metallic orange in the candlelight. The groom is a red-haired American with a deep laugh. They are both very young, and they both cry while they say their vows. They didn't want to write their own vows because a vow is not something you write. A vow exists already and all you have to do is mean it when you say it.

Theo is the ring bearer. He gets bored mid-ceremony and swings the pillow for the rings round and round as if he is a baseball player about to pitch a fast one. One of the rings bounces across the tiles, and everybody has to bend down to find it.

Emily asked me to write a poem for the ceremony. For a long time I felt I wasn't equal to the task. I wanted to say how much I loved Emily and how proud I was. I wanted somehow to include those tears over math homework done years ago and teaching her to swim. I wanted to say something true about being in love. And I wanted the poem to be short and funny, and best if it rhymed a little, I thought.

One line is: Because you both lived through that storm in Halifax where a bride had to ride to the church in the shovel of a snowplough.

Eva's Question

Eva said, I think you have to make clearer in this essay how you *really* feel about having children.

I want life – and here I am thinking of Mrs. Ramsay's dinner table, Minta Doyle all flushed and trippingly late, her lost brooch, first love, the lid on the French stew, all of the children, the salt shaker, the seashells and open windows and the sweeping band of light catching it before everything is swept irrevocably into the past – I want all that *and* to be able to write it down at the same time.

Eva on the Subject of Eggs

We have three margarine containers full of red, orange, and blue dye. My friend Sophie sits across from me. The top of the egg pressed against her lips. Her eyes are squinted a little and her cheeks are red. But her fingers are gentle. Undeveloped baby chicken slides out of the bottom of her egg in mucousy strands as she blows. I tap the top of my egg with a needle, and I'm surprised by how hard it is to break the surface. I wrap a checked dishcloth over the tip of the needle and dig it deep into the egg. When I slide the needle out, it is glistening.

Sophie takes another egg out of the carton. She places the rounded bottom in the palm of her hand and curls her other hand around the top.

You know if you squeeze an egg like this, no matter how hard you squeeze, it can't break, she says. She presses her hands together, applying pressure to both ends of the egg, and a bluish vein lifts in her wrist. The egg pops. Bits of shell and slimy yellow insides cover her forearm and the tablecloth. We both laugh hysterically. She uses the same dishcloth I was dulling the needle tip with to wipe up the egg. We are still laughing and a part of me realizes our friendship depends on these moments.

Junior High Graduation

Mom, look, that's one of the guys who egged our house, Eva whispers.

We are in the lobby of Brother Rice Junior High, and there is a crush of parents and kids in prom dresses and Kleenex carnations on the lattice archway borrowed from Complete Rentals, across the street. Everybody is waving programs and flashbulbs pop all over.

The boy she means is standing very close with his back to us. Beyond the boy are his parents, standing side by side, preparing to take a picture of their son.

He is a tall boy with blond curly hair and an oversized, retro tuxedo jacket, powder blue. His father is peering through the viewfinder, then he lowers the camera and looks, and then focuses again. But he lowers the camera once more, and now he is looking straight at me. I realize I am in the background of the picture and all the tiny muscles in my face are pinched up into a scowl. He has seen me, through the viewfinder, glaring at his son with a near homicidal intensity, and he is extremely puzzled and can't bring himself to take the picture.

Are you going to say something, Mom? Eva asks.

No, I say. We'll write about it instead, that will be our revenge.

She raises an eyebrow.

Yeah, she says dryly, that'll show him.

The Inevitable Shape of a Story

My friend Rose calls to say that on the Equinox – and it is the Equinox – you can put an egg on its end, and it will stand all by itself.

It has to do with the axis of the earth, she says.

I turn on a lamp and get out the marble cutting board. The cutting board is black and veined with pink and grey. The egg casts a perfect oval shadow. I am gradually removing my finger from the tip of the egg. Rose said to do it slowly.

The shell is so white and smooth, except for a speckle of grit here and there, and these small dots catch the light too and cast minute shadows. The egg has weight. It is blue-white. The egg, in order to do what it has to do, must be exactly the way it is. The shell is semi-permeable to allow a flow of oxygen; it is tough enough to protect the embryo, but fragile enough to allow the chick to break out. Maybe stories should be like that too, form following content in some perfect way.

I take my finger off and the egg falls over. The story is uncontainable. It should be perfect, we strive for it to be perfect, but it always cracks unexpectedly. Out streams the lurid yellow yolk.

SHANI**MOOTOO**

Poetry Lesson

One is always grateful for poetry where it's expected, but discovering poetry where it's least expected is like a gift without occasion from a lover who wants nothing, not even your gratitude or joy, in return.

The route my family's driver took to the wrought-iron gates of the convent school I attended as a child in Trinidad skirted Carnegie Library, which was situated on the hectic traffic island known as Library Corner. I didn't know anyone who patronized the library, since to do so would have meant climbing over the contorted bodies of those who used the corner and the steps of the once magnificent building as bedroom, bathroom, and flophouse. There were apparently girls, bad girls, who made their way to that corner, where men lurked chatting up the girls, who subsequently became pregnant. So it was said that one would never come across a convent girl at Carnegie Library. Passing through that busy intersection on the way to school, I took care not to look too closely at the goings-on there, for fear that I too might be called bad, and even find myself pregnant.

Still, once we were inside the convent's gates, which were pad-locked as soon as assembly began, even the eight-foot-high, steel-blue concrete walls surrounding us could not keep the iniquities of the outside world entirely away. Over those walls floated the distracting aromas of Indian-style finger foods, forbidden because they were said to harbour gastrointestinal bugs, and deep-fried on the spot by the multitude of competing vendors on Library Corner. When a tropical breeze was whipped up, whatever cooling effect it provided was often tempered by the nostril-singeing stench of pee that wafted into our classrooms. More often than not, the voices of our teachers would be drowned out by the constant blaring of traffic, the greetings shouted between shoppers on their way to the open-air market and abbatoir on the other side of the library, and calypso music booming from a passing car. Best and worst of all were the endless soaring musical interludes from the five-hour Bollywood movies that played back to back all day at the Indian-language cinema that shared a wall with my school. The time would come when a song spiralled high, and though we might not have understood the language of that song, we stopped listening to our teacher and hummed along.

In those days, St. Joseph's Convent was run mostly by Irish nuns. My first poetry teacher's method of introducing us to that subject was to teach us an incomprehensible jumble of mostly strange words by, say, Ogden Nash, Blake, Tennyson, or Coleridge. We had to learn entire poems by these men, by heart. But as far as memory goes, I have no heart. I have never been able to remember even the simplest jokes, riddles, or songs, least of all lines of poetry. I have always envied people who can burst into song or verse at any occasion. For me, the second line of any poem is always, *Let me count the ways,* as in:

Tyger! Tyger! burning bright, let me count the ways.

I do remember scents, emotions, situations. Situations like my so-called poetry teacher spending an inordinate amount of time on something about AA, BB, CC, and AB, AB, etc., which was too much like the wall-erecting-in-the-mind kind of math puzzles that asked "if *a* equals two *b*'s, and two *b*'s equal one *c*, then what do *a* plus *c* plus *b* plus *c* plusplusplus equal?" But as far back as this memory is able to reach, that was all she ever tried to teach us about poetry. The rest was recitation.

Eleven a.m. The equatorial sun makes no distinction between indoors and outdoors, or sun and shade. The air is thick and hot, and the breathing is shallow in a small room crammed with forty perspiring children sitting at forty desks from which arise the odours of wet-season mould and unwashed bottles of souring fruit juices, and yet the teacher wants to know, "Who else did not learn the poem? You want to waste my time? Come. Come to the front of the class." It has been too long since breakfast, and lunch is still forty-five minutes away. Hunger in this heat is dizzying. The scent of roasted nuts from over the wall distracts. Bara and curried channa. Hot oil. Coconut fudge. Forty-five minutes to lunch.

The teacher divides us into four rows of ten students each.

On the street outside a man and a woman begin to fight. They are screaming at each other, yet every word is clear; from our classroom we can pick sides. The unusual stop and start of an ambulance's siren tells us that the vehicle is stuck in traffic a street or two away. Ah! There is a cooling breeze, but with it comes the funk of what wanton men do against the exterior of the convent's walls.

On the teacher's command, the first row of students recites:

It is an ancient Mariner,
And he stoppeth one of three.
"By thy long grey beard and glittering eye,
Now wherefore stopp'st thou me?

When they reach the second stanza, the second row of students begins the poem from the very top. From the other side of the wall, I can hear the tassa drums begin and the string orchestra laying the groundwork for the sitar-imitating voice of a woman declaring her devotion in a South Asian language while those in the first row are reciting:

The Bridegroom's doors are opened wide,
And I am next of kin;
The guests are met, the feast is set:
May'st hear the merry din."

I am in the third group. The fear of forgetting guarantees forgetting. The wall in my mind has been erected; I cannot recall even the first line. The outside world has been drowned out now by the cacophony inside the class. If I could hear the classmates beside me, I might be able to pretend to mouth the words, but I hear only the racket of students with better memories becoming boisterous and uncontrollable with this strange and dubious freedom.

He holds him with his skinny hand,
"There was a ship," quoth he.
"Hold off! unhand me, grey-beard loon!"
Eftsoons his hand dropt he.

Before the fourth group has reached the end of the first stanza, the teacher has walked down the aisle and plucked me from my row. She ushers me to the blackboard, and I am made to write out the first four stanzas. I am given a bad mark that will, of course, count against my house-team, and my penance is to stay in the following evening and copy out the entire poem three times.

The first book I ever stole – the first of three to date, and all lifted, I will quickly add, within the space of a few weeks during one term in high school – was a small book of poems by Carl Sandburg. This little transgression took place at the same convent, whose notion of a library consisted of a modest bookshelf of donated books. I am not proud of how this book came to me. But how can I not be at least a little pleased that I would make a thief of myself for a book of poetry? In this book, whose pint size is what first caught my attention, I came upon a poem called "Was Ever a Dream a Drum?":

> Was ever a dream a drum
>   or a drum a dream?
> Can a drummer drum a dream
>   or a dreamer dream a drum?
>
> The drum in a dream
>   pounds loud to the dreamer.

Here were plain words in what I had come to recognize as the form of poetry, yet words I was able to understand, and sounds and rhythms and dilemmas that thrilled me. Was ever a dream a drum? Or a drum a dream? What play! And that play got published! I no longer have that book – where it has gone is a mystery – but the poetry in it pounded loud and clear to the dreamer in me. Around that time I began scribbling my own dilemmas in similar fashion.

In the early eighties I left Trinidad and its equatorial midday sun behind and migrated to Canada. One brisk and drizzly Vancouver day, as I was spring cleaning and making decisions about which books to keep and which to take to the second-hand bookstore, I came across the volume of T.S. Eliot poems I had laboured over with marginal success for my Advanced Level English exams. The once cream-coloured pages had by this time yellowed. I flipped through the book, which had imprisoned between its covers memories of the odours and sounds of the Carnegie Library Corner in San Fernando, and I found "The Love Song of J. Alfred Prufrock." It was a poem that for some reason I had never been able to hold in my head, with a word in its title I had been mortally afraid of mispronouncing. But far away from the pressures of grades and from the judgments of those who might deem me "stupid," the words rose off the pages, struck and awakened me. This poem, that particular reading, sealed in me a long-lasting love affair with language, meaning, sound, and, ultimately, with writing poetry.

Distance is usually measured in kilometres. But having emigrated to Canada and then not returned to my childhood home in Trinidad for a long time, I find that I measure distance in memories.

When I returned to Trinidad after a long absence, I discovered that people from my childhood had passed away, that the landscape in my memory no longer exists, that buildings that played some role in my shaping have been torn down. The convent building as I knew it is gone. Library Corner is unrecognizable, but I can't pinpoint why. The park I played tennis in has been divided up to make way for a traffic bypass. The Town Hall has been moved and the hospital expanded, its once familiar and comforting contours now – to my mind – disfigured. And suddenly, distance is measured in memory. But memory itself becomes a political tool, for me, a measure of my loyalty to a people, to a place, to a history, to my own presence then and point of view now. Memory is rendered most volatile and interesting when it can be confirmed or contested by at least one other person. And so I find my migrant's memory of Trinidad pitted against the authority of those who remained behind. For this migrant, then, memory is an imperative, an urgent truth that, in my case, only fixing it to paper can calm.

But which brand of words to use to do this? For me, the wordiness of prose gets in the way of truth by creating rather than revealing it, so I turn to poetry when I know that what can be captured of a truth is fleeting.

> If this pen
> could cut a path
> I would walk it,
> carry plaster and paint
> outline each porthole,
> frame a view
>
> of slow chop, lull of ocean,
>
> of horizon line,
> demarcation precise
>
> of equatorial sky,
> haze impregnable,

of oil rigs for perspective, flames on top,
a freighter here
a frigate
cloud

Still the air
tastes of blood, salt, and rust,
the flavour of drinking water

Here is the cracked floor
of an outdoor bathroom stall
where a shower dripped water,
salty, singed the cornea

concrete walls wept,
spawned moss,

the crab cradled
in the bed
of slime-green moss

salt lichen florets flourished
on forearms, neck, and legs

There was a camera, too –
in my hand and loaded –
but I could not bring myself to use it
for fear of what I would make:

realism
a theory

fiction
iconography

romancing the crumbling

As an immigrant in Canada, I have a foot in two landscapes, one foot crazy for the feel and cold of mountain snow, the other yearning for the sear and sizzle of asphalt bubbling in the equatorial midday. Writing, and writing poetry in particular, allows me to set these landscapes, past and present, so that they cannot be taken away by time or by others. When individual and collective memories collide, poetry becomes my drum and exclamation mark.

ALICE**MUNRO**

Writing. Or, Giving Up Writing

July 2005

A year ago I had one book finished and another book three-quarters finished. The first book was published last September, and during the ten months since then, I have worked, when I got the time, on the other book. Now it is finished – at least I think it is, though the editors may think otherwise, and I may still have some fiddling around to do. I have been saying in public and private that I have written my last book, and though most people may have taken that to mean the book already published, I meant this one. When it comes out, if it comes out, I have been telling myself, it's to be the last.

My reasons for this:

Writing is too nerve-racking. I mean, writing with interruptions is too nerve-racking. For instance, just as I typed these words, the phone rang. It was for my husband, who is working in the backyard. I went out and yelled for him in a shrill, aggrieved voice until he heard me and came in. I didn't need to answer the phone, but I feel very uneasy if I let the message go on the machine. The phone rings a lot, and it's usually for me, and if the call is being made during office hours, it has to be answered during office hours, so I may as well deal with it right away. Most times it's somebody wanting me to do something. Requests come in one after another, and present me with public and private ways of being a useful citizen, a champion of literacy or literature, or just making some-body's birthday very happy by autographing a book and getting it wrapped and standing in line with it at the Post Office. In other words, in order to have time to do my work I must continually refuse to do things that other people think perfectly reasonable and even obligatory for me to do, and sometimes I get mad enough to tear out my hair.

I should say, while we're on the subject, that I don't think many writers get uninterrupted free time, men or women, teachers or housewives, old or young. Writing fiction is seldom something that *has to be done that day*. And sometimes I am unhappily convinced that real writers, other writers, manage to do all the things I feel I can't do, and they still come out with a solid book every year. I have a nasty cringing feeling that I shouldn't complain.

Too late now.

Of course my stopping writing won't stop the requests, but they won't be interrupting anything, and I may even change into the decent person I always pretend to be.

Maybe the real reason for giving up writing is that I'm getting older. Old. When that happens it takes more time and concentra-tion to do the things you have to do. Paying bills and keeping your dates with the garbage-truck, being a conscientious recycler, getting money off to all those worthy causes you once promised yourself to support as soon as you could afford to. Maintaining order around you. Disorder is a lot more threatening than it used to be –

it's no longer forgivable and disarming, a proof of creativity, but a signal of the arrival of old-age mess and teary turbulence, decidedly un-charming. As a matter of fact it's *always* less charming – mess is – in women than in men. The same goes for keeping your physical self in presentable shape. It takes more and more effort, not even to halt the deterioration but to slow it so that it's bearable to yourself and others. Pills and tests and exercises. No more hammering out the end of a story at three in the morning. You can't just let go and Be a Writer, all temperament and bad habits and Screeching Genius, like in the old movies. Not that I ever did (I don't recall any of those geniuses being women), but the notion used to be in the back of my mind that someday I might try.

So – I can quit writing, in the interests of a manageable life. And in the knowledge that it's very rare for outstanding work to be produced in these later years, so one or two books fewer won't really be anybody's loss. Certainly I won't miss the harried trying-to-get-it-done, or the sheer awfulness of waiting for the book to come out and then putting on a brave face and going out to be responsible for it in the Great World. (It does really seem then as if the world of publishing, reviewing, reading, is a great world, when in fact it is small enough that most people in your own country, your own town, will never know your name.)

Not really my loss, either.

But wait a minute – what was so wonderful about it? What made it irresistible? What made nonsense of all these drawbacks? When is the really good point, with writing? For me, it's not when you're doing the work, not when you're sending it out, not when you see it in print, or (God forbid) when you read from it in public or when it gets on a bestseller list (then you have to worry about how long it will stay on), not even when it wins a prize, though you have to admit that's better than not winning.

Isn't the really good time when you are just getting the idea, or rather when you encounter the idea, bump into it, as if it has always been wandering around in your head? There it is, still fairly featureless, but shapely and glowing. It's not the story – it's more like the spirit, the centre, of the story, something there's no word for, that can only come into life, a public sort of life, when words are wrapped around it. (Of course you never say anything like this, when an interviewer asks you how you came to write a story – you don't want to sound *fey*.)

Still unspoiled, untampered-with, this intimation. In finer fettle than it will ever be again, after all your pushing and pulling it into sentences.

Suppose you could be satisfied with that encounter, just recognize it and leave it alone? How would that be?

We'll see.

SUSAN**MUSGRAVE**

Inventing Herself

"Musgrave cuts such a colourful figure in her writing that she distracts her readers, tempting them to look for the author in and behind the work. However, it is in the work itself where Musgrave is to be found; she is the creator and the product of her own creation."
– *Border/Lines*, Fall 1990

Hector Aristizabal, the Colombian human-rights activist and psychologist, was imprisoned and tortured in his native country after soldiers found "subversive" literature in his home. "Each of us who survives must create meaning from the experience," he says, in a recent interview in the magazine the *Sun*. "We seek meaning by creating narratives about our lives."

Susan Musgrave came of age cocooned in a middle-class Canadian family. Torture, for her, was having to crawl out of a warm bed in the morning; her biggest struggle was finding meaning in a privileged life. She wrote subversive free verse on the injustice of having to walk to school in the rain, and being imprisoned every summer aboard her father's forty-foot yacht. In the Summer of

Love she ran away from the place of safety that was home and dropped LSD at a Be-In in Stanley Park. Her antics did not result in her being imprisoned and tortured by the RCMP; instead her parents had her committed to a mental institution where authorities threatened her with electroshock therapy.

Shortly after she celebrated her sixteenth birthday, confined to Room 0 of the psychiatric ward, she had a visit from the poet Robin Skelton. Skelton, who had met her psychiatrist at a party, asked to read some of her work. "You're not mad, you're a poet," he told her, and went on to publish six of her poems in the *Malahat Review*. (He also left her copies of Allen Ginsberg's *Howl* and Sylvia Plath's *Ariel*, books whose influence can be seen in her subsequent verse.) With her hundred-dollar earnings she purchased her first portable typewriter.

When her first book, *Songs of the Sea-Witch*, was published, Musgrave was, in her own words, "too young to have a biography" and seemingly ignorant of the literary world into which she was about to be launched. She wrote, she maintained, not because she was interested in immortality or fame, but because she loved the shape-shifting of words. "Getting published doesn't excite me as much as the process of 'getting there.' My challenges are in the world of the next poem struggling to be born."

Critics portrayed her as "a tormented sea-witch with Medusa-like hair" and "the chance daughter of Allen Ginsberg and Sylvia Plath." Her wraithlike appearance and the fact that she'd called her book *Songs of the Sea-Witch* destined her to become, in the media's eye, the sea-witch personified. (Robert Graves's "white goddess" in her primitive guise – as sea-witch, Circe, death goddess – is the persona of the book.) And the label stuck. In 1995, a reviewer of her *Selected Poems* described Musgrave as having gone from a "sea-witch to a sea-hag," illustrating with "before" and "after" photographs. The "sea-hag" is a mature Musgrave, somewhere in her late forties, while the "sea-witch" is her eighteen-year-old self on a camping trip in the wilderness. "I had swallowed my first birth control pill of the month and had been sick in my hair," she wrote, in 1972, in a letter archived at McMaster University. None of that is apparent in the picture, which has an ephemeral quality: she looks like a wood nymph, coaxing to life a reluctant fire.

Victoria Girl Witch and Poet

"Among other idiocies, the Canada Council is responsible for the proliferation of expensively printed and bound volumes of poetry, which are often unreadable and largely unread. One such volume of rubbish is *Songs of the Sea-Witch*, by Susan Musgrave, a 19-year-old roamer who seems to see herself as the resident poet of Long Beach."
– Victoria *Colonist*, October 1970

"She may not be any great shakes as a poet, but this girl's doing all right," wrote the Victoria *Colonist*'s book reviewer Colonel E.D. Ward-Harris of what Musgrave now calls "her first slim volume of sorrows." The Colonel decided it was his task to bring her down a notch, and chastised the Canada Council, the CBC, and all the literary magazines that had first published her, for leading her to believe she was anything but superficial.

The same month her book began getting attention in the press, Musgrave left Canada to live in the west of Ireland, where she received little news from the rest of the world. Her mother kept the review from her, in any event, "perhaps thinking it would further retard my creative genius," and it wasn't until she returned to Canada, several years later, that she read the Colonel's prognosis of her "juvenile skirt-liftings."

Tall, Blonde, Obsessed with Death

> "She lives in isolation in a log cabin on a cove some 25 miles from Victoria, B.C., and nobody can understand her."
> – *Chatelaine*, 1978

Before she turned twenty-five, Musgrave was being celebrated as a poet of "death and darkness, the *enfant terrible* of Canadian letters, a prophetess with an apocalyptic and haunting vision who explores sexuality at the primal level of bone hurt." It didn't matter how vociferously she proclaimed her innocence, the witch-hunters had decided her fate. In the mid-1970s, a full-page photo of her appeared in *Chatelaine*. "Hi, I'm Susan Musgrave, symbol of vulnerable womanhood, witchery and madness. And I'm going to be Canada's next poetry superstar. Move over, Margaret Atwood," read the words, in Gothic lettering, issuing from her mouth.

"Witch" Poet Fights Her Image

> "The word 'witch' turns up in every headline about her. In the past, she seemed determined to live up to every last detail of the mad-poet persona, West-Coast style, at least in media accounts."
> – Kitchener-Waterloo *Record*, October 1983

Musgrave acknowledges that living in relative "isolation" (in the west of Ireland and on the Queen Charlotte Islands/Haida Gwaii) is one reason she has been able to separate herself successfully from her public persona. "I'm at home in myself and I'm confident enough about my world that it doesn't matter what anyone says about me. People are always telling me how it's dangerous to be so open and honest; I think my vulnerability is a disguise to cover my real vulnerability. The very fact of revelation is a way of hiding."

"But," she adds, "it's not something I do consciously."

Writers help – albeit inadvertently at times, and in varying degrees – to create and shape their personas; perhaps they feel compelled in some strange way to play to the public's curiosity. "It seems incumbent upon writers these days to find a way to step back from themselves and become the kind of celebrity that will interest the industry pushing books as well as the book-buying audience. These personas can work for us, it's true, but they can also become a huge liability," Musgrave says. She goes on to illustrate: "Sylvia Plath was described recently, in the Calgary *Herald*, as 'best remembered for writing angry poems about men.' Imagine having your whole life's work reduced to a line like that!"

She mentions Germaine Greer, too, a serious thinker whose deeper discoveries about the accomplishments of women in history are often obscured by her own lurid public persona. There's also the plight of the "confessional poet" Anne Sexton. "She cries, every time, right here on stage . . ." was how she was introduced to a crowd who had come to see her, shortly before she killed herself, a horrifying example, Musgrave says, "of how an image that precedes us can also trap and diminish who we are." (Sexton took the box of tissues she was offered and did, in fact, leave the stage weeping.)

How private a writer's life remains depends on her ability to balance her personal needs with her public persona, giving away only as much of herself as she can safely afford to give. "I have a public persona, and what I do with it now *is* to have fun with it," says Amy Tan, author of, among other books, *The Joy Luck Club*. Tan explains:

> I used to resent feeling that I was giving away bits and pieces of myself – that my privacy was being invaded – but now I happily give away this part of my persona which is just the fun part. I used to dread the readings, and go home and gnash my teeth, and now I just do it and it's over. I forget it and I just go back to the non-persona, the private persona, which can be fun too. I don't take it seriously. I know that *that* name is out there.
>
> At times when I don't want to be bothered with that name, when I'm buying underwear or dandruff medication and someone says, "Aren't you Amy Tan?" I just look at them and I say, "You know, I've [met] other people who've thought that too."

Zadie Smith rattled the literary world with her first novel, *White Teeth*. The book scooped numerous awards, but it was the combination of her youthful good looks and Jamaican ancestry that established her reputation as the hot new flavour-of-the-week writer on the scene.

The recipient of the kinds of labels that make writers cringe ("black, bookish babe"), Smith delivers a subversive version of her persona when she compares her home-based writing lifestyle to that of a prostitute: "The neighbours think I'm a whore. I stay in all day, I wear nothing but a nightslip, sometimes men come to my door bearing brown envelopes. I don't do any work yet I seem to have money."

Her second novel, *The Autograph Man*, was described as "a snarky parable about the subterfuge of celebrity, as well as the intrinsic disconnect between person and persona." But Smith has grown weary of discussing her image. "Although I do have a public persona, it's not my life. I do my job and that's the end of that."

Still, it obviously rankles Smith that a perception of who she is inevitably precedes her:

> It's so unnatural. Some *thing* I do – which if I was some-body else, nobody would notice – is an insult. Like if I don't go to a lunch date where there's 50 people for lunch, it's, "Oh, she thinks she's too good to come."
>
> If it were anybody else, it would be, "Who gives a shit? So what if she doesn't come to lunch? There's 50 of us." But if I don't come, it's an issue. You have to be aware of it because you end up insulting a lot of people if you don't remember.

A Writer Whose Life Is Stranger than Fiction

> "Susan Musgrave is a writer whose personal life overshad-ows her writing. That's not surprising when you consider that this Victoria-raised poet has led a life that reads like a tabloid newspaper reporter's dream.
>
> She posed nude for *Saturday Night*. She married Stephen Reid, a bank robber, while he was still in prison. She has variously been called one of Canada's foremost poets, a witch, a madwoman, a writer of great daring and wit.

And she thinks she may have done her work a disservice by having what Al Purdy calls 'a genius for publicity.' "
– Vancouver *Province*, September 1989

"As her life grew ever more sensational she created an image of herself that doesn't necessarily reflect the real Susan Musgrave," one interviewer wrote. And Musgrave recognizes that. "People find my life more interesting," she says, "and that's the burden I have to carry because I created that perception, at least partly." Musgrave's actions away from her writing desk feed the media what they want. They dwell on her non-literary exploits, she says, because it's easy and makes a better story than writing about her craft.

But Musgrave admits to being frustrated by claims that her life upstages her art. "I don't contrive to live my life so that it will make an exciting press release. I do what all writers do – plunder my life experiences for my writing. I don't like to think some biographical details might cause the work to get lost in the shuffle."

Sea-Witch Under His Spell

"His hair is greying and in the dim light it's hard to see the knife wounds that made the cops label him 'Scarface' when he was on the FBI's Most Wanted list, but he has a cool, watchful presence and looks as if he could spring into instant action if necessary. He touches [Musgrave] lovingly, but his past is never far from his mind."
– *City Life*, 1995

In the fall of 1984, at the beginning of her second year as Writer-in-Residence at the University of Waterloo, Susan Musgrave received a manuscript from a convicted bank robber. Musgrave read the manuscript and fell in love with the novel's protagonist. She began to correspond with the book's author, Stephen Reid, a member of Canada's notorious Stopwatch Gang who had served ten years of a twenty-year sentence for a gold heist in Ottawa. The correspondence touched off a romance, a bestselling novel, *Jackrabbit Parole*, and eventually a maximum-security wedding: three camera crews, including one from the *fifth estate*, filmed the couple saying "I do," and Musgrave was commissioned by *Vancouver Magazine* to cover her own three-day honeymoon in a cottage on the prison grounds. Reid was released on full parole in June of 1987. "That person seems like an ancestor of mine," he said, recently, of his days in the Stopwatch Gang.

After her prison marriage, Musgrave acquired a new persona, "the bank robber's wife." When, in 1998, the CBC produced the *Life and Times* documentary "The Poet and the Bandit," Musgrave decided to have fun with both their public images, even orchestrating a photo-shoot where they posed as Bonnie and Clyde, restaging a famous shot of the two outlaws where Bonnie holds her partner-in-crime hostage at the end of a gun.

"Outlaws, when they succeed, raise the exhilaration content of the universe," writes the American novelist Tom Robbins. "They even raise it a little bit when they fail." In June 1999, six months after the documentary was broadcast, and after years of being everybody's favourite reformed bank robber, Reid raised the exhilaration content of Victoria's peaceful Cook Street Village: when he filled his body with heroin and took down a fully loaded ATM machine at the Royal Bank in Fairfield, shooting at the police afterward, during a high-speed car chase. (His escape route has since been mapped out in a book called *The Alternative Guide to Victoria*, and three years ago a Japanese television program, *World Surprising*

News, made a film based on the robbery, paying the police to re-enact the car chase and fire blanks out the window.)

At the time of the offence many members of the public vilified Reid. Everyone had loved him when he had *been* a bank robber: he could talk flash talk and write books and was civilized and tamed enough to be a highly sought-after guest at dinner parties. But rob a bank? The media seemed to take his fall from grace personally. "Stephen, how could you do this to me?" one local journalist wrote. His relapse was the subject of morbid speculation: Was this an attempt at suicide? Was Reid trying to destroy his redeemed bank-robber image?

Musgrave has come to the conclusion that she fell in love, ini-tially, with Reid's persona. "I remember when he got his first day-pass and we went clothes shopping. He wanted to buy an eel-skin bow-tie and I was furious. This didn't suit my image of what an outlaw should wear! Same thing when he put on a baseball cap, backwards. It took me a long time to find, and fall in love with, the real person inside."

She recalls the words of anthropologist Paul Bohannan, who wrote that North Americans tend not to marry for economic, polit-ical, or family reasons. According to Bohannan, Musgrave says, "We marry for love and to accentuate, balance out, or mask parts of our private selves. That is why you will see a reserved account-ant married to an exotic dancer, or perhaps why I was attracted to Stephen."

In December 2005, Musgrave was invited to a festival in the Italian Alps. Her novel *Cargo of Orchids* had been published in Italy and her publisher hoped to generate some interest from the media. At her first press conference she was introduced as the "Calamity Jane of Canadian Literature," and the majority of the questions directed at her through translators dealt with her marriages to a marijuana smuggler in 1980 and then to an armed robber in 1986. Did she ever attempt to reform her husbands? Why was she attracted to brutal men, to outlaws?

In her most recent book, *You're in Canada Now . . . A Memoir of Sorts*, Musgrave grapples with her fascination with the outlaw persona. In one essay, she writes:

> Perhaps our pursuit of money has something to do with our respect for those who go after it with guns blazing. Our esteem for the hold-up artist is mirrored in the language we use to describe his line of work – beginning with the word "artist" itself.
>
> Outlaws are just more *interesting* than inlaws, which may be the simple reason why our society is obsessed with them. Novelists, playwrights and folk singers have perpetuated a romantic outlawry tradition in which the bank robber has been awarded the most glamorous image of all. They are the ones who do our dirty work for us, thumb their noses at authority, spit into the wind. Outlaws represent an almost childlike freedom we wish we had.

Referring to a scene in *Butch Cassidy and the Sundance Kid* where Butch takes Etta for a ride on his bicycle as B.J. Thomas sings "Raindrops Keep Falling On My Head," Musgrave writes:

> Butch is a threat to orderly society with boy-next-door appeal; it's impossible *not* to like him, especially when his movie role is played by Paul Newman with those regulation killer-blue eyes. Men look up to him, women fall for him. There is perhaps nothing more appealing than a man who is half outlaw, half good citizen.

This is how she would still characterize her husband, now serving an eighteen-year sentence.

Bank Robber's Wife Feels Trivialized by Labels

"Poet Susan Musgrave is fed up with all the labels that have stuck to her. The sea-witch. Bank robber's wife. Druggie. Crazy.

'I spend my life sitting in a room with a word processor,' she says. 'How exciting is that?'"

– Victoria *Times Colonist*, 1998

"Unlike many other famous individuals in our society, writers can't really fake it," argues Maralyn Lois Polak, editor of *The Writer as Celebrity*. "They can't really be permanently levitated by hype; their product, the book, poem, play, or article, speaks for itself; a bad writer ultimately unmasks himself on the page."

Musgrave pauses as she shelves the endless files of press clippings about her life and times (including those she has unearthed as research for this essay), recalling a small item she once read on the back pages of the *New York Times*, next to a cure for balding: "Actress smothers under avalanche of personal press clippings." "It's a good reminder," Musgrave says, "to put all this stuff away where you don't risk getting suffocated by it."

The Life and Art of Susan Musgrave

"Susan Musgrave is a renowned B.C. author with more than 20 books to her name. She is also the wife of accused bank robber Stephen Reid. Does any poet need this much torture?"

– *National Post*, August 1999

"Those of us who've been tortured need to see it as simply one more event in our lives, not a defining characteristic of who we are," says Hector Aristizabal. Musgrave adds that although Aristizabal may not let his past hardships define his own view of himself, once he has declared himself a survivor of torture, the experience becomes central to our understanding of him. His moral authority stems from his political activism and the persecution he suffered as a result.

Both the myths that writers have created about themselves and the myths that have been imposed upon them – in Musgrave's case those of the sea-witch or the *enfant terrible* attracted to outlaws – become the lens through which the public comes to view them. "It is not that you are misunderstood by the media or by the public," Musgrave says, "it is that they perceive you through a transitory and partly exaggerated narrative that is only a small part of your life story. But if you assist in the creation of your own persona," she maintains, "then you usually have the awareness, the self-efficacy, the sense of humour, to transcend the public image and live as an authentic person in your own right, not as a self defined exclusively by one aspect of your life."

Musgrave is adamant: any writer who buys into the myth of his own public persona, no matter how seductive or profitable it may be to do so, is doomed. She cites Hunter S. Thompson as an example. After the success of *Fear and Loathing in Las Vegas*, and then *Fear and Loathing on the Campaign Trail '72*, Thompson's larger-than-life reputation eclipsed the man-behind-the-mask. He became a caricature of himself, hamming it up in interviews, playing to his own mythology. His writing, too, reached a predictably gonzo edge. As others have noted, Thompson "*became* the story, our own countercultural literary dancing bear."

"The myths we start defining ourselves by, to try and make sense of our lives, can also be addictive and destructive," Musgrave says. "In some cases they exact a deathly price."

Poet's Public Persona Waxes Outrageous in Toronto

"Victoria's Susan Musgrave and her public persona are sitting in a bright, near-empty restaurant in Toronto.

Musgrave is the quiet one.

Her persona is its usual outrageous self, shocking, provoking and adding dark confirmation to her status as a death-obsessed witch poet."

– *Canadian Press*, 2004

What did Musgrave do this time to confirm her status as "a death-obsessed witch poet"? She shrugs. "Who knows? Maybe it had to do with these bones I wear around my neck?"

I am indebted to the following authors for their insights on the writer's persona: Camille Dodero for her interview with Zadie Smith, "Q&A: A Writer's Truth," *Boston Phoenix*, July 18–24, 2003; and David Walley for his article "Hunter S. Thompson: Fear, Loathing, and the Dancing Bear," *New Partisan*, February 22, 2005.

ANNA**PORTER**

The Master Storyteller

It's a long way from Halifax to River Bourgeois. After the Causeway and the spewing paper mill at Port Hawksbury on the way to Sydney, there is still that stretch of gravel road before you see the barn that is no longer a barn but headquarters of the Mowat Environmental Institute. Out front there is a weather-worn mailbox, arm raised to signal uncollected mail. The lettering on the mailbox announces: MOWAT.

Farley and Claire live here for the warmer half of the year in an old Nova Scotia white wood house with a grey peaked roof, tall bramble bushes, spruce forest, and narrow paths leading to the bay below. It's a clear summer day with a wild, whirling wind that smells of the sea. We walk on the beach in the late afternoon. Chester, the small black lab, is chasing seagulls, pirouetting on three legs, scratching a sore spot on his side with the fourth. "His back hurts," Farley explains. The dog, like Farley, is listing slightly to the left. Though he has a long record of supporting the Left, this is not all political persuasion: Farley hurt his back putting fresh paint on the house, getting it ready for the winter. Chester, so much younger, is aping sympathy.

An osprey circles overhead; its thin, sharp cries stop abruptly when it dives for its supper. Farther out a few seals pop their heads above water to peer at us. There are discarded bottles and cans amongst the stones at the edge of the sea. "I haven't been able to change one goddamn thing," Farley declares. "I thought I could make a real difference, force people to see what I see. Devastation. Death. We're dying in our own waste. Killing everything." He stops for a moment, watching the bird grab a fish with its outstretched talons and struggle to lift off again. "*Sea of Slaughter* was too dark, maybe. Too grim. Once they put it down, people wouldn't pick it up again." *Sea of Slaughter* was first published in 1984. There was still a Newfoundland fishery then. Cod was still king. But the age of the great whalers had already emptied the seas of most whales. The facts were numbing, but they have since become worse. "And they are still blaming the seals," he says, his eyes scanning the horizon for those few bobbing black heads. "The slaughter goes on." In April, the good ship *Farley Mowat*, captained by Farley's friend Paul Watson, sailed to the ice floes' killing grounds with a small group of Sea Shepherd Conservation Society folk. Armed with only their cameras, they tried to confront sealers carrying clubs and high-powered rifles.

"I couldn't go this year," Farley says apologetically. He is eighty-four years old.

I have known Farley Mowat since he handed in his manuscript for *Sibir: My Discovery of Siberia*. Early 1970. His publisher, Jack McClelland, had just hired me as some sort of junior editorial busybody and thought it would be interesting to send me to talk to Farley about his new book, an almost uncritical immersion into Siberia, and his love affair with the Russians. As Jack knew, I was born in Hungary. I had known a side of the Russians Farley had not seen. I was a kid during the 1956 Hungarian Revolution and had seen people face Russian tanks and die. He was the son of a librarian from Belleville, Ontario. He had fought in the Second World War when the Russians were allies. He had visited the Soviet Union and liked the people he met there. He assumed that they would be more responsive to his messages about disappearing wildlife. His book *Never Cry Wolf* had been published in Russian with the title *Wolves, Please Don't Cry*, and it raised such a public ruckus that the government decreed a moratorium on wolf hunting. The killing of wolves has not been banned in North America. Farley had seen the dark side of Western civilization and deplored it.

Predictably, we fought and argued, yelled at and harangued each other, more or less as Jack McClelland had intended we should. I am not sure why that resulted in a kind of friendship, but Jack had been fairly certain it would and he knew his Mowat well.

They had been friends since before the publication of Farley's first book, *People of the Deer*, an indictment of the Canadian government's policies in the North. It was around 1948. They had both endured the war – Farley had volunteered with the Hastings and Prince Edward Regiment, his father's, and fought his way up from the heel of Italy; Jack had been in the Atlantic on a Motor Torpedo Boat, harassing German U-boats – and they had both had enough of war.

Farley described Jack as this athletic-looking blond guy, tall, slim, casual, collar unbuttoned, feet on what might once have been a fine pine desk. Jack loved the book business. Against all good family advice, he wanted to be a publisher. Jack used to tell the story of how Farley first appeared in his office. A small, red-haired wild man with a passion to change the world. More than anything, he had wanted to be a writer. He thought words had the power to change the world.

As it transpired, they both got their wish. Jack became one of the last great, personal publishers, a believer in authors ("not just books," he said), a much loved, rather romantic breed that included the likes of Alfred Knopf and Roger Straus in the United States, and Billy Collins and George Unwin in the U.K. And Farley became one of the most prolific writers in Canada. Thirty-nine books and he is still up in his study every day – working on the next one.

"This one," he tells me, picking green beans in their small vegetable garden, "is definitely my last."

"Oh, Farley," Claire admonishes.

They have been together for more than forty years. She has just published a memoir of her own called *Travels with Farley*. It is a warm-hearted but clear-eyed exploration of what it is to be part of another's "writing life." She has been there through the adventures and the sadness, the delights of success and the disappointments; she was first mate on the boat they sailed around Newfoundland, the one that almost killed both captain and wife; she joined him in the battle for *A Whale for the Killing*; she commanded the home front on the Magdalen Islands. She knows that if he ever stopped writing he'd stop living.

I suggest he could maybe write something lighter, less harrowing, maybe even funny. He had often threatened to write a book about Albert, the dog he loved as much as he had loved his first dog, Mutt, hero of *The Dog Who Wouldn't Be*. It would be easier on his heart.

"Nothing wrong with m'heart, kid," he says, grinning, "it's the rest of me I'm not so sure about." Besides, in one of his letters to Jack, Farley had promised not "to grow old gracefully. I'm going down the drain snarling all the way."

He has been shouting his anger at the senseless killing of other species, the destruction of other ways of life, the cruelty, stupidity, and greed that have characterized our world, the driving need to conquer and possess. "It will, of course, destroy us. No, I am not worried about the Earth any more," he says. "The Earth will take care of itself. There have been other upheavals in its life. This tsunami, the hurricanes, the melting of the Arctic icecap, this is just the beginning. What I worry about is my tribe. Humanity. There will be no more stories. No more words. We shall become extinct."

When *Sea of Slaughter* was republished recently, David Suzuki said, "The tragedy of our time is that we have failed to act on the alarms and have continued the massacre. . . ." Twenty years ago there was still a chance. Farley is convinced that it is too late now. "Of course, the book won't sell," he says. "Crazy idea to publish something no one is going to buy. Also, it's bad business." He glares at me over the beans in the kitchen. "And don't interrupt."

I had been trying to tell him that it is good business, but Farley is convinced I have been publishing books for reasons other than commercial acuity.

The fortieth book will not be about these things, after all. It is, he says, grinning at both Claire and me, a personal "adventure" in the ancient tub of a boat whose engine would rarely obey commands, whose hull leaked, whose masts untwisted, who stubbornly refused to go where she was steered. Mowat fans will remember her as the *Happy Adventure* of his 1969 book, *The Boat Who Wouldn't Float*.

The Mowats winter in Port Hope, Ontario. Last spring the town threw a bash in honour of its most famous inhabitant. The Capitol Arts Theatre was packed with admirers and well-wishers. At 8 p.m., when he was piped into the building, everyone stood and clapped wildly. Farley, jaunty in his kilt and socks, bounced along to the music, waving this way, shaking hands that way, hugging some, kissing the women, trying, resolutely, not to be maudlin with all the adulation.

That evening followed the publication of his thirty-ninth book, *No Man's River*, a gripping tale set in the Far North. Its time is 1947. Having left behind the devastation of the Second World War, the young Mowat seeks a cleaner world far from man-made insanities. What he finds is a tragedy unfolding, and a great adventure that brings him to an understanding of the ancient people of the Arctic. The story is as vibrant and vivid, as well told, as if he had just returned from the journey.

He is still the passionate, pugnacious guy Jack McClelland first met in his office at the end of the forties, still telling his stories, the truth, the *real* truth – not just the barren facts, as he likes to point out.

Watching him onstage, bowing to the applause, thanking the speakers, I am crying – as is most of the audience. Reflecting on his life, those thirty-nine books in twenty-four languages that have sold more than twenty million copies worldwide, I think that the thing about Farley, the most important thing, is that he is the quintessential storyteller. He loves to entertain. Sure, there is also something he desperately wants you to know, that he cares about passionately, but he never wants to bore you, the reader. His descriptions are always apt, his dialogue works, you can believe his characters existed and several may still be wandering about in Newfoundland or in the Arctic, in Africa, or on some old Saskatchewan farm. He is a stylist, a wordsmith, the perfect teller of tales.

If only words could change the world, Farley, you'd have us all live in a better place.

EDEN**ROBINSON**

The Author Reading That Made Me a Woman

I was on a book tour of schools in northern B.C. The audience was four hundred grade eight students packed into a darkened auditorium. One of the teachers had decided to keep the rowdies under control by placing them all in the front row.

I can't remember how I got involved in the tour. I do remember how I drove around the snowy northern highways in a badly heated rental car with two other writers, another novelist and a poet. I'm not sure the teachers had been told we were coming or what we had written. My first assignment was to read to a kindergarten class. I flipped through a mental list of suitable material to read to six-year-olds. My only published book at that point was *Traplines*, a collection of stories about homicidal sociopaths and their dysfunctional family dynamics. I switched with the poet and read to a grade twelve English class, who stared through me. They leaped up when the lunch bell rang and charged for the door while their teacher shouted their assignments after them.

The poet had a beatnik charm, black turtleneck, and hand drums. The other novelist had a delicate presence, lyrical writing, and stage training. They would tutor me on public speaking as we drove between gigs. We would do warm-up exercises and practise relaxation techniques. I had already had two years of Toastmasters, acting and improv classes, voice training and hypnotherapy. But I was still obviously uncomfortable in front of an audience. I also loathed interviews, especially live interviews. It had taken two Gravol and an Imodium to get me through my *Morningside* interview with Shelagh Rogers.

Receptionists don't have to do this, I thought, looking out at the audience from behind the stage curtain. The poet was reading and the rowdies were whispering to each other. On the other hand, receptionists were the first point of contact in any company and they got the flak when the irate needed to vent on someone harmless. I'd manned the phones in an Unemployment Insurance office when a new rule came down that employees would not get UIC if they were fired. I had been dithering about renewing my government contract until that day, when the switchboard lit up with strangers questioning my parentage and telling me to place different body parts in impossible positions. Job security could take a flying leap. I celebrated my last day of work with co-workers who shook their heads and said I could always come back if freelancing didn't pan out.

I love writing. I love daydreaming for a living. But writing is barely half of an emerging writer's career. The other half is hustle, or, more politely, promotion. Any chance you get, you hump your work through schools, libraries, literary festivals, bookstores – anywhere that will give you a podium and an audience. I was drawn to the solitude of writing, but forced by the job description to perform publicly on a regular basis. I did my duty but I didn't enjoy it and, judging from the way my tour buddies were trying to coach me, no one else was enjoying it much either.

As the other novelist started to read, the grade eight audience was riveted by one of her lesbian erotica segments. Seeing the students leaning forward in their seats, rapt, I wished I'd written lesbian erotica. She wasn't reading anything graphic or distasteful, but the teachers in the back of the auditorium formed a concerned huddle.

We had developed a routine where we introduced each other to keep the reading moving briskly. She finished up by reciting a brief blurb about me and then she left the stage to resounding applause, which dimmed and quickly died away as I walked toward the podium.

I mumbled into the microphone.

"What?" one of the rowdies shouted.

"What? What? What?" the others chorused.

I raised my head out of my book to plead silently with the teachers in the back to intervene and discovered that they had all left the auditorium. The other writers were backstage, and I knew from experience they were probably in the green room, drinking coffee and laughing. I was alone with four hundred thirteen-year-olds. I cleared my throat. The front row cleared their throats, turning to each other and clearing their throats again and again, pausing only to snicker.

I could either slink off the stage or stick it out long enough to save face. A quick five-minute reading, I decided, and then I would run to the hotel room and phone my sister for solace. I stuck my head in my book and ploughed through.

"You suck!"

"Hey, loser! Yeah, you! Get off the stage!"

"Boooring."

I was booed. Loudly. Crumpled paper started piling up at my feet. I stopped reading and looked up.

I had always feared that this would happen, that people would absolutely loathe what I had to say. This was the worst-case scenario that kept me up the night before every reading. It did hurt but I wasn't devastated. I had expected to dissolve into a puddle of shame and wretchedness but instead I was annoyed. Damned if a bunch of rowdies were going to drive me offstage.

Out of spite, I read the most gratuitously violent, curse-laden segment in my book. To my surprise, I was cheered. No one had ever given a performance of mine anything more enthusiastic than a golf clap. The teachers had returned by now, and one of them gave me a desperate cut-off signal. Some of the kids stayed behind and we talked and I signed their notebooks. It was the first time I felt like a real author. I can't say I immediately became a great reader or performer, but after facing down one of my biggest bogeymen, I relaxed a little more into my own skin and became less afraid of engaging an audience.

MARILYNNE**ROBINSON**

On the Reader:
An Excerpt from an Essay in Progress

Why, as a girl, was I staggered by *An American Tragedy*, by *Of Human Bondage*? I have never gone back to either of those books, which figure in my imagination like the dark old ritual places in Freud's imagination of primal consciousness. I feel as if, when I read them, something happened that had to happen, an initiation into the mythos and cultus of mortality itself. What if, going back, I found nothing there to frighten me, nothing there that I could mourn? I do not want to risk the loss of those heavy-hearted moments when it seemed that I lost myself, and found myself. Whatever the books actually said or meant, they told me an astonishing thing, that the world would break my heart. And I learned at the same time that there was a place in my soul prepared almost to welcome the injury. My mother might have been cooking supper, my father might have been reading the paper, while I, in that charmed secrecy of the enthralled, was learning from a battered library book what they would never have thought to tell me, perhaps hoped I would never know. I would have put the novel down with the usual reluctance, dealt quietly with my mashed potatoes, dealt distractedly with dishes and homework, and then returned again to those tales of long-drawn grief and guilt as if I had returned to a place more my own than my parents' house could ever be.

For a while last year I was receiving brief, unsigned emails from a woman in China. She was alone in a city where she knew no one, and it was very cold. She had whiled away her solitary time translating my novel *Housekeeping* into Chinese. She wrote to me because in that city the snow was falling. She wrote to me because on a certain day she had left her room and gone out to the street. She wrote to say that she had a friend in Rhode Island, and if she came here to visit she might also say hello to me. The serene formality of her foreign English, so precise, as if it were a language only meant to speak of winter solitude in a nameless city, as if we are in error who make such indiscriminate use of such a language – what can I say, except that that woman on the other side of the planet met me on the terrain of the imagined world and divulged a thrilling sorrow to me there. It is a very deep thing, this reading of books, an unaccountably primal thing, clearly much deeper than history or culture.

Mass literacy and the ready availability of books are very recent developments. This tiny excrescence on human existence we call the modern period has, as one great cause and one great consequence, the omnipresence of the written word. We need not look back very far, a century or two, to find a time when to own a book, to have read a book, would have been a mark of privilege anywhere in the world. So why should it be that literacy is an expectation we can have of most people in any population? I have read that writing and speech are negotiated in different regions of the brain, that when we write we have another, larger vocabulary than we use in speech. Why should we be so well adapted for a skill very few of us, historically speaking, would have had any chance to acquire or any occasion to use? When the word is a mere sign – *this end up, exit, caution* – it can be thought of as analogous to finding the footprint of an animal or noting the drift of the constellations, the sort of thing we have been up to forever. But reading a book is a much deeper thing than interpreting a series of signs. Words can inform, but they can also enlist, and it is this power to engage consciousness, so that a fiction becomes the reader's own experience, that is remarkable. There is a power, as of ritual or initiation, which claims a place in deep memory, and which remains integral and complex. Every novel we call great has by now a penumbra of interpretation surrounding it. But at the core of it all is the irreducible complexity of the fiction itself, for which no equivalent language can be found. This is the music that has as its instrument the consciousness of the reader.

There is a story we have told ourselves for a long time, that primordial human experience was more potent than our own. I have invoked this notion with my allusions to ritual and initiation. Like all of us, I learned what I know about them from Freud and assorted anthropologists, not one of whom I am much inclined to credit. I am pretty sure that certain among our forebears, hunkered around the communal fire, wished the shaman would just get to the point, so the sheep could be slaughtered and immolated and then they could all dance around a little and go home. I think it is fair to assume that our forebears were tired most of the time, and that they had practical worries all that business with smoke and feathers could not wholly assuage. There is an obvious condescension in supposing that people whose material culture was rudimentary were therefore childlike. And there is condescension in assuming that people whose material culture is complex – ourselves – are therefore estranged from the possibility of experience that makes us feel our humanity deeply. So when I speak in the terms Freud has supplied, perhaps I am, and he was, retrojecting experience that is indeed available to moderns like ourselves. He invokes those great Greek fictions, the tragedies, which are meditations on the variants of human guilt, error and entrapment, and which are tragedies because no rituals of expiation preclude or resolve the offences against the gods which the gods occasion or permit and also punish. If they and sacrifice have the same subject, the yearning for encounter with forces on the hidden side of the mortal mystery, so does, for example, *King Lear*. So does *Crime and Punishment*. So does *The Sound and the Fury*. It is true at the moment that our literature seems to incline toward terror a good deal more than it does toward pity, unless its subject is the writer herself or himself. But there are only a handful of great books in any generation, and perhaps, when the epiphenomenal literature falls away, we will find that we have contributed our share to the sum of them.

Nor do I want to dismiss the fictions I have called epiphenomenal, mysterious as their appeal might seem in another decade. Nor do I wish to imply that only tragedy has value. I read *The Trail of the Lonesome Pine* because Gertrude Stein said that when she read to wounded American soldiers in the hospitals in France during the First World War, it was the book they always asked to hear. It is charming to think of that abstruse old poet reading to injured farm boys just back from a brush with the worst war the world had seen, and longing to hear a very sentimental story one more time. She did not know what they saw in it, but she read it again and again. Maybe they were the true modernists in the room, having looked into the future from their trenches and bunkers. And maybe sentiment was a balm to them, and a very profound thing, too, in that moment, on that account. To her great credit, Stein made no attempt to elevate their tastes.

People seem to have been judged by their taste in books for as long as there have been books enough to make one's choices among them meaningful. To be a reader of French novels once reflected darkly on one's character. Fiction itself was suspect when most of the books published in America were still collections of sermons. And of course there is nothing like prohibition to raise the value of whatever is forbidden. The earliest American novels were tales of incest, perhaps in response to the presumption that fiction was itself a kind of transgression. And perhaps that presumption lingers with us, and is reflected in the very widespread tendency among writers to try to find a way to scandalize their readers, if only a little. Among the arts the novel is a new form, just as the cheap production of books and the broader distribution of time and privacy are new features of life. The novel has antecedents, of course, but its presence as a major and highly available experience for readers is a recent development. To tell or hear stories as our ancestors did, even to be read to, is different from curling up on a couch with a novel, or reading on the subway. There is at least the society of two involved in telling and hearing, whereas the reading of a novel – apart from the mysterious communion of book and reader – is a quintessentially solitary experience. If one were to look for things to compare, for their engaged isolation, with the reading of a novel, they would be dreaming, meditation, and prayer. And perhaps it is this manifest individualism it induces, this being alone and engaged over time in a powerful present, unshared and essentially incommunicable, that makes the novel an eccentric and often a suspect form.

Words that are associated with modern or contemporary life, here individualism, are widely assumed to have negative connotations. I love individualism, and only wish there were more of it. It has been associated, recently and arbitrarily, with competition, with self-seeking. But this assumes that an individualist would accept the definition of success that is general in his or her society – how else to engage in competition? by what other standard to measure relative success? In other words, the present notion of the individualist is of someone neither self-sufficient nor self-directed. This inversion of meaning may reflect the general loss of respect for inwardness, or perhaps a loss of faith in the existence of inwardness except in pathological forms. If the strange, enthralled isolation imposed by the novel seemed suspect when the form was emerging, and if the intimacy of the reader with the book encouraged, for example, Laurence Sterne to forget his priestly decorum and confide a certain pleasure in rakish humour, or Zola to dwell on the painful particulars of life in regions of society the polite did not mention, then the vitality of the form, which is to say the need for it, has to do with just that isolation, that shared terrain of special trust between the writer and the reader.

We tend to think we are wise and worldly and have outlived these quaint anxieties. I suspect we should think again. When I was in college, certain of my friends, girls from very urbane and enlightened families, were told by their parents that they could experiment with psychoactive drugs so long as there was a doctor present. And some parents seem to have orchestrated these events, with obliging doctors and high-quality drugs, in non-threatening environments of the daughters' choosing. Whether they succeeded in neutralizing the lure of Haight-Ashbury I do not know. I suspect the presence of anxious parents and of hovering medical assistance might have diminished the thrill of transgression a little, and perhaps that was the point. In any case, girls from such families seemed bent on lives in investment banking, so inoculation was probably not necessary to begin with. It seems to me that there is something of the same tendency in the way fiction is taught these days. That solitude, that venture into intense inward experience, must be disrupted for the reader's own good. The educated reader is told – you should not do this alone. You will need the assistance of a qualified professional. He or she will protect you from the effects of contaminants in the authorial worldview, instructing you in the dangers of adulteration with thought crimes and thought misdemeanours, those conceptual impurities which otherwise produce a toxic response when ingested. You can have the experience of reading a powerful book, but do it safely, with expert help, under our anxious parental gaze. This is a long way of saying that the individual is not now trusted, that interest and value are not conceded to individual experience. Perhaps I romanticize the issue. It may be truer to say that the fact of the individual is not strongly valued among us at this time.

What happens to a fact when it is not credited? One thing we know is that facts utterly pertinent to human life and to the norms of behaviour within and among societies can be denied so thoroughly that they are suppressed almost beyond retrieval. And we know also that this suppression is a consistent feature of human life and culture. The intelligence, sensitivity and moral competence of the great majority of people in any society is, at best, radically underestimated on grounds that are familiar to us all – race, gender, ethnicity, disability, and so on. We may be unique among the generations for the emphasis we have put on eliminating these inequities. Ironically, however, we have at the same time generalized these presumptions against intelligence, sensitivity and moral competence so that they now seem to apply to the whole of the population. So whatever justice we extend with one hand we take away with the other. Those members of the population who were once denied the social franchise education in this society has traditionally conferred are now offered a future as economic helots – right along with most others in their age cohort, of course. That is the new equality. They have been liberated into the age of declining expectations. We hear all the time about the downward drift of one or another aspect of collective life. . . .

PETER**ROBINSON**

Turning to Crime

There are so many misconceptions about crime fiction and its practitioners that it is hard to know where to begin. I should know. I held most of them myself when I was a stuck-up English student publishing poetry in small magazines. Crime writers, so the stereotype went, were lurid types who wrote to a formula and, even more to the point, were only in it for the money. We all knew that. Of course, at the time, I hadn't read any crime fiction. I did know Samuel Johnson's oft-quoted dictum, "No man but a blockhead ever wrote except for money," but I took it as a tongue-in-cheek remark. We literary purists knew that the only reason we wrote was because we had something very important to say. It was only later I learned that I write because I have to, because I love it, and because there's nothing else I can do as well. But that's another story.

I say that I hadn't read any crime fiction, but this is only partly true. I certainly hadn't read any recent mysteries – I had been too immersed in Shakespeare, Coleridge, Keats, Hardy, and Dickens – and I hadn't read Agatha Christie, Dashiell Hammett, or Raymond Chandler. But, in a way, it was the crime fiction I read as a child that got me interested in writing in the first place, and reading it later was a return for me rather than the new departure it sometimes appeared to be.

In his essay "The Lost Childhood," Graham Greene has this to say about the importance of childhood reading and its influence on our later lives and work: "In childhood all books are books of divination, telling us about the future, and like the fortune teller who sees a long journey in the cards or death by water they influence the future." We may not realize this at the time, but it is true.

Greene notes the excitement of finding a new novel by Rider Haggard, Percy Westerman, Captain Brereton, or Stanley Weyman. Each generation, as well as each country, has its particular childhood favourites, and while some names, such as Rider Haggard, stand the test of time, many, such as the other three, don't. Like most English children of my generation, my early reading began with Enid Blyton. Blyton started out as a kindergarten teacher and ended up publishing over six hundred children's books between 1922 and 1966, including the "Noddy" series and, perhaps more important for a budding crime writer, the Famous Five, Secret Seven, and "Adventure" series.

During the 1960s, Enid Blyton came in for a lot of criticism from librarians for her books' limited vocabulary and their perceived sexism, snobbery, and racism; her Noddy books were later recast in a form more acceptable to the politically correct nineties. However, her contribution toward getting a generation of children to love reading cannot be overstated, and she brought most of us to reading via adventure stories and mysteries. I recently bought a couple of old Famous Five first editions at an antiquarian book fair in North Yorkshire, but I haven't been able to bring myself to read them. Somehow, I fear, they won't match up to my memories of our first encounter.

✳ ✳ ✳

With the onset of adolescence came a sudden dissatisfaction with the rarified world of Julian, Dick, Anne, and George and their dog, Timmy, and the yearning for something more exciting. Sherlock Holmes made a good starting place. I especially loved the old Basil Rathbone movies, most of which had nothing whatsoever to do with Conan Doyle's stories, which I read and read over again. The Holmes stories are far less the dry exercises in reason that some people imagine, and far more *Boy's Own* adventure stories, filled with exciting chases and frightening villains. *The Hound of the Baskervilles*, with its eerie evocation of Dartmoor and its central struggle between reason and superstition, remains one of my favourite crime novels to this day.

But there was one ingredient missing from Sherlock Holmes's exploits that a fourteen-year-old boy was very much interested in: sex. In my search for something a bit racier, The Saint and James Bond seemed to fit the bill nicely: handsome, daredevil, debonair heroes, who always got the beautiful girl and always defeated the mad, evil genius intent on world domination. At least James Bond did. Simon Templar's adversaries were often a lot more down to earth, and much of the satisfaction of reading Leslie Charteris's series came from seeing The Saint put yet another one over on Inspector Teal, much like Sherlock Holmes did with Inspector Lestrade. My entire generation must have thought that Scotland Yard was staffed by bumbling idiots, an image borne out again later when I read Agatha Christie and watched Hercule Poirot run rings around the hapless Inspector Japp.

Both The Saint and James Bond had become pop culture icons by the mid-sixties, the former via television and the latter via movies, and these media, perhaps even more than books, fed my adolescent craving for adventure, thrills, and the promise of sex. What teenage boy can forget Ursula Andress walking out of the ocean in *Dr. No*? Or Shirley Eaton's nude, gold-painted body in *Goldfinger*? Yet the Bond books were even sexier – Honey Rider was *naked* when she came out of the sea in Ian Fleming's novel, and Bond always seemed to be reaching for some girl's left breast, something we weren't shown in the movies. I have managed to reread a number of the Ian Fleming novels over the past few years, and he turns out to be both a much better and a much worse writer than I had remembered. Better because he actually *could* write decent action and description, worse because the books are full of irritating authorial interferences, usually to give opinions on everything from women drivers to communism.

There were others, of course – Sexton Blake, Bulldog Drummond, The Toff and The Baron, but The Saint and James Bond were the true heroes of my early adolescence.

❋   ❋   ❋

In my late teens, however, my literary tastes took a swift about-turn when I encountered the Beats, especially Allen Ginsberg, Jack Kerouac, Lawrence Ferlinghetti, and Gregory Corso. I still have many of those well-thumbed little City Lights "Pocket Poets" books – *Howl*, *A Coney Island of the Mind*, *Gasoline* – and I still make my pilgrimage to the City Lights Bookstore every time I visit San Francisco. Just as the new music, with its daring and often incomprehensible lyrics from the likes of Bob Dylan, the Grateful Dead, the Incredible String Band, Roy Harper, and Captain Beefheart began to replace the more insipid "boy meets girl" songs of the early Beatles, Elvis Presley, Roy Orbison, and the rest among my favourites, so the works of Ginsberg and his fellow Beats replaced Fleming, Sapper, Doyle, and Charteris and fired my imagination anew. There was no room in the brooding, surrealistic, and engaged world of the Beats for the frivolities of a James Bond or Bulldog Drummond. Interestingly, I now find rereading the Beats as problematic as I find rereading the works of my early crime fiction and thriller heroes.

At school, poetry had always seemed a distant and unattainable vocation, reserved mainly for lords and the upper classes in general, but after reading the Beats I realized that anyone could write poetry. You just wrote about your feelings and your thoughts about the world, God, the universe and stuff and broke it into uneven lines. It didn't even have to rhyme or make sense. What could be easier? From that moment on, I decided that I was a poet. It wasn't until several years later that I discovered poetry is a far more complex literary undertaking that has a lot to do with things other than "my feelings" or my views on the world, and that, even if it doesn't have to, poetry is rather nice when it does actually rhyme and make sense.

The late sixties and early seventies were a mad whirl of books, talk, pubs, rock concerts, drugs, and girls. I joined a group of itinerant poets and musicians and we travelled around the U.K. doing poetry readings at arts labs, festivals, colleges, pubs, anywhere that would have us. More often than not we got paid in beer, if we got paid at all. It didn't matter. We were like Sal Paradise and Dean Moriarty in *On the Road*, prattling away like maniacs as we hurled through the night, ideas crackling like electricity in the air around us. One cold and windy January evening in Blackpool, we even did a gig with the American rock band Spirit, and I once found myself working as a roadie for the support band to The Who at Manchester University. If anyone had told me at that time I would end up writing about a police inspector, I'd have laughed in his face. I spent most of my time avoiding the police, not seeking them out.

Sometimes I forgot that I was university student and that I was supposed to be reading *Tristram Shandy* or *Humphry Clinker* rather than *Siddhartha* or *The Ticket that Exploded*. But I did manage to get my BA Honours degree in English Literature, and I graduated from the University of Leeds in the spring of 1974.

✳   ✳   ✳

So where does the crime kick in again? Not until a while later. Poetry carried me though my MA in English Literature and Creative Writing at the University of Windsor, where I studied under Joyce Carol Oates, a wonderful teacher who encouraged by example and made anyone who cared about writing feel that it mattered, and that *they* mattered. Joyce also had a table piled with books by the door of her office, and she encouraged us to borrow freely every time we left a seminar. Often I'd just make a random selection, but sometimes she would guide me in certain directions – Robert Creeley's poetry, for example, or Robert Duncan – and I would take it all in. I was writing exclusively poetry at the time and I couldn't imagine ever writing anything else.

After Windsor, I went into the Ph.D. program at York University, in Toronto. By that time I was starting to publish in magazines such as the *Malahat Review*, *Matrix*, *Quarry*, the *Antigonish Review*, and *Queen's Quarterly*. In 1979, I published my first volume of poetry, called *With Equal Eye*, with Gabbro Press, which consisted of Gail Noble and me, our spouses, and an old letter press in the basement. We handset the type ourselves, printed two hundred copies, and had them bound. Then we left them on consignment in every bookshop we managed to visit. Years later, I found a copy in the Gotham Book Mart in New York. I didn't know whether to feel thrilled that it was still there or sad that it hadn't sold. In 1982,

I published a pamphlet called *Nosferatu*, also with Gabbro, in a signed and numbered edition of one hundred copies.

By this time, I was working on my Ph.D. thesis, *A Local Habitation: The Sense of Place in Contemporary British and Irish Poetry*, examining the work of Philip Larkin, Ted Hughes, Seamus Heaney, Basil Bunting, and Geoffrey Hill. I helped to organize regular poetry evenings at Winters College, under the guidance of the college master, Maurice Elliott, and our readers included such luminaries as Christopher Dewdney, Al Pittman, Eli Mandel, Paul Muldoon, Susan Musgrave, Lorna Uher (as Lorna Crozier was known back then), and Patrick Lane. I was also writing a quarterly column on poetry for *Poetry Canada Review*, and I contributed an essay on Robin Skelton's poetics to *Skelton at 60*, published in 1986.

My own poetry was changing dramatically, moving away from the loose Beat structure to more formal meditations and narratives, and I was quickly beginning to feel that the kind of forms I wanted to write in, and the stories I wanted to tell, were actually beyond the scope of what narrow poetic talent I possessed. As it turned out, they weren't the sort of poems that magazines wanted to publish at the time, anyway. I suppose one obvious sign that the end was near was that I was spending far more time reading books about poetic form and structure than reading or writing poetry itself.

*   *   *

One surprising thing I had discovered during my academic journey was how many professors and "serious" literary types read crime fiction. My thesis adviser was a big fan of Robert B. Parker, for example. Robin Skelton loved mysteries and was kind enough to give my early books some good notices. He had, in fact, written a number of crime novels himself and was always disappointed that they were not published.

But still, it seemed, I resisted.

Until one rainy day in Leeds – I was back home in Yorkshire for the summer – when out of boredom I picked up one of my father's books, a cheaply printed omnibus of three Raymond Chandler novels. The first of these was *The Little Sister*, and from the second paragraph I was hooked. Interestingly enough, it wasn't plot at all that got me excited. Chandler couldn't plot to save his life. It was the *voice*, the vivid descriptions, character, place, the witty dialogue, writing with muscle. Read chapter thirteen. It has no business being there because it doesn't further the plot in the least; it reveals character and place. But it's a gem of a prose poem. Or the opening paragraph of "Red Wind." Sublime.

Chandler always suffered from what he called "the redlight segregation of detective stories from 'novels' by reviewers," and he was thrilled when, in 1954, *The Long Goodbye* was reviewed as the work of "a Novelist" in the London *Sunday Times*. Many consider that book his greatest work. It is certainly a "novel," and a fine one at that.

Encouraged by my enjoyment of Chandler, I ventured on to Georges Simenon, another favourite of my father's, partly because the Parisian settings reminded him of his days in Paris just after the Liberation. Again, plot was a minor concern. Usually someone got killed and Inspector Maigret spent his time hanging around bars and nightclubs talking to petty criminals and prostitutes and having a thoroughly good time. Sometimes he went into the provinces, and the stories he got involved in there seemed reminiscent of the Chabrol or Truffaut movies I was watching at the time.

While Chandler's Philip Marlowe and Dashiell Hammett's Sam Spade represent the prototypal American private eye, Inspector

Maigret is perhaps the true forebear of contemporary fictional police detectives, including Alan Banks. The books drip with atmosphere, from the sound of coins clinking on zinc counters to the rain-soaked streets of Montmartre, or the deserted crossroads of a provincial town. Maigret empathizes with people, with killers, thieves, dancers, bankers, and shop clerks alike, but one suspects that he prefers the company of the working girls and the petty criminals to the upper echelons of Parisian society he sometimes has to deal with. Psychology is his forte; Maigret understands people, their needs, what pushes them over the edge, and it is often with great sadness that he hauls the killer off to jail at the end.

The closest American equivalent is probably Ed McBain's long-running 87th Precinct series, though McBain put the emphasis on teamwork rather than individual detection. McBain's characters and ensemble set-up have formed the unacknowledged basis for any number of network cop shows, from *Hill Street Blues* to *NYPD Blue*.

Among the American private detective novelists, though I always hold a special place in my pantheon for Hammett and Chandler, Ross Macdonald and his Lew Archer series quickly became my favourite. Here was a tough but remarkably intelligent and compassionate man digging up the buried secrets of California's wealthy elite. Macdonald could plot. In fact, he once wrote, "I see plot as a vehicle of meaning. It should be as complex as contemporary life, but balanced enough to say true things about it." From *The Galton Case* (1959) onward, Macdonald was to tell very much the same story over and over: a wealthy family has a secret that is causing dysfunction in the present, which often results in a murder or disappearance, and the solution usually requires a heavy dollop of Freudian psychology. Whatever else he accomplished, Macdonald added a lot more psychological depth to the literary panache that Chandler had already brought to the private-eye novel.

*   *   *

Imagine my surprise and pleasure on discovering that not only could Simenon, Hammett, Chandler, Macdonald, and McBain write, but they could write intelligent stories that probe the world in which we live on both social and psychological levels, and keep me turning the pages at the same time. I began to crave more, and next I turned my attention toward British writers.

One of my early discoveries was Ruth Rendell, and she remains a great favourite to this day, as much, if not more, for her psychological thrillers such as *A Demon in My View*, *Live Flesh*, or *A Judgement in Stone* as for her Wexford police novels. It is interesting to consider that the best screen adaptations of Rendell's work have been made by European directors. Claude Chabrol did a fine job with *A Judgement in Stone* (*La Cérémonie*, 1995) and *The Bridesmaid* (*La Demoiselle d'honneur*, 2004), and Pedro Almodóvar made a quirky and intriguing version of *Live Flesh* (*Carne trémula*, 1997).

Though I enjoyed many British crime writers, including Ruth Rendell, Reginald Hill, and P.D. James, I found myself drawn more to the Europeans, such as the Swedish couple Maj Sjöwall and Per Wahlöö, who set out to write a series of ten police novels featuring Martin Beck between 1965 and 1975, in which they mapped the social changes in Swedish society through crime and criminal investigations. Then there was Nicholas Freeling's Van der Valk series, set in the permissive atmosphere of sixties Amsterdam, where personal freedoms were often set against the needs and ideologies of post-war Dutch society as a whole. A little later came Janwillem van der Wetering, who brought a decidedly zany, Zen element to policing Amsterdam. (Van der Wetering had, in fact, spent a number of years in a Zen monastery in Japan, an experience he wrote about with great humour and insight in his memoir, *The Empty Mirror*.) It was beginning to seem that the depth and breadth of crime fiction were full of infinite possibility.

*   *   *

Of course, the main ingredient of most crime novels – and the reason why many members of the literary establishment often dismiss crime fiction out of hand – is a corpse. There also needs to be some sort of investigation into how there came to be a corpse. This can be carried out by a talented (or even an untalented) amateur, or by a professional, and it can be serious, comical, incompetent, or skilled. But in most cases, it has to be done. To some people, this smacks of formula. I could argue that it's no more formulaic than a sonnet or an epistolary novel or a picaresque novel, all of which make demands on the writer in terms of their form and structure. In some ways, one could also argue the crime novel is a sort of bastard offspring of the comedy of manners and the sensational novel. But that's a whole other argument, and one I don't have the time or space to go into here.

The point I want to make, and I think it is an important one, is that in the best crime writing, the murder is a catalyst to set things in motion. Hitchcock used to call the secret documents, or whatever it was that everyone was chasing in his movies, the "McGuffin." In a crime novel, the murder is the McGuffin. It is what allows the writer to throw a spanner in the works of normal life and examine people under pressure, peel back the surface to look at their motives, backgrounds, secrets and lies, along with their relationships to one another and to the society in which they live.

That said, though, it has always been one of my contentions that the main character in a crime novel is not the detective, but the victim. In this sense, one speaks for the dead, who cannot, of course, speak for themselves. And the central mystery, to me, is what combination of circumstances, of deliberation and coincidence, brought this person to this end at this time? In order to discover this, one must reconstruct the life of the victim through the often unreliable recollections of others and through the imagination of the detective himself, who puts together the fragments until a picture emerges, then comes into focus like a distant figure in a telescope. If this bears an uncanny resemblance to the way a writer constructs a novel, it is probably because, in a way, the writer shares with the detective the important qualities of curiosity and imagination, and both writer and detective often find themselves speaking for the voiceless and imagining the lives of others.

Crime novels inhabit that landscape where individual needs and desires clash with society's taboos; they examine how far people will go, and for what. A character's world is not seen in isolation, but in the context of his times, and the particular crimes a society suffers says a lot about that society, its problems, and its values.

More and more, in contemporary crime writing, this world view is expanding, and the best writers make us aware that even the most remote village is not immune from the problems of drugs and violence, and that the fallout from not-so-distant wars, such as those in the Balkans, can be seen in the plight of asylum seekers and sex trade workers in the larger towns and cities. The aftermath of imperialism and colonialism comes home to roost with a vengeance in large numbers of displaced and disaffected people and in terrorist acts in New York, Bali, or London. You can't ignore this. The best crime writers, like all writers, write with the uneasy knowledge of genocide in Rwanda and the suffering of women in wartorn countries like Sierra Leone. They also know that sometimes it is the one small, silent death among the shrieking mass of wholesale slaughter that says the most.

One of the questions I am often asked is, Do I mind being regarded as a second-class citizen by the literary community and arts media? Well, of course I bloody do! I would have thought that was self-evident. All writers want the respect they feel they deserve. Of course crime writers want lengthy, well-considered reviews, not just a skimpy column inch along with the four or five other crime novels published that month, and they want to be asked to join in discussions on writing and literature on TV and radio. So, yes, I do mind, and I'm one of the luckier ones in terms of media coverage. But I don't mind that much. You see, I know I'm in very good company.

JOHN RALSTON SAUL

Writing in the No-Go Zone

I was travelling through China in 1979 when the Gang of Four wasn't long gone. We were a little group of three and everywhere we went writers took us in hand. They were all from the old Chou En-Lai school of sophisticated Marxist mandarins, mainly in their seventies or eighties. Many had been on the Long March. They spoke three or four languages, chain-smoked with ivory cigarette holders, their Mao jackets were well-cut and their sense of humour wry.

Thirteen years before, the Cultural Revolution had turned them from heroes of the revolution into traitors. They had only recently been released from hard labour on pig farms or from prison or house arrest. Many other writers had been killed or had died from the conditions in which they had been forced to work.

One of those accompanying us had written the long ode to Chou En-Lai which, using his death, had provoked the demonstration in Beijing that brought this particularly destructive period to an end. And now the old guard of intellectuals was back, eager to talk, eat well, drink. The secretary of the Writers' Union who travelled everywhere with us had been confined to his small office for years, during which he had become obsessed by bonsais, an obsession suited to his condition. The Minister of Culture, an aged novelist now back in favour, was famous for a novel of the Communist–Kuomintang civil war. He interrupted our highly formal meeting to muse over what part of his writings might survive.

He was convinced one line would make it into eternity – one line in which he had written life. It involved describing a woman's breasts as artillery shells. The importance of this wasn't entirely clear to us at first, but he argued that there were hundreds of thousands of descriptions of women already in place. It was virtually impossible to invent something entirely new. He was convinced he had.

None of these writers talked about the civil war or the Long March or their taking of power or their use or misuse of it, let alone the Cultural Revolution. Instead they chatted on about literature. If you didn't know already, you would never have known from them what their half century of adventures had contained. They belonged to an elegant tradition in which talking about such things in public would be a sign of weakness, while writing about them was a strength. Their life was all there in their writings.

*   *   *

I was obsessed at that time by André Malraux and, more importantly, by the patron saint of writers like Malraux – Joseph Conrad. I'm still obsessed by Conrad. He discovered a new way to capture life by pretending to embrace reality while actually freeing us from it, at least long enough to consider our existence. He pretended to tell stories of life while he was evoking its impossibility in a certain kind of world.

I have a rare signed photo of him hanging over me while I write. He signed it for my godfather's stepmother in New York in 1919 when he made a single appearance as the great modern master.

But on this trip to China my particular obsession was Malraux and *La Condition Humaine*. The importance of the novel can't be questioned, but what interested me was the relationship between these great Chinese writers I was meeting and the Westerner who has written – thanks to his involvement with the revolutionaries, his role in the revolution – the great novel of the revolution, the great novel of modern China. Although younger than Malraux, they would have known him, I was sure, talked with him, perhaps even been influenced by him. Throughout his life, Malraux had returned to his own obsession with China and to the meaning for humanity of its half century of turmoil.

As we travelled about the country we would meet daily with new groups of Chinese writers and I would ask them what they thought of Malraux, how well they had known him. They would look blank and ask me to spell his name, describe his books. No one had heard of him. It became a running joke with Adrienne Clarkson and Charles Taylor, the former *Globe and Mail* China correspondent, the other two of our group. Eventually, I gave up asking.

So Malraux was not a great figure in the myth of the Chinese revolution. He was great in his own myth. But *Man's Fate* was/is a masterpiece. It emits some inexplicable reflection of life. And so out of his mythomaniac depth Malraux had been able to drag a greater truth than reality. Put another way: Conrad had to continually abstract himself out of the reality he knew in order to create it. Malraux had to abstract himself in. And this conundrum lies for me at the heart of writing life.

* * *

Either way, these survivors of multiple Chinese upheavals were not writers who could have been taken seriously if they decided to argue that art existed for art's sake. Or that they merely wrote for themselves, for no one else. Or that what they did as writers was something they had learnt as a skill in a schoolroom.

✻　　✻　　✻

A year or perhaps two years later, I was in Bangkok, thinking about what to write. I had a large *Conradian* project in mind – a series of novels filled with struggling, awkward, faltering, mythomaniac Westerners blundering through Asia and Africa. Friends introduced me to the Buddhist philosopher Sulak Sivaraksa. He was, and still is, more than a philosopher: a writer, a proposer of other ways of thinking, the man the Thai military disliked most because he questioned their legitimacy and because he did it from within local values, the ones the military claimed to be protecting each time they ran a coup d'état.

Over the years Sulak had been arrested, beaten, had to flee into exile, part of it in Canada, his publishing company had been blocked, his bookstore ransacked. He came from a family of the royal court, but dressed in traditional country clothes. While the rest of the Bangkok elite lived in an air-conditioned, mechanized cocoon, he walked everywhere and made do with simple fans. More to the point, he believed – believes – that there is a Buddhist way to modernization. Not something derivative of the West.

In the late eighties, he had to flee into exile again and we made him an honourary member of PEN Canada. By then we were good friends. He had become one of those markers of continuity necessary in every life – a constant reminder that if you write life you risk life. In Canada, the risk is at worst to your career, your reputation, your pocketbook. In other places putting a word on a page is a way to risk your life.

What I have noticed each time Sulak talks to a Canadian audience is just how unprepared people are for someone so tough, so rigorous, so demanding. The Western idea of Buddhism assumes something soft, gentle. With Sulak the public sees a man who indeed seems to move gently or at least with restraint – as he gets to his feet. Then, as the words flow, they are drawn out of the lives which brought them to that hall, and on into another form of imagining, another way of life.

Not too long ago Sulak went up into the jungles in the steaming humidity of full summer. He had decided to protest the use of slave labour in the building of a pipeline from Burma to Thailand. He walked into the camp and blocked the work with himself. Hours later two police cars made their way up the work road to arrest him. They were horrified when he accepted, but refused to get into the car. He said he would walk to the police station, kilometres away. I've often noticed that in a place where using free speech can cost you your life, comedy and tragedy are more deeply intertwined. The once leading thinker, writer and disturber is now the symbol of ethical behaviour and an elder. The officers wouldn't lay a hand on him without orders from above. So they drove out of the jungle, a police car on either side of Sulak, their air-conditioning on full and directed out their wide open doors in an attempt to cool the great man. The last thing they wanted was for him to collapse in the heat while under arrest.

*　　*　　*

About the time Sulak became part of my life, I began spending ever more time wandering about in border areas where there were vacuums of power. These borders were not lines, but vague, undefined no-go areas with private armies and guerrilla forces jockeying for power. I took to setting myself little goals – meet the world's leading drug lord; enter into the world of art smugglers; pass myself off as a silk merchant in order to get into areas of Burma closed because of ethnic warfare; travel across those mutant borders in order to convince a guerrilla army to take me up the most active, new drug trail; talk my way into a wild fifteen-hundred-kilometre dash across the war zone of the Western Sahara in an old Land Rover driven by the Polisario Guerrillas.

There was nothing odd about all of this. What else should curious individuals do in their thirties? The odd thing was the way friends and publishers and later on journalists felt a need to put all of this in a utilitarian context. What I was doing, they said, was researching novels. And for the purpose of explaining these novels, I didn't argue with them.

The truth was somewhere else. You don't research novels. Fiction is not a manufactured product of manufactured experiences. I spent those years living the life I wanted to live, while the books cooked away in that invisible place reserved for the unwritten. To return to the conundrum with which I began, I was either abstracting myself in or out of reality in order to write some version of life.

*   *   *

When I moved back to Canada in the eighties, it struck me that PEN was the organization I should give time to. From its beginnings, my decade-old life as a published writer had been filled with experiences, stories, friendships, crises, all revolving around the fragility of freedom of speech, and for that matter the freedom to read and to listen. Friends had been murdered, crippled. Some were in prison. Some in exile. Some stayed silent to stay alive.

The dramatic lives of writers in China, Thailand, Burma, Morocco, Algeria and on and on, lay at one end of this tension between speech and power. But in France, even Britain, I had seen how the system was constructed to limit troubling expressions of reality. In Canada the libel laws served those seeking to limit freedom of speech better than those seeking to protect it. Libel chill was a new elite fashion. Sue anyone who criticizes you. Tie them up in expensive pre-court procedures. If necessary, bankrupt them.

PEN does now what it did then, only more of it and with the sophistication of too much experience. Why too much? Because you keep hoping that these sorts of problems will shrink away. Some do. Some don't. Some appear out of nowhere. In the meantime PEN keeps people alive in prisons, gets others out, brings others here to a dignified exile. I remember Timothy Findley working to get Martha Kumsa out of an Ethiopian death camp in the 1980s. Now she is a professor here. I remember Duo Duo, the Chinese poet, who was outside of China during the Tiananmen Square Massacre. He spoke up in defence of free speech and so could not go home. We brought him here and worked to get him citizenship.

Now we have a Writers-In-Exile network with dozens of universities, libraries, cities and others involved. This is the largest program of its sort in the world. And it is one way for Canada to demonstrate at home what it preaches abroad.

*   *   *

I was in Kabul over New Year in 2003–4. The city was over half flattened. There was no electricity, only generators in selected areas. Most people walked great distances to collect water. There were refugee camps devoted to orphans.

Adrienne and I spent most of our time with our soldiers or the Afghan officials or looking at various bits of reconstruction work. A school built by our soldiers. A wonderful medieval park – Babur's Gardens – was being restored by the Aga Khan in the ruined city centre. Canadian NGO workers, who lived in an atmosphere of uncertainty, gathered together to talk about what they thought was happening.

The one thing I insisted on was meeting with the new PEN centre. There had never been one in Afghanistan. And on the surface nothing could have seemed less likely in this flattened city in which several million people camped. But, led by the Swedes, some money had been found and a house had been rented – a safe haven, if you like – and young writers, men and women, had come together.

The problem was that our security forces wouldn't allow me to go there without armoured vehicles. And that might attract too much attention to what the writers were doing. What were they doing? They were writing, that most dangerous of activities for those who believe that force is truth.

In the end we met in a neutral place and the writers talked of the need to be able to publish. That was not a difficult problem. A bit of money and some computers would produce a desktop publishing possibility. Our Ambassador, Chris Alexander, said he could make it happen.

Twelve months later I was back in Kabul for the next New Year. This time part of the city had electricity, buildings were being rebuilt, many women were in the streets with scarves, not veils, there was food in the market. The city was still mainly in ruins, but the museum had been reopened. Most of the early Buddhist statues smashed by the previous regime had been carefully put back together. We went off to a small house where women were learning journalism. Babur's Gardens were finished and becoming a place where people could gather to talk and relax, as if life were normal and war an illusion.

And this time the security was just good enough that I could go off to the PEN house. Some of the writers were gathered there. The money was coming in to support publishing. And we sat around and talked in heavy coats because there really wasn't much heating in the city.

And this is the point of my story. When I got up to leave, they took me out to the old dining room of the house. Inside there were almost twenty young writers reading their poetry to each other. What were the words? I do not know. What I do know is that in this city of rubble, where the president scarcely dares leave his palace, and soldiers attempt to keep the peace, young people were reading their poetry to each other, reminding themselves that civilization lies in the word.

SHYAM**SELVADURAI**

Opening for Mr. Davies

For me, the writing life involves two personas. There is the writer who wanders around in stained track pants talking to himself, standing at windows and gazing out, his lips moving silently before rushing to the computer to compose something; who is often so lost in an imaginary world that he forgets to buy groceries or feed the cat or fails to listen when his partner is calling to him. Then there is the author who goes out to public events and readings neatly dressed and clean; who is gracious and chatty and extroverted; who answers questions, signs books, and travels by car, bus, plane, and train to far-flung places in order to flog his latest novel.

At the readings and lectures I do, people always want to know how I became a writer and I have many answers to this. But what about being an *author*? How and when did I learn to become that?

Not long after my first novel, *Funny Boy*, came out, my publisher had the brilliant idea of sending me on a tour of Southwestern Ontario with Robertson Davies, who had just published his latest (and what would turn out to be his final) novel, *The Cunning Man*. The idea was that readers would come out for the great Robertson

Davies and, in the process, hear me as well. My publicist enthused about what a marvellous marketing ploy this was. She told me that hundreds of people came out to hear Robertson Davies read and I would sell just a ton of books. I also learned from her that Southwestern Ontario – including Toronto, of course – was known as the Golden Horseshoe in publishing. It was the area where the most books were sold in Canada. From this, I conceived the idea of Southwestern Ontario (our tour would include London, Guelph, Hamilton, and Waterloo) as a sort of make-or-break point in a writer's career. And I felt sure that I would make it. After all, my novel had come out to great fanfare and, at the few readings I had given in Toronto, I had drawn a large crowd and sold a lot of books. So, Southwestern Ontario would be a cinch. It was surely already mine, and I could not help fantasizing about the readings I would give with Robertson Davies. I imagined the event from the audience's point of view. Imagined them coming out to hear the old man read, but before he did so, a young Sri Lankan novelist would come up onstage, and he would start to read, and they would be enraptured. A star would be born overnight on the touring circuit of Southwestern Ontario.

The part of the reading tour I was not looking forward to was being in a van for hours with Robertson Davies. I had heard he could be a curmudgeon and that I would have to be extremely careful about what I said around him as he was liable to fly off the handle if you disagreed with him. It was entirely likely that this might happen. To me, Robertson Davies represented everything I disliked most about Canada and the white male establishment. I had heard that his *Fifth Business* was mandatory reading in various upper-crust university frat houses, those bastions of white male power. Then there was his stint as Master of Massey College, which I had heard was a rather anachronistic institution at the University of Toronto where fellows drifted about in gowns and generally carried on as if they were at Oxford or Cambridge. Having gone to York University, which I considered pluralistic and forward-looking, I looked down on the University of Toronto as stuffy and snobbish and colonial-minded.

A van had been rented for the occasion of our first reading and, once the publicists had picked me up, we made our way to Mr. Davies' home up on Avenue Road. Then, there he was, the man, the legend, coming out to us. He had a great white beard and wore a black fedora at a rather rakish angle. Over his black suit, he sported a black cloak, and he walked with a cane. He looked the very image of a senior man of letters and, supporting him by the arm, was his wife. She herself looked rather formidable, sort of like the Queen, with her hair backcombed into a perfectly coiffed helmet and, just like the Queen, she wore a rather severe suit and carried one of those hard handbags.

Robertson Davies was by now in his eighties, and the van was too high for him to climb into. So the publicists had brought along a stool that he could use as an intermediate step. I had been asked to sit at the very back, so the Davieses could have the middle row. After much heaving by the publicists, and quite a few tries, Robertson Davies finally made it into the van. He collapsed in his seat panting, then, once he recovered his breath, he wiped his face with a large white handkerchief and turned around to me in the back. He greeted me affably and we shook hands. His wife did the same, and then they turned around to the front and we were off.

I had decided that the only way to survive this tour was not to speak unless I was spoken to, and then to say only the very minimum that needed to be said, to avoid in any way offending the great man. So we drove mostly in silence all the way to London where we were going to read at the University of Western Ontario.

When we arrived we were met by a professor of English and his wife. No sooner had the van drawn up in front of the designated building than they rushed to the van and drew the door back. "Ah, Mr. Davies," he cried, "welcome, welcome, this is a tremendous honour." Then he proceeded to help the Davieses out of the van, telling them all the while what a delight, what a privilege it was to have them here. I received a very cursory greeting from the professor before he scurried ahead to bow and scrape Mr. and Mrs. Davies toward the lounge that had been set aside for us to sit in before the reading. The man was beside himself to be meeting the great Robertson Davies, who was clearly one of his literary heroes. He had ordered some sandwiches and other refreshments and he made Mr. Davies a plate, leaving me to my own devices. I sat with my publicist in a corner, largely ignored, growing more and more annoyed by the minute.

Finally it was time for us to read, and we were led into a hall. It was packed. In fact, there were so many people that they were seated on the steps of the aisle and standing along the sides of the room. My spirits immediately picked up. Here they were, the promised book buyers of Southwestern Ontario. They might have come to hear Robertson Davies, but they would leave with my book as well.

I was to go first and I had been allotted fifteen minutes. Then Mr. Davies would read for, well, as long as he wanted. I waited for the professor to get through mispronouncing and mangling my name, and give my oh-so-short bio, and then I stood up from the front row of the auditorium and went up onstage. There was a polite smattering of applause as I walked toward the podium. Then I started to read.

Within a few minutes, I saw that it was not going well. This was a section I had read many times before, and I knew the first point at which the audience should laugh. Here, however, there was hardly a titter when I got to that part, and soon I could feel coming toward me the thing that writers at a public reading just dread – waves of boredom. A woman coughed, someone rustled a program, two men were whispering. A quick glance at the audience showed me that one elderly man had actually drifted off to sleep. I began to read faster and soon I was stumbling over my words in my anxiety to finish. Finally I was done and I hurried back to my seat.

Now it was Robertson Davies' turn. Or rather, first, it was the professor's turn to give a long-winded and effusive description of Mr. Davies' bio and heap praise on him. Then the old man, the legend, stood up, straighter than I had ever seen him stand so far. He picked up his cane, gave it a little twirl, a little flourish, and, at this gesture, a thunderous roar of applause swept through the room. He walked grandly toward the steps that led up to the stage. I could see that he was lapping it up. The professor came forward gallantly to offer his arm, but Robertson Davies refused it. He made his way up the steps, then stood for a moment to catch his breath. The applause was still going on and he raised his hand in acknowledgement of it, then walked over to the podium, put down his cane, slipped on his glasses, and began to read. A hush came over the auditorium. The great Robertson Davies read for forty-five minutes, and the audience listened intently. I could feel it, the thing all writers at a reading hope and long for, the waves of rapt attention passing me on their way to the stage.

The applause when he finished was tremendous. Some people leapt to their feet. It went on and on as Robertson Davies slowly (I thought rather *purposefully* slowly) made his way across the stage, down the steps, and along the front row to his seat. Before he sat down, he raised his hand once more.

Now it was time for the book signing. I sat at one end of the hall, Mr. Davies at the other. What happened next was not unexpected.

The entire audience began to line up to get their books signed by Robertson Davies. The line was so long that it actually snaked right past where I was sitting and, occasionally, as people passed by, they stopped to utter some insincere praise with falsely polite smiles on their faces. I think I must have signed two books that evening. I sat at that table for well over an hour twirling my pen, until my publicist finally took pity on me and said, with a wry smile, "I don't think you're going to be signing any more books tonight." She ushered me back to the lounge. I sat there munching on a rather dry egg-salad sandwich, humiliated. The fact that, over the next few weeks, there were going to be three more such readings filled me with dread and despair. How would I be able to get through them? I simply could not go through such humiliation again.

Finally Robertson Davies returned to the lounge, triumphant. We were loaded back into the van and delayed while the professor made his effusive goodbyes to Mr. Davies, and then we set off back to Toronto.

After we had been travelling a little while, Mr. Davies turned in his seat and regarded me over his spectacles with an odd twinkle in his eyes. "Let me tell you about a reading I did once at a bookstore in Kingston. We arrived in the middle of a snow storm, having driven all the way from Toronto, to find that nobody had turned up. There was just me, my wife, and the lady who ran the bookstore. The poor woman was mortified, of course, but what was to be done?" He shrugged. "She suggested that perhaps we should forget the reading altogether, but I said to her, 'Madam, I have driven all this distance and I will do my reading.'" He laughed. "So I got up and I read to my wife and the woman who owned the bookstore." He gave me a long stare. "I've read to two people and I've read to five hundred, and I'll take anything in between."

I was glad it was dark in the back of the van, because suddenly I was blushing with shame. For I saw that I had misjudged the old man on numerous levels. On the most obvious level, I had let all the hearsay and gossip about him prevent me from being open to knowing him at all. But, more important, I saw that the tremendous adulation he had received tonight was something he held slightly apart from him; that his theatricality, the cape, the fedora, the walking stick, the white handkerchief that he brought out periodically to mop his brow, were all part of a theatre performance that in a curious way kept the audience, not to mention the professor, at a distance; a distance that I have now come to understand as vital, if one is to return from being an author promoting a book, to that solitary kernel within, from which the work flows.

Over the rest of our tour, things were never quite as dismal as they were at Western, but still the audiences had come for Robertson Davies, and I continued to spend large amounts of time sitting at my table twirling my pen. But I used that time to study this senior writer, to see the way he handled himself around his readers. When he read I watched him carefully and learned. Like Timothy Findley, Davies came from the theatre and, just like Findley, he approached the act of reading as a piece of theatre. From watching him do the same reading over and over again, I realized that everything about his reading was staged, the way he would use his cane at certain moments, the fact that he always withdrew his handkerchief at a point of suspense and mopped his brow, keeping the audience waiting in anticipation. I certainly don't have such a flair for the theatrical, but I learned from him to approach a reading as a piece of theatre – for example, never to read impromptu, to practise in advance, to mark the section you are reading with appropriate points where you will pause, and to prepare in advance an introduction that gives the listeners all the information they need to follow along.

But the most important thing I learned was that the success I was enjoying with my first book had begun to eat away at my writing self. I had confused the two roles of writer and author. Only by keeping them distinct would I be able to write the work I wanted to create, rather than the work I thought others expected of me. This is not an easy thing to do, and I am sure that Mr. Davies still struggled to keep them separate. But the struggle is necessary.

We never became friends or even good acquaintances. There was just too much that was different between us. Still, though we journeyed for the most part in silence, there were occasional moments when we talked as writers about writing. The most memorable of these was when I told him about an awful review I had received in *Maclean's* magazine. After consoling me, saying that he had received numerous bad reviews over his career, he lifted his chin and said with an imperious bark of a laugh, "Critics! My books are still on the shelves and where are their reviews today?"

I think I have become much better at not confusing who I am as a writer with who I am *as an author*. As for readings, I do have an extroverted side of me that enjoys going out and giving them and meeting readers. It provides a nice break from the tedium of writing and the boredom of one's own company. And the travel has allowed me to see parts of this country and the world that I would have never been able to visit otherwise. It is disappointing if you have a poor turnout, and annoying if there has been very little effort to publicize your event. And there are times when I find myself reading with a writer whose popularity far outweighs my own, and again I sit at my table while the line snakes past me.

Yet I have learned not to invest too much of myself in what happens on the reading circuit. Now, when I turn up to give a reading, having sometimes travelled in all sorts of weather across great distances, I say to myself, "I too have read to two and I've read to two hundred, and I'll take anything in between."

RUSSELL**SMITH**

Flying

In dreams I fly like a rocket – just take off, straight up. I can feel the propulsion under my feet, and I soar. It feels like being lifted by a current of air. But I just will it and rise. My speed comes from my will. And when I fear or doubt my hovering ability, I lose velocity and buoyancy, and in disappointment I begin to float downward. Then I realize I have simply forgotten how to fly. I just touch down gently, trying to remember what I thought or did before I rose, puzzled and frustrated and wondering if it was true, if I ever actually flew at all and if so how I learned to do it and why I can't now remember it.

If the airborne hesitation is sudden, I plummet. I see the ground rushing up, my heart thumping.

And sometimes just standing at the bar waiting for my beer after another vanished day of telephone calls and computer games, tapping my fingers in frustration, I feel my arms spreading, as if I knew, for a second, that I could turn on the engines and rocket up and out and away and be there simultaneously, raise my arms and blast, soar and fly – in a vague space, I'm not sure if I have left and entered the sky or if the chatty young people in the bar are still watching me – with the waitress – the waitress is always with me, watching me.

She has a bare belly and bare arms and full breasts and bare legs, and her fingertips are just touching mine, and that pulls her along with me, watching me and smiling and laughing little bursts of stars or mercury or floral scent, crushed yellow petals.

Back in the bar, I shake my head and look at her, and she actually does smile at me – and in fact she does have a lovely round bare belly which quivers slightly, and skin like caramel – and I smile nervously and look down at my beer.

If only she knew I were a rocket. Or at least that I think like one, and that I am so close to the secret.

And in fact I know, I do know, that I am close. That if only I could focus and relax enough I could just open my arms, and I would feel it spreading upward in me – it would just be a question of abandoning myself to it, of not trying too hard, of not trying at all.

Sometimes in the subway I am so tired I think I will shout or lie down in the aisle and close my eyes, and that my throat has been scratched and stretched by rusty fingers; it hurts to swallow; and everybody around me looks the same or worse: they are lumbering and pockmarked, they carry plastic bags, they wear sad boots, greasy clothing that, even when new, even the very day it was bought new in the shop, already bore signs of futile nostalgia, utter helplessness and pointlessness – it is then that I close my eyes involuntarily and for a moment I feel the vibration under the soles of my feet – it vanishes instantly – that was about to take me up and away, blasting through the roof of the tube, through the asphalt street like a missile unleashed from a submarine. As soon as I open my eyes it is gone.

And perhaps, I realize, it was that I was thinking of describing this scene in words, perhaps it was the euphoria of leaving the subway car and the stale smells and the tangle of impenetrable lives by painting these hard surfaces over with words, picking them up in my hand and weaving them together until they mesh with the sparks on my screen and appear the same but now complicated by coloured threads leading elsewhere, calming everything down, sorting it and classifying it and linking it up and painting it like a child with a spray can, forcing it into images and plots, clues and hidden doorways – or turning it into something else entirely, some set of images that are full of undertow, of connections, full of nearly glimpsed memories and logical subsets and upset belly. Something like an angel.

At night, when I am clean and quiet and I have soaked myself in alcohol, scrubbed and soaked and sunk into quiet and the city is still and buzzing, I see an image of words dripping from my fingertips. If I hold a pen, the words seem to come out of my arm, effluent, propellant. And if I type at the keyboard, they materialize as incandescent light on this screen, shifting, darting bits of self. And I fly, and I know this is flying.

ROSEMARY**SULLIVAN**

Writing Lives

Biography is an act of revenge against death, a rebellion against the impossible fact that a life can disappear so easily – all the energy, passion, humour that constitute an individual life can one day simply stop. By definition, then, biography is an elegiac art; it is a gesture of remembering.

The biographer begins by admitting the artifice of her conventions. How do you *tell* a life? One of the most difficult things in writing a biography is the pull of narrative itself. You know that this is where the energy of biography comes from. But you also know that as soon as any life is turned into a story – and there is no other way to tell it – the daily ordinariness of real life is distorted, and the life is inflated into a kind of myth. This "spotlighting effect," as the novelist and biographer Victoria Glendinning calls it – focusing on one person as central to the scheme of things – inevitably magnifies that person, and one runs the risk of "author-theology." Yet the isolating of a model, a paradigm, is really what biography is all about. All lives, or at least the lives of artists, turn inevitably into quest stories: for artists, the search for the fulfillment of the artist's gift.

Biography is an exacting art, fraught with responsibilities: responsibility to the living, responsibility to the dead, responsibility to the facts. The ethics of biography are ruthlessly straightforward. Implicitly the biographer makes a pact – with the subject and with the reader. To accord the subject the respect one would demand of others if one's own life were examined. To assure the reader that nothing will be made up.

The assumption is often made that the biographer's task is to dig up secrets. During a symposium on biography at Concordia University I was asked by a young woman: "Was there a deep, dark secret that Elizabeth Smart told you, a secret she begged you never to tell? And if so, what was it?" Astonishing! The biographer as betrayer is clearly not a role one willingly takes on.

But as a biographer begins to tell the story of a life, offering an hypothesis about how that life was lived, the complexity of the life takes over. And if a biographer can record a life with enough compassion, many secrets can fairly cease to be secrets. As moments that are part of the logic of a life, they are no longer shameful. I remember when the poet Andrew Motion published his eloquent biography of Philip Larkin, revealing the supposedly shocking detail that Larkin read pornography. But Motion's revelation said less about Larkin than about British society in the 1950s: how sad and inadequate was the intimacy in families; how pernicious were the racism, classism, sexual repression, and misogyny that pervaded society. Larkin had tried to rise above that in his poems – few have written so well about male loneliness and emotional crippledness – even as he backslid into it in his life. The point is that biography is not just about the subject. It is about all of us.

In 1988, I was asked if I would like to write a biography of Elizabeth Smart, author of *By Grand Central Station I Sat Down and Wept.*

Elizabeth Smart had been a friend. I'd first met her in London, England, in 1978 and had come to know her when she returned to her native Canada as writer-in-residence at the University of Alberta and then at the University of Toronto in the early eighties. When she died in 1986 at the age of seventy-two, I wrote a memoir for *This Magazine*, where I worked as an editor. I called it "Muse in a Female Ghetto," because, for me, the mystery of Elizabeth Smart was her silence. How, after writing her masterpiece, *By Grand Central Station*, had she fallen into a writer's block that lasted thirty years before she wrote her second novel, *The Assumption of the Rogues & Rascals*? What had stopped her?

I had never thought about writing a biography, let alone one of Elizabeth Smart. It would have felt like trading on a friendship, but when I was invited to do so, I thought: Yes, I would like to try. But where to begin?

I decided to start with the documents. Elizabeth Smart's papers were housed in the National Library in Ottawa. There were ninety boxes of material. It seemed she had saved everything. She had kept a trunk in her basement and stuffed everything into it. All the chaos of a lifetime was there: passionate love letters, her own lover's letters of betrayal ripped into tiny shreds in an agony of jealousy but saved, the journals she had crafted lovingly by hand for her children, fan letters, the ring and miniature horse of a dead daughter burning my fingers – the detritus of a lifetime. Why had she saved all this? It was not simply ego – that she had lived a life she knew was worth recording, though there was that. It was as if she were saying, poignantly, that everyone leaves behind only a confusion of details. In these boxes was the record of a lifetime – joy, passion, anger, the whole thing. *Don't be afraid of it. This is what you are writing about.* As a person Elizabeth always had enormous guts, "bashing on regardless." She thought only appetite mattered. She used to say that it takes enormous desire to live, with all the attendant risks.

I discovered the most important task in writing a biography is to establish the relationship you will have with the family or literary executors. Will you be free to write what you must? I began by visiting Elizabeth's daughter, Georgina Barker, in London. It is not easy to say to a complete stranger, "I want to write your mother's life," with the implication being that *you* will *all* be in it. But as I met the rest of the Barkers, I soon discovered that none of the family was afraid of exposing secrets. They had been brought up in a madcap bohemian world of books and writers. Where biography was concerned, they were afraid only of banality and bad writing. Over lunch, Georgina, as beautiful as Elizabeth, with the same romantic swath of red-blonde hair, told me: "Yes, write about my mother, but don't sentimentalize. The book will be useless unless it's the whole picture. Put the hard bits in, my mother would have wanted that." The question was: Was I brave enough to enter the terrain of this family that, like all families, had its silences, its emotional violence, its love? I discovered that's what it means to be a biographer.

There was one encounter I had in writing this book that sits in my mind as perhaps the most extraordinary. George Barker, Elizabeth's lover and the father of her four children, had taken the notion of the priapic, bardic poet – womanizer, drinker, agonized romantic – which his society offered as mandatory for the authentic poet and lived it to the hilt. When Elizabeth met him he was married, and after his relationship with her he had another three *wives*. In all he had had five wives (though only two marriages) and fifteen children. I needed to meet the children from his first marriage who had been lost to him fifty years ago. I needed their permission to quote from the letters to Elizabeth written by their mother, Jessica Barker, whose place Elizabeth had usurped in George Barker's life.

I finally tracked down the woman I was looking for, Anastasia Barker, and found myself travelling to a remote farm district in the blue hills of Kentucky to meet this complete stranger, carrying to her the stories of a father she had never known. Her mother had told her in her childhood: "Your father was a poet. He went to a poetry reading at Harvard and never came back." "It was said in such a way that you knew the conversation was over," Anastasia told me. "You weren't allowed to ask anything more." She and her brother had grown up in Greenwich Village in New York. Though they lived in England for a year when she was a teenager, it had never occurred to her to look up her father. George Barker was only a poet they had read in school.

I gave Anastasia photographs I had brought of her father – she had never seen them. And there was I, an outsider, the carrier of her family history – at that moment, the only one who could, however awkwardly, pull the threads together. Had I come to visit a few years earlier, Anastasia told me, she probably wouldn't have been willing to meet me. But her mother was dead – Anastasia had nursed her through several years of Alzheimer's. Giving in a way that one must to someone so sick had been the most moving experience of her life. It had transformed her. "I'm tired of secrets. Secrets destroyed my mother's life." Her mother had remained embittered about George Barker, locking that rancour in her heart. She never spoke of him, but her children all lived under the weight of his unspoken existence. And their lives became a geography of lost and missing pieces. Anastasia wanted everything told. "Publish anything you need to tell the story." What she was saying to me, I understood, was profound. It is the secrets that keep us locked inside private agonies. But the secrets turn out to be ordinary lived experience. George Barker's mistress, as Anastasia called Elizabeth, had been freer than her mother. She had spread her life generously.

Elizabeth sent me on many unanticipated journeys, but one was particularly intriguing. As I read her first novel for perhaps the tenth time, it occurred to me that one aspect of the plot was mysterious. As they travel across the United States, the unnamed protagonist and her lover are arrested at the Arizona border and imprisoned under the Mann Act, an archaic act designed to counter prostitution. If an unmarried couple were caught crossing a state border and the woman was under twenty-eight, they could be arrested. As Elizabeth put it: "You could fornicate in any state, but not cross a state line for the purpose."

Elizabeth and George Barker had actually been arrested in the autumn of 1940 as they drove into Arizona. Because Barker's British papers were in order, he was released, but she was detained when it was discovered she was in the U.S. illegally. By chance, her passport had not been stamped when she entered the country. She was kept in jail for three days until her father's influence got her released.

I had always passed over this incident matter-of-factly until I asked myself the question: how do you get arrested at a state border when the border was open and there were no checkpoints. Were Elizabeth and George under surveillance? I wrote the FBI asking to see their file on Elizabeth Smart.

To my surprise I received a reply. The FBI *did* have a file on Elizabeth Smart, but in the interests of national security it could not be released. Citing the Freedom of Information Act, I demanded an explanation. I was told that Elizabeth's file was cross-referenced with that of another individual who was still considered a threat to national security. The only explanation I could imagine was that there must have been exiles from the Spanish Civil War at the writers' colony in Big Sur where Elizabeth was living: *Communists*, who were deemed potential *fifth columnists*. After almost fifty years, the FBI didn't want their secret surveillance operations exposed.

In the course of writing my biography of Elizabeth Smart, which I called *By Heart*, I came to feel that the search for the details of another's life is as compelling as the complex process of narrating those details. I also came to feel that it would be important for the reader to have some sense of the biographer's search. How does a biographer come to know the things she does? And how does she arrive at the judgments she makes? Isn't it important for the biographer to admit what is fact, what is speculation, what can and can't be known about another's life?

I decided to write a second biography. I chose the Canadian poet Gwendolyn MacEwen as my subject because, unlike Elizabeth, she had been so productive, writing more than twenty books in thirty years. But I wrote this book differently. I included my own voice as a biographer searching for the narrative of MacEwen's life. As I wrote in my Preface to *Shadow Maker: The Life of Gwendolyn MacEwen*:

> I decided to follow the clues as they came, recording the voices that surrounded Gwendolyn, all those versions of her life she had left behind. It would mean that I would not be able to pretend, as biographers sometimes do, that one can turn a childhood into a seamless narrative when one is following forty years after the fact, and constructing a childhood from the multiple versions of the survivors who are left behind. I would have to track down her lost lovers, from whom there would be no letters and whom friends remembered only as a shadow or a name. Even then who was to say that the man I would meet and

the man Gwendolyn had loved bore even the slightest resemblance to each other. What debris had gathered in the pockets of memory? To be faithful to the mystery that was Gwendolyn, I would have to lay bare the bones of my search for her, with little of the biographer's illusions of omniscience or objectivity.

Gwendolyn MacEwen was a great poet who died at the age of forty-six in mysterious circumstances. Some people suspected suicide. I had known Gwen; we had friends in common. How was I to write about her? Above my desk I kept an extract from a poem by the German poet Nelly Sachs to remind me of what I was doing:

> When someone lifts us
> He lifts in his hand millions of memories
> Which do not dissolve in blood
> like evening.
> "Chorus of the Stones"

Gwen had expected a biographer. She left instructions to her sister in her will to set aside certain papers for her biographer. Yet she didn't talk much about her life. She was a house with many rooms. As a friend, you were invited into the one that most suited you, while the others remained secret simply because you lacked the key. What did people know of Gwendolyn MacEwen? What would I discover?

We believe the roots of a lifetime are hidden and entwined in childhood. A biography begins its archaeology there. The first person I had to speak to was Gwen's sister Carol Wilson.

This time, I was deeply aware that I was entering the lives of *real* people. Carol sat across from me in her small-town Ontario kitchen. Eight years older than her sister, she seemed a photocopy of what Gwen would have looked like at her age. She described how, in 1950, when her family moved to Winnipeg, she and her sister witnessed their mother's attempted suicide. Carol recounted the story to me in a halting voice full of pain. "This is not easy for me," she said. What did Gwen see that night? she wondered. She also spoke of a loved father, broken by family tragedy, who died prematurely of alcoholism.

On one of my visits, Carol handed me a sealed envelope, on the back of which Gwen had scrawled her name in large childish letters. Carol told me it contained the pencil with which Gwen wrote her first poem at the age of ten. She also told me that Gwen changed her name. The family had always called her Wendy, but at age twelve, she insisted that her name henceforth would be Gwendolyn. She said she thought one day she might be important and Wendy was not the name of somebody important.

The astonishing thing is that, out of the pain of that childhood, Gwen MacEwen was able to construct such a powerful life for herself. For her, it seems that art became a way to make sense of life. It required training, discipline, love. And she had a remarkable mind, perpetually in gear.

I discovered she had been very secretive about her life. Only a select few knew of her mother's mental illness or her father's alcoholism. I had to build her story from clues left behind. I went to libraries and searched through city directories to locate the many places she had lived. I found her letters in writers' archives across the country, echoes of her lost voice. I consulted the Mormons in Salt Lake City to trace her genealogy. I phoned Edinburgh searching for details about her father's life. I wrote hospitals for files. And I tracked down many of the witnesses who shared, however peripherally, in her life. The story grew. How, after leaving school, she roamed the back streets of High Park until she found a small *chaider*, or Hebrew school, and walked in asking them to teach her Hebrew. If she was to know the Bible, the Zoar, the Gnostics, she must read them in the original language. There was her amusing anecdote about the night she was at the Wah Mai Café on Queen Street when the cops raided and began to haul in the prostitutes. They inquired about the kid in the brown corduroy jumper. She told them she was there because she was training to be a writer: "I'm just a page now but one day I'll be a book."

I found letters to and from her father, whose life had begun with such promise, though it degenerated into alcoholism. Margaret Atwood, who had been Gwen's friend, gave me their correspondence, which amounted to almost a hundred letters. These offered a portrait of two young female mavericks, poets confronting the world together at a club called the Bohemian Embassy. I began to watch magic shows. Gwen loved magicians. "Poets are magicians without quick wrists," she said.

One of the most mysterious figures I had to find was a lost lover. He was simply a name in one of her last and most delicate poems: "Letter to an Old Lover." Beginning the poem "Salah, I have not forgotten you," she imagines him lost to her somewhere in Cairo.

Margaret Atwood remembered Salah as a handsome young Egyptian, studying for an MA in chemistry at McGill University in the late 1960s. She did not remember his last name. When I phoned the chemistry department at McGill, I was told all the old files had been burnt in a fire. But the secretary I spoke to was willing to search for a lost lover with a mysterious first name. It had something to do with nostalgia – we have all had lost lovers – and with the fascination we feel for memory, for recovering broken-off pieces of the past. The secretary found me a likely name. When I inquired at the Egyptian Embassy, I was advised to advertise in the Cairo *Gazette*. But then, serendipitously, I discovered that Salah still lived in Montreal. It took days before I gathered the courage to phone him. Who was I that I should walk into his life carrying his past? When I phoned there was silence and then he said: "Yes, I am the one who knew Gwendolyn. I knew she had died. How did she die?"

After I published *Shadow Maker*, much to my surprise, I received an extraordinary number of letters. Many people identified with the tragic life of Gwendolyn MacEwen. I was moved that they would take the time to write, and that almost all said that they had gone out and bought her poetry and were reading her entire work. But there was something that disturbed me. Some people began to ask why I identified with dark, self-destructive, romantic female extremists. But that was not how I saw either Gwendolyn MacEwen or Elizabeth Smart. They were writers of remarkable courage, who had succeeded against the odds, as all writers must, and the difficulties of their lives had come from where most difficulties do: in large measure from the patterns scripted in childhood. Theirs were individual stories and it was risky to use their lives to generalize about the Ur-pattern of the artistic life.

I remembered Margaret Atwood commenting once that there is no common pattern to the artist's life. The only thing that writers have in common is that they write. I found myself thinking about writing a book about Margaret Atwood. Would that be possible? And why would I presume? I had two motives. First, this would be another kind of story, a narrative about a woman who had managed to take control of her artistry *and* her life. And, secondly, she would be there to talk back. This intrigued me. I was skeptical about the way many biographers claim to know the motives of their subjects after they are dead.

I decided to write a portrait of Margaret Atwood's early career. My book would be about confidence, about how you find the courage to believe in yourself as an artist. It would be a cultural history. It would also be about the creative process itself.

In my head I thought of this book as a not-biography. There would be no intimate journals or letters as sources. These were still in private hands, though Margaret Atwood allowed me to read her restricted files in the Thomas Fisher Library that houses her papers and we had a lively email correspondence. I also knew that people would be guarded and protective of her. Why, then, write the book? I wanted the third version of the female artist's life. Elizabeth Smart had been trapped in silence – after her masterpiece she had lost her nerve as a writer. She said she felt the maestro of the masculine sitting on her shoulder, telling her she could never be good enough. Gwendolyn MacEwen had been killed by the secrets behind which she hid. Margaret Atwood had produced a brilliant and extensive body of work and was content in her life.

In the course of writing my previous biographies, I had experienced the nostalgic, elegiac feeling of following after. The subjects were gone and had left only their words behind. Writing about Margaret Atwood was, of course, completely different. I was driven by curiosity and intrigue, and found myself saying: *Ah, so that's what it was like.*

Research took me back to the 1950s when Margaret Atwood was a teenager. It was an astonishing period, the decade of brand names, miracle synthetic products, and the clutter of consumerism: pop-up toasters, electric frying pans, Mixmasters, and the newly invented television. For a young girl the fifties meant unrelenting propaganda about marriage: you were expected to marry at the age of twenty-one. It was amusing and poignant to watch Margaret in this world.

I sat in the Vic College library at the University of Toronto, a stone room with high windows like a pseudo church and brown sepia-toned portraits of eminent Victorians lining its walls. Green-glassed desk lamps lined up on the study tables like sentinels. The library hasn't changed much since Margaret sat there as an undergraduate.

I trekked down to Harvard, where she'd gone to graduate school, and visited the Lamont Library, which, as a female student, Margaret hadn't been allowed to enter. Apparently it was felt that the presence of females would distract the young male students. And I saw where Founder's House, her graduate residence at Radcliffe, had been, and thought of her description of the sexual perverts who, like aphids, had scaled its walls. With her roommates, she had gone to court to testify against one voyeur who had been caught on the roof, but he'd been released on bail and had long disappeared. "At Harvard," she would later say, "I learned about urban violence."

And I thought of the costume party she and her friend Jim Polk had organized at Founder's House. It was meant to be a Roman orgy. She'd gone as Cleopatra's breast, wearing a birdcage covered in a flesh-coloured towel, and he went as the asp. As I walked through Harvard, I also saw what Margaret would come to make of that intimidating institution when it became the headquarters of a fundamentalist dictatorship in *The Handmaid's Tale*.

Every life has a great deal to do with timing, but particularly the artistic life. Margaret Atwood remarked that had she been born a decade earlier, like Mordecai Richler, she would probably have had to leave Canada in order to write. Her growth as a writer coincided with Canada's growth as a culture. These two stories are central to the book I called *The Red Shoes: Margaret Atwood Starting Out*.

In the end every biographer has to admit that a curious osmosis takes place between biographer and subject. It's impossible to live so intensely in the details of another's life without strange things happening. I have dreamed about each of the women whose stories I've written. But readers often assume that the biographer is seeking to live vicariously through their subject. For me at least, that is not the seduction of biography. I have written in other genres: poetry, short fiction, travelogue, essays. What makes biography unique is that it lives on the knife-edge between fact and fiction. If you go deeply enough, you discover that lived lives are as dramatic as fictionalized ones. But while the fiction writer has the liberty to invent, the biographer must stick to what actually happened and then interpret those facts. To write biography, to enter the life of the subject, one must call upon all one's emotional intelligence and all one's lived experience. This means that biography is not only an elegiac art, but also a celebratory act. "To be alive," Philip Roth once said, "is to be made of memory." Memory-making is the biographer's responsibility and gift. But no biographer escapes from the writing unscathed. Then why write biography? I go back to the image of Elizabeth's trunk into which she had tossed the disconnected details of her life. Her biographer was meant to connect them. Only by writing the biography of a life can we hope to save, however partially and inadequately, the record that time would so ruthlessly efface.

SUSAN**SWAN**

The Education of a Novelist: Making Things Up and Getting Them Right

As a novelist, I'm in the business of making things up. But in the last decade, I've become self-conscious about representing other cultures in my fiction.

I trace my loss of innocence back to the early 1990s, when aboriginal writers in Canada objected to white writers describing their experience. Native writers like Lee Maracle and Leonore Keeshig-Tobias asked white novelists like Anne Cameron, Rudy Wiebe, and M.T. Kelly (all of whom had written books sympathetic to aboriginal experience) to step back and give native writers a chance to tell their own stories. I was sympathetic to their view. It felt rather as if white writers had been telling aboriginal stories at a literary banquet without offering aboriginal authors the chance to speak. Until the storytelling stick had been passed more fairly around the table, I thought it was a transgression for white novelists to keep writing about First Nations experience.

However, I disagreed with the notion that writers should only tell stories drawn from their own first-hand experience. At a literary gathering in London, England, in 1993, I was publicly denounced by the audience when I said that it was misguided to ask writers not to imagine other lives. Rows of enraged women rose to their feet and shouted that a white woman had no business writing in the voice of a black character. I tried to explain that I personally wouldn't write about black experience, but the shouts simply grew louder. I left the auditorium feeling frustrated and misunderstood.

Since then, many black and aboriginal novelists have made a name for themselves, and there's no longer much controversy here about voice appropriation. After all, this is what novelists do – we appropriate voice.

But I understand more now about the limits to anyone's understanding of other cultures. I may share a beating heart with members of another society, but I don't necessarily share the same cultural norms and values, let along storytelling tropes. Ultimately, every story set in another culture is a story about the narrator, as Joseph Conrad suggested in *Heart of Darkness*.

I realized I would be wrestling with the new self-consciousness when I began my last novel, *What Casanova Told Me*, although I had no idea how deeply embedded my stereotypes about Muslim societies were. I was setting part of my book in eighteenth-century Muslim Constantinople (as Istanbul was then known), the seat of the Ottoman Empire in what is now modern-day Turkey. In his celebrated memoir, *History of My Life*, Giacomo Casanova (1725–1798) had described a visit to Constantinople in his youth during which he nearly married the daughter of a wealthy Turk. The condition for the marriage was that Casanova should adopt the Muslim faith. Although tempted, he declined and went on with his travels through Europe. Because I felt I understood the character of Casanova, it wouldn't be hard, I surmised, to imagine how he would behave in Constantinople on a return visit.

At the same time, I knew that I needed to be wary. If I wasn't careful, I would find myself indulging in Orientalism, the term coined by the late critic Edward Said, who criticized the West for projecting its prejudices onto the East. Said argued that Western writers either demonized its peoples as savage and barbaric or painted them as romantic and quaint.

I'd chosen Constantinople as a destination because it was the sort of setting that would interest my heroine, Asked For Adams, the fictitious young cousin of the American president John Adams. In my novel, Casanova returns to Venice at the end of his life, but he is still charming and appealing enough to persuade Asked For to leave her father and fiancé and help him find his lost love, a French woman who was part of the Sultan's harem in the Ottoman palace of Topkapi.

I should point out that the French woman I was sending Casanova in search of was a real person who lived in the harem of the Ottoman Sultan, Abdul Hamid, in the 1790s. Her name was Aimée Dubucq de Rivery, and there have been a few romantic novels written about her recently, since her life was so fascinating.

Born on the Caribbean island of Martinique to a noble French family, Aimée attended a French convent school near Nantes until it was closed because of the political agitation in the French countryside before the French Revolution. On her way back to Martinique, she was captured by Barbary pirates and sold to Sultan Abdul Hamid, who was delighted by her fair hair. Soon she gave birth to their son, who later became the Ottoman sultan known as Mahmud II.

Aimée was real; Casanova was real. Asked For was imaginary. Not that it mattered. I was interpreting all their lives in the mysterious brew of fact and fiction that's characteristic of many historical novels. Whoever read my novel would need some appearance of cultural verisimilitude in order to believe the story. So I began asking around at my university for scholars who knew about the Ottoman Empire. One of my colleagues told me about Irvin Schick, a Muslim scholar who grew up in Istanbul. Schick is a mathematician at MIT in Boston, and his side interests are Ottoman history, art history, and the practice of calligraphy in the Ottoman Empire.

We started an email correspondence and, right from the start, I was impressed with his courtesy and by the thoroughness of his historical knowledge. He spoke several languages besides Turkish and English, and was widely read on subjects like contemporary gender theory. I realized he could be my trustworthy wormhole into eighteenth-century Ottoman culture. I started sending him sections of my novel to check for historical accuracy, and he emailed me back, noting in detail the stereotypes about the Ottomans that had crept into the narrative. Didn't I know that Jews and Christians were not persecuted under the Ottomans the way Muslims had been persecuted by the Christians in parts of Europe? Or that from 700 to 1200 AD, Islam had led the world in power, refinement of manners, humane legislation, and religious tolerance?

No, I did not. In fact, I was beginning to see that I had a monolithic notion of Muslim cultures. I didn't differentiate much between countries like Turkey and Syria and Iran. I began to read more generally about the Middle East and was surprised to discover the extent of the famous flowering of Islamic civilization between 750 and 1200 AD. From Islam came our Western notions of cleanliness; the ribbed vaults in the design of medieval cathedrals; the tradition of courtly love; knowledge of astronomy, medicine, physics, mathematics; papermaking techniques; even scientific terms like algebra, zero, cipher, zenith, almanac, alembic. The extent of these contributions from Islamic civilization was mind-boggling and hadn't been acknowledged in my general arts education at university. Eighteenth-century Ottoman culture was a later historical development and again more sophisticated than I had realized.

My relationship with Irvin progressed online, and our discussions ranged from street names in Istanbul to the way a turban is made to sit on the head. We also discussed representation in old Turkish calligraphy and grammatical points such as whether the noun *archives* is singular or plural. Irvin, I discovered, was a stickler for spelling and punctuation in all the languages he spoke; he could have been employed as an editor in a publishing house. I started to send him longer drafts asking for his insights. Meanwhile, the list of the mistakes he found grew longer and a note of irritation had slipped into his replies. Why was I still making references to harem women being stuffed into sacks and thrown into the Bosporus if they displeased the Sultan? (I had persisted in a scene describing this even though he had tactfully suggested that such cruelty was a Western fantasy.) Didn't I know that beheading and strangling were the preferred punishments in that part of the world?

And why did I depict the lives of the Ottoman slaves as if they were living on a plantation in the Barbados? Didn't I realize that Ottoman slaves were seen as dependents and allowed to rise in rank depending on their skills and abilities? In a scene in an early draft, I had described Asked For and Casanova in Ottoman-dominated Athens watching a Muslim man stone his wife for having committed adultery. Irvin reminded me that stoning wasn't a common punishment in the Ottoman Empire, although a respectable Ottoman chronicler had written once about a woman being stoned for adultery. The fact that he had written about it, Irvin said wryly, suggested that it was an unusual occurrence. Otherwise it would have been overlooked.

I made some changes to that scene, including a new name for the Turkish husband. According to Irvin, Zak wasn't a Turkish name but a pseudo-Turkish name invented by Western chroniclers who thought it sounded exotic. And why, Irvin chided, was this Zak character speaking Arabic? Although Arabic is spoken in the entire Arab world, people in Turkey as well as Iran, Pakistan, and other non-Arab Muslim countries use Arabic only as a religious language. "Arabic is sort of like Hebrew which is spoken in Israel," Irvin wrote. "But everywhere else Hebrew is only a liturgical language."

I confessed that most of my notions about the Ottoman Empire came from accounts by European travellers, and Irvin was astonished by my naivete. He felt that most of these Western travellers were frauds who had never learned a word of Turkish. They either tried to jot down what they heard phonetically or they took their information from unreliable sources. I felt slightly ashamed of myself for taking these accounts as historical verity. My characters might think in stereotypes, but I didn't want to be lazy with my prejudices and assumptions. If, as a writer friend once said, writing fiction involves a search for truth, and truth is also the enemy of clichés and stereotypes, it makes no sense to keep false notions in play. Still, I was proud of my effort to understand eighteenth-century Constantinople. Not many writers would bother to research in this much detail, I reassured myself.

Then, a few emails later, Irvin wrote a scalding dismissal of my work-in-progress description of Casanova and Asked For sailing into the isolated port of Marmaris in Turkey. In this section, Asked For Adams saw barely clad dancers on wooden rafts surrounding the Sultan's ostentatious galley ship:

> The rafts were beautifully ornamented as were the boats
> containing the spectators who formed an outer ring

around this vast floating theatre. One vessel was particularly sumptuous. Golden banners hung from its masts and
music poured out from its sides and into the air like
perfume – the high clear notes of these songs were as intricate and pleasing as anything I have heard in my life. On a
nearby barge, young women dressed as galley slaves undu-
lated and quivered around two sea captains. I realized the
sea captains were women too, and they were drinking
from bottles of wine and crossing scimitars in a burlesque
of male duels. On another barge, we saw male dancers,
whose heads and arms were concealed with shawls, shaking
and undulating. Their bare bellies had been painted to
look like female faces on their stomachs. As the dancers
contracted or expanded their stomach muscles, the painted
female faces smiled or drooped.

Irvin said my description of the Sultan's galley surrounded by
rafts of belly dancers was outrageous and implausible. For one
thing, Ottoman sailing vessels weren't decked out in gold banners,
and the Ottoman sultans were known for their austere public pre-
sentations. My description of the dancers was ridiculous because
men and women commingling with female dancers simply didn't
happen in Ottoman society. I sent off a hasty email suggesting I
switch my scene to a local Ottoman fair, but he said that was
equally ludicrous.

I, too, felt annoyed and frustrated. I was fond of my scene with
the Sultan and the dancers even if it was orientalist. My job was
not to compile an accurate historical account but to create a story
that the reader would enjoy and accept. Irvin had gone too far, I
decided. He'd forgotten that a natural tension exists between the
scholar and the novelist. Granted too much sway, the scholar's

insistence on historical accuracy could sink the imaginative flights of the writer.

Irvin and I didn't correspond for a while. In the interim, I found myself wishing I hadn't chosen to send Casanova to Turkey. Still, I was too far into the story to change Casanova's destination. What to do?

I knew I couldn't really continue without Irvin or someone like him. I wanted historical authenticity to reinforce the illusion of the world I was creating.

Without giving away all of my story, let me explain that Casanova had shown Asked For Adams, his young travelling companion, letters from Aimée Dubucq asking Casanova to rescue her from the sequestered life in the harem. Asked For was moved by these letters from Aimée, which were full of fanciful stereotypical descriptions of the harem much like my orientalist scene with belly dancers on floating rafts near Marmaris.

But what if I re-jigged the narrative so that the letters written by Aimée had actually been written by Casanova as a way of enticing Asked For Adams to travel with him? In the original version of my novel, Casanova was in love with Aimée and Mahmud was their son from a liaison that had occurred shortly before her capture by the pirates. However, it would be far more interesting if Casanova (who was something of a dissembler anyway) made up these letters as a seductive ploy. And Asked For, not Aimée, would be the woman whose heart Casanova secretly hoped to win.

Now my characters' eighteenth-century accounts of life in Istanbul could be truly orientalist because Casanova would be no different from any of the other Western travellers in that part of the world; he would take Asked For there with a full set of Western assumptions about the Ottoman court and Asked For herself would not know any different. Suddenly, I had a far more interesting novel on my hands. I'd also lightened the burden of scholarly accuracy while still relying on it to reinforce my tale. As I tell my creative writing students, the needs of the story must come first.

In the end, every human complexity is grist for fiction's mill – including the challenge of setting a narrative inside an older Muslim culture. Toward the end of the novel, I even added a section where a descendant of Asked For Adams makes many Irvin-like comments about the baroque prejudices of Western travellers in Turkey in the eighteenth century.

I'd taken the dramatic and what sometimes felt like the fool-hardy step of inviting a scholar into my creative process. But it turned out that my dialogue with Irvin had affected my novel, not only in lending it an air of historical truth, but also in creating a plot that was more exciting for me (and I hoped for the reader). Our email discussions continued. I stopped bristling if I thought Irvin's objections went too far because I felt more comfortable with the tensions between our viewpoints.

And so did Irvin. In the present-day section, for instance, a character visits Istanbul and is harassed by a hotel clerk who tells her she can't go to Topkapi Palace without a male escort. Irvin wrote that no Turkish man would be so silly as to suggest this and that I was perpetuating stereotypes of Turkish men in Istanbul. I fired back an email explaining that this was what I had experienced first-hand; I'd been astonished at the naive ideas some of the city's hotel staff had about Western women.

"You are the boss," he acknowledged wistfully. "This is a novel, after all."

Did I mention that I deleted the belly-dancing scene? And that Irvin and I had finally met when he visited Toronto to give a talk? Not so long ago, I bought him dinner, the only payment he would accept from me.

He was fair-haired and looked more European than I expected, but by then I'd learned to distrust my assumptions about his part of the world. He had taught me things about another culture and another time that I could use. And our disagreements had led me into a more interesting story, while never really impairing my freedom as a writer who makes up stories. And for me, as a novelist, this was a happy ending.

MADELEINE**THIEN**

After the Flood

In the spring of 2000, I stood on the harbour of Sandakan, a small city on the coast of North Borneo, and a place I had imagined since my childhood. Behind me, the road lifted away from the sea, twisting past the market, up the slope and into the jungle. I remember the cobalt blue of the sea, how it glimmered in the early morning, how the chalk hills of the nearby islands glowed red in the moments before sunrise.

This place has a resonance for me in both time and space; it marks the beginning of five turbulent years, and the physical start of the novel I had long wished to write. The novel's beginnings lie in the story I was told of my grandfather's life and death. What I know is sparse, and there are only two details of which I am certain. During the Second World War, after the defeat of the British in North Borneo, my grandfather, well-educated and wealthy, was forced to work for the Japanese military; and in September of 1945, after the war was over but before the town was liberated, he was executed by Japanese soldiers. My father was six years old at the time. He remembers, one morning, watching his father being led away, and then never returning.

At the harbour, my elderly aunt, Margaret, held my arm, guiding me forward. We had met for the first time only days ago, but we had fallen into step together. She had offered to accompany me through the eastern towns and villages.

On that particular morning, we had breakfast with her friends, all octogenarians. When they saw me, many of them touched my face, holding it in their hands for a moment, thoughtful, as if to guess its weight. I felt both old and childlike, and I wondered if they recognized in me someone they had known in their youth, my father or my grandparents. Together we drank coffee, watching the boats that jostled in Sandakan harbour.

At the time of the Second World War, these men and women were in their twenties, younger than I am now. When I asked what they remembered about the war, the one consistent response was *hunger*: the deep, psychic pain of starvation. They could barely meet my eyes when they said this. I felt that I had the capacity to hurt them with my questions, my curiosity, and so I held back. For most of our time together, we sat beside the sea and drank our coffee. They talked about people they knew, about their children and grandchildren. People here, Margaret said, as an addendum, don't like to remember the war. There is humiliation in being laid so low, in having experienced the desperation – she used the word *shame* – of wanting to survive.

Of the rest, the bombs and the dying, they said little: only that it happened.

My extended family in Southeast Asia is generous, big-hearted. I had come by way of Thailand, peninsular Malaysia and Sarawak, and they were surprised to see a young woman travelling alone. When they heard that I was researching a novel, they wanted to take me everywhere, into plantations, temples, a fishing village built over the water, balanced on stilts and boardwalks. In the market, where almost everything was new to me, they pressed exotic fruits and packets of sweets into my hands. Margaret took me to the Australian War Memorial just outside of Sandakan, then shooed me inside while she herself waited patiently at the entrance.

Now, five years later, my recollection of that trip to Southeast Asia has crystallized into particulars: a long conversation with a cousin in Singapore, as we walked through a deserted landscape of temples and rivers. He told me about his mother's death from cancer, how she had succumbed after years of living in poverty, just when her children were coming into their own. In Sandakan, four of us gathered around a kitchen table, sharing a large, spiky fruit whose name I could not catch. We ate the flesh off the seeds, and they argued amongst themselves, about politics and family, and the way the war is remembered here in Southeast Asia.

They looked at me, this newfound family, and I could see the curiosity in their faces.

– And your book?

– No, no. It isn't finished.

In truth, the book was barely started. When they pressed for details, I could only shake my head. Back then, the book was no more than an idea, as fragmentary as a dream.

At night, listening to the beat of the fan, I thought about my family in Canada, how I was writing out of love for them, and also from a place of estrangement. Writing to make sense of life for myself, to make palpable in fiction what I could not hold in life. I wanted to write about the Second World War because it is the dark heart of our century, a conflict that brought the world, individuals, to the precipice. Afterward, people said never again, but the Second World War, carrying the world to Auschwitz, to Nanking, ending in Hiroshima, remains a nightmare of what may yet be. In my head, I carried words spoken by a character from Rachel Seiffert's

The Dark Room: "I can never explain and you can never understand." I wanted to write my way into these words, to learn how far the effort, the reaching, could bring us. "Understanding," writes Erna Paris, in her book *Long Shadows*, "is the road this child, and her generation, needs to travel."

When my mother died suddenly in 2002, my life came undone. Grief is a knife in the chest, twisting the core of what we are, breaking us off, for a time, from the world. I could not bear that she no longer existed, that her physical presence in the world was lost to me. I was twenty-eight years old then, and I wanted answers that would not come. Of all my family, she was the one to whom I was closest, to whom I turned. In the days after, I found, among her possessions, a story I had written for the local newspaper; she had searched for it on the Internet and printed a copy for herself. I cried over all the words that had passed between us, and over these words too that had circled in cyberspace, making their long journey away from me, into the public realm, and then home again to us both.

Soon after, I left Canada, moving with my fiancé to the Netherlands. We had planned this departure long ago, and I simply kept going, one step following the other.

In our one-room flat in Scharnegoutum, in the north of the country, we occupied two corners, the attic roof sloping around us. My fiancé was writing his dissertation on human motor control, trying to map the neural net running from our minds to our bodies, analyzing the flicker of electric signals. I worked on the novel I had begun in Sandakan, rewriting it again and again, thinking of myself and of the world, reflecting the two against each other. The drafts, fragmented, always falling short, accumulated. Hours passed with only the occasional tapping of the keyboard, the flutter of pages turning. On Tuesday mornings, we rode our bicycles to the market, then treated ourselves to coffee and cake at a nearby restaurant owned by his cousin. It was a dimly lit, smoky place where the tables were covered by thick carpet. At night, we unfolded the couch into a bed, falling asleep under a skylight. Once, in the winter, we came home in the early hours of the morning to see coloured lights twisting in the sky. A UFO landing, I said. My fiancé smiled. No, the aurora borealis. I had my bicycle with me and I leaned it against my hip. I stared up and thought, *Remember this. Try to remember.*

On days when I could not write, I read anything that I could find. Books in English were, in our village, a rare commodity. From bookshops in the U.K., I ordered out-of-print tomes on Southeast Asia and the former British North Borneo, collections of photographs, books on political philosophy. Around me, I felt the world was shifting. The planes that flew into the World Trade Center, the wholesale destruction of Falluja, the pitting of one kind of fundamentalism against another, these conflicts reshaping politics and the polity, wiping out the middle ground – the place where divergent perspectives meet, where they can be heard, understood, and made to matter.

By chance, after writing an article for a newspaper in Canada, I was contacted by a woman in a nearby town. She had lived in Toronto, while working for Médecins Sans Frontières, and her husband worked for the United Nations in Nepal. Over dinner, we talked about where life takes us, the choices that must be made. Her husband had devoted his life to street kids, and he had an aura around him of capability, the will to see things through to the end. I admired them both deeply. There was a time, I told them, when I thought I would work overseas, commit my life to my ideals. But instead, my track was more predictable, university and then travelling. One day in the future, marriage and children.

After my nights with them, I would return home, turn on the computer, and stare at the words I had written. Back in 2001, I had gone to a lecture delivered by Carol Shields. *Use everything*, she had said. Don't save it up, don't put it aside for another story. Life folds and buckles. Give everything now. I looked at my novel and wondered if what I wrote reflected the life that I knew, the lives in the past I had tried to imagine. My words seemed always to be scratching at the surface, dodging the centre, stumbling.

In the novel, a boy witnesses the death of his father. It is September 1945, and the Second World War has ended. Day after day, I sit with him, watching the same scene repeat itself, trying to glimpse his future. I write him falling in love, comforting his first child. I imagine him as a much older man in a much different country, but through all of this, the wound remains, more potent than simply a memory, yet just as ghostly. In my head, I carried reams of notes, so much history, but what I wanted to know was what had happened to this boy, and to those around him.

How to fulfill the obligations of both art and documentation? Because, overwhelmingly, this feeling remained with me: a sense of obligation. Faithfulness to facts, to history, on the one hand; to story, art, on the other. Two halves each struggling to hold sway, twin poles of reason and imagination, and the words walking a wire between them. I think that a story, like life, is a great balancing act, acrobats spinning through the air, the impossible made to look effortless. The lines of construction, of support, should be invisible. I look at the books that I admire and I think, in wonder and joy, look what human hands have wrought.

Within a person, too, the lines of construction, of support, are not easily seen. In current research into the mind, scientists are learning that the "I" is shifting, recreated moment to moment, a neural map of the body and emotions. Consciousness emerges from physical matter, molecules and synaptic charge; thought and imagination arise by the grace of the architecture of our physical, molecular selves.

We can measure the brain's activities, track the chemical bursts, make an educated guess as to where the story comes from. But there is a point at which we lose the trail. There is darkness, and then a leap of faith.

For a long time, this is where I have felt I am writing from, the leap of faith which, by its nature, can make no promises. Perhaps, when I jump, I will succeed in carrying the narrative line with me. Perhaps I will reach out my hand and grasp only air. But writing at least mirrors the web of my feelings: that I am falling, that I am letting go of so much I once held sacred. The narrative line is a construction made from words, each one pinned hopefully to the next. Sometimes strong enough to bridge the distance. Sometimes a lesson in falling.

It is life we are trying to set down, and we are working against the limitations of the lonely, solitary mind, of a single lifetime. Writing is a way of contributing a particular sensibility to the world, the belief in imagination, in empathy. The belief that, without these human capacities, there can be no meeting place. Without imagination, we will continue to be a society where power rules, where the weak are left behind, abandoned to their fate because we had not the foresight or the will to imagine another way.

The past five years have been marked, brutally, in the world: the Southeast Asian tsunami, Beslan, Iraq, the devastation of AIDS in Africa. In my own life, many things have changed. The death of an aunt, then my mother, then a friend. I am married. My best friend, who lives in Madison, Wisconsin, gives birth to her first child under difficult circumstances, and when I arrive there, I want to gather up her small family, hold them close, never let go. During these years, work sees me through. The book becomes one of the few constants in my life. Oddly, I start to feel a debt to it. It sits waiting for me, growing thick around the waist, tottering on spindly legs. For hours, I drink coffee and examine its carriage and heft, the timbre of its voice. Editing, when it happens, feels surgical. The book is creaky. At some point, I must remove the knees, and then build them again from scratch. For a long time, I am constantly pouring life into it, and then, suddenly, it becomes necessary to stand back. Pare down, tread lightly.

Over and over, my husband and I pack up our things, moving from one home to another. We move a total of 19,163 geodesic kilometres; eventually, we just start leaving our things behind.

In 2004, before driving from Vancouver to Quebec, we packed up the contents of my mother's house, which, until then, had been stored in a warehouse. Because of the looming start date of my husband's new job, we worked ceaselessly, and the task was finished within days. Decisions on what to keep and what to discard were made quickly, practicality trumping sentiment.

On the day before we were due to drive east, we stood at the Vancouver landfill, an open pit covered by a high, tin roof. I could not stop looking at the detritus – a couch, a broken mixer, shoes – all the objects we had gathered but could no longer carry, all the bits and fragments that had seen us through the joy, the sorrow, and the mundanity of our hours. At the recycling bins, the same. A worker, a man my mother's age, appeared wearing heavy gloves. He touched a button that I could not see and the bin leaped into motion. It began to compress my mother's belongings – papers, notes. From where I stood, I could see the faint line of her handwriting covering the pages. I watched until every sheet had disappeared, and then I turned away. The same feeling I'd had when she died came back, that I could know nothing, that I could keep nothing safe.

In the span of these years, I have left many things behind. Sometimes we change for the better; sometimes we only harden ourselves against future loss. In the moment, it is hard to tell. There were times when all I wished was that the days would pass, that they would accumulate and carry me into the future.

Use everything. The words on the page are just a flicker, an imprint of the tide that passes through our minds. It isn't this flood, I think, that Carol Shields was calling up, but the way in which this tide has reshaped our selves, the marks left behind, the places hollowed out or filled in. What I hope for in my writing has become simpler, that I let my imagination flourish, so that I'm not bound by my solitude, my own lifetime, my landscape and time.

Sometimes I think about what I would do if I could no longer find my way into stories. If writing goes, how would I reimagine my life? Would I get up from my desk, finally, go into the world as I imagined I would, and make something useful of my days?

We tell stories, Hannah Arendt once said, in the hope that our telling will bring about a change. She said that we are taking part in a great common venture, that humanity cannot be acquired in solitude. "We start something. We weave our strand into the network of relations. What comes of it we never know."

I'm not religious, but there is a kind of faith here. That when I speak, someone is listening. That when you speak, we are listening. And I think this faith changes the words we use, it makes the story more than experience and more than art. It is one-half of a call and answer, a conversation within myself, and between you and me. In this way, the writing life is both a challenge and a solace, a challenge to get the words right, to make the inexpressible concrete. And a solace because writing is an entry into that "network of relations" on which our hope for change depends.

When I think back to that day in Sandakan, I see a time when my mother was still alive, when barely a page of the novel was written; there are questions unformed in my mind, so many questions I had not thought to ask because the need for an answer had not yet arisen. Back then, the novel I wanted to write was only intention, it was possibility, light and buoyant.

Now, in Quebec City, the seasons are changing. It is fall and the novel, nearly edited, waits. My husband and I have been talking about five years here – and then, who knows? I think what I desire is so common. Let writing and life unfold, let me have another chance to get it right. Now, this moment.

JANE**URQUHART**

Writing Sisters

I. Charlotte Brontë Waits for a Letter

Winter's ghost armies of rain
Autumn's blood stain of heather
The hills she walks near dry stone
Willing his ink to appear in her hand

A sequence of fickle weather
Patterns supervise
This ancient exercise in stasis
This aching patience

Transparent paper in her morning mind
And words in a foreign language
The ear on the pillow listens
For the whisper of a knife she keeps
To open vellum

Elsewhere he writes on a black board
Sentences that never reach her
Somewhere he walks on parquet
And the unwritten letter follows
Loyal as a pet

It has arrived in her dreams
A thousand times before she knows

It will not arrive
The moor streams out like a scarf
From her small neck
In a strong wind

All waterways are frozen

Jane Eyre, Villette
Begin to grow like tumours
Darkly in her brain.

II. Emily's Dog Keeper

> "An interpreter ought to have stood
> Between her and the world"
> – Charlotte on Emily Brontë

He is large and golden
And stands between
Her and the planet

Keeping the world and then
Keeping it out

He moves like an arrow
Over the landscape
She places his shadow
On bog water, mud path
Keep that, she says
Measuring bruised distance
Her arm cutting through wind

He keeps hoar frost for her
And keeps the flowers out
Keeps only damaged stars
And the blade of a moon
In troubled air

Strangers flicker on the edge
Of a cold, grey village
Keep them out she whispers
He does

Now the secret kingdom's
Ample population is marching
Through her weather
Keep that she says
Caressing his thick neck

Now granite cliffs are
Homes for nightmare's children
These he keeps for her
Closest to his heart
She loves him

She loves him
His teeth when he shows them
Shine

1984, 2006

MICHAEL**WINTER**

A Galapagos Wave Strikes Newfoundland

This past summer I spent a week on my own – driving all the rough roads left on the Avalon Peninsula, in Newfoundland. I was in my seventeen-year-old Honda Civic, a car I called Jethro. When my mother heard its name, she said, Why would you call a car Death Row? My brother had warned me about getting attached to old cars, so at the end of this trip I was going to drive Jethro along the muddy road of Vatcher's Salvage and throw the key into the woods. Jethro didn't know this yet. I was keeping it secret. I would walk away from him. So on this last venture I loaded the trunk with a tent, a fishing rod, a Coleman stove, a small Styrofoam cooler, and some CDs from the public library: Hank Williams and Glenn Gould.

I hauled Jethro over to the side at every brook for a trout. I ate orange trout and speckled trout and very pale dubious trout. Once I caught an errant salmon. I slept on barren hilltops overlooking the ocean, built fires to cook fish and steak and eggs and pasta. I felt lonely, but it was a loneliness I had volunteered for. It was as if I was shifting through the gears of loneliness and enjoying the power of gasoline. Whenever I got too lonely, I put on Hank or Glenn and rolled down the car window.

I grew filthy and enjoyed the greasiness of my hair. I boiled coffee in the morning or drove to a gas station, and was pleased that not once had I unpacked the Coleman stove. The fire kept me company, and the coals of a fire are more absorbing than television. In a convenience store in Colinet I watched a woman warm formula in a take-away cup of hot water, and I considered that enough of a reason to live.

On the last day of my dirt-road search I drove out to Brigus. I wanted to take a picnic out to the house I had written about in my latest novel. I wanted to present the novel and say thank you in a quiet solitary fashion. I like sneaky, private affairs. I have left things in the woods, like roofracks, and picked them up a year later. No one looks for things in the woods.

The book is a fictionalized memoir of *Moby-Dick*'s illustrator, Rockwell Kent. The artist lived in Newfoundland in 1914, but was kicked out for being a German spy. Kent's story was a chance to assume the emotions of a man quite different from me. But I didn't want to write a staid history book. And now that the book was out and published, I was wondering if I'd done the right thing. For instance, research – maybe I should have done more of that? I'd never been inside the house Kent had lived in. It's been owned for the last fifty years by an American, Jake Folensbee. Jake would arrive in August and leave again for Seattle on Labour Day. He was in his eighties and he dyed his moustache. I'd come out and knock on his door. Yes, he'd say, from around a corner. Me: I'm that guy writing a novel set in this house. His voice, weary: It's not a good time for a visit.

The house is on the west side of the town of Brigus, which is in Conception Bay. Brigus is an old merchant port, and so a lot of it is preserved. But this wooden house sits alone, and as you walk out to it, the twenty-first century peels away. You're in the woods and there's the sea and there are no modern things like powerlines or roads, so you can easily slip back a hundred years.

I've lived in small houses throughout Newfoundland, old houses that people were only too happy to let me live in, as long as I kept them warm and fixed the roof. One of these houses was in Heart's Desire, a Catholic community not far from Brigus, where I lived one winter. When I moved in, the pipes had frozen. I hauled water in two five-gallon buckets from a neighbour who had framed pictures of Jesus across his kitchen wall. He had so many that the frames touched. The post office was across the bay, so I took to walking over the ice – it was the shortest way. One day, in February, I heard some kids talking by the bus stop. He's the fellow, one said, who walks across the water.

Is there something odd about that?

This is the first time in seventeen years, the boy said, that bay has frozen over. You'd have to be half out of your mind to walk on that.

✳   ✳   ✳

I live in Toronto now, but I grew up in Newfoundland. The first three books I wrote were influenced by things that happened to me in Newfoundland. My early stories were largely autobiographical, and when you write from that kind of material, you learn how to make it interesting to a reader who knows, or cares, nothing about your life.

All this changed when people I loved started to tell me they were hurt by the way I was writing about them. My brother, for instance, said that if I wrote about him again, he'd deliver a punch to my head from which I might not recover.

So I decided to write an historical novel. I saw a travelling exhibit of Rockwell Kent's Newfoundland work and thought his life would make a good novel. He was pretty much forgotten, out of fashion, but in his day the *New Yorker* published this ditty:

> That day will mark a precedent
> which brings no news of Rockwell Kent

I thought a memoir of an old man reflecting on his foolish youth would make a good book, and it would solve the issue of my writing about people I know and love.

But I'm not very good at research.

Also, I'm not convinced that the world a hundred years ago was that much different from today. Yes, the surfaces might appear different, but when I read diaries written a century ago, the feeling I get is, *how modern*. Also, when I read contemporary novels that describe how people salted fish and how they hoisted the spanker, I get a little seasick from the information. I prefer the emotional life, and life related first-hand, or works so masterful you are convinced that what's being described is a matter of life and death.

I think I was jarred into realism by reading Norman Levine. I met him in 1993, when he came to St. John's to promote the new edition of *Canada Made Me*. I didn't know much about Levine, until my friend Larry Mathews, who was my first creative writing teacher, made me read Levine's stories, his novel, and his memoir. The images and voice stayed with me. There was something small and quiet that worked deep down in the nervous system. I had grown up in a small town: Corner Brook. I didn't know what to do with myself. There was nothing around me that told me I should try being artistic. When I was eight, my father took me to the Arts and Culture Centre to see the world-famous American outdoorsman Lee Wulff. Wulff delivered a slide show on big game hunting to an audience made up of fishermen and their sons. After the screening, Lee Wulff appeared at one end of the stage, holding a fly rod. He cast out a figure-eight of line in the air above us, and rolled that length of line across the floorlights until a red bow, tied to the end of the line, came to rest on top of the head of a man in the back row. We all exploded into applause. For years afterward, I associated theatre with the experience of watching a man flick a fly rod into the audience.

It was my older sister, Kathleen, who gave me the idea to write. God knows how it came to her. Kathleen took a degree in journalism at Carleton University. In the summers she returned to Corner Brook to work at the local newspaper. I delivered the papers that had her column in it. She also worked for the TV *Guide* and told me, privately, that she'd often rewrite the text for the sitcoms. She'd have Jack Tripper have an affair with Ralph Furley, or the whole cast of *Taxi* would get in a cab and travel to Morocco. No one complained. On the side she wrote short stories and sent them to little magazines. She wrote on a manual typewriter on the picnic table in the backyard. I remember one rejected story that received this note from the editor: "Interesting, if a little cryptic."

I asked her what *cryptic* meant, and she told me about being obscure, about not saying exactly what you mean, about being oblique and mysterious.

And I realized that was how I acted in the world, and yet I was not encouraged to be that way, especially in print.

The first real art show I saw was in the summer before I left Corner Brook. I was eighteen. There was a touring exhibit at the Arts and Culture Centre. The artist, Marlene Creates, had taken black-and-white photographs of Newfoundland fields. These were fields where she had spent the night as she travelled across the island – she had taken a snap of the impression her body had made in the land. You could see aluminum-coloured blades of grass beginning to perk up again. At the horizon were the posts of a fence, the legs of a cow, a strip of ocean.

The photos made me angry. There seemed to be nothing in them. And yet, the pictures stayed with me. The work was a reaction against monumental art, my sister told me – art that is supposed to last through time. Marlene Creates wanted to capture that fleeting moment when we make an impression in the world. Her work was bereft of vanity, and yet, oddly, it contained something lasting, a snapshot of the intangible, passing moment. It made me realize how often, while I was falling asleep, I'd remember a moment of the day, and that moment might be as inconsequential as seeing a woman's dress billow out of a payphone booth.

∗   ∗   ∗

When I moved to St. John's, I met people like Larry Mathews and Lisa Moore. Lisa and I would learn to write together. I became an editor of a small magazine, *TickleAce*. When Norman Levine came through town I wanted to interview him. It was his first visit to Newfoundland. He was concerned about how small the place was, but he liked it. He asked if I had interesting friends. Yes, I said. Good, he said. Then you can live here.

I had just returned from travelling. I had wanted to go to Greece, Turkey, Israel, and Egypt. In Greece I stayed in a little youth hostel in Crete. On the bookshelf was a novel by Percy Janes called *House of Hate*. As I learned, it was all about growing up in Corner Brook, Newfoundland. No one had told me about this book, and I had to come to Crete to discover it. It made me think of my own experience of Corner Brook, and perhaps of writing about it.

That was how I began writing thinly veiled autobiography while living in little houses in outport Newfoundland. Then my brother told me he was hurt by what I wrote. What was it, I asked, that crossed the line? Was it the time he thought about robbing the bank?

No, that was good.

Was it all the sex and drugs?

It was what I had written about his dog. We're in the truck, he said, and I'm braking for a red light. And the dog's nose makes those snout marks on the windshield.

All this to say, you never know what kind of exposure will hurt someone you love.

*　　*　　*

Those boys in Heart's Desire, they knew when I got up, because they'd see smoke climbing out of my chimney. They'd arrive after school and watch me make lunch. One of them had never had real butter, just margarine. He'd never had a poached egg before, and he certainly didn't grind pepper on it. Once, while the pipes were still frozen, I brought some water from St. John's.

That town water?

I watched him look at the plastic bottles of water lined up by the woodstove.

When you got the best water in the world right here?

I explained the situation with my pipes, and I asked him if he'd ever tasted water from the city. He took a taste. That's healthy, he said. It was his first taste of the outside world.

*　　*　　*

One morning I woke up to a whiteness and discovered a curling wave of snow sitting in my kitchen, from a storm that had blown open my porch door. It looked like something out of *Doctor Zhivago*. The snow was white and quiet as a sand dune, and I spent the morning shovelling the tongue of it back out into the yard.

I wrote it down and knew I could use it. I knew they shovelled snow a century before, just as we still hang clothes on a line to dry them. I'd never been in Rockwell Kent's house, but I'd been in houses. I knew what it felt like, generally, to be inside an outport house. I knew the walls were not insulated, and that you can sit in one house and hear what's being said in another.

✳   ✳   ✳

I walked out to the Brigus house that I'd written about, with the book that had the house in it. This time the windows were wide open and there were bright figures inside. A lot of people. I knocked on the door. A man answered. I told him who I was.

Oh yes, he said, we've heard all about you.

It was Jake Folensbee's nephew. Jake had died over the spring. And they had come up to settle his affairs. Inside were the Brigus Historical Society. I handed them the copy of my novel, and they said I should take a tour of the house.

It was small. I had to crouch for the six-foot ceilings. On the kitchen cupboards were two small red roses that Rockwell Kent had painted.

It was an odd moment, to be inside the house I had written so much about. And I was glad to have published the book without being inside. For the book, I realized, is not about being accurate to surfaces and objects. It's more about emotions and psychology, and my belief that the thoughts people had a century ago are similar to those people have today. I told this to the nephew and he said yes, society was more polite and mannered, but the inner life remains the same.

I had written a sex scene set in this house. I hadn't wanted it to happen in a room, because that would be predictable, so I had Rockwell Kent and the woman who took care of the children, and I put them in the stairwell. But I had never seen the stairs. And now there they were in front of me, so small, and I realized how impossible it would be for two people to perform such an act on them.

*   *   *

In my tent that night I thought about how little time Rockwell Kent had spent here. And that he wrote my book in his private voice, and as an old man. That's the conceit. I could get things wrong about this place because they happened so long ago to a man who had spent very little time here. I was listening to Hank Williams and Glenn Gould as I arrived at this reassurance. I sometimes think about Hank, how he'd be in his early eighties if he was still around, and how eerie it is to hear his grandson, Hank III, sing. The old Hank Williams affected a southern accent – he'd pronounce "window" as "winder." It was false and yet there was something more genuine in the affectation. Then I listened to Glenn Gould. Gould had once been in Newfoundland. He had made a wild recording here, blending a series of waves – grinding waves and slooshing waves, all from Newfoundland. He had recorded one-on-one interviews with Newfoundlanders, and he was weaving these voices within the waves. He was dropping his own voice out of the recording, so it sounded as if these people were talking amongst themselves, when in fact they were speaking to him. But Gould was frustrated with the range of available sounds. He was missing something. He found other sea tapes: exotic radio tape from the Galapagos Islands. He listened to them. There was a Galapagos wave he wanted and he spliced it in – in the middle of Newfoundland. It sounded right, he said. It was more truthful.

The last bit of rough road was out to a lighthouse in Cape Race. I camped at the lighthouse and studied the slow orb of its candle power strobe across the Atlantic, the dense particles of fog triggering the digital sensor on the foghorn. It was an unmanned station, but it was a pointer to ships at night, long oil tankers flying Liberian flags of convenience, plying their double hulls through the worst seas in the world, dumping waste before they hit Boston. A hundred years ago, two telegraph operators named Dot and Dash relayed sealing disasters, the fate of the *Titanic*, war.

In the morning, as I drove back to St. John's to park Jethro at the salvage yard, I spotted a man in chest waders in the river, fly-fishing. He had an English setter standing in the water with him, full of attention. The man was good at casting and he would catch fish. He looked like me, if I had stayed in Newfoundland.

PATRICIA**YOUNG**

The Writing Family:
Trimming Curtains the Length of Light

The heart of my family's life is a barn: post-and-beam construction, board-and-batten siding, woodpile foundation. It sits rather grandly on a sloping rock outcrop. In fine weather its living space expands and spills out on three sides: covered veranda, cedar deck, brick patio.

Mice live and die within its walls. Squirrels scrabble in the gap between shiplap ceiling and corrugated tin roof. From the bedroom windows we can see deer stepping through the high yellow grass. Carpenter ants chomp through the phone wires. In the woodbox, a shrew gives birth to babies smaller than a fingernail. Once, I heard an explosive scuffle, and then a weird shrieking, cries more human than animal. For days afterward, a musky stench rose up through the floorboards.

Built in 1891, the barn has come to us through the generations. It has lasted through winter storms and breathless summer afternoons. It stands in all its strange organic beauty.

One way or another we all write out of this place.

*　*　*

Up ahead, Terence pedalled hard on his black Carleton Cobra, wanting to get there, wherever *there* was. The chain on my own ten-speed kept slipping from its sprocket, and I had to keep getting off to coax it back on. It was messy work; my fingers were numb.

I rode slowly, in no hurry to catch up. He didn't stop or turn around or seem to care that I was lagging farther and farther behind, and I started to hate him a little, this boy I'd been admiring, not too discreetly, for months in the school cafeteria.

Green hills and long shadows, the forest rising up on both sides. His red jacket disappearing over the horizon. Where the hell were we?

* * *

People ask how I feel when my children write about me. How do Liam and Clea feel when I write about them? How does Terence feel when I write about him? How do I feel when he writes about me?

It's a tricky business, I say.

Every family draws lines in the sand. You can go this far but no farther.

Terence: That spaz you had in the toy department yesterday? If you're thinking of using it – too late.

Clea, at thirteen: Hello? Earth to mother, my life isn't exactly an open book.

Liam: Hey, I drove a truck into the lake. That's *my* story.

A tricky business indeed.

* * *

The barn was dark and mysterious and rarely visited. Rooms had been carved out of the interior with wooden partitions, but the roof was so high the rooms had no ceilings. When Terence was young, he'd climb up to the rafters and look down on the floor plan. From up there, he said, it was like watching a play.

Though primitive, the timber-framed building was furnished with ornate mirrors and wardrobes and marble-topped wash-stands. Heavy silverware and enormous platters with family crests. A windup Victrola, its cabinet full of seventy-eights. Inside the swollen drawers: moth-eaten woollen bathing suits, tins of ancient-smelling talc, *Liberty* magazines.

Framed photographs of Terence's relatives hung on one wall: Aunt Cecil squinting in a flowery print dress and dark lipstick; Terence's mother, May Queen at sixteen; his grandmother in a rowboat, surrounded by water lilies, a thick braid draped over the front of her body; his great-grandfather, Charles Dumbleton, remittance man and congenial drinker; great-uncle Ernst, a month before he was crushed to death in a gold mine in Mexico.

I pointed to a little boy in a sailor suit. Who's he? I asked, but Terence didn't know. It seemed no one knew. He'd been asking about that kid for as long as he could remember.

If the mother in Clea's story is a depressed psychiatrist who flies into a rage every time her daughter uses the clothes dryer, that's okay with me.

If the wife in Terence's story is a pot-smoking, laser-tongued misanthrope, that's also okay with me.

I understand: I am not all mothers, all wives.

If the vegan mother in Liam's story sparks a family feud because her visiting brother-in-law innocently fries up a few strips of bacon (*This house is a meat-free zone, for Christ's sake! How could you not know that?*), it has to be okay.

If it weren't, none of us could write.

*   *   *

We pulled up chairs and put our feet inside the oven. Night closed in and despite the kerosene lamps, the room was dark and shadowy. Terence began to talk about B.C. Hydro expropriating the neighbour's land – land that had once belonged to his family – and razing the forest to build massive electrical pylons. He said that he and his friends regularly tramped over the stolen land, removing the right-of-way markings, the surveyors' ribbons and stakes.

After what seemed like forever, the kettle on the woodstove began to hiss and we became aware of ourselves, the strangeness of being alone and together and far from anywhere, though in fact we were only ten miles outside of Victoria. We sipped Lapsang Souchong, and I might have told him I wrote poetry because he disappeared through a heavy curtain and returned with a book of poems. Someone called Pablo Neruda. I have forgotten countless mornings and afternoons and evenings of my life, but those few hours huddled in December darkness, Terence reading aloud ("And it was at that age . . . Poetry arrived / in search of me. / I don't know, I don't know where / it came from, from winter or a river"), remain so immediate I can still smell the tea's smoky fragrance.

*   *   *

Is Clea's choice to write actually a choice?

When she was very young and Terence and I were going to university, we lived in the barn, which meant no TV or neighbourhood friends. Just toys and paper and library books and records. I read to her for hours at a time, or she'd sit on the couch and listen to *Alice in Wonderland* on the turntable, four LPs, eight sides, repeating along with the heavily accented British voice. Sometimes she'd ask me to drape a dishtowel over the photograph of the little boy in the sailor suit, because, she said, he spied on her when he thought she wasn't looking.

Terence built her a little desk, which she wanted right beside mine. While I typed poems on an electric typewriter, she drew pictures and printed her name, the *C* always backward. Often she'd sidle over and climb onto my pregnant lap, and together we'd look out at the forest, the winter gloom pressing up against the glass.

She wrote all through her childhood, filing drafts of stories and poems in manila folders, making little books, sewing the pages together, imitating perhaps, but also forging her own way. One day she walked into the kitchen and asked me to read a story she'd written. She needed a title. Did I have any suggestions?

We were living mostly in the city by then, but her story was based on something that had happened a few years earlier, when the barn was still home: a little girl believes fairies live inside the cedar house that sits over the well, believes there are also tiny beds and lamps and tables and chairs, believes all this because her mother has told her it is so, has told her in fact that there is a fairy who looks just like the girl, except the fairy-girl wears flower petals and dew drops instead of jeans and sweaters.

The girl in Clea's story believes these things until the day she watches in horror as her father dismantles the rotting well house, exposing an ugly rusting pump.

I had been chopping onions, but now, through tears, considered: *Childhood as Garden of Eden. The Loss of Innocence.* I suggested *The Well House.* Clea pondered this for a moment. No, she didn't think so. A little while later she returned and asked what I thought of *Trimming Curtains the Length of Light.* I stopped what I was doing and looked at her face, serious, wanting my approval, but also resolute. This title that had nothing to do with her story was exactly what she'd been groping for – words that sang.

I tossed the onions in the olive oil along with the garlic. I love it, I said. Really, honey. I wish it were mine.

* * *

Mirrors within mirrors within mirrors. But within a single family? People ask, Does this complicate things or make them easier?

Give me a writer any day, I answer. Someone who understands the process.

No matter how many times I tell my sister, the massage therapist, that it takes many lives and many people to construct a single character, she doesn't hear me.

Sister: That Marianne in your story has a lisp and smokes menthol cigarettes.

Me: Your point being?

Sister: Plus, she took highland-dancing lessons as a kid!

Me: So.

Sister: So? *So?* You're writing about me again! How many times do I have to tell you not to write about me.

Me: You don't smoke menthol cigarettes.

Sister: And her vacuous inner life, her stupid little Pomeranian!

Me: We all loved that dog.

Sister: So you admit it. You admit you walked in on me and that guy.

Me: What guy?

Sister: That guy you were supposedly nuts about – excuse me, that *Marianne* is nuts about.

Me: You knew I liked him. You knew very well how I felt.

It goes in circles. It goes on all the time.

*   *   *

After Liam was born, we continued to pack up our lives at the beginning of each July, and drive out to the barn, which Terence continued to work on – a second floor, an outdoor shower, an indoor bathroom. He and my father built a wood heater, compressing, then welding six feet of coiled hollow steel they'd bought for next to nothing from Wilson's Cold Packing and Storage. The Armadillo – as we have come to call it – radiates so much heat it's hard to believe freezing brine once flowed through its pipes.

One summer night, Terence wound the Victrola's spring and put on a record, and I went out to the veranda with a bottle of wine and two glasses. The children, two and seven, might have been asleep, though they might just as well have been lying in their beds, listening to "Congratulations" or "Where Were You, Where Was I," funny old songs from the twenties, a time we imagined more innocent and magnanimous than our own.

Terence lit a cigarette and we leaned on the railing, looking out at the fir trees silhouetted against the sky. The record ended and in that silence the forest grew loud with crickets and frogs. He smoked thoughtfully for a few minutes, and then said on nights like this he always imagined himself a passenger on a doomed ocean liner.

Why doomed? I asked.

Something about this place, he said. Something about leaning over this railing, this glass of wine, this cigarette, the twenties music. Something about the way he'd been etched into the actual building, the way his growth had been scratched into a doorjamb. What had been charted, however, was not gain but loss. He said the barn had always evoked in him a kind of gentle grief for all that had passed away.

✳ ✳ ✳

Even in her nineties, Terence's grandmother told fantastic stories in which she was often the heroine. Once, when we went to visit her at the Gorge Road Hospital, where she had lived for years, crippled with rheumatoid arthritis, she talked about her father, Charlie Dumbleton. In need of money, he'd apparently sold the house, the lake, the barn, and the surrounding 350 acres to the son of a German count. She wasn't clear how long the son of the count had owned the property, but when the First World War broke out, the Canadian government, suspecting him of espionage, expropriated the land and lake and buildings and returned them to Charlie.

Terence and I glanced at each other and rolled our eyes.

As far as we knew, Charlie, a gentleman farmer with a penchant for good times and pretty women, incurred so much debt in the thirties he'd had to sell off everything but the barn and the four surrounding acres. Until then we'd never heard anything about a shadowy German colluding with the Kaiser to install a gun emplacement on Scafe Hill, which has a view of Esquimalt Harbour.

For years Terence and I attributed his grandmother's story to a vivid and morbid imagination. Until last summer, that is, when, because I could, I googled *German Count+Real Estate+Vancouver Island+First World War*, and up came Gustav Konstantin Alvo von Alvensleben. It seems that a son of German nobility, with family ties to the Kaiser, *had* bought up land all over B.C., building one of the largest financial empires in the history of the province. There is even a photograph of him: tall, clean-cut, athletic-looking. A Prussian aristocrat decked out in a hunting suit.

* * *

By the time Clea was fourteen she'd had it with our summer retreats. Even a few weeks out in the freakin' boonies with her freakin' parents was more than she could endure.

On the phone to a friend: Save me. I'm dying.

Liam, who imitated most of what Clea said and did, from her sudden modesty at ten to her sudden scorn of the barn now, decided he'd also had it. He wanted to be elsewhere, grinding his skateboard against a city curb. One night, perhaps to emphasize his point, he announced: No more bedtime stories.

Me: Okay. Fine. You can read by yourself then.
Him: Why should I?
Me: Because you want to.
Him: What if I don't?
Me: Don't what?
Him: Want to read by myself.
Me: That's impossible. Of course you want to.

And just like that, the bedtime story, an almost sacred ritual, was forever eradicated.

Over the next few years I pushed books in his direction, non-fiction, mostly, because teachers and librarians had advised that boys prefer action/adventure books. My mother bought him a subscription to *National Geographic*. When he asked for a subscription to *Thrasher*, a skateboard magazine, for his birthday, I was overjoyed. At least he'd be functionally literate.

He was fifteen when we argued about my latest offering, *The Perfect Storm*, a novel I'd been told no boy could refuse. Liam's position was unchanged. He wasn't interested. Feeling personally rejected, and a little heart-broken, I said, Well, I guess I must have failed somehow.

He patted my arm: Don't worry, Mum. It's not your fault. Maybe you just overdid it.

Overdid what?

You know, the reading thing.

∗   ∗   ∗

As Terence and I moved into married life, he supported my passion for poetry. While not particularly driven to write himself, he always imagined that he *would* write sometime in the future. In the meantime he taught high-school French and English, dabbling now and then, writing a few poems, publishing the odd short story.

His grandmother died, and then his father, followed by my father. A dear friend committed suicide, another died in an inexplicable boating accident, another of a brain tumour. With each death we rang the rusting 1928 Buick brake drum, which hangs from the veranda's main beam.

The desire to write intensified when Terence began to teach a creative writing class. Now he was spending time not just with Shakespeare and Milton and Donne, but with the finest practitioners of modern poetry and fiction. This material, along with the work of his students, inspired him. He also began to feel slightly fraudulent. How could he teach writing unless he himself wrote?

It seemed we were ringing his grandmother's dinner gong more and more often now. The future was upon us, it was right here, and then one night we came home from a party, and while Terence got into bed and I stumbled around drunk, trying to get out of my clothes, I heard him say, offhandedly and almost to himself: Once, there were just days. Now there are the days we have left.

What did you say? I asked.

I said . . .

I know what you said, it's just I'd never thought of it like that. I've never thought of it quite like that.

He laughed and turned off the light.

The following September he took a two-year leave of absence from teaching and did an MFA in Creative Writing at the University of British Columbia.

*   *   *

Somewhere along the way I had convinced myself that I didn't have the mind for fiction. In her late teens, Clea was like me; she wrote only poems. Perhaps she had also settled on this notion of a "poetic sensibility." For a first-year writing class, however, she had to write a short story, which she read to Terence and me one night after dinner. I recognized places and details, people from whom she'd drawn, a boyfriend, a gruff old caretaker out in The Highlands. But her actual characters and story were fresh. They were her own.

I was very impressed.

How had she done this thing? I asked. Could I do it too?

I don't know, Mum, she said, it takes a lot longer than writing a poem. I'm not sure you have the patience.

*   *   *

In the summer between grades eleven and twelve, Liam picked up *Blood Meridian* by Cormac McCarthy and read it. And then he read *Disgrace* by J.M. Coetzee.

All through July and August he sat on the deck, a multi-coloured Rasta hat on his head, reading Alice Munro, F. Scott Fitzgerald, Raymond Carver, Leon Rooke, Malcolm Lowry, Richard Ford, Herman Hesse, Ernest Hemingway, Denis Johnson.

Despite the activity of the past years – the basketball, soccer, snowboarding – it seemed his brain had been in some sort of dormant state, suspended, waiting to become.

In his last year of high school, he signed up for English Literature and, most surprising of all, a writing class. He wrote a story about a boy whose father, an obsessive compulsive, goes a little nuts when his wife leaves for unknown reasons. The story ends with the son and father heading out to a barn in the forest for the father's birthday, because this is the only place he feels truly relaxed.

The following summer Liam kept going: Dostoevsky, Bill Gaston, Lorrie Moore, Dave Eggers, Elizabeth Bishop, Don DeLillo, Herman Melville, Sharon Olds, Patrick Lane, Mark Strand, Joy Williams, José Saramago, Annabel Lyon, Ha Jin, James Tate, Amy Hempel, Barry Hannah, John Gould, Margaret Atwood, Jim Harrison, Mark Jarman, John Metcalf, ZZ Packer, whatever he could find, whatever was close at hand, every *New Yorker*, *Harper's*, George Saunders, William Trevor, John Ashberry.

Eight years of deprivation. Now he gorged.

*   *   *

The best thing about being married to a writer: the brutally honest feedback. The worst thing about being married to a writer: the brutally honest feedback.

Having decided to try to write fiction, I heard voices all the time, lucid, demanding voices with stories to tell. Unfortunately, I lacked the skill to get them down on the page. The years of writing poetry had not prepared me for the task of writing fiction. I was enthusiastic but inept, and, as Clea had predicted, impatient.

I gave Terence a draft of something I'd written and after he'd read it I saw the pain in his face. He offered a few suggestions, but it was clear he thought the story was dead in the water. I was hurt and frustrated and defensive and demanded he explain himself more fully, but he sensed, quite rightly, that whatever he said from then on would be the wrong thing, and so he refused to say anything.

Later, walking along the waterfront, I looked over and saw his jaw set like his father's – I'd never seen his jaw set like that – which infuriated me even more. But no matter what I said or how I pleaded he would not be drawn into further discussion.

It was a beautiful afternoon, sailboats on the water, kids on roller skates, old people pushing walkers, and it occurred to me that after all we'd been through – our darkest hour and the darker hours that followed – my awful story might be the end of us.

*   *   *

Over the years Terence has maintained the pump, jacked up the foundations, insulated the walls, scraped moss off the roof, devised gutters, replaced broken windows. Without his constant attention, the barn would have collapsed in on itself years ago, become uninhabitable. He has brought down trees and split fresh shakes for the woodshed, built chimneys, a new outhouse, poured a cement septic tank. Last summer he laid down new kitchen counters, using tongue-in-groove fir flooring, which he sanded and then varnished three times.

I wonder: Is the barn a stone he polishes for the sheer pleasure of polishing a stone? Or is the endless shoring up his way of holding back not just the subdivisions and box stores encroaching on all sides, but the inevitability of death.

＊　　＊　　＊

My family's love of this place is somehow intertwined with our love of words. In my mind, at least, the two are inseparable. I would say this love of words unites us as a family, but I can hear Liam groan in mock agony because – although it's true – I, his mother, have said it, and it is embarrassing to hear your mother talk about your family and what unites it, particularly if the word *love* is involved.

Reading a poem Terence wrote a few years ago, I was struck by how the barn informs our writing, even when it doesn't figure literally. In "Brave," he writes about an evening in Mexico. Though not sitting on the veranda in The Highlands, looking out at the forest, we could be, because there it is, at the end of the poem, the image of passengers on an ocean liner, the sense of doom.

. . . but aligned seaward as we all were on our chaise
lounges – my son, my daughter, my wife and I – our legs extended,

backs upright, heads tilted to the sky, I couldn't help thinking – maybe
it was the Spanish refrain, I don't know, some hint of a hopeless cause

like love or war about to begin – that the four of us were courageous,
though not in the way heroes are said to be courageous, those people

who snatch small children from debris in the middle of swollen rivers,
but brave as my mother used the term on those occasions when another

pet sank beneath the soil of our back garden, or when on a morning
of rain and gloom I walked out the front door to school, lunch kit in

hand, the drawstrings of my hood pulled tight around my face, another
pointless day with the substitute teacher. "You're a brave boy," she'd

say, and I believed her, as I believed my family was brave simply for
sitting there on that tropical evening, like passengers on an ocean liner

who had left behind a country on the brink of ruin only to discover there
was no safe port left in the world, no haven that would take them in.

*   *   *

Now, when Terence and I go out for the summer with books and laptops, he sets up a desk with his back to the wall of photographs of his mostly deceased relatives. I prefer a table on the deck, facing the gravel road, which is now gated at the fork so that only the occasional horse or mountain biker passes by. Dappled light filters down through the maple leaves, and quails thrash through the underbrush. Fir needles drop into the spaces between the letters of my keyboard. A circling raven makes a sound like amplified water drops plunking into a washbasin.

Liam and Clea drive out for dinner and afterward we all walk down to the lake for a swim. Later, drinking tea in the living room, I tell them about their great-great-grandfather selling everything to the son of a German count. I tell how the count's son disguised himself as a woman and caught a night train to Seattle to escape British intelligence, but was later picked up somewhere in the States and interned near Salt Lake City for the rest of the First World War.

A spy? Clea says. No way. A spy?

There's a moment of silence and then, as though drawn by something beyond our control, we all turn to the boy in the sailor suit, his long, imperious gaze.

ABOUT THE CONTRIBUTORS

Sari Ginsberg

André Alexis was born in Trinidad in 1957 and grew up in Canada. His debut novel, *Childhood*, won the Chapters/*Books in Canada* First Novel Award, shared the Trillium Book Award, and was shortlisted for the Giller Prize and the Rogers Communications Writers' Trust Fiction Prize. He is also the author of a collection of short stories, *Despair and Other Stories of Ottawa*, which was shortlisted for a regional Commonwealth Writers' Prize; a published play, *Lambton Kent*; a children's book, *Ingrid and the Wolf*; and a forthcoming novel, *Asylum*. André Alexis lives in Toronto.

George Whiteside

Margaret Atwood is the author of more than forty books of fiction, poetry, critical essays, and books for children. Her most recent works are *The Tent*, a collection of mini-fictions, and *Moral Disorder* (fall 2006). Her other books include *Oryx and Crake*, a finalist for the Man Booker Prize and the Giller Prize; the 2000 Booker Prize–winning novel *The Blind Assassin*; *Alias Grace*, winner of the Giller Prize and the Premio Mondello in Italy; *The Robber Bride*; *Cat's Eye*; *The Handmaid's Tale*; and *The Penelopiad*. Margaret Atwood lives in Toronto with novelist Graeme Gibson.

Emma Dodge Hanson

Russell Banks has received numerous prizes and awards for his work, including the O. Henry and Best American Short Story Awards, the John Dos Passos Prize, and the Literature Award from the American Academy of Arts and Letters. Russell Banks lives in upstate New York.

Thomas Fricke

David Bergen is the author of the novels *A Year of Lesser*; *See the Child*; *The Case of Lena S.*, winner of the Carol Shields Winnipeg Book Award and a finalist for the Governor General's Award for Fiction; and *The Time in Between*, winner of the Scotiabank Giller Prize. He is also the author of a collection of short fiction, *Sitting Opposite My Brother*, which was a finalist for the Manitoba Book of the Year Award. David Bergen lives in Winnipeg.

Jean Mohr

John Berger is a novelist, storyteller, poet, screenwriter, and art critic. His previous books include the *Into Their Labours* trilogy (*Pig Earth*, *Once in Europa*, and *Lilac and Flag*), *About Looking*, and *Ways of Seeing*. He was awarded the Booker Prize for *G.* and received a Lifetime Achievement Award from the Lannan Foundation. Born in England, John Berger has, for many years, lived in a small rural community in France.

Sarah Warren

George Bowering is a poet, novelist, essayist, critic, teacher, historian, and editor, and one of the most prolific writers in Canada. He is a two-time winner of the Governor General's Award, and his most recent collection of poetry, *Changing on the Fly*, was shortlisted for the Griffin Poetry Prize. In November 2002 he was appointed the first Canadian Parliamentary Poet Laureate. That same month he was made an Officer of the Order of Canada. In 2004 he was awarded the Order of British Columbia.

Michael Elcock

Marilyn Bowering (www.marilynbowering.com) has received a number of awards for poetry, including the Pat Lowther Award, the Dorothy Livesay Prize, and several National Magazine awards, and she has been shortlisted twice for the Governor General's Award. Her fiction has won the Ethel Wilson Prize, been shortlisted for the world-wide Orange Prize, and been recognized with the designation of Notable Book by the *New York Times*. Her new novel is *What It Takes to Be Human* (fall 2006). She now lives with her family in Sooke, British Columbia.

Steph Beeley

Joseph Boyden is a Canadian with Irish, Scottish, and Métis roots. His first novel, *Three Day Road*, won the Rogers Writers' Trust Fiction Prize and the McNally Robinson Aboriginal Book of the Year Award, and was a finalist for the Governor General's Award. Boyden is also the author of *Born with a Tooth*, a collection of stories that was shortlisted for the Upper Canada Writer's Craft Award. Joseph Boyden divides his time between Northern Ontario and Louisiana, where he teaches writing at the University of New Orleans.

Walter Isaac

Di Brandt is the author of five collections of poetry, including *questions i asked my mother*, *Agnes in the sky*, *Jerusalem, beloved*, and *Now You Care*, a finalist for the Trillium Book Award and the Griffin Poetry Prize. Her numerous awards include the Gerald Lampert Award, the McNally Robinson Manitoba Book of the Year Award, a National Magazine Award, and the CAA National Poetry Prize. Brandt recently accepted a Canada Research Chair in Creative Writing at Brandon

University in Manitoba, and is delighted to be back on the prairies, her beloved home landscape, after teaching at the University of Windsor for eight years.

John Reeves

Barry Callaghan is a novelist, poet, journalist, publisher, and man of letters. The winner of the inaugural W.O. Mitchell Award, Callaghan has received numerous honours for his work and for his contributions to literature. His books include *Hogg: The Poems and Drawings*, *The Black Queen Stories*, *A Kiss Is Still a Kiss*, the memoir *Barrelhouse Kings*, and two volumes of collected non-fiction, *Raise You Five* and *Raise You Ten*. His writing has been published around the world and translated into many languages. Barry Callaghan lives in Toronto.

Karen Engle

Lynn Coady's latest novel is *Mean Boy*. She is also the author of *Strange Heaven* and *Saints of Big Harbour*, and a book of short stories, *Play the Monster Blind*. Lynn Coady lives in Edmonton.

Tim Leyes

Susan Coyne is an actor and writer living in Toronto. As an actor, she has appeared in leading roles in theatres across Canada and is a founding member of Soulpepper Theatre Company. She adapted her memoir, *Kingfisher Days*, for the Tarragon Theatre, where she is a writer-in-residence, and where her latest play, *Alice's Affair*, had its premiere. She has also adapted plays by Chekhov for the stage, and Carol Shields's novel *Unless* for CBC Radio. She has been nominated for a Gemini and won a Writers Guild of Canada award for her work on the TV miniseries *Slings and Arrows*.

Holly Hogan

Michael Crummey is a full-time writer living in St. John's. His bestselling first novel, *River Thieves*, was a finalist for the Giller Prize, the Commonwealth Writers' Prize, the Amazon/*Books in Canada* First Novel Award, and won the Thomas Raddall Atlantic Fiction Award and the Winterset Award. He has written three books of poetry, a collection of short stories, and, with photographer Greg Locke, published *Newfoundland: Journey into a Lost Nation*. His latest novel, *The Wreckage*, was a finalist for the Rogers Writers' Trust Fiction Prize.

Sam Green

Margaret Drabble has published sixteen novels and various works of non-fiction, including biographies of English novelists Arnold Bennett and Angus Wilson. She is also the editor of the *Oxford Companion to English Literature*. Drabble is a patron of the Cambodia Trust and the Guantanamo Human Rights Commission. She was awarded the CBE in 1980, and became a Foreign Honorary Member of the American Academy of Arts and Letters in 2002. Margaret Drabble lives in London and West Somerset.

Michael Mitchell

Bernice Eisenstein is a writer and artist whose drawings and illustrations have appeared in a variety of Canadian magazines and periodicals. She has also worked as a freelance literary editor. Her recently published illustrated memoir, *I Was a Child of Holocaust Survivors*, is scheduled for publication in the U.S., the U.K., and in translation throughout the world. She lives in Toronto, with her husband and two children.

Howard Engel is the creator of the enduring detective Benny Cooperman, who has become an internationally recognized fictional sleuth. Two of Engel's novels have been adapted for TV movies, and his books have been

translated into several languages. In 2001, Howard Engel experienced a stroke that resulted in *alexia sine agraphia*. Soon after, despite his inability to read, he wrote *Memory Book*. In March 2005, he received the Matt Cohen Prize for Lifetime Achievement. He lives in Toronto.

Damon Galgut was born in 1963 in Pretoria, South Africa. He is the author of five books, the latest of which, *The Good Doctor*, won a regional Commonwealth Writers' Prize for Best Book and was a finalist for the Man Booker Prize and the International IMPAC Dublin Literary Award. He lives in Cape Town.

Jonathan Garfinkel is the author of a book of poetry, *Glass Psalms*, and the plays *Walking to Russia* and *The Trials of John Demjanjuk: A Holocaust Cabaret*. His most recent play, *Blind*, about a divided house in Jerusalem, was presented in June 2005 at the National Arts Centre in Ottawa. An article about his travels in Palestine and Israel is forthcoming in the *Walrus*. He is a recent graduate of the University of Toronto's MA program in Creative Writing. Jonathan Garfinkel lives in Toronto.

Greg Gatenby is the author of several books of poetry and non-fiction, most recently, *Toronto: A Literary Guide*. He was, until recently, the Artistic Director of the world-renowned International Festival of Authors and of the weekly Harbourfront Reading Series in Toronto. Under his directorship, the program featured readings and talks by more than four thousand authors from more than ninety nations. Gatenby was one of the five founding members of the reconstituted PEN Canadian Centre, and one of the four principal organizers of the PEN World Congress in Toronto in 1989. He is currently writing a history of the First World War.

Camilla Gibb is the author of three novels, *Mouthing the Words*, winner of the City of Toronto Book Award, *The Petty Details of So-and-so's Life*, and *Sweetness in the Belly*, a finalist for the Giller Prize.

Charlotte Gray is the author of five bestselling, award-winning books of biography and popular history, including *Sisters in the Wilderness: The Lives of Susanna Moodie and Catharine Parr Traill*, *Canada: A Portrait in Letters 1800–2000*, and *A Museum Called Canada*. In 2003, Gray received the Pierre Berton Medal for distinguished achievement in popularizing Canadian history, and her biography of Pauline Johnson, *Flint & Feather*, won the University of British Columbia medal for biography. Her latest book is *Reluctant Genius: The Passionate Life and Inventive Mind of Alexander Graham Bell* (fall 2006).

Elizabeth Hay's books include the award-winning novels *Garbo Laughs* and *A Student of Weather*, and the story collection *Small Change*. Born in Owen Sound, Ontario, she worked as a radio broadcaster before becoming a full-time writer. She lives in Ottawa, where she's at work on a new novel about the North.

Susan Carr

Michael Helm's most recent novel, *In the Place of Last Things*, was a finalist for the regional Commonwealth Writers' Prize for Best Book and the Rogers Writers' Trust Fiction Prize. His first novel, *The Projectionist*, was a finalist for the Giller Prize and the Trillium Book Award. His essays on fiction, poetry, photography, and painting have appeared in various North American magazines, including *Brick*, where he has served as an editor since 2003.

Lee Towndrow

Sheila Heti is the author of the story collection *The Middle Stories*, the novel *Ticknor*, and the musical *All Our Happy Days Are Stupid*. She is the creator of Trampoline Hall, a popular lecture series out of New York and Toronto, at which people speak on subjects outside their areas of expertise. She studied art history and philosophy at the University of Toronto, and playwriting at the National Theatre School of Canada.

Rick Loughran

Annabel Lyon is the author of the fiction collections *Oxygen* and *The Best Thing for You*. Her short fiction has been published in *Toronto Life*, *The Journey Prize Anthology*, and *Write Turns: New Directions in Canadian Fiction*. In addition to creative writing, Annabel Lyon has studied music, philosophy, and law. She lives in Vancouver.

Nigel Dickson

David Macfarlane is the author of *The Danger Tree*, winner of the Canadian Authors Association Award for non-fiction, and *Summer Gone*, a finalist for the Giller Prize. His play, *Fishwrap*, was performed at Toronto's Tarragon Theatre in 2005. Macfarlane has been the recipient of several National Magazine Awards and a National Newspaper Award. He is currently completing books on the marble quarries of Carrara and on Toronto.

Ted Rhodes

Alistair MacLeod is the author of the short-story collections *The Lost Salt Gift of Blood, As Birds Bring Forth the Sun,* and *Island: The Collected Short Stories.* His celebrated first novel, *No Great Mischief,* won numerous awards, including the International IMPAC Dublin Literary Award, the Thomas Raddall Atlantic Fiction Award, and the Trillium Book Award. Alistair MacLeod and his wife, Anita, live in Windsor.

Greer Gattuso/
Palm Beach Daily News

Margaret MacMillan is the Provost of Trinity College and a professor of history. Her bestselling book *Paris 1919: Six Months That Changed the World* won the Samuel Johnson prize for non-fiction among others in the U.K. and the U.S.; and in Canada the 2003 Governor General's Award for Non-Fiction.

E.C.

Alberto Manguel is internationally acclaimed as an anthologist, translator, essayist, novelist, and editor. He is the author of several award-winning books, including *A Dictionary of Imaginary Places, A History of Reading,* winner of France's Prix Medicis, and *Reading Pictures,* a finalist for the Governor General's Award for Non-Fiction. His most recent book is *Stevenson Under the Palm Trees.* Manguel was born in Buenos Aires, became a Canadian citizen in 1982, and now lives in France, where he was named an Officer of the Order of Arts and Letters.

Danielle Schaub

Yann Martel is the author of a collection of short stories and two novels. His last novel, *Life of Pi,* won the 2002 Man Booker Prize and was published in more than forty countries. He is torn between living in Saskatoon, where he was writer-in-residence at the Public Library in 2003–4, and Montreal.

David Laurence

Anne Michaels's first novel, *Fugitive Pieces*, garnered high acclaim and numerous awards internationally, including the Orange Prize for Fiction, the Trillium Book Award, the Chapters/*Books in Canada* First Novel Award, the *Guardian* Fiction Award, the Giuseppe Acerbi Prize in Italy, and a Lannan Literary Award for Fiction. She is also the author of three poetry collections, *The Weight of Oranges, Miner's Pond*, and *Skin Divers*. Anne Michaels lives in Toronto.

F. Mistry

Rohinton Mistry is the author of three novels, *Such a Long Journey, A Fine Balance*, and *Family Matters*, and a collection of short stories, *Tales from Firozsha Baag*. His fiction has won many prestigious awards internationally. Born in Bombay, Rohinton Mistry has lived in Canada since 1975.

Barbara Stoneham

Lisa Moore has written two short-story collections, *Degrees of Nakedness* and *Open*, a finalist for the Giller Prize. Her first novel, *Alligator*, was a finalist for the Scotiabank Giller Prize and winner of a regional Commonwealth Writers' Prize for Best Book. She lives in St. John's, Newfoundland. Her daughter, Eva Crocker, won the Newfoundland and Labrador Arts and Letters short fiction prize for 2003 and 2004.

Aline Brault

Shani Mootoo was born in Ireland and grew up in Trinidad. She has lived in Canada since the early 1980s. She is the author of a book of poetry, *The Predicament of Or*, a collection of short fiction, *Out On Main Street*, and two novels, *Cereus Blooms at Night*, a finalist for the Giller Prize, the Ethel Wilson Fiction Prize, and the Chapters/*Books in Canada* First Novel Award, and, most recently, *He Drown She in the Sea*. Shani Mootoo lives in Edmonton.

Derek Shapton

Alice Munro is the author of thirteen books of short fiction, most recently *Runaway* and *The View from Castle Rock* (fall 2006). During her distinguished career, she has been the recipient of numerous prizes, including the W.H. Smith Prize, the National Book Critics Circle Award, the PEN/Malamud Award, the Rea Award for the Short Story, the Governor General's Award, and the Giller Prize. Her stories have appeared in the *New Yorker*, the *Atlantic Monthly*, and the *Paris Review*. She and her husband divide their time between Clinton, Ontario, and Comox, British Columbia.

Charlotte Musgrave

Susan Musgrave has been labelled an eco-feminist and an anti-feminist, a stand-up comedian and poet of death and darkness, a femme fatale and enfant terrible, sea-witch and sea-hag, and "the bank robber's wife." On her days off she writes books, the latest being *You're in Canada Now . . . A Memoir of Sorts*.

Jeff Nolte

Michael Ondaatje is the author of the novels *In the Skin of a Lion*, *The English Patient*, and *Anil's Ghost*. His other books include *Running in the Family*, *Coming Through Slaughter*, *The Cinnamon Peeler*, and *Handwriting*. His most recent book is *The Conversations: Walter Murch and the Art of Editing Film*. Ondaatje was born in Sri Lanka and came to Canada in 1962. He lives in Toronto.

Thies Bogner – Bogner Photography

Anna Porter has been an editor and publisher for thirty years. She is happy to have had a chance to work with extraordinary writers, including Farley Mowat. She is the author of four books, most recently *The Storyteller: Memory, Secrets, Magic and Lies*.

Arthur Renwick

Eden Robinson finishes a book every five years or so. She's written two novels, *Monkey Beach* and *Blood Sports*, and a collection of short stories, *Traplines*. She lives in Kitamaat, a reserve on the northwest coast of British Columbia.

Nancy Crampton

Marilynne Robinson is the author of the novels *Housekeeping*, winner of the PEN/Hemingway Award, and *Gilead*, winner of the Pulitzer Prize and the National Book Critics Circle Award, and two books of non-fiction, *Mother Country* and *The Death of Adam*. She teaches at the University of Iowa Writers' Workshop.

Biserka Livaja

Peter Robinson is one of the world's top writers of crime fiction and the author of the internationally acclaimed Inspector Banks novels. The series has won numerous awards, including the Edgar Award (U.S.), the Dagger in the Library Award (U.K.), the Grand Prix de Littérature Policière (France), the Palle Rosenkrantz Award (Denmark), and several Arthur Ellis Awards (Canada). Robinson was born in Yorkshire, England, and immigrated to Canada in the early 1970's. He lives in Toronto.

Hilary Sherker

Constance Rooke is the President of PEN Canada and the editor of two previous PEN Canada anthologies, *Writing Away* and *Writing Home*. An academic who has served as Chair of the Department of English and Associate Vice-President Academic at the University of Guelph, and as President of the University of Winnipeg, she is presently Director of the University of Guelph's new Master of Fine

Arts Program in Creative Writing at the University of Guelph-Humber. She is the author of several books, including *Fear of the Open Heart: Essays on Contemporary Canadian Writing*, and for ten years was Editor of the *Malahat Review*. She lives in Toronto.

Sophie Boussols

John Ralston Saul's latest book is *The Collapse of Globalism and the Reinvention of the World*. His philosophical trilogy and its conclusion – *Voltaire's Bastards: The Dictatorship of Reason in the West, The Doubter's Companion: A Dictionary of Aggressive Common Sense, The Unconscious Civilization* and *On Equilibrium: Six Qualities of the New Humanism* – has impacted political thought in many countries. Former President and now Honorary Patron of PEN Canada, Saul is a Companion in the Order of Canada and a Chevalier in the Ordre des Arts et des Lettres of France. In 2004, he received the Pablo Neruda International Presidential Medal of Honor.

Sari Ginsberg

Shyam Selvadurai was born in Sri Lanka, and came to Canada with his family at the age of nineteen. He is the author of two novels, *Funny Boy*, winner of the W.H. Smith/*Books in Canada* First Novel Award and the Lambda Literary Award in the U.S., and *Cinnamon Gardens*, a finalist for the Trillium Book Award; a young adult novel, *Swimming in the Monsoon Sea*, a finalist for the Governor General's Award; and the editor of *Story-Wallah: A Celebration of South Asian Fiction*. He lives in Toronto.

Shawn Benjamin

Russell Smith grew up in Halifax and now lives in Toronto. His most recent novel, *Muriella Pent*, was a finalist for the Rogers Writers' Trust Fiction Prize and the Toronto Book Award. He writes a weekly column on media in the *Globe and Mail*.

Juan Opitz

Rosemary Sullivan is an award-winning Toronto writer and author of ten books. *By Heart: Elizabeth Smart/A Life* was nominated for the Governor General's Award for Non-Fiction in 1991; *Shadow-Maker: The Life of Gwendolyn MacEwen* won the Governor General's Award for Non-Fiction in 1995. Her latest books have been *Labyrinth of Desire: Women, Passion, and Romantic Desire*, and *Cuba: Grace Under Pressure*.

Beth Perkins

Susan Swan is a Toronto novelist and Humanities professor at York University. She is also the vice chair of the Writers' Union of Canada. Her novel *What Casanova Told Me* was published in Canada and in the U.S., and will be published in Spain, France, Serbia, and Russia.

Willem J. Atsma

Madeleine Thien's first book of fiction, *Simple Recipes*, won four awards in Canada, was a finalist for a regional Commonwealth Writers' Prize for Best First Book, and was named a notable book by the Kiriyama Pacific Rim Book Prize. Her debut novel, *Certainty*, is scheduled for publication in the U.S. and the U.K., and in countries around the world. Originally from Vancouver, Madeleine Thien currently lives in Quebec City with her husband, Willem.

Elsa Trillat

Jane Urquhart is the author of six novels, *The Whirlpool*, *Changing Heaven*, *Away*, *The Underpainter*, *The Stone Carvers*, and *A Map of Glass*. Her fiction has won numerous awards, including Le prix du meilleur livre étranger (Best Foreign Book Award) in France, the Trillium Book Award, and the Governor General's Award. She is also the author of a collection of short fiction, *Storm Glass*, and four books of poetry. Jane Urquhart lives in southwestern Ontario.

Christine Pountney

Michael Winter is the author of the novels *The Big Why* and *This All Happened*, and the short-story collections *Creaking in Their Skins* and *One Last Good Look*. He has won no major prizes. He lives in Toronto.

Terence Young

Patricia Young's eight books of poetry have won numerous awards, including the Pat Lowther Award, the B.C. Book Prize, the Dorothy Livesay Prize, the League of Canadian Poets National Poetry Competition, the CBC Literary Competition, and a National Magazine Award. Her most recent collection, *Ruin and Beauty: New and Selected Poems*, was a finalist for the Governor General's Award. The manuscript for her first collection of short fiction, *Airstream*, won the Metcalf-Rooke Award.

ACKNOWLEDGEMENTS

We are grateful to SoftProbe and Friesens for their generous contribution to the production costs of this anthology.

* * *

The lines from the poem "Berryman" on page 8 are taken from *Flower & Hand: Poems 1977–1983* by W.S. Merwin. Copyright © 1997 by W.S. Merwin. Reprinted by permission of The Wylie Agency.

The excerpt on page 13 is from *Fifth Business* by Robertson Davies. Copyright © 1970 by Robertson Davies. Reprinted by permission of Pendragon Ink.

The excerpt from "Cortes Island" on page 14 is taken from *The Love of a Good Woman* by Alice Munro. Copyright © 1998 by Alice Munro. Reprinted by permission of McClelland & Stewart Ltd.

The italicized lines on page 106 are taken from an untitled poem from *Agnes in the sky* by Di Brandt, published by Turnstone Press.

The excerpt on page 206 is from *Suttree* by Cormac McCarthy, published by Alfred A. Knopf, a division of Random House, Inc.

ACKNOWLEDGEMENTS

The italicized excerpt on page 217 is from the short story "Song," from *Oxygen* by Annabel Lyon, published by McClelland & Stewart Ltd.

The lines from the poem "Was Ever a Dream a Drum?" on page 292 are taken from *Harvest Poems, 1910–1960* by Carl Sandburg. Copyright © 1960, 1958 by Carl Sandburg. Copyright renewed 1988, 1986 by Margaret Sandburg, Janet Sandburg, and Helga Sandburg Crile. Reprinted by permission of Harcourt Trade Publishers.

The excerpt on pages 294–96 is from the poem "Beach Composition III," from *The Predicament of Or* by Shani Mootoo, published by Polestar Book Publishers, an imprint of Raincoast Books.

The Amy Tan quotation on page 306 is from "Ghost Writer" by Gretchen Giles, *Sonoma County Independent*, December 14–20, 1995.

The Zadie Smith quotations on page 306–7 are from "Q&A: A Writer's Truth" by Camille Dodero, *Boston Phoenix*, July 18–24, 2003.

The excerpts on page 311 are from *You're in Canada Now . . . A Memoir of Sorts* by Susan Musgrave, published by Thistledown Press.

The excerpt on pages 373–74 is from the Preface to *Shadow Maker: The Life of Gwendolyn MacEwen* by Rosemary Sullivan, published by HarperCollins Publishers Ltd.

MEMBERSHIP IN PEN CANADA

Membership in PEN Canada is open to everyone. There are three categories of membership: writer members, associate members, and student members. Criteria for the category of writer members are set out on our website (www.pencanada.ca). All other members, with the exception of student members, are termed associate members. For both associate and writer members, dues are $60/year; dues for student members are $25/year. All members have the same rights with one exception: only writer members may vote at the Annual General Meeting.

Benefits of PEN Canada Membership

All members receive:
- A PEN Canada membership card
- A charitable receipt for the full amount of membership fees
- Acknowledgement in PEN Canada's Annual Report
- *Bulletin*, PEN Canada's twice-yearly newsletter
- A monthly e-bulletin
- Annual Report
- Notice of all PEN Canada events
- Opportunities to serve on PEN Canada's committees
- Opportunities to participate in Rapid Action Network appeals

How to Become a Member

We urge each reader of this book to think seriously about becoming a member of PEN Canada. Please call us or email us to indicate your wish to join, or to get more information. Thank you so much for your support of PEN Canada.

PEN Canada
24 Ryerson Avenue, Suite 301
Toronto, ON M5T 2P3
Phone: (416) 703-8448
Fax: (416) 703-3870
Email: info@pencanada.ca
www.pencanada.ca